RAISING

Bringing Up

NUESTROS

Latino Children

NIÑOS

in a Bicultural World

GLORIA G. RODRIGUEZ, PH.D.

FIRESIDE BOOKS

FIRESIDE
Rockefeller Center
1230 Avenue of the Americas
New York, NY 10020

Copyright © 1999 by Gloria G. Rodriguez, Ph.D.

FIRESIDE and colophon are registered trademarks of Simon & Schuster Inc.

DESIGNED BY PATRICE SHERIDAN
PRODUCED BY K&N BOOKWORKS INC.

Manufactured in the United States of America

10 9 8 7 6 5 4 3 2 1

Library of Congress Cataloging-in-Publication Data is available upon request.

ISBN 0-684-83969-5

Dedication

This book is dedicated to *mi madrecita*, Lucy Villegas Salazar, *a quien quiero con toda mi alma y corazón*. My mother made me realize there was no other role more important in life than being a parent and thus, she became my inspiration for initiating Avance in 1973.

This book is also dedicated to *mi familia querida: mi marido maravilloso*, and my better half, Salvador C. Rodriguez, *y nuestros niños*, Salvador Julián, Steven René, and Gloria Vanessa, whom we love dearly and who have enriched our lives immensely, as did our little angel in heaven, Sonya Yvonne. May this book help *nuestros niños* in their future parenting roles and in preserving our beautiful, rich Hispanic culture. What we desire for our children, we desire for all Latino children.

Foreword

More than twenty years ago I was invited to witness the blossoming of a national treasure. In 1973, Gloria Rodriguez, a young and intelligent Mexican American woman, newly graduated from college and with every option for individual material success before her, decided to give up her teaching job and go to work in the most deprived of San Antonio's West Side housing projects. I remember so well the depressing and threatening surroundings as I walked on that gray February day, through the unfamiliar honeycomb of buildings that led to the first Avance Center. Even more forbidding was the task before me: to help strategize ways to use the initial foundation grant that was fast running out. Inside, the room was warm, filled with the smells of *café y tacos* and the chatter of about a dozen young girls, some with infants in their arms and others with infants still in their very young tummies. They were sewing sock puppets, as Gloria's new partner, Carmen Cortez, talked to them about language development in very young children. When Gloria Rodriguez approached the table, they proudly displayed their handiwork and the chattering reached a crescendo as each one made a commitment to return for the next session. The program wrapped itself around my heart, never to let go. I understood then that no one of conscience who saw what Avance meant in the lives of these young women could fail to support its work.

Over the ensuing quarter century, scholars, policy makers, surgeons general, a passel of First Ladies, and even the Prince of Wales would traverse the path to that converted housing-project apartment. What was created in that impoverished setting would be replicated in sites across two states and in eleven chapters. The philosophies and methodologies of Avance have spread throughout the U.S. and Latin America due to the influence of the Avance Training Center. The handwritten Avance curriculum would progress from a series of worn yellow legal pads to a sophisticated comprehensive system that allows for replication. The original 35 young mothers would eventually be joined by more than 80,000 mothers and fathers. The staff has grown to number in the hundreds. Avance would transform many lives—the lives of young mothers (and now fathers) whose futures were once defined by a sense of hopelessness. Now they were being empowered to take charge of their lives through completing high school, going on to college, receiving job training—and most of all, becoming competent, confident, optimistic parents capable of transforming the lives of their own children. Avance's success soon became indisputable. The questions that persisted for scholars, policy makers, and others skeptical of such social programs, however, were "Why does it work and how does it work?" The social scientists would take the program apart and put it back together only to discover that it was impossible to pinpoint why the program was so successful.

This book, from its focus on the Virgen de Guadalupe to its guidance on Piagetian principles of child development, provides some answers to those questions. More important, it extends the power of Avance to Latino families, whether they are headed by teen-age girls struggling through high school, upwardly mobile professional couples, or individuals with doctorates in child development. Avance works because it is founded on unconditional acceptance of the young Latino mothers and fathers who come to its centers, on unequivocal belief in their potential, and on the creation and celebration of lasting intimate, supportive relationships as parents engage the most demanding job in life. Avance works because highly vulnerable young parents find they can trust in its teachings. This book is an invitation to those teachings, a celebration of those teachings, and a *bienvenido*, welcome, to the intimate family joys, struggles, and triumphs of Latino families.

This book, like the program built by the author, is propelled by the energy of its creator, an energy that infects most who come into contact with Avance and with Gloria Rodriguez. It is an energy that will not be constrained by traditional structures and that insists everything is possible, for anyone. It is an energy that is an amalgam of the deeply held beliefs and traditional child rearing wisdom of Latino families; the power inherent in our contemporary scientific understanding of how children develop physically, intellectually, emotionally, and socially; and the common sense lessons that are acquired in the struggle for dignity and full participation of a historically excluded community. Even more valuable, this book is fused with the richness of Gloria's own family history, tradition, and experience—a richness with which all Latinos will identify.

In many ways the book is like the community it is designed to inform and to serve. The Latino community represents the eruption of new energy in this country. This powerful force of demographics and spiritual and cultural energy will in many ways define America's twenty-first century much in the way that the baby boom generation defined the twentieth century. Growing to 25 percent of the U.S. population in the next fifty years, Latinos will impact every institution and the life of almost every American. The nature of that impact depends largely on our ability to develop in our children the capacity for contribution to and participation in U.S. institutions while strengthening rather than destroying the familial, ethical, and spiritual assets that are the hallmark of our traditional deep culture in all its diversity.

Professionals in education, child development, health and social services who work with Latino families can find in this book not only deep insight into the interplay of culture, mind, and spirit in this community, but countless tools for reaching out to Latino families. I would recommend that readers use this book as a resource for their children and families, a sourcebook of songs, recipes, and *dichos* so important to Latino culture, meant to be treasured and passed down through generations.

Latino parents will find themselves and their parents and their grandparents reflected and celebrated in these pages. Whether of Mexican, Puerto Rican, Dominican, Central American, Cuban, or South American origin, whether Indian, Black, White, or Mestizo, Latinos in the United States will be challenged and excited by the possibilities of raising strong children—*que no le piden nada a nadie*—who know who they are and the wonderful gifts that they bring to this beloved country in the exciting century they will shape.

—*Blandina Cardenas*
Associate Professor, University
of Texas at San Antonio;
Former Commissioner of the
Administration for Children,
Youth, and Families

Acknowledgments

First and foremost I wish to acknowledge and thank my immediate family for their patience and support while I was writing this book. I also want to thank my nuclear family, my extended family, my husband's extended family, and the Avance family, for the wonderful memories and for making this book possible. I have tried to share my life experiences, my Latino cultural pride, as well as my knowledge and professional training to help all parents and future parents who read this book.

I want to especially thank Elena Cabral and Rebecca T. Cabaza, two great Hispanic writers, for sharing their literary and editorial talents with me. I also want to thank Cami Licea for translating the book into Spanish, Blandina Cardenas for doing the foreword, and the many people who shared their recipes, *dichos*, games, songs, and lullabies.

Most important, I want to recognize and give thanks, praise, and glory to Almighty God for His love, blessings, guidance, and strength. It is He who sustains me. I would not have been able to complete this book without His presence in my life, since in the middle of writing *Nuestros Niños* I lost my dearest friend, Carmen P. Cortez, whose friendship and beautiful smile I truly miss.

Contents

Part Three
The Three Pillars of Effective Parenting: Marriage,
Family, and Community

Introduction

In 1970, as a freshman in college studying sociology and education, I learned that I was a "child-at-risk." As the daughter of a single mother, who raised me and seven other children in the barrios of San Antonio, I was, according to some experts, not supposed to have made it to my high school graduation. At a time when statistics had begun to paint a grim portrait of Hispanic youth in crisis, with alarming rates of school drop-out, low academic achievement, and juvenile delinquency, I marveled at the fact that by society's standards, I was a mystery.

When I read those foreboding numbers, I began thinking back to the Alazán Housing Project and our tiny wood-frame house on Colima Street in the city's West Side, where my mother, a widow with no more than a third-grade education, successfully raised her children in spite of the drugs, violence, and crime that threatened the streets. I asked myself, just what was it that this woman did, what secret or strange magic did she possess to have successfully raised her children despite the odds?

Several years of study, a Ph.D., and three children of my own later, I found out that it was no secret or spell. For my mother, Lucy Salazar, it was a combination of her unwavering faith, her deep sense of commitment to family, and the support she received from the extended family and neighbors in el barrio that made her unique. The greatest support came from my grandfather, Lázaro "Papayo" Villegas, who became for me, at the age of two, a loving father figure after my father died. Central in my family were an unconditional love, dedication, and high expectations for the children. There was also a profound sense of commitment to la cultura, which they so proudly bestowed on us as a special gift that needed to be preserved and cherished.

In spite of the fact that we were poor, I remember always coming home to a loving mother who prepared a table of food, complete with a plate of warm tortillas piled high. Although we had a small yard where we lived, my mother always managed to fill it with fragrant perennial flowers and beautiful rose bushes, which, along with the pecan trees, made the yard beautiful and made it seem bigger than it was. Though my mother taught us the importance of humility, she also emphasized el orgullo, or pride, stressing that we should always hold our heads high. She had my sisters and me dolled up in gloves and pretty hats to show off the brightly colored petticoat dresses she sewed for la Navidad and

Día de Pascuas. Each one of us was made to feel important and special. An intense sense of obligation to *la familia* took shape during those early years, for as sisters and brothers we were expected to look out for one another. As children, we were expected to show *respeto* to our elders. As Latinos, we were infused with a sense of pride and *dignidad* because we were part of *nuestra gente*, our people.

My mother's favorite *dicho*, or saying, *no hay mal que por bien no venga*, out of everything bad comes something good, became a familiar creed in our house. Though she relied on my grandfather for support, my mother served as both father and mother to me. She was, like my mother-in-law, *la Doña*, always making clear in no uncertain terms what she expected from her children and never deviating from the rules she set. Like many Hispanic parents, among those things she considered most important was *nuestra educación*, a learning that included not just what we read in books, but how we behaved, our attitudes, our principles, and beliefs. To be *bien educados*, to be well educated, meant not only that we knew how to read and write, but that we possessed the virtues of respect, loyalty, compassion, and hard work, and the ability to distinguish right from wrong.

One of the most vivid memories of my childhood takes me back to when I was not more than four years old. I was standing on the sidewalk in front of my building in a housing project when an older child plowed into me on her bicycle, sending me flat on my face as she pedaled away, indifferent to my injuries. My mother, who saw the incident from the second-story window of our building, was so enraged and upset that she called the police, and the incident, much to the surprise of my neighbors, was even reported later in the local newspaper. What stayed with me long after that day was the way my mother, always vigilant, courageous, and headstrong, never failed to use every one of her resources and energies to keep her children standing. *Mientras que hubiera aliento en su cuerpo* (as long as there was breath in her body), she was determined to make sure that no one was going to knock us down and keep us from becoming who God intended us to become.

This woman who had so little, managed to fill us with so much love, hope, and pride that we could never imagine not meeting her expectations to stay out of trouble and pursue our goals. Both she and my grandfather made sure we knew that we were special. I remember my grandmother telling us, "*Dios cuida a los huérfanos y las viudas*," "God takes care of orphans and widows." "He has a special purpose for each of you."

My purpose in life these past twenty-five years, besides my family, has been Avance, a nonprofit organization that has been recognized worldwide as a leading parent-education and family-support organization and wins praise from both the mainstream and Hispanic media as well as politicians on every side of the political spectrum. Dignitaries including Prince Charles, Barbara Bush, Jesse Jackson, Governor Ann Richards, Surgeon General David Satcher, and U.S. Senator Bill Bradley have visited the Avance programs. Avance has been recognized in books written by three First Ladies: Barbara Bush's *First Teachers*, Hillary Rodham Clinton's *It Takes a Village*, and Rosalynn Carter's *Helping Someone with Mental Illness*. In 1997, an Avance family and I were invited to the White House by President Bill Clinton and First Lady Hillary Rodham Clinton to represent Avance as a model program at the White House Conference on Early Childhood Development and Learning. Avance was able to expand its parent education and family support services because of the support of the largest foundations and corporations in the United States, including Carnegie, Ford, Kellogg, Rockefeller, Hilton, Mott, Hasbro, and Kraft/General Foods.

This book brings the strategies and principles, which have helped so many Avance parents from the neighborhood where I grew up and beyond, to all Hispanic parents. The model that Avance has cultivated over twenty-five years of research and experience is based on meeting children's four basic needs: the physical, cognitive, social, and emotional. In addition to these, for the purposes of this book, I have added a fifth need that is interwoven throughout the Hispanic cultural fabric: our faith and spirituality. Using activities that embrace and celebrate the traditions of *nuestra raza*, our people, I show parents how their culture can enhance the experience of child rearing. I build on our strengths as Latinos, namely our language and cultural values, as I help parents acquire knowledge and skills essential to becoming better parents. These values include devotion to children, marriage, family, faith, and community. *Nuestras costumbres*, our customs, are powerful forces that can shape children's minds and hearts, creating proud and confident individuals who have something very special to offer society.

All of us want to see our children become healthy, happy, competent, and successful human beings. We want them to excel in school and grow up to be honest, compassionate, hard working, and responsible individuals. Of course, children do not automatically come with these virtues, nor do they come with instructions. Likewise, effective parenting does not come naturally; it is an art and includes skills that must be learned, like any other important role in society. You already possess many of the essential ingredients for effective parenting, including the love, hopes, and dreams you have for your children. With the right tools, parenting can be the most fulfilling and gratifying experience of your life.

Hispanic Americans, about to become the largest ethnic group in the United States, face great opportunities and challenges. As mothers and fathers, many find themselves struggling to navigate their children through an increasingly urban, mobile, and impersonal competitive society, where negative influences seem to lurk around every corner. The natural support systems associated with *la familia*, a strong marriage and a network of uncles, aunts, friends, and neighbors, is still strong among many Hispanics, but must be reinforced as families become more mobile and Americanized. My husband and I are like many working Hispanic parents who want to maintain old traditions in this ever-changing world while coping with the demands of two careers. I know the obstacles that many of you face. Nevertheless, I also know that there are ways to merge the best of both worlds, the Latino culture and the American culture, to help maintain a strong marriage and family and to help your children succeed in a bilingual, bicultural world.

With my training in the fields of education and child growth and development, I can provide you with the most up-to-date information and research to help you guide your children. Certainly, children around the world have the same basic needs. However, as a Latina who is raising three children and who has worked with countless other Hispanic parents, I want to discuss these principles with a voice that speaks to our community. In doing so, I will draw upon my experiences from my own upbringing, my professional training and development, my teaching experience, and examples from the Avance and the Rodriguez family. I will also apply the knowledge I have gained from my own sons and daughter, Salvador, Steven, and Vanessa, as they learned about their world and their rich Hispanic heritage and as they developed their enormous potential. My children have served as my laboratory while I have tried to apply the theories that I learned in child growth and development to each of them through every developmental stage. Parenting can certainly be a challenge as our children test the limits and strive for autonomy and independence. At times humorous, often harrowing, the anecdotes I will share are, above all, full of heart, for they let you know that you are not alone in your frustrations and fears, nor in your hopes and dreams for your *niños*.

Through anecdotes, *dichos*, songs, and games, this book will offer you a rich cultural framework for absorbing the information you need for parenting. These elements may teach, entertain, humor, and perhaps even surprise you. But mostly, they will remind you how unique and important your culture is and how it can enrich your family and community and help you fulfill your parental roles and responsibilities. At a time when families and communities everywhere are looking for new buffers against the forces that pull them apart, you will find that the *consejos*, or words of advice, in this book still hold a message that speaks to all people in the twenty-first century. The sanctity of the extended family, the belief in community and our unique sense of *compadrazgo*, godparenthood, reflect our devotion to relationships. For generations, these ties have held Hispanic families together. Like the countless elders who counseled my mother and whose words of wisdom were passed on to me and to my own children, this book will offer some *consejos* on how to bring about *un niño bien educado*, a well-educated, well-rounded child.

This book covers the first twelve years of a child's life. With the last of my three children, Vanessa, having just turned thirteen when I began writing this book, I marvel at all that she and my two sons, Sal and Steven, learned during the first twelve years of life. Important milestones take shape during this critical period, from children's ability to learn basic concepts, languages, and values, to developing their self-esteem and personality. These are the important years when they establish their character and when their interests and talents emerge. Half of what children learn between the time they are in the womb and the age of seventeen is learned by the age of four. The critical message of this book, therefore, is that there will never be another person who will have a greater influence in the development of your children than you. If you lay a good foundation and establish a strong parent-child relationship during these important years of life, then the likelihood of your children doing well in school and life will be even greater.

This book is for individuals who are parents or who are planning to become parents. I want to help you understand what is expected and needed during these years so that you will create the right kind of environment for your children. Being an effective parent requires a great amount of time, energy, patience, and commitment, knowledge, and skills. I hope this book will help you acquire the information and skills to help you improve the way you interact with your *niños*. Just as was true for my mother, a combination of your faith, your deep sense of commitment to your culture and your children, as well as the support that you will receive from your spouse, family, neighbors, friends, and community will help you in your parenting role and in enabling your children to reach their potential.

As you read this book, I want it to appeal to your mind as a rational adult who wants to provide the best upbringing for your children. But I also want it to touch your soul as a Latino or Latina who recognizes and is proud of your cultural roots. It is clear that we have much to be proud of. I want Hispanic parents or those individuals married to Hispanics to be able to help their children find a place in the world where they can shine. As *nuestros niños* learn about their rich cultural Latino heritage, history, and language, while absorbing the American culture and English language, they will be ready to assume their leadership roles in this country and in the world.

Over the years, I have received numerous awards and recognition for my work in parent education, from Hispanic magazines, including *Hispanic*, *Hispanic Business*, and *Latina*, and from the mainstream media, including the *New York Times*, ABC's *World News Tonight*, Lifetime Television, *Parent's* magazine, and *Working Mother* magazine. While I may be considered by some to be an expert in the fields of parenting and early childhood education, I do not profess to be the perfect mother, nor my children model children. I doubt if there are such individuals. I certainly have made some mistakes in child rearing and, in retrospect, could have done some things differently. However, I do know from experience that effective parenting, with some training, guidance, and support, can be achieved to a great measure. As with everything in life, you, too, will deviate from the mark, but with a strong foundation, you will find you can survive the pitfalls and find the experience as joyful and fulfilling as I have.

You may remember being told the following words by a parent or grandparent: *Hijo eres, padre serás, según lo hiciste, así lo verás.* Loosely translated, the refrain says, Child you are, parent you will be, just as you have done, it will be done to you. As a strong-willed child, my mother used to tell me, "*Vas a pagar todas las que debes,*" You will pay back all that you owe. This was a warning that I remembered with a sense of excitement mixed with fear upon the birth of each of my children. I asked myself, was I prepared in the same way that my mother was to meet the enormous challenges of raising these tiny human beings who would surely grow up to be strong-willed individuals like their mother? How could I take the lessons of her experience and apply them to my own reality?

These are the kinds of questions that you, too, may be asking yourself as you begin the greatest journey of your life preparing the next generation of leaders, citizens, workers, and parents. I hope that the pages that follow will give you some answers as you proceed *paso por paso,* step by glorious step.

Nuestros Niños:
Our Children

Nuestros Niños are like beautifully scented roses
in a cool spring morning in May.

Our Children are like glorious picturesque sunsets,
etched in our minds forever to stay.

Nuestros Niños are like soothing and raging winds,
they stir every emotion by what they do and say.

Our Children are like radiant warm sunbeams,
they can cause us pain and make us gay.

Nuestros Niños are like sweet-sounding birds,
they fill the air with laughter and joy as they play.

Our Children are like metamorphosing butterflies,
they unfold their unique talents each day.

Nuestros Niños have, like rambling brooks,
a rich heritage in their veins from yesterday.

Our Children have, like life's awesome wonders,
a unique beauty and radiance to display.

Nuestros Niños are the greatest of God's gifts,
to love, to care, and to show the way.

—*Gloria G. Rodriguez*

Part One

Destined for Greatness:

Teaching Hispanic Children

Who They Are,

Where They Came From,

and Where They Are Going

Chapter 1

Destined for Greatness:
Hispanic Demographics
and History

¿Quiénes Somos?

NUESTROS NIÑOS: HISPANIC CULTURE'S GREATEST TREASURE

By virtue of our past, we Hispanic parents already have much to help prepare our children for the future. Essentially, to be Hispanic is to value children. We love and treasure our children, and many of the things we do, we do for them and with them. To witness this, one only has to attend a Hispanic wedding or *quinceañera*, where children can usually be seen playing in the middle of the dance floor, dancing proudly to *cumbias, polkas, salsas,* or *merengues.* At these events, children are displayed and introduced to friends and relatives as our most prized possessions. Rarely are children as welcomed and visible with adults as in the Latino culture. Indeed, *los hijos son la riqueza de los padres, son nuestro gran tesoro,* children are our greatest treasure. They enrich and give meaning to our lives. While *nuestros niños,* like all children, can cause us stress and anxiety as they go about exploring their world and testing their limits, they can also give us enormous pleasure and gratification. They are *nuestra vida,* the core of our existence.

Los padres tienen la esperanza y el deseo, hope and desire, that their children succeed, and they feel *un gran orgullo,* a great sense of pride, when they do. *Esta esperanza y orgullo de los padres,* this hope and pride, become tremendous driving forces for Latino parents. Knowing this was what helped me successfully reach poor Hispanic families twenty-five years ago when I began Avance. I knew that Latino parents, regardless of their status in life, had hopes and dreams for their children, especially when they were very young. I thought that even if parents had lost hope for themselves, or had resigned to their status in life, that there would still be a flicker of hope for their children. When I knocked on the doors of parents in an effort to recruit them to Avance, I would ask, "Do you love your children? Do you want the best for them?" Every time the response was a resounding, "¡Sí, cómo no!" Yes, of course. I learned that Hispanics will do whatever is needed to help their children develop well, succeed in life, and obtain their derechos, their basic rights, to dignity and respect.

In order to help nuestros niños, we must help them draw upon their rich cultural heritage and history for strength and a sense of identity. If we want our children to have confidence and a healthy self-esteem, they must get this empowerment from knowing what it means to be Latino. Let us take a moment to consider who our children are, where they trace their origins, and how their destiny is connected to their spirituality.

As a parent, it is critical that you realize the changing demographics of this country. The face of America will not be White Anglo-Saxon for long. It will soon be mostly Hispanic and with it comes a great destiny for our children. Marvelous and extraordinary things await our children. Blessed with a legacy of achievement and a rich heritage from their ancestors as well as an array of talents and capabilities, our children have much to build on, as they will one day become the largest ethnic group in America. Like any plant that must be well rooted in order to grow strong and healthy, our children must understand their roots in order to reach their destiny. They must understand who they are, where they came from, and where they are going. They must appreciate the hopes, struggles, and triumphs of our ancestors. You must help them recognize that they are a link in a long chain and are the beneficiaries of the quest for a better life sought by our antepasados. They stand on the shoulders of people that came before them so that they can further climb the ladder of success and reach their unique goals and potential. Not only will they be in a position to help themselves and their family, but they will be able to use their talents, skills, and positions of influence to improve the quality of life of the many Latinos that will follow them.

To be able to bear fruit, a plant not only must be well rooted, but also must be grounded on a solid and rich foundation. By helping your children understand the strength of our culture and their relationship to history, you are preparing the rich soil from which they can proudly creep out into the world and grow strong, helping them reach for their dreams. From that foundation, you, too, will be able to draw strength, pride, and energy as the competent gardener who cultivated and produced your greatest treasure.

¿QUIÉNES SOMOS?—WHO ARE WE?

According to demographers, in 1997, Hispanics comprised almost 30 million people, or 11 percent of the U.S. population, while non-Hispanic Whites comprised 73 percent. By the year 2000, Hispanics will comprise 15 percent of the population, or 39 million. By the year 2010, Hispanics will surpass the African-American population, with a population projected to be 41 million compared to a projected Black population of 37.5 million. If you had a child born in 1998, by the year 2010, your child will be under the age of twelve and will not only be among the largest minority group in America, but together with other minorities, they will comprise the majority. By the year 2050, the Hispanic population is projected to almost triple in size to 87.4 million, comprising about one-fourth of the population of 392 million. Because of Hispanics' high fertility and immigration rates and because non-Hispanic Whites are projected to continue to decline in population, Hispanics are projected to one day become the largest group in America.

Hispanics as a group are young. The median age for Hispanics is twenty-five years compared to thirty-four for the general population. About one-third are children under the age of fifteen, which reflects the youth of our population, compared to 20.4 for non-Hispanic Whites. The average household size is 3.6 versus 2.6 for non-Hispanics. According to the National Center for Health Statistics, in 1992, the White fertility rate was 1.8 children compared to 3.0 for Hispanics and 2.5 for Blacks. Mexican Americans have a higher fertility rate than other Hispanic groups, with a mean of 3.78 children per family, followed by 2.85 for Puerto Ricans. Statistics for Cuban Americans are more comparable to Whites.

From classrooms to the marketplace, our influence is already being felt in nearly every sector of society. In many schools today, especially in states with large numbers of Hispanics like Texas and California, Hispanic children already comprise the majority. Our $350 billion purchasing power has spurred new trends in fashion, publishing, and film, and our strength was felt in the last several presidential and gubernatorial elections at the national level because of the concentration of Hispanics in key political states like California (35 percent), Texas (20 percent), New York (10 percent), and Florida (7 percent). This economic and political influence was felt in spite of the fact that the average Hispanic family income is $25,561 versus $33,864 for all families.

HISPANIC HISTORICAL ROOTS

We as a people are known by different names: Latino, Hispanic, Chicano, or Latin American, all of which I will use interchangeably throughout the book. Sixty-four percent of Hispanics are Mexican Americans, 11 percent are Puerto Ricans, 13 percent are from the Caribbean and Central and South America, almost 5 percent are Cuban Americans, and 7 percent are other. Within those labels lies a tapestry of experiences that distinguish the *mexicano*, *cubano*, *puertorriqueño*, *dominicano*, *nicaragüeño*, *venezolano*, and *peruano*. Hispanics have distinctive socioeconomic backgrounds, histories, education, and political affiliations.

The origins of the Latino population have long been the subject of intense study and debate. Some have linked Latinos to the nomadic people who crossed the Bering Strait from Asia, some 11,000 to 20,000 years ago, forming the basis for our indigenous "Paleo-Indian" ancestry, or the first "Americans," whose descendants later migrated throughout North, Central, and South America as well as the Caribbean Islands. The oldest human presence in the Americas was traced to Monte Verde, Chile, dating back 12,500 years and to Clovis, New Mexico, 11,200 years ago. Many of *nuestros niños* are descendants of the great Indian nations including the Olmecs, Mayans, Toltecs, Aztecs, Incas, Tainos, Quechuas, Anasazis, and Mogollons.

According to legend, the Aztec people spoke of having emerged from caves in a mythical place called Aztlán, which is said to be located somewhere in the Southwest section of the United States. From there, guided by their sun god *Huitzilopochtli*, they searched in the wilderness for their prophetic sign, an eagle with a snake in its beak perched on a prickly pear cactus. They would find it in 1323 in *Tenochtitlán*, the location where they built their empire, which is present-day Mexico City.

Today Hispanics look elsewhere in their genealogical searches. A light-skinned, curly-haired Puerto Rican I know, who is proud of her African roots, can also trace some of her ancestors to the Vikings from Sweden and Norway, who inhabited the Caribbean Islands and Latin America many years before Christopher Columbus ever set foot there. Those newcomers intermarried with the Indians, then with the Spanish, and later with the African people who had been brought to this area as slaves.

Other Hispanics make strong connections to Africa, where all of human civilization originated more than three million years ago. As one Hispanic saying goes, *todos tenemos negro detras de las orejas*, we all have black behind the ears. However, many Latinos look to the voyage of Christopher Columbus in 1492 in Mesoamerica, which includes Mexico, Central America, and the West Indies, as the birth of the Latino people, which came about because of *el mestizaje*, the mixture of Spanish and Indian bloods and the blending of their cultures.

The tapestry of divergent races and cultures coming together in the Hispanic world has often carried with it special names. The descendants of the first Spanish settlers were known as *criollos*. *Mestizos* were the product of Spanish and Indian bloods, just as *mulatos* were the product of Black and Spanish mixing. Blacks who intermarried with the Indians had children who were called *cambujos* and the mixture of *mulatos* and *criollos* were called *chinos*. Even the Native-American Indians who acculturated to the Spanish culture were called the *jenízaros* and *jenízaras*.

COMING TO AMERICA

It is important that you provide your children with a Latino historical perspective, which is usually missing in the school textbooks. Take them to the library and see if they have a Latino collection of books. From these books, you will see that the migration of Hispanics to America has multiple origins. As Latinos, we can take pride in the fact that Spanish explorer Pedro Menéndez de Avilés established the first permanent settlement in St. Augustine, Florida, in 1565, forty-two years before the pilgrims arrived at Plymouth Rock in 1607. Even Santa Fe, New Mexico, was settled before, in 1598.

Many of the original settlers and their descendants eventually migrated to what is now the Southwest of the United States. February 2,

1848, is considered by some to be the official birth of Hispanic Americans in the United States. This is the day that the Treaty of Guadalupe Hidalgo was signed after the American victory in the Mexican-American War. Under the terms of the Treaty of Guadalupe Hidalgo, Mexico sold to the U.S. the states of California, Texas, Nevada, Utah, and parts of Arizona, Colorado, Kansas, New Mexico, Oklahoma, and Wyoming for $15 million and then readjusted the boundaries in 1853 with the Gadsden Purchase. All the people living in these regions automatically became United States citizens. Thus, many families living as Mexicans prior to this war were now Americans, or Mexican Americans. They became, like so many Latinos, hyphenated Americans, or people of two worlds and two cultures.

Because of war, the Puerto Ricans had a fate similar to that of the Mexicans in becoming citizens. With the victory of the Spanish-American War of 1898 and the signing of the Treaty of Paris in 1899, Puerto Rico became a territory of the United States. Later, the Jones Act of 1917 made Puerto Rico residents U.S. citizens and gave them the right to travel freely between the mainland United States and the island. Large groups of *puertorriqueños* settled mostly in New York, New Jersey, and, until recently, in Florida. Between 1940 and 1960, more than 545,000 Puerto Ricans came to this country looking for work because of the island's poor economic conditions. The men, for the most part, came to this country first, moved in with relatives, and then later brought the rest of the family.

Other Hispanics came to America driven by wars and severe economic conditions in their countries and lured by the promise of a better life in *los Estados Unidos*. Until 1924, people could travel freely between Mexico and the United States. But when the U.S. economy suffered and there was a scarcity of jobs, the U.S. Bureau of Immigration was established to control immigration, only to conveniently open the border gates again when the economy improved. In 1900 there were between 380,000 and 560,000 Mexican Americans living in the United States and approximately three million in 1930. Between 1900 and 1940 there was a great demand for cheap labor to build railroads and work in mines and factories. Laborers were also needed in cattle and sheep ranches and on farms doing agricultural work, picking cotton, and harvesting fruits and vegetables. Many Hispanics came to this country through work permits or labor contracts. Their strong work ethic took them to the steel mills, auto factories, canneries, and meat-packing plants, dispersing Mexicans throughout the United States, particularly in Texas, California, Arizona, New

Mexico, Colorado, Washington, Montana, Idaho, and parts of the Midwest (especially the Chicago and Kansas City areas).

When the jobs ended, many Hispanic families stayed in those cities and became citizens through marriage and their children became U.S. citizens. Many of my Hispanic friends in the Southwest have a parent who is Mexican or Mexican American and another who is Native American from such nations as the Navajo or Pueblo. The Repatriation Program of 1939 deported about 500,000 people of Mexican descent. This program caused a great deal of resentment, humiliation, and anger for Hispanics who had been living in this country for more than a decade. Some were deported even if they had become citizens. But then again there was a demand for Latinos to fill the great U.S. labor shortage during World War II. The government-sponsored Bracero Program, which began in 1943, encouraged many Mexicans to take low-paying menial jobs. Again, many of these people married and settled in this country and became U.S. citizens. The Hispanics who went to war had better opportunities to further their education and improve their quality of life through the GI bill. Many became community leaders and fought tirelessly for equality and civil rights for Hispanics through such organizations as Lulac (the League for United Latin-American Citizens) and the GI Forum.

Other Hispanics came to this country, just as my own ancestors did from Mexico, escaping persecution and wars. My grandfather, Lázaro Villegas, proud of his Indian and Mexican heritage, brought his wife, Rosario, and son, Pascual, to America because of the turbulent times brought about by the Mexican Revolution of 1910. My paternal grandfather, Julián Garza, known as "el general," was a *Carrancista* who fought in the *revolución* against Pancho Villa. He died fighting to protect his land and the honor of his family as Villa forces raided villages and raped *mestizo* and *criollo* women, including one of my relatives. It was during this tumultuous period that my widowed grandmother, María de Jesús "Chita" Lombraña Garza, mostly of Spanish blood, migrated to the United States with her children.

The most recent wave of Latinos to the U.S. came from Spanish-speaking countries in Central America, the Caribbean, and Cuba. Approximately 200,000 Cubans came to the U.S. escaping the Cuban Revolution between 1959 and 1962. Another 50,000 arrived between 1962 and 1965 and 250,000 more came during the airlifts from 1966 and 1973. In 1980, there was a massive exodus of 125,000 "Marielitos" whom the Cuban government sent by boat to Miami from the port of Mariel, and in 1994, thousands more Cubans fleeing poverty and political oppression arrived, many making the journey on small, homemade boats.

The Dominicans who immigrated to the United States between 1945 and 1959 were like the Cubans, who also left their country for political reasons, many of them similarly affluent and educated. Most Latinos from Central America came to the United States through Mexico seeking asylum from the ravages of civil war when they were under military rule. These included death squads and civil rights atrocities against the guerrillas who rebelled for equity and a more just distribution of the nation's resources. Thousands of people mostly from Guatemala, Nicaragua, and El Salvador were forced to leave their countries due to war. With great emotional scars, they traveled through dangerous conditions seeking asylum in the U.S. However, most were rejected by the government due to United States policy regarding these countries, forcing many to enter the country illegally. South Americans came to the United States to work and study. Many Latinos eventually married and became legal citizens while others stayed illegally.

The Immigration Reform and Control Act of 1986 gave amnesty to all illegal immigrants who had been in this country since January 1, 1982. Because of this Act, there were 2.3 million Mexicans and 100,000 South Americans who, between 1986 and 1992, became legal permanent residents.

HELPING OUR CHILDREN FIND THEIR ROOTS

In helping our children study their cultural roots in a bicultural world, many of us discover that our courageous ancestors came to this country seeking asylum, freedom, and a better life no different than European immigrants who arrived at Ellis Island. The ancestors who left their much beloved countries, whether *cubanos*, *mejicanos*, *salvadoreños*, or *dominicanos*, did so out of concern for the safety and well-being of their children. I have heard stories about the brave journey taken by many single women, including my own grandmother, who crossed the border into the United States with their children to begin a new life of hope and opportunity. As with many Hispanic families, such a journey has marked the beginning of a new chapter in the family's history.

My grandmother María de Jesús Garza and her children settled in Zuehl, Texas, as sharecroppers. Many years later, my father and grandmother moved to the "big city" of San Antonio where my father worked as a butcher for his uncle in the barrio. My mother was born in Laredo, Texas, in 1920, soon after her parents crossed the border. She settled with her parents a few blocks away from where my father lived and worked in the barrios of San Antonio. She worked as a pecan sheller along with her mother until she married my father and then they moved next to her parents' home. It was for them a time of extreme determination and sacrifice, of memories left behind and of new beginnings in that small wood-frame house on Colima Street.

The daughter of a Mexican father with Spanish roots and a first-generation American-born mother with mostly an indigenous Indian background, I am proud of my mixed heritage. Like other Hispanics, I probably have African roots as evidenced by my very curly hair, or Chinese lineage, shown in my oriental-looking eyes, or even some Jewish heritage, since the original Garza settlers in Mexico, I was told, were Sephardic Jews from Spain. I share all of this with you to make a point that as Latinos, each one of us has a historical account and genealogical journey that is both rich and unique.

Do you know your genealogical roots? How far back can you trace your family lineage? It would be a very interesting and important family project to trace and record your family ancestry. I wish I had videotaped my grandfather, aunts, and uncles before they passed away. Have your children videotape and interview their *abuelitos*, elderly *tíos and tías*, or other individuals who knew your family before they first came to this country. Visit your family's birthplace, as I did when I went to Nava, Mexico, to see my father's birthplace. To my surprise, I talked to people who knew my father and his family very well. Put together a scrapbook consisting of old family photos that go back to the '30s, '40s, and earlier, if possible. Do a family tree with names of all your relatives, beginning with your immediate family and going back as far as you can. My husband cut out small wooden trees and inscribed them with the names of his family and gave one to each of his siblings for Christmas.

Have a family reunion. I am so fortunate to have attended family reunions in family ranches around Nava, Mexico, and in Zuehl, Texas. Up to 400 family members attend the annual family reunions from throughout the United States and Mexico. Each branch of the family tree wears a particular color T-shirt. We have a wonderful time sharing fabulous stories and exchanging priceless pictures of our ancestors. We have even taken a panoramic picture of the Garza clan. One can see the joy of the wise elders as first, second, and third cousins embrace, and as everyone puts them in a place of honor. I see the pride in the children as they feel a sense of connection and belonging. As the "official" historian, I get a great deal of satisfaction as I gather new information to further fill the family tree, which I share with other family members. My cousins compiled a cookbook of their mother's favorite recipes. From playing Mexican bingo, volleyball, and sack races to riding horses, breaking piñatas, and listening to mariachis and dancing, everyone has a superb time.

Interview people and ask them where they came from, when, how, and why they came to this country. Were their ancestors in this country before the Treaty of Guadalupe? Some Hispanics are very proud to be fifth-generation Hispanics. Tell them to close their eyes and remember something about their childhood. Tell them to think of all the sights, sounds, and smells as they answer some of these questions.

1. Describe your house, your neighborhood. Where did you go shopping?
2. What were some games, songs, *dichos*, celebrations, folk tales, lullabies that you remember?
3. What musical instruments did you play or did you hear played in your community?
4. What kinds of foods did you eat? (Get favorite recipes.)
5. Describe the flowers, trees, and landscape of your country.
6. Describe your schools. What did you study? How about your siblings? What skills did you learn?
7. How would you spend your weekends?
8. How did you get around? What form of transportation did you use?
9. Describe your religious upbringing.
10. What job did you have?
11. What were your happiest and saddest moments and why?
12. Describe your personality. What did you like to do?
13. Which relatives do you look like physically?
14. What kind of clothes did you wear?
15. How many languages do you speak?
16. Describe your journey to America.
17. Help me plot your family tree. Name all family members you recall.
18. Are there any exciting or interesting stories that you can remember about your family or town?

LEGACY OF ACHIEVEMENT AND RICH HERITAGE

As members of what will be the largest ethnic group in our nation's diverse multicultural society, our children need to be confident and proud that they are the inheritors of at least two great cultures, two languages, and centuries of history. We want them to know the English language and feel comfortable with American culture and traditions, but we want them also to speak the Spanish language, and preserve their Hispanic identity. We want them to know their historical roots and to be proud of their legacy and rich heritage.

History books in American schools do not emphasize enough about our ancestors and our history. Our children are not exposed enough to the great accomplishments of the Aztecs, Olmecs, Toltecs, and Incas. These great empires, built around 200 B.C. to 400 A.D., had populations of up to 30 million people, larger than any empire at that time. They built huge pyramids and palaces of stone with hundreds of rooms. It is amazing to know how they were able to do this. They had religious temples, recreation centers, schools, plazas, prisons, barbershops, gardens, and zoos, just like a major metropolitan city of today. Architects and engineers also constructed avenues, canals, bridges, reservoirs, and irrigation systems. Inquisitive astronomers analyzed the skies and invented the most precise calendar to date that was used to plan religious ceremonies, planting, and harvesting. Hispanic people produced glittering creations throughout thirty spectacular centuries of art, from fine jewelry and ornate pottery to tapestries and magnificent statues displayed in museums throughout the world. In these empires, Hispanics built military forces, established trade, and celebrated religious, social, artistic and recreational events. I tell my children that they are good at math, science, and art because of the rich Hispanic heritage that flows in their veins. Maintaining this complex social order required great management skills, an elaborate form of government, as well as a large, skillful, and intelligent workforce.

There are many ways to bring this rich cultural history to your children. Take them to the library and check out books on the Mayans, Aztecs, and Incas. Take them to museums to learn about the pre-Columbian era. If you have opportunities to travel, take them to see the Pyramid of the Sun near Mexico City, to Mayan ruins found in Chichén Itzá, Uxmal, and Palenque in the Yucatan Peninsula and in Tikal in Guatemala, the magnificent Incan ruins in Machu Picchu in Peru, or the ancient Spanish fortress of El Morro and the governor's palace, La Fortaleza, in Puerto Rico. Your children will surely be proud to be connected to the magnificent archaeological finds and historical sites that are greatly admired by millions from throughout the world. The Discovery Channel on cable television and *National Geographic* magazine occasionally feature stories relating to our ancestors. Since the schools present more of a Western European perspective of America, it is up to us as parents to offer our children the missing history chapters to give them a source of pride and a sense of identity in their Latino roots.

LA RAZA CÓSMICA AND OUR CHILDREN'S DESTINY

The arrival of Spaniards to the Caribbean in 1492, to Mexico in 1519, and to Peru in 1532 would change the course of history and culture for our people. José Vasconcelos, Mexico's former Minister of Education, referred to this phenomenon as *la Raza Cósmica*, a varied mix of every race and ethnic group. October 12, the day that celebrates Christopher Columbus's discovery of America, is commemorated by many Hispanics as *Día de la Raza*. Latino children today are the product of many mixed marriages and the blending of numerous races, creating a rainbow of beautiful shades of skin colors. Hispanics differ in the color and shape of eyes and the color and texture of hair. Regardless of our physical, historical, and subtle linguistic differences, we are linked by a rich and varied culture that includes enduring traditions and basic fundamental values, such as a strong belief in the sanctity of children, family, community, and spirituality.

HISPANIC ORIGIN AND SPIRITUALITY

Besides the ancient ruins, the Aztec calendar, and the beautiful folk art, our ancestors left us a strong spirituality that has guided our thoughts and actions. I see our children, who represent the blending of many ethnic groups and diverse religious beliefs, as having risen, in a sense, from the ashes of great civilizations and mighty empires to assume the prominent roles for which they are destined.

There are many recorded accounts of the mysterious events that occurred prior to the rise and subsequent destruction of magnificent civilizations of the Aztecs in Mexico and the Incas in Peru, and to the appearance of the *Virgen de Guadalupe*. These incredible events are recounted in numerous books, including Richard E. W. Adams's book *Prehistoric Meso-America* and Earl Shorris's book *Latinos*. It appears that every incident, as incredulous as it may seem, was divinely crafted and orchestrated.

Among the first of these mysteries was the prophetic sign that the Aztecs were searching for in the wilderness that would tell them where to build their empire. One hundred fifty years later, they encountered a magnificent eagle on a prickly pear cactus with a snake in its beak, on an island in the middle of a lake in *Tenochtitlán*, which is present-day Mexico City.

Then there is the prophecy that was foretold and recorded before Christopher Columbus arrived in the Caribbean concerning the decimation of the Taino Indians. Earl Shorris cites Fray Ramón Pane's *Account of the Customs of the Indians*, in which he mentions that the Tainos saw in their country "a clothed people who were to rule over them, and slay them, and they would die of hunger." The Taino Indians in Puerto Rico and Cuba were indeed decimated and the Arawaks were also completely annihilated by the Spanish.

In her book *Kingdom of the Sun*, Ruth Karen illustrates the coincidental timing of the arrival of the Spaniards. The Inca Empire fell in thirty-three minutes largely because two royal Inca brothers had just been at war with each other and were exhausted. Before the war, the dying royal father was given the following prophecy by his diviner: "The moon, your mother, tells you that *Pachacuti*, the creator and giver of life, threatens your family, your realm, and your subjects. Your sons will wage cruel war, those of royal blood will die, and the empire will disappear." His prophecy turned out to be accurate, but unfortunately, he was executed for having disclosed it.

The Incas believed that the Spanish explorer Pizarro was the fair-skinned, bearded hero-god who, according to Inca legend, had come to teach them about the "important arts of life" and then left to the East promising to return by sea. The Aztecs had a similar legend. They believed Hernán Cortés was *Quetzalcoatl*, god of light, truth, and goodness who had left *Tenochtitlán* and promised to return from the East. The Aztecs had many other gods, including *Huitzilopochtli*, the god of war, who demanded regular human sacrifices to enable the sun to rise. *Quetzalcoatl* left Tenochtitlán in 895 because he was very much against these human sacrifices.

This Aztec folklore and prophecy set the stage for the drama of the Spanish conquest. The real-life drama had suspense, human drama, and much bloodshed. Right before the arrival of the Spaniards, the Aztecs recorded several unusual events and omens. First, a three-headed comet appeared during the day over *Tenochtitlán*. Second, the temple of *Huitzilopochtli* was burned to the ground in an unexplained fire, and a bolt of lightning from a great storm damaged another *Huitzilopochtli* temple. Third, *Nezahualpilli*, the Texcoco king of the Aztec *Náhuatl* nation, predicted that in 1519 their god *Quetzalcoatl* would return from the East as a large man with blue eyes and blond hair and that the Aztec civilization would come to an end. In 1519, in accordance with that prophecy, a white Spaniard with blue eyes, Hernán Cortés, arrived from the East.

In addition, it is recorded that some Aztec fishermen received a prophecy of "strange-looking people being taken to the Aztec king Moctezuma." Those strange-looking people who requested a meeting with Moctezuma turned out to be the Spaniards, who later took the Aztec king prisoner. Hernán Cortés took advantage of the fact that the Aztecs thought he was a god and the Aztec subject states were not loyal to Moctezuma. Although the Aztec forces won a great victory in 1520, known in Spanish history as "*la Noche Triste*," the sad night, one year after this battle, nine hundred Spanish soldiers and thousands of Indians from the Aztec subject states conquered the Aztec dynasty.

After the conquest, the Spaniards brought great pain and suffering to the Aztecs, including those who had aligned themselves against Moctezuma. The families were torn apart. They were starved, tortured, and forced to become slaves; their culture, religion, and worldview were abruptly changed. One of the greatest civilizations of all time had been destroyed.

The main character, who eventually led to the Christianization of eight to nine million Aztecs in a ten-year period and to the gradual blending of two cultures, was *la Virgen de Guadalupe*. She was the cultural and spiritual bridge between the Aztecs and the Spaniards. The appearance of the Virgin Mary to a poor Aztec *Náhuatl* Indian named Juan Diego in 1531 was the climax in this incredible drama. Because she appeared as a dark-skinned *Mestiza* and spoke the *Náhuatl* language, the Mexican people could identify with her.

According to Jeanette Rodríguez's book titled *Our Lady of Guadalupe: Faith and Empowerment Among Mexican-American Women*, Juan Diego said that *la Virgen de Guadalupe* told him: "...to all the inhabitants of this land and to all who love me, call upon me, and trust in me. I will hear their lamentations and will remedy all their miseries, pains, and sufferings." When *la Virgen de Guadalupe* appeared to Juan Diego and healed his ailing uncle, she told him her name was *Tlecauhtlacupeuh*. The name sounded like *Guadalupe*, the name of the Virgin that the Spaniards brought from Extremadura, Spain. But in *Náhuatl* it means, *"la que viene volando de la luz como el águila de fuego,"* she who comes flying from the region of light like an eagle of fire.

The Aztecs had their own virgin mother god, named *Tonantzín*, who was mother to *Huitzilopochtli*. She was worshipped by the Aztecs on December 12 by the European calendar. The *Virgen de Guadalupe* miraculously appeared to Juan Diego on that same day, December 12, on the hill of Tepeyac, the place where *Tonantzín* was worshipped. The *Virgen de Guadalupe* eventually replaced *Tonantzín*, and the god *Huitzilopochtli* was replaced by the Christian God that the Spaniards brought from Spain.

The miraculous appearance of Our Lady of Guadalupe to Juan Diego occurred during a period when the *Náhuatl* people were in turmoil and suffering greatly. Our Lady wanted a church built in Tepeyac to show all of her love and to comfort those in need. She brought them hope and gave them strength.

LA VIRGEN DE GUADALUPE: OUR CULTURAL SYMBOL OF HOPE AND STRENGTH

That same hope and strength that was given to the Náhuatl people, she has given to Hispanics throughout Latin America and the United States. This is especially true for the many Latinos who migrated to the United States without a social support system or without knowing the language or customs or knowing what was expected of them in this new land. Because of her miraculous appearance and the important role she has played to so many Latinos throughout the Americas, *la Virgen de Guadalupe* was officially recognized by Pope Pius XII as the Patroness of the Americas. She continues to be regarded as a protectress against evil forces, which are sometimes symbolized by snakes and dragons.

Once, in the Mirasol Housing Project in San Antonio where the first Avance center was located, a hideous drawing of a dragon with fire coming out of its mouth and the numbers 666 written next to it covered a wall near the Avance office. This was about the time when drug dealers and delinquent teenagers were causing a great deal of pain and suffering to the residents. An Avance board member, who is Hispanic and a devout Catholic, was so appalled when he saw this drawing that he put up the necessary funds to replace it with a mural of *la Virgen* embracing a Hispanic mother and child. This mural was untouched by graffiti because of the respect and devotion the people have for her. In that Hispanic community and in many others, she appears as an invincible force watching over families. She provided a source of strength and courage to those families, enabling them to challenge the drug dealers, who were destroying their youth and forcing them into a life of drugs and crime. Because of their unity and strength, the parents eventually drove the drug dealers out of their community.

Nuestra Señora de Guadalupe has left us her incredible wonder, the phenomenal *tilma* that Juan Diego wore the day she appeared to him. When Juan Diego dropped the roses from his *tilma* as proof of her authenticity to the Bishop, the image of *la Virgen* miraculously appeared on the cloak. Despite the coarseness of the fabric, the incredible image of the Virgin Mary has remained on Juan Diego's cloak since 1531 and still exists today at the *Basílica de Nuestra Señora de Guadalupe* in Mexico City.

There are many interesting sites on the Internet dealing with *la Virgen*, including http://ng.netgate:net/~norberto/eyes.html. If you explore that site and read the section on the mystery in the eyes of Our Lady of Guadalupe, you will learn about various discoveries of silhouettes in the pupils of both eyes of the Virgin Mary, images that appeared on the original *tilma*. At the center of one of *la Virgen de Guadalupe's* pupils is an image of a family with various children, one of them a baby carried on the mother's back with a *rebozo*. I believe that *Nuestra Señora de Guadalupe* continues to speak to Latinos in a healing voice today as she did at the time of the Aztecs.

That revelation made me think that perhaps *Nuestra Madre*, known by many names, is trying to tell us something about the family. Perhaps she knows that the family is under serious attack in our modern world as the *Náhuatl* people were so many centuries ago. Possibly, she is trying to tell us that she hears the lamentations of many Hispanic families who are suffering because their children are falling victim to drugs, alcohol, and crime. The adults are faced with too much illiteracy, unemployment, and discrimination. Among the children, 15 percent go to bed hungry, almost 50 percent drop out of school, and almost 40 percent live in poverty. Love of money and material things can also destroy our children and families. The Virgin Mary may be sending a message to look to her and God, her Son, for strength and guidance.

I believe that in order to keep families strong, we must begin by rebuilding a foundation from our cultural strengths: our spirituality, as well as the value we place on children, marriage, family, and community. The family, with so many forces threatening it, can survive if we embrace the cultural richness that we have inherited.

The roses that miraculously sprang from Juan Diego's mantle are a metaphor for the rebirth of a new Latino race at a time and place when no one expected them to appear. Like the countless varieties of roses, Latinos reflect a beautiful assortment of colors and varieties. Just as those delicate blossoms thrived with proper nourishment, persistence, and love, so too will our Latino children flourish and become a promise for a better future. Our children have been destined to lead and create a better nation and a better world for all people.

Chapter II

The Hispanic Culture

La Cultura Hispana

Culture is a way of life that encompasses everything from what we believe and how we celebrate, to what we eat and wear. It includes our language, food, religion, music, traditions, and values. Culture consists of how we relate to other people, how we think, how we behave, and how we view the world. Culture is the way a child is socialized from birth beginning with the family, and later from institutions such as the church and schools in the community and the environment around him. The most impressionable is the culture of the home, which is passed down from one generation to the next and learned early during the critical period of life. The Hispanic culture is rich and vibrant, full of traditions, celebrations, and strong relationships. Our culture includes lively songs, delicious foods, strong religious beliefs, and the Spanish language. It is the way we live, it is who we are as Latinos.

From *el bautismo* to *la quinceañera*—a celebration commemorating a young girl's rite of passage into adulthood—Hispanic parents have celebrated events that bring family and friends together to proclaim the child's importance with plenty of food, music, merriment, and spiritual meaning. Hispanics believe in celebrating life. Our culture is imbued with invigorating and uplifting music that restores and energizes the human spirit. Each celebration has its own special songs that heighten our sensibilities and touch our soul, as when "*Las Mañanitas*" is sung at Mexican birthdays, "*Madre Querida*" is sung to *las madrecitas* on Mother's Day, or *Las Posadas* are reenacted with song and drama at Christmas. Guitars, *marimbas*, conga drums, *claves, güiros, maracas*, accordions, and trumpets are some instruments typically used to produce a range of upbeat Latino music, from *cumbias* and *polkas* to *salsas* and *merengues*, all of which are appreciated throughout the world.

El Día de los Muertos, one of many Hispanic traditions, helps us deal with death in a positive way. Our bright and colorful *fiestas* help us cope with life's heavy burdens. In the Hispanic world, life is celebrated with music and brilliant colors. Like the bright paper flowers and colorful ribbons at our celebrations, a child's imagination and creativity abound through our rituals and folklore. Singing, dancing, clapping, and shouting *gritos* such as "*ahua*" energize us and keep us happy and healthy. Ceremonial rituals bring us together with God, family, and friends. Although Hispanics are known to have a powerful work ethic, we also believe in enjoying life. This concept is emphasized in the *dicho Come, bebe, que la vida es breve*, eat, drink for life is short, and the popular Latino toast *Salud, amor, pesetas, y tiempo para disfrutarlas*, health, love, money, and time to enjoy them.

Our culture has played an important role in keeping the family together and keeping it strong through traditions and rituals. It has enabled families to celebrate life and has helped build strong and lasting relationships. These connections to our children and to the extended family, neighbors, and friends are evident as we come together in happy times to celebrate Christmas, Thanksgiving, Easter, Mother's Day, birthdays, *bautismos, quinceañeras*, and weddings, and in sad times as we share the grief with our loved ones at *velorios*.

Hispanics throughout the United States are recapturing their rich heritage in countless ways. They may teach their children to appreciate folklore such as *mariachi* or *jíbaro* music or through *cuentos*. They may also encourage their children to study traditional dances. If we do not expose our children to these cultural traditions, they will surely disappear, along with the special benefits they bring. Parents should make every effort to teach their children the Spanish language, guiding their behavior with insightful *dichos* and taking pride in the traditional mouthwatering dishes of our people. Even some of our traditional folk remedies and herbs, such as *té de manzanilla, té de canela*, and *yerba buena*, have been found to have beneficial medicinal value.

Hispanic parents, along with their children, need to celebrate the fact that they are unique and special because they are Latinos. For many generations in America, there were never many rewards for being Hispanic. When I was in school, for example, if students were caught speaking Spanish, they would be met with a swift *golpe* on the hand with a ruler or they would endure the humiliation of having to stand with their nose facing the inside of a circle on the blackboard. I spent many afternoons with my nose pressed against the *pizarrón* because I entered school speaking mostly Spanish. Like many Hispanics, some of my friends would also hide the *taquitos* their mothers made them inside their paper lunch bags as though ashamed that they did not have a ham and cheese sandwich. None of us want our children to be ashamed of who they are. We do not want our children to go through what many of us experienced in our youth. Those who have succeeded came from parents who encouraged us to know who we are and to be proud of our identity. At a time when our music and artwork are treasured by millions and our cuisine, including tacos, burritos, and salsa, is as popular as hamburgers, pizza, and catsup, it may be easier for Hispanic children to celebrate their cultural heritage, *con gusto, confianza, y orgullo.*

OUR NAMES

Hispanic names speak volumes about our history and culture and remind us of who we are. Many Hispanic names have religious significance, including the name *Guadalupe* or *Lupe*, in honor of Our Lady of Guadalupe. My male cousin and female sister-in-law are both named Guadalupe, both called Lupe for short. You can hardly enter a Hispanic neighborhood without finding a treasure trove of Marys or Marías as in *María Elena, María Antonietta, María Luisa, María de Jesús, Ana María* or Mary Ann, Mary Lou, or Mary Helen. I remember that as a teenager, whenever I would go to the outdoor drive-in with my girlfriends, the boys would inevitably call out to us saying, "Psst, psst, hey, Mary." They knew that the probability of one of us being named Mary was high. Even men in our culture carry the name María, including my great-grandfather who was named José María. Hispanic names reflect the liveliness and spirituality of our culture, from Luz, which means light, to Esperanza, which means hope.

And of course another religious name that is commonly found among Hispanic families is the name of Jesús in English and Spanish. My sister Susie's birth name is *Jesusita,* after my grandmother María de Jesús. Other traditional Hispanic names that have religious significance include names of disciples: *Juan, Lucas, Pablo,* or *Pedro.* The saints and other Biblical and religious figures are remembered in names like *Lourdes, Teresita, Ana, Tomás, José, Moses, Israel, Lázaro, Ester, Magdalena, Marta, Rebeca, Raquel, Mercy, Angel, Angélica, Santos, Gloria,* and *Luz.*

My son Salvador Julián came home from school one day very upset because the boys in his first-grade class said that his name was as long as a snake. He no longer wanted to be named Salvador. He wanted a short name like Tom or Bill. My husband and I sat down with him and explained how special he was to carry the names of his father and two grandfathers and the name of our Savior that translates to *salvador* in Spanish. "There is no greater name than that," we told him. My son responded by saying, "I know that my name is special. I don't mind having a long name at home, but, in school, is it okay if I let them call me Sal, for short?" "Of course," I said, "Daddy is also called Sal by his friends. But he knows that his real name is Salvador and he is proud of it, as we want you to be."

If you live in an ethnically diverse community or your children go to a multi-ethnic school, you may find that people who are not accustomed to hearing Spanish names may treat your child differently, perhaps even tease him. We as parents must help our children deal with negative remarks and sensitize teachers so that they will do likewise. Let the teacher know that you do not want your child's name changed or anglicized for convenience, such as calling a Rafael "Ralph." When you speak to the teacher, pronounce the name the way you want it to be said. They may not be able to roll the R's as well as you, but they will get the picture that your child's name is important and meaningful.

If you believe that names have significance, you should take pride in those names that give your children a sense of their history. Increasingly, we hear names like Valerie, Crystal, Brian, or Jeffrey together with surnames like Garcia or Hernandez. These combinations suggest that we are at a crossroads between two cultures and that we are able to embrace both. In some cases, like my daughter and my son, Gloria Vanessa and Steven Rene, Hispanic children may carry one name from one world and one from the other. Many names like Ana or Benjamín can accommodate both worlds.

Do you have a special name for your children? Nicknames are often better known among Spanish friends than given names. A person may be called *la Araña* if he has long legs, *la Güera* if she has blond hair and fair skin, or *Chino* if he has curly hair. I was called GoGi; Yolanda, the youngest sibling in my family, was called Baby; Susie was *Tuti;* Rosa

Linda was *Chata;* and the eldest in the family is usually called "*Mami.*" My husband was called *Nuni,* because he was a Junior in the family, and one of his brothers was called *Mito* for *hermanito.* Many Hispanic names are shortened to nicknames. For example, *Enrique* is often changed to *Quique, Antonio/Tone; María de Jesús/Chita; Gregoria/Goyo; José/Pepe; Guillermo/Memo; Ignacio/Nacho; Alberto, Gilberto, Roberto/Beto; Jesús/Chuy; Consuelo/Chelo; Luciano/Chano,* and *Rosalía/Chayo.* By adding *ito* and *ita* to some names they become "names of endearment," such as *Juanito, Rosita,* and *Panchito.* Other terms of endearment are *mi hijita, mi amor, mi cielo, mi corazón,* or *mi luna de miel.*

Sometimes words like *gorda(tita), negra(tita), ñaquita, viejito* are *solamente una expresión de cariño.* Unless one is immersed in the culture, one may find it difficult to understand the cultural nuances, just like when I call my daughter "mi Mamita," "mi princesita," "mi hijita," and "mi chulita." She may be my princess, my daughter, my cutie, but she is certainly not my mother.

Did you ever have a special nickname growing up? Do you use any Spanish terms of endearment with your children? Doing so is a great way to celebrate our culture and to create a warm lasting relationship with your children.

OUR RELIGION

An examination of our culture's most enduring aspects might begin with what I consider one of our greatest strengths, our faith. Hispanics represent a host of denominations, including Baptist, Methodist, Jehovah's Witness, Seventh Day Adventist, and Judaism. But because many remain a product of our history, 75 percent of Hispanics are Catholic. Each organized religion has its valuable doctrines, traditions, and practices and most Hispanic people are profoundly spiritual, regardless of ideology. My husband and I were each baptized Catholic and we are raising our children Catholic. As a Catholic, I would like to share with you how integrated the Catholic religion is in the Hispanic culture. Some people may have converted to another religion but have retained many of the Catholic practices that have come to be considered Hispanic because these practices have remained with us for so many centuries.

For example, our strong religious traditions are reflected in the sacred objects that adorn many Hispanic homes bringing blessings, peace, and harmony to our lives. From the *Ojo de Dios,* eye of God, mobiles that hover over a Latino baby's crib, the *rosarios* that we proudly hang on rearview mirrors, and the religious candles, crucifixes, *virgencitas* that are on *altares*, these are some symbols that reflect the Hispanic family's connection to the spiritual world. You see it on the *medallas* and *angelitos* that people wear and in the *santitos, retablos, bultos,* and *nichos* that are prayed to or displayed. Many Hispanics make pilgrimages to shrines like San Juan de Los Lagos in the Texas Rio Grande Valley, praying to the Virgin Mary for *milagros* or to make *promesas*. In many Latino churches, you can pray for a *milagro* for your child by leaving his picture at a special room in the church and lighting a candle, or by attaching a pin in the shape of the body part you want healed to a statue of a particular saint. Crutches, wedding dresses, and even military medals that are found in these rooms signify that many prayers were answered.

Many Hispanics put their faith, hopes, and petitions on *santitos,* such as *Santa Ana.* Songs ask *Santa Ana, la Virgen,* or *Jesús* to hush and lull their babies to sleep as they look over and protect them. As the mother of the Virgin Mary, Saint Ann is the patroness of mothers and grandmothers and she stresses for Hispanics the importance of mother-child relationships and the extended family. Another saint that may play a role in the life of a Hispanic family is Saint Anthony or *San Antonio de Padua,* who cares for sick family members or helps find lost animals. Other popular saints include *San Judas Tadeo,* patron saint of hopeless causes; *Santa Rita de Casia,* for women searching for husbands; *Santa Inés* (Agnes), known for protecting the purity of young girls; and *Santa Bárbara,* who protects against lightning and child abuse. A favorite saint to many Hispanics in Mexico and New Mexico is the *Santo Niño de Atocha,* the patron saint of children, prisoners, and those with illnesses. The saint is also known to protect travelers, as is Saint Christopher. You can use the stories of the saints to teach your children positive behaviors, like kindness, and to discourage others, like selfishness. For many generations of Latinos, *los santitos* have served as moral role models.

Retablos are two-dimensional pieces of Hispanic folk art made of tin, copper, canvas, or wood, which depict the faces or deeds of saints or biblical events. *Nichos* (niches), small boxes that enshrine a *bulto,* a three-dimensional carved wooden sculpture of Jesus, the Virgin Mary, or a saint, are becoming as popular today as they were in the twelfth century. *Nichos* come in all sizes, colors, and designs. You can introduce your children to these beautiful works of art in museums and folk art shops.

In times of bereavement, Catholics also find great peace and strength as they turn to Our Holy Mother through the rosary. Throughout Latin

America, she is known by many names, including *María*, *la Madre Dolorosa*, *la Madre de Socorros*, *la Virgen de Caridad del Cobre*, *la Virgen de San Juan de los Lagos*, *Nuestra Señora de Alta Gracia*, and *Nuestra Señora del Rosario*. She is also known as *Nuestra Señora del Carmen* and *Nuestra Señora de la Luz*. Our Lady of the Angels and Our Lady of the Immaculate Conception are seen as protectors from monsters or evil. But best known is Our Lady of Guadalupe. Along with the Holy Trinity and the Angels, she is seen as a protectoress, healer, comforter, intercessor, and a source of empowerment to Latinos. As a cultural and religious figure, she gives us a sense of identity, purpose, and value.

HONORING *LA VIRGEN DE GUADALUPE*

As you take your children for a drive in Hispanic communities, point out the many shrines built in *la Virgen's* honor in yards and in prominent places in people's homes. Some people, like my mother-in-law, have shrines of *la Virgencita* that are decorated with candles and flowers. I have a picture of her over the fireplace mantel, in my bedroom, and in my car. My neighbor, who prays to *la Virgen* every day, has a shrine that is surrounded by a cloud of cotton with a ceiling lamp shining on the *Virgencita*. Some altars become the central focus of the room where pictures or icons of the Virgin Mary, arranged in a collage, share space with images of Jesus, saints, and members of the family. These *altares* bring the divine and the earthly worlds together. Today, you can still see yard shrines to the *Virgen* called *grutas* (mini grottos) made of rock, tile, seashells, and flowers or her statue as part of fountains in backyards. Her image is depicted on candles, medallions, murals, and even in tattoos on the chests, backs, and arms of brawny men.

Devout Catholics honor Our Lady of Guadalupe on December 12. But all year long, the *Guadalupanas* and *Guadalupanos*, a group of Hispanic women and men dedicated to serving and honoring her, put fresh roses and candles in front of the statue of the Virgin. They are also responsible for organizing the celebration held on her feast day. Throughout the week, there are various masses, *rosarios*, *velorios*, and festivals that feature special dancers. In Mexico, there is a pilgrimage to Tepeyac, the location where she first appeared to Juan Diego. Thousands of people from around the world come to pay her homage. It would be an awesome cultural and religious experience to take your children to witness such an event, as well as to observe the original *tilma* that can be found in the *Basílica de Guadalupe*.

Every year, my husband faithfully joins other choir members beginning at five o'clock in the morning to serenade *la Virgen* on her special day. Each time I attend these gatherings, I am so moved to see the devotion of the many people who wake up so early to sing the beautiful songs written especially for her. They include *"Buenos Días, Paloma Blanca"; "Adiós, O Virgen de Guadalupe," "La Virgen Ranchera,"* as are the ones sung to all mothers, *"Madre Querida," "Canto a la Madre,"* and *"Las Mañanitas."* There are Spanish songbooks with the melodies of these songs in Catholic bookstores, especially in cities where there is a large Hispanic population.

Buenos Días, Paloma Blanca

Buenos días, Paloma Blanca,
hoy te vengo a saludar,
saludando tu belleza
en tu trono celestial.

Eres Madre del Creador,
y a mi corazón encantas;
gracias te doy con amor.
Buenos días, Paloma Blanca.

Niña linda, niña santa,
tu dulce nombre alabar;
porque eres tan sacrosanta,
hoy te vengo a saludar.

Reluciente como el alba,
pura, sencilla y sin mancha;
¡Qué gusto recibe mi alma!
Buenos días, Paloma Blanca.

Qué linda está la mañana,
el aroma de las flores
despiden suaves olores
antes de romper el alba.

Mi pecho con voz ufana,
gracias te da, Madre mía;

en este dichoso día
antes de romper el alba.

Cielo azul yo te convido
en este dichoso día
a que prestes tu hermosura
a las flores de María.

Madre mía de Guadalupe,
dame ya tu bendición;
recibe estas mañanitas
de un humilde corazón.

Adiós, O Virgen de Guadalupe

Adiós, O Virgen de Guadalupe,
Adiós, O Virgen del Salvador,
Desde que niño nombrarte supe
Eres mi vida, eres mi vida, mi solo amor.

Adiós, O Virgen, Madre querida;
Adiós refugio del pecador.
Eres mi encanto, eres mi vida,
Dulce esperanza en mi dolor.

Adiós, O Virgen de Guadalupe,
Adiós, O Madre del Redentor,
Ante tu trono siempre se agrupe
Todo tu pueblo lleno de amor.

Adiós, O Madre la más amable,
Aquí te dejo mi corazón;
Adiós, O Virgen incomparable,
Dame, Señora, tu bendición.

La Virgen Ranchera

A ti Virgencita, mi Guadalupana,
Yo quiero ofrecerte un canto valiente
Que Méjico entero te diga sonriente.

Yo quiero decirte lo que tú ya sabes
Que Méjico te ama, que nunca está triste
Porque de nombrarte el alma se inflama.

Tu nombre es arrullo y el mundo lo sabe
Eres nuestro orgullo, mi Méjico es tuyo,
Tú guardas la llave.

Que viva la Reina de los Mejicanos
La que con sus manos sembró rosas bellas
Y puso en el cielo millares de estrellas.

Yo sé que en el cielo escuchas mi canto
Y sé que con celo nos cubre tu manto
Virgencita chula eres un encanto.

Por patria nos diste este lindo suelo
Y lo bendijiste porque era tu anhelo
Tener un santuario cerquita del cielo.

Mi Virgen ranchera, mi Virgen morena,
Eres nuestra dueña, Méjico es tu tierra
Y tú su bandera.

Que viva la Reina de los Mejicanos
La que con sus manos sembró rosas bellas
Y puso en el cielo millares de estrellas.

In many Hispanic communities, extravagant festivities on December 12 include special dancers called *Concheros* and *Matachines* who create music with rattles, shell anklets, flutes, and *conchas* of armadillos. They are dressed up in bright, sequined costumes with ribbons, feathers, beads, mirrors, and beautiful headdresses representing their ancestral Aztec culture. The *Matachines*, or sword dancers, perform up to twelve different dances, including "The Maypole," "The Battle," "The Cross," "The Procession," "El Abuelo," "The Maypole," and "El Toro."

This ritual sword dance was originally performed in medieval times to represent the conflict between the Moors and Christians. It was brought to Mexico and the Southwest to symbolize the resistance of the Indians to the Spanish Conquest and the later subjugation and discrimination that they experienced. On December 12, the drama of *la Virgen de Guadalupe's* appearance to Juan Diego is portrayed within the context of the clash of religions and cultures that resulted from the meeting between Cortés and Moctezuma. It is also reenacted to mock the role *la Malinche* played in the conquest through presentations in which young boys dress up as girls with funny or grotesque masks, wigs, and costumes that portray her. Through drama, humor, and symbolism, they depict the transformation of a people.

Get your child the book by Sylvia Rodriguez entitled *The Matachines Dance* to learn more about these ritual dances and their meaning. If you live in a community where *la Virgen's* feast day is celebrated, introduce your child to this rich part of our culture. Your son or daughter may be interested in playing one of the roles in the ceremony, where you may have to make elaborate costumes, as are worn today by the Pueblo Indians and *Hispanos* of New Mexico. I am sure your child will never forget the day he or she plays one of these characters, if they're lucky enough to be selected. Adults also play various roles and have even more fun than their children. It is said that voluntary participation brings honor and blessings to the performer's family and the community in general. If groups who perform these ceremonies do not exist in your community, perhaps you can begin one.

OUR CELEBRATIONS

Many of our traditions, beliefs, practices, celebrations, and rituals revolve around religion. They are centered in church services that bring family and friends together for baptisms, first communions, confirmations, *quinceañeras*, and weddings, as well as religious holidays including Christmas, New Year's Eve, *Día de Pascuas*, and *El Día de los Muertos*. There are also many religious *fiestas* and festivals that are celebrated with plenty of delicious food, colorful paper flowers, and lively entertainment that, along with the spiritual significance, make our life more exhilarating and joyful.

Celebrating *La Nochebuena*, Christmas Eve

At sunset on Christmas Eve or *Nochebuena*, Hispanic families throughout the Americas prepare for *Las Posadas*, a Spanish word meaning lodging. The traditional reenactment of the journey by Mary and Joseph to find shelter at Bethlehem is celebrated for nine days in Mexico and other Latin American countries beginning on December 16. Each night a group of neighbors carrying candle *farolitos*, tin lanterns, walk to several houses in the neighborhood with statues of Mary and Joseph on a donkey. *Luminarias*, brown paper bags weighted down with sand and a votive candle, illuminate the night and guide the travelers or *peregrinos* on their journey. Perhaps your family can participate in a *Posada* sponsored by your church or you or a neighbor can begin one in your community. Improvise making shepherd costumes and instruments, or plan the event with the whole pageantry and regalia of a Christmas scene.

Following is the traditional song that is sung. The *peregrinos* knock on the door of a neighbor's house and ask for lodging, singing the following song (*Afuera*). The family members of that house similarly respond in song (*Adentro*):

Las Posadas

Choir:

(Joseph, Mary, and the group of travelers sing)

Afuera

1. *En nombre del Cielo,*
Os pido posada,
Pues no puede andar
Mi esposa amada.

Head of the House:

(The family opens the door and the head of the house responds)

Adentro

2. *Aquí no es mesón.*
Sigan adelante.
Yo no puedo abrir.
No sea algún tunante.

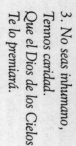

3. No seas inhumano,
Tennos caridad,
Que el Dios de los Cielos
Te lo premiará.

4. Ya se pueden ir
Y no molestar,
Porque si me enfado
Los voy a apalear.

5. Venimos rendidos
Desde Nazaret.
Yo soy carpintero
De nombre José.

6. No me importa el nombre.
Déjenme dormir.
Pues ya se los digo
Que no hemos de abrir.

7. Posada te pide,
Amado casero,
Por solo una noche
La Reina del Cielo.

8. Pues si es una Reina
Quien lo solicita,
¿Cómo es que de noche
Anda tan solita?

9. Mi esposa es María,
Es Reina del Cielo
Y madre va a ser
Del Divino Verbo.

10. ¿Eres tú José?
¿Tu esposa es María?
Entren, peregrinos,
No los conocía.

11. Dios pague, señores,
Vuestra caridad,
Y así os colme el Cielo
De felicidad.

12. Dichosa la casa
Que abriga este día
A la Virgen pura
La hermosa María.

ENTIRE FAMILY:

(When the door opens the host family responds)

Ábranse las puertas, rómpanse los velos,
Que viene a posar el Rey de los Cielos.

Entren, santos peregrinos, peregrinos.
Reciban este rincón,
No de mi pobre morada, mi morada,
Sino de mi corazón.

As the people enter the house, they kneel down before the nacimiento, a manger, in remembrance of the birth of Christ, the true meaning of Christmas. On Christmas Eve, families bring out a doll representing the baby Jesus and the owner of the house selects a woman whom

she likes who will become her *comadre* for three years. As the *madrina* of the baby Jesus, she will *arrullar*, or rock, the *Santo Niño* before she puts him in the manger. Everyone sings the following lullaby, which is followed by the breaking of the piñata and its corresponding song.

El Roro

A la rururu, niño chiquito.
Duérmase ya mi Jesusito.
Los animales grandes y chiquitos,
guarden silencio, no le hagan ruido.

Noche venturosa, noche de alegría.
Bendita la dulce, divina María.

Coros celestiales, con su dulce acento,
Canten la ventura de este nacimiento.

La Piñata Song for Las Posadas

En las noches de Posada, la piñata es lo mejor
Aun las niñas remilgadas, se animan con gran fervor.

Con los ojitos vendados, y en las manos un bastón
La olla rómpela a pedazos, no le tengas compasión.

Dale, dale, dale
no pierdas el tino.
Mide la distancia
que hay en el camino.

Que si no le das
de un palo te tiro.
Que si no le das
de un palo te tiro.
Dale, dale, dale.

Many go to Mass to present a gift in front of the *nacimiento*, which can be a poinsettia plant, food for the poor, or a *promesa*, a pious offering to behave better. The neighbors prepare special foods like *pan dulce*, cookies called *bizcochitos*, *chocolate Mexicano*, or *ponche y dulces*. Each of the nine days includes festive, colorful sights, joyous sounds, and luscious smells. One can find sweet treats, a colorful *piñata*, music, and singing that leave lasting impressions on any child.

As part of a *Las Posadas* celebration, make these traditional foods with your children. Enlist an older family member to help you out if you have never tried making these on your own. Chances are that past and present generations will find lots of common ground as you make these delicious traditional treats. Perhaps your children can help you cut out the cookies, roll the dough into spheres, or put the cinnamon and sugar mix on the cookies.

▼▼▼▼▼▼▼▼▼▼▼▼▼▼

Bizcochitos
Anise Cookies

1   pound (2 cups) lard
1   cup sugar
2   eggs, beaten
1   teaspoon vinegar (only if using orange juice)
2   tablespoons aniseed
6   cups flour
3   teaspoons baking powder
1   teaspoon salt
⅓   cup orange juice, or ¼ cup brandy, cognac, sherry, or bourbon (whichever you prefer for taste)
⅔   cup sugar plus 1 teaspoon ground cinnamon, for coating

Preheat oven to 350°F. Cream together lard and sugar in a bowl until light and fluffy. Add eggs, vinegar (if using), and aniseed, beating until creamy. In a separate bowl, combine flour, baking powder, and salt. Add the flour mixture and the orange juice alternately to the lard mixture, beating until the dough is firm. On a floured surface, roll out dough with a rolling pin to ½ inch thick. Cut out dough with small (I prefer a 1-inch) cookie cutter of your choice and dredge with sugar/cinnamon mixture. Place on an ungreased baking sheet and bake for 10 to 20 minutes, or until light brown. Makes from 4 to 12 dozen cookies, depending on size.

Pan de Polvo

¾ cup (2½ ounces) aniseed
5 3-inch cinnamon sticks
3 cups water
1 package (¼ ounce) active dry yeast
1 cup sugar
1 pound (2 cups) lard
1 pound (2 cups) vegetable shortening
12 cups flour
⅔ cups sugar plus 1 teaspoon ground cinnamon, for coating

Preheat oven to 350°F. In a one-quart saucepan, boil the aniseed and cinnamon sticks in water for several minutes to make anise/cinnamon tea. Remove from the stove and set aside until warm. Dissolve yeast and sugar in warm tea. Stir together lard and shortening until creamy. Add the flour and tea to the lard mixture, beating until the dough is firm. On a floured surface, roll out dough with a rolling pin to ¼ inch thick. Cut out dough with small (I prefer a 1-inch circle or heart shape) cookie cutter of your choice. Place on an ungreased baking sheet and bake for 15 to 20 minutes, or until light brown. Press warm cookies in the sugar/cinnamon mixture. Make 6 to 8 dozen, depending on size. Cookies can be stored in a sealed tin container for up to 4 weeks. These cookies are served at weddings and *quinceañeras*.

Polvorones de Canela
Cinnamon Cookies

1 cup (2 sticks) butter or margarine, cut into pieces
½ cup confectioners' sugar
1 teaspoon vanilla extract
2½ cups flour
1 teaspoon ground cinnamon
¼ teaspoon salt
1 cup finely chopped pecans
1 cup confectioners' sugar plus 1 teaspoon ground cinnamon, for coating

Preheat oven to 350°F. With an electric mixer, cream butter until fluffy, then mix in sugar and vanilla. Gradually beat in two cups flour, cinnamon, and salt. Stir pecans into remaining flour, add to dough mixture, and beat until well mixed. Cover and chill dough for 2 hours. Form chilled dough into 1-inch balls, place on an ungreased baking sheet, and bake for 15 minutes. While still warm, roll cookies in sugar/cinnamon mixture. Makes 4 to 5 dozen cookies.

▼▼▼▼▼▼▼▼▼▼▼▼▼▼▼▼▼▼▼▼▼▼▼▼▼▼▼▼▼▼▼▼▼▼

Pasteles de Bodas
Wedding Cookies

1   cup (2 sticks) butter, cut into pieces
1   teaspoon vanilla extract
½   cup confectioners' sugar, plus additional confectioners' sugar for
     coating
2   cups flour
¼   teaspoons salt
1   cup finely chopped pecans

Preheat oven to 350°F. With an electric mixer, cream together butter and vanilla until fluffy. Beat in sugar. In a separate bowl, mix together flour and salt; beat into butter mixture. Beat in the pecans. Form dough into 1-inch balls and roll into log shapes about 1¼ inches in diameter. Refrigerate for 2 hours until firm. Slice logs into ½-inch thick rounds, place on an ungreased baking sheet, and bake 15 to 20 minutes. While still warm, sprinkle with confectioners' sugar. Makes 24 cookies.

Although some Hispanics in America still celebrate *Las Posadas* for nine days, most people hold a condensed version on Christmas Eve. In my family, the children dress as angels and shepherds. In a truly bicultural celebration, the youngest male child usually plays the part of the drummer boy, a tradition of North America.

In my old neighborhood, the *peregrinos*, or travelers, walked to shelter stations (huts) set up throughout our large front yard to symbolize Mary and Joseph's journey to different inns. Each family would sing a response from their hut. When we moved to the suburbs, neighbors were invited to participate in *Las Posadas*. As family members walked to the neighbors' homes through streets lit with Christmas lights and paper *luminarias*, we sang Christmas carols in both English and Spanish. My husband led the crowd playing the trumpet. At our first stop, we knocked at the door, and when the neighbors opened it, we sang "*Las Posadas.*" Since they were all having their own family gatherings, they invited us in for a drink and cookies. We wished them *una Feliz Navidad* and then went on to the next neighbor's house. Our house was the last stop where the whole group entered after the singing to enjoy much food and merriment. First, though, everyone is to kneel before the *nacimiento* while the baby Jesus is laid on the *pesebre*, cradle, where he remains until *Día de los Tres Reyes Magos*, The Epiphany.

Right before midnight, the whole family usually rushes to *La Misa de Gallo*, named for the legendary story of two roosters, one who stood on the manger on the First Christmas and announced "*¡Cristo nació!*" Christ has been born, while the other answered, "*¡en Belén!*" in Bethlehem. At midnight Mass we partake of the Eucharist, watch a reenactment of the birth of Christ, and sing popular Christmas songs, like "*Noche de Paz,*" Silent Night.

Noche de Paz

Noche de paz, noche de amor,
Todo duerme en derredor,
Entre los astros que esparcen su luz,
Bella, anunciando al niñito Jesús,
Brilla la estrella de paz, brilla la estrella de paz.

Noche de paz, noche de amor,
Todo duerme en derredor,
Sólo velan en la oscuridad
Los pastores que en el campo están;
Y la estrella de Belén, y la estrella de Belén.

You can have joyous memories decorating your house for Christmas with your children. At my house, Steven takes pride in building the *nacimiento*, adorning it with moss, Christmas lights, angels, shepherds, animals, and figurines of the Virgin Mary and Joseph. It is then placed in a prominent location in the house. Adjacent to the *nacimiento* is a snow-covered village that becomes the family project, where everyone decides where the many houses, buildings, and townspeople that I have collected through the years go. Some "villages" in Latin American homes take up a wall from floor to ceiling with animals, shepherds, and townspeople, a snapshot of how they envision that special night. Try building one with your children. I can assure you, this experience will have lasting memories.

Beautiful decorations—*angelitos*, snowballs, candles, and floral centerpieces—can be used to create the spirit of Christmas. Garlands decked with pinecones, angels, and ornaments can embellish the fireplace mantel and staircase. A majestic-looking Christmas tree is put up in my living room and covered with every *angelito* imaginable as well as flowers and birds. The second Christmas tree, which we have in the game room, is decorated with Mexican ornaments made of yarn and glimmering colorful beads.

You can have another memorable family project creating the nativity scene in your front yard. My husband's pride is a large manger that the family builds annually, trimmed with Christmas lights, *nochebuenas*, and a huge star that illuminates the sky. There are also plastic life-size figurines of Mary, Joseph, and baby Jesus inside the manger, with wooden cutouts of kings, a shepherd, camel, donkey, and lighted iron-wrought angels. This outdoor Christmas scene always attracts attention and causes cars to stop to take a second look. You, too, can help your children make some of these religious characters or even Santa Claus and his reindeer. Get the child with the artistic talents to sketch out the design on plywood and get an adult to cut out the designs. Then let your children paint and decorate the characters. Even I got involved in decorating the Three Kings with artificial jewels and the camel with a "saddle" made from a piece of carpet and decorated with tassels. These kinds of activities are a great deal of fun and enjoyment and are sure to make your Christmases extremely memorable.

CHRISTMAS DAY

Our family celebrates Christmas twice: on Christmas Eve with my husband's extended family and on Christmas Day with my extended family. Both days can produce captivating and exhilarating moments filled with sounds of laughter, the aroma of delicious foods, and the glimmer of holiday lights. We have a big spread that includes tamales, rice and beans, *chilitos*, vegetable salads, and a table full of delicious desserts from pecan pies to *bizcochitos* and empanadas.

Tamales

A tradition that is making a great comeback among Hispanics during Christmas is tamale making. It is a family affair or the time for female friends and family members to come together to complete the time-consuming and laborious task. Increasingly, more men are joining in the making of homemade tamales. It is hard work and an all-day event. However, it can also be a time to catch up on the latest *chismes*, gossip. Some people have a tradition of the entire family making tamales on Christmas Eve to have their big meal of warm tamales on Christmas day. Others cook them weeks and days in advance and freeze them. Tamales are so delicious, but so fattening. Oh well, as the *dicho* goes, *Una vez al año no hace daño, una vez al mes tal vez*, Once a year it doesn't cause harm, once a month perhaps it does. If you would like to make some traditional foods for the holiday season, try some of these recipes for making empanadas and tamales. Again, your child can help you make the spheres, roll them, or prick the empanadas. Have your child separate the dried husk, soak the leaves in water, and fish them out when they are ready. The older ones can help you spread the *masa*. Making tamales is a lot of work, but the homemade tamales are so good and the tradition of making them must continue. It would be wonderful if your child had at least one experience making tamales, so that he can continue this tradition with his own children.

There are so many varieties of tamales. You can make the traditional ones out of *cabeza de marrano* and *piernitas de marranito*, while tamales made of pork and beef roast are now becoming more popular. You can also find tamales made of deer, beans, raisins/cinnamon/sugar, and for those who are more conscientious of their weight, replace the lard with vegetable oil and the meat with fresh vegetables such as squash and corn. Of course, there is always the stack of tamales that have chili and those that do not.

My sister Rosa Linda and her family make 20 to 25 dozen tamales every year for Christmas, putting some in her freezer to be warmed up when friends and relatives come to visit. Her tamales are bigger and meatier than the average. She has learned some rules of thumb in the process of making tamales. According to her, she uses one pound of meat to make one dozen tamales. For every pound of *masa*, she uses one teaspoon of salt, one teaspoon of chili powder, and ½ teaspoon paprika. She never lets the water touch the tamales when they are cooking. She no longer makes all 20 dozen in one day as she used to, but makes them in two days. The first day she prepares all the meat and makes one batch, then she finishes the rest the next day.

Most Hispanic families I know will not go through the trouble of making tamales unless they make enough of them to freeze. Therefore, the following recipes are for large quantities. In the first recipe, you can divide all the ingredients in half to make 10 to 12 dozen, or by 5 to make 5 dozen. The second recipe uses fresh chiles minced in the blender instead of chili powder, and the tamales are cooked standing on end rather than lying flat.

20 to 25 Dozen Tamales

10 pounds pork roast
10 pounds beef roast
5 teaspoons salt (or to taste)
2 to 3 cups water

2 cups lard
1 cup flour
6 cups hot water
2 tablespoons salt
4 teaspoons pepper
4 ounces prepared Gebhardt chili powder
4 tablespoons paprika
4 tablespoons cumin
8 cloves garlic, minced

Preheat oven to 350°F. Cut the roasts into 1-pound pieces. Place meat in a large roasting pan. Add salt and water and cook for 3 hours. Turn meat and cook for another hour until very tender. Turn the oven off and let meat simmer for thirty minutes. When cool enough to handle, shred meat and mix together. Pour off the remaining broth and divide in thirds, refrigerating one third to use in *masa* the following day.

Divide all remaining ingredients in half and prepare meat in 2 batches. In 2 5-quart Dutch ovens, melt lard over low heat. Add flour and stir until brown. Add hot water and stir constantly, scraping the bottom, until gravy starts bubbling. Add salt, pepper, Gebhardt chili powder, paprika, cumin, garlic, and one-third of the reserved meat broth and simmer for thirty minutes. (If gravy becomes too thick, add a little more water and let it simmer for another 10 minutes.) Add more salt if needed. Stir meat into the gravy a little at a time and simmer, stirring constantly, 20 to 30 minutes. Turn off heat and let meat cool, stirring every 15 minutes, until cool enough to handle. Refrigerate, covered, overnight, leaving the lid slightly open.

Masa

4 pounds lard
20 pounds prepared *masa*
Reserved meat broth
10 teaspoons salt
10 teaspoons chili powder
5 teaspoons paprika

Melt lard over low heat and set aside to cool. In a large pan, mix *masa* with lard a little at a time with your hand for 30 minutes to an hour. Add reserved meat broth, salt, chili powder, and paprika to the *masa* after 15 to 30 minutes. Divide into 2 batches.

Making the Tamales

20 to 25 dozen corn husks
Prepared *masa*
Prepared meat

Remove the silk from the corn husks. Right before you spread the *masa* on the tamales, rinse the husks twice and soak them, 6 to 8 dozen at a time, for about thirty minutes. Working with one husk at a time, place the husk, smooth side up, on your palm with the point of the husk toward your fingers. Spread a tablespoonful of *masa* on the husk. Spread *masa* evenly over the bottom two-thirds of the husk; do not put *masa* on the pointed top third of the husk. Place a spoonful of prepared meat in the middle of the *masa* and with your fingers pat it into a strip down the center of the *masa*. Fold one-third of the husk lengthwise over the meat, then fold over the other third. With your fingers, flatten the tamale slightly and fold the pointed end over the top of the folded sides. Set the tamale aside, folded part down. Make five dozen at a time before putting them in the pot.

Cooking the Tamales

In a 5-gallon pot with a wire rack set in the bottom, arrange just enough unused husks to cover the rack, leaving a 2-inch opening in the center and a 1-inch gap at the sides of the pot to allow steam to pass through to cook the tamales. Going around in a circle, stack each tamale flat, folded side down and the open end away from the center, leaving a ¼-inch gap between tamales and leaving the center open. Start the second layer by placing the first *tamal* on top of the ¼-inch opening between tamales on the first layer, again leaving a ¼-inch gap, until you complete the circle. Continue until all tamales are in the pot. Pour in about 6 cups of water, or enough to reach ¾ of an inch up from the bottom of the pan. Cover, allowing steam to escape slowly, and cook for 1 hour and 15 minutes over moderate heat. If too much steam is escaping, cover two-thirds of the edge of the pot with foil. Remove the top dozen and a half tamales, add a cup of water, and cook another 30 minutes to ensure that the tamales in the center get cooked. Before you peel the husk off, open the tamale and let it simmer for 1 minute. If the cooked tamale easily slides out of the husk without sticking, it is cooked. If white spots of *masa* stick to the husk, they need a little bit more cooking. Repeat the stacking and cooking for each 5 dozen tamales. *Buen provecho.*

▼▼▼▼▼▼▼▼▼▼▼▼▼▼▼▼▼▼▼▼▼

A Different Way of Making Tamales

This recipe makes 14 dozen tamales.

Meat

7   pounds pork roast
6   cups (approximately) water
5   cloves garlic
2   teaspoons salt

Chili

15   or 16 dried red chile peppers
     Hot water
1   teaspoon cumin
4   cloves garlic

Place pork in a 3-gallon pot and add water to cover. Add garlic and salt and boil over moderate heat for 2 hours, or until fully cooked. Pour off liquid from roast, reserving 4 cups; set aside. Tear pork into tiny shreds.

Soak chile peppers in hot water to cover for 1 hour. Discard stems and seeds. Fill a blender halfway with chiles, add 1 cup of water, cumin, and garlic, and puree. Repeat the procedure, using chiles and water, until all the chiles are used. Pour each batch into a large Dutch oven and mix thoroughly. Add shredded pork and mix. Cook over moderate heat just until liquid comes to a boil.

Masa

3   pounds lard at room temperature
1½   teaspoons baking powder
10   pounds prepared *masa*
2   tablespoons salt
4   cups reserved warm pork broth

With an electric mixer, beat lard and baking powder for about 30 minutes, or until fluffy. Working in batches, in a large bowl or pan, add some *masa* and some warm broth to lard and mix with your hands until well blended. Fill a glass with cool water and drop a small piece of *masa* in. If it floats to the top, it is ready. Mix in salt.

Soaking Husks

Soak husks in hot water overnight. Rinse husks, making sure corn silk is removed. (You can also clean the husks right before you make the tamales, but make sure that they are cool before using.)

Spreading the *Masa*

Place the husk in your palm with the pointed end of the husk toward your fingers. Place a tablespoonful of *masa* on the husk and spread from side to side in a rectangle, making sure to leave at least ¼-inch margin on sides and bottom. Do not put *masa* on point of husk. Place a tablespoonful of meat filling in middle of *masa*. Fold sides of husk over to enclose filling, then fold point of the husk down over folded sides.

Cooking the Tamales

In a 5-gallon pot, place enough unused husks to cover the bottom of the pot. Place a wire rack on top of the husks. Pour in 4 cups of water. Place tamales upright on the wire rack with open end up. Start in the middle and work your way around. (Do not lay tamales flat.) Arrange more unused husks on top of the tamales, and cover with 2 layers of cheesecloth to hold in steam. Cover and cook over high heat for ½ hour; reduce heat to moderate and continue cooking for 45 minutes. Turn heat off, leaving pot covered for another 30 minutes. If the cooked *tamal* slides easily out of the husk, it is done.

Empanadas

Just like tamales, empanadas come in different varieties.

Fresh Pumpkin Empanadas

Filling

1 medium-size pumpkin (7 to 10 pounds)
2 cups brown sugar
1 teaspoon cinnamon
1 teaspoon cloves
Pinch of salt

Dough

1¼ cups (4 ounces) aniseed
2½ cups water
7½ cups flour
2½ cups (5 sticks) butter or margarine
½ cup sugar
1 tablespoon salt

Preheat oven to 375°F. Wash the pumpkin, and stem and seed it. Cut into 5-inch by 3-inch pieces. Place, skin up, in a large pot and cover with water. Bring to a boil over high heat, then reduce heat to a simmer and cook until soft. Peel pumpkin and place pulp in a large saucepan. Add brown sugar, cinnamon, cloves, and salt and mash the pumpkin. Cook over low heat until mixture looks pasty; set aside.

For the dough, boil aniseed in water for several minutes; remove from heat and set aside. Mix together flour, butter, sugar, and salt. Gradually add anise liquid to flour mixture, and knead until a firm dough forms.

Pinch off pieces of dough and form into 2-inch balls. On a floured surface with a rolling pin, roll each ball to ¼ inch thick. (Or roll entire amount of dough out to ¼-inch thick and cut into 3-inch circles.) Put a tablespoonful of filling on one-half of the circle. Fold circle in half, seal edges with a fork, and prick top three times with fork. Place empanadas on an ungreased baking sheet and bake 20 to 25 minutes, or until brown. Makes about 24 empanadas.

Easy-to-Make Empanadas

Filling

1   cup solid pack pumpkin
⅔   cup sugar
1   tablespoon aniseed
1   tablespoon finely crushed cinnamon stick

Dough

⅔   cup water
2   tablespoons sugar
½   teaspoon salt
1   or 2 pinches finely crushed cinnamon stick
1¼   cups shortening
1   drop yellow food coloring
3½   cups flour
2   teaspoons baking powder

Preheat oven to 375°F. Stir filling ingredients together until sugar is dissolved. Do not cook.

In a mixing bowl, combine water, sugar, salt, cinnamon, shortening, and food coloring. Mix together flour and baking powder and add to the shortening mixture. Knead lightly to form dough. If sticky, add more flour. Avoid overmixing. Cut dough into 12 to 15 pieces and roll into balls a little bigger than a golf ball. On a floured surface with a rolling pin, roll out dough to ¼ inch thick. Place filling in the center of the circle and fold over and seal with a fork. Place on an ungreased baking sheet and bake 20 to 25 minutes, or until brown.

We have a tradition in our family of dressing a family member as *Papa Noel*, or Santa Claus, to pass out the Christmas gifts. As the children are brought to the front of the Christmas tree, my sister Susie and I, the two schoolteachers, lead the children in singing Spanish Christmas carols like "*Feliz Navidad*" and "*Noche de Paz*." We also sing "Jingle Bells," "Frosty the Snowman," and "Santa Claus Is Coming to Town." Hearing his cue at the end of this song, *Papa Noel* comes down the stairs with his white beard, which sometimes reveals his black mustache, and his disproportionate (stuffed) potbelly. He sits on his special rocking chair by the Christmas tree and joins the excited children with one or two Christmas carols before he distributes the gifts. The very young children are enthralled by this character as they try to figure out if he is the real thing. The older ones usually go along with it. Every year the adults look forward to seeing Santa's wife or girlfriend sit on his lap to get her present, in addition to her kiss.

Then comes the finale, the time when some of the children take center stage and demonstrate their musical talents. We have Iris, who annually sings Selena songs and Nadia who sings "Silent Night." Other years we have been entertained by Sal, Monica, and Melissa who have played the piano, Rene the violin, Tony and Manuel the guitar, and Steven the accordion. If your children have a special musical talent, make them feel important by asking them to play their instruments, sing a song, or play a part in a Christmas pageant.

There is so much preparation and effort to produce the seemingly perfect and memorable holiday celebration. In many homes, the women still do more than their share of the cleaning and food preparation with some help from *los hombres*. I realize that in some families, if the women are not determined or willing to keep certain traditions alive, these traditions surely will not survive. It is a truism when people say *la mujer hace el hogar*, a woman makes the home. She is the glue that keeps the family together. But it is important that all members of the family do their part in creating the enchanted moments.

Los Pastores — The Shepherds

Los Pastores is a religious folk play that originated in the twelfth century in Europe and was brought by the Spanish missionaries to the New World as a means to Christianize the indigenous people. Since the Spanish did not speak the same language as the Indians, they tried to teach many of their religious beliefs through folk drama and traditions. The drama of the birth of Jesus, based on the Biblical account in Luke

2, is still alive today. This semicomic shepherd's play is performed by Hispanics in neighborhood backyards, churches, and community courtyards during the month of December and the early part of January. The characters include a hermit, an old spiritual man with a white beard who carries a rosary and a cross, several devils, Saint Michael the Archangel, and some shepherds. The theme revolves around the devils coming to earth to attack Man while Jesus is still a baby. Ultimately goodness prevails.

The play begins with an angel of the Lord telling the shepherds of the good news of the birth of Christ. The shepherds became very happy and set out to see the baby Jesus in the manger. One of the shepherds runs into an old hermit and tells him that the Messiah has come. The shepherd invites the old hermit to his camp to inform the others about the Messiah. There they find the shepherds arguing and carrying on, especially a married couple. The devils appear to one of the shepherds who wandered away from the camp. Frightened, he runs back to the camp and tells the other shepherds about the devils. The devils' plot against Man begins with tempting the hermit to kidnap one of the female shepherds. While the shepherds are beating up the hermit, Saint Michael the Archangel fights the devils and sends them back to hell. The play ends with the reenactment of the birth of Christ, a lullaby, and a farewell.

If you can't find a *Los Pastores* celebration in your community, watch the video with Linda Ronstadt and Los Lobos entitled *Los Pastores*. This has become a classic and is shown on many PBS stations during the holiday season. Here is a traditional song about the shepherds, called "*Amigos Pastores*."

Amigos Pastores

Amigos pastores, es tiempo de ver
a la Virgen Pura y al Niño también.
Venid, venid, venid a Belén.
Venid, venid, venid a Belén.

Amigos pastores, vamos a Belén,
ha nacido un Niño llamado Emmanuel.
Venid, venid, venid a Belén.
Venid, venid, venid a Belén.

Los Tres Reyes Magos

In some Hispanic families, especially among Puerto Ricans, *Día de Los Tres Reyes Magos*, which falls on January 6, twelve days after the birth of Christ, is celebrated as faithfully as Christmas. And no wonder. This holiday commemorates the day when the Three Wise Men followed the bright North Star to a manger in Bethlehem to bring gifts to *el Niñito Jesús*, the Messiah. This day is also called the Day of the Epiphany. For Hispanics, this story is transformed into a tradition that becomes a day of more gifts and lessons for the children after Christmas. Family members wait to exchange gifts among themselves, and the children receive up to three special gifts from the "visiting" Kings in the same way American children do from Santa Claus.

On January 5, have your children place straw for the camels in boots or shoes left outside their doors or under their beds. Have them leave a glass of water and fruit for the Kings. In the middle of the night, replace all these gifts with treats the children like. When the children awake, they will find the straw, water, and fruit gone, and in the boots or shoes they will find small presents and goodies.

Parents should try to make this a joyous day for their children while teaching them its true religious significance. In Mexico, this is the day the *madrina*, who rocked the baby Jesus on Christmas Eve, gets to "*levantar*" *el Niño* from the *pesebre* and dress him, like the *Niño de las Palomas* and *Niño de Atocha*, to be baptized in a church. Some lavish the baby with an extravagant christening gown, a long, beautiful white dress made of lace. On the *madrina's* third year the baby is crowned with a king's crown and cape. The newly baptized *Santo Niño* is brought back from the church and placed on a special chair or bed on an altar where he remains until February 2, when he is put away and the Christmas season is officially over. People from Mexico who migrated to the United States have brought this tradition with them and have taught it to others. "*Las Mañanitas*" is sung as *el Niño* is lifted. Instead of taking the baby to the church, perhaps you can invite a priest to your home to lead a group of people in a rosary and to officiate over the "*levantado*" ceremony. Perhaps you may just want to build or buy a special chair and let your child have the privilege of placing the baby Jesus in his place of honor.

Among some Mexican Americans, *Día de los Tres Reyes* is celebrated with family or neighbors and with *champurrado* (an *atole* made with *harina*, *canela*, sugar, chocolate, and milk) or *horchata*, which is made out of the juice of rice, evaporated milk, cinnamon, and vanilla. Sometimes, among Puerto Ricans, the event involves a big meal with a feast of *paste-*

les, *arroz con grandules*, *lechón asada y tostones* (fried plantain bananas).
Try these recipes with your children on a cold rainy day.

Horchata

1½ cups whole grain white rice
1   gallon (16 cups) water
2   cinnamon sticks
1   cup evaporated milk
1   tablespoon vanilla extract
1½ cups sugar (or to taste)
    Ice

Soak rice and cinnamon sticks in water overnight (or at least 4 hours).
Working in batches, liquify rice mixture in a blender. Stir in evaporated
milk, vanilla extract, and sugar. Pour through a strainer to remove any
remaining rice. Serve cold.

Champurrado

2   cups Quaker Masa Harina de Maiz
4   cups milk
4   ounces Mexican chocolate
1   cup sugar
1   cinnamon stick

In a large bow, mix *masa* and milk until the *masa* is completely wet. Add
sugar and place in a 5-quart saucepan, along with the cinnamon stick.
Cook on low heat for 15 minutes. When the mixture starts to boil, add
chocolate, stirring constantly so it won't stick to the bottom of the pan.
Add more milk if you like it thinner and less if you like the mixture
thicker. Makes six cups.

You can sing the follow song *"Chocolate"* to your children while you
are preparing *champurrado*, or *chocolate atole* in Spanish.

¡Uno, dos, tres–cho!
¡Uno, dos, tres–co!
¡Uno, dos, tres–la!
¡Uno, dos, tres–te!
(Rub hands together as if using a *molinillo*.)
¡Cho–co–late, cho–co–late!
¡Bate, bate el cho–co–late!

▼▼▼▼▼▼▼▼▼▼▼▼▼▼

Champurrado
Variation

2	cups masa harina
8½	cups water
1	cinnamon stick
1	cup milk
1	cup sugar

▼▼▼▼▼▼▼▼▼▼▼▼▼▼

Place *masa* in a large bowl. Stir in 1½ cups water and knead until a firm dough forms. Bring 5 cups of water and the cinnamon stick to a boil in a large saucepan. Pour the remaining 2 cups of cold water into a small bowl. Break the *masa* dough into small pieces and put in the cold water to dissolve. Slowly pour the dissolved *masa* mixture through a large strainer into the boiling cinnamon water, stirring constantly. Reduce the heat to low and cook about 30 minutes, or until soft and slightly thickened. Remove from heat and stir in the milk and sugar. Return to heat and bring to a simmer before serving. (For the chocolate *champurrado*, substitute 1 cup brown sugar for the white sugar and add 3 1-ounce squares of unsweetened chocolate. Makes 12 cups.

Some people serve a Three Kings cake, which is known as *Rosca de Reyes* to some Hispanics and *Marzán* to others. This ring cake is decorated with jewels made of colored dried fruit and fresh cherries in the shape of a crown and with a tiny porcelain baby Jesus baked inside. Have your children help you decorate the cake or place the baby doll inside the cake by making a slit in the side of the cake and pushing it in. Then they can cover the slit with icing.

Rosca de Reyes Cake

2   packages (1/4 ounce each) active dry yeast
½   cup warm water
1   cup (2 sticks) unsalted butter
½   cup sugar
4   eggs, or 6 egg yolks, lightly beaten
½   teaspoon salt
5   cups flour
1   cup candied fruit, plus extra for decoration
½   cup chopped pecans, plus extra whole pecan for decoration
½   cup raisins, plus extra for decoration
2   tiny dolls that will not melt
1   egg lightly beaten with 1 tablespoon water, for glaze

Icing

4   tablespoons unsalted butter plus ½ cup sugar
    or
½   cup orange juice plus 2 cups confectioners' sugar

In a large bowl, dissolve the yeast in warm water. Melt the butter and set aside to cool. With an electric mixer, beat together butter, salt, sugar, and eggs; add yeast mixture and beat well. Add 3 cups flour and beat well again. Gradually add the remaining flour until dough is firm and not sticky. Turn dough onto a lightly-floured board and knead until elastic, adding additional flour if necessary. Cover dough with plastic wrap and set aside in a warm place for about 1½ hours, or until double in bulk. Turn dough onto a lightly-floured surface, punch down, and divide in two. Knead half of the candied fruit, pecans, and raisins into each batch of dough. Roll out the dough and join the ends together to make two thick rings. Push a baby doll deep into each of the two rings. (The dolls can also be inserted after the cake is done by cutting a slit and decorating over it.) Place rings on a buttered baking sheet, cover, and set aside to rise for 1 hour. Preheat oven to 375°F. Before baking, brush loaves with egg-and-water glaze. Bake rings 30 minutes, or until lightly brown. Prepare icing by mixing together either the butter and sugar or the orange juice and confectioners' sugar. Spread sugar mixture on the rings while they are still hot and decorate with whole pecans, raisins, and candied fruit.

We have celebrated this event with several families in the neighborhood. A member of each family takes turns cutting the cake equally. If the baby Jesus is not found on the first round, then the eldest member of each family continues to cut a slice until it is found. The person who finds the baby in the cake is the *madrina* or the *padrino* and is said to have good luck for the rest of the year. They are to dress the tiny porcelain baby found in the cake in a white robe made of silk material or tissue paper. The *madrina* or *padrino* is responsible for holding another celebration in their home forty days later, on February 2, which is also known as *La Candelaria*. This tradition is similar to the *cuarentena*, the tradition observed by Hispanic women who stay in bed for forty days after the birth of a child. This tradition may have originated from the Feast of the Presentation held on February 2, signifying the forty days Mary had to wait before she could present Jesus to the Lord at the Temple. According to Mosaic law, a Jewish woman having given birth to a son was unable to touch anything sacred or enter the temple until forty days after the birth, when she was considered purified of the flow of blood (Lev. 12:2–8).

Among Puerto Ricans, *Día de los Tres Reyes Magos* is also celebrated with *parrandas*, a group of individuals who go to people's homes singing *aguinaldos*. These are songs that are often improvised spontaneously as they drink *coquito* (eggnog) or other holiday treats. My Puerto Rican friend, Isaura Santiago Santiago, shared with me two of these impromptu verses.

Si me dan pasteles, dénmelos calientes
Pues pasteles fríos empachan a la gente.

De las montañas venimos a invitarles
A comer ese lechoncito en su barra
Y Don Pitorro* a beber.

* homemade rum

The following is sung to the tune of the traditional English Christmas carol "We Three Kings."

Los Reyes de Oriente

Reyes de Oriente son,
Van en busca de Jesús,
Por la tierra van guiados
Por una estrella.

O bella es la santa luz,
la maravillosa luz
Que los guía al pesebre
Del divino Rey Jesús.

EL DÍA DE LOS MUERTOS—THE DAY OF THE DEAD

El Día de los Muertos is another tradition that is celebrated by Latinos throughout the United States and Latin America. With roots dating back to ancient times in Mesoamerica, the tradition evolved simultaneously with All Saints Day and All Souls Day, both of which are celebrated in many countries. Like the Aztecs, the Spanish believed in showing respect for the dead. They believed in the continuum between life and death and that, once a year, the spirits of the dead join the living. In Puerto Rico, the Spanish tradition was combined with the traditions of the Taino Indians of the Caribbean to make *El Día de los Muertos*. The Taino Indians believed that when the family spirits joined the living they revisited those things they enjoyed when alive.

El Día de los Muertos is celebrated twice. First, on November 1, loved ones go to the cemetery to remember the young children who are deceased, a day also known as *Día de los Angelitos*. The next day, November 2, is set aside for adult loved ones who have passed away. The holiday provides a more cultural and less commercialized extension of the Halloween festivities. The tradition of *El Día de los Muertos* helps Hispanics confront death and accept it as a natural part of life. It teaches that death is not a tragedy or something to fear, but part of a journey to the next phase of life. It is the point where the world of the living and the world of the dead intersect in a festival of sights and sounds. The ritual of *El Día de los Muertos* connects us with the spirits of our ancestors and with the spirits of those that we care for. It is said that the value of a person's life can be determined by his death, and that the occasion marking his passing keeps him alive. Children who participate in this ritual observe the importance of that person's life and learn how one's life can touch many others. It teaches them to be compassionate and to honor the living just as one should honor the dead. It makes them reflect on how they would like to be remembered after they die, and perhaps they will strive to live their life accordingly.

On *El Día de los Muertos*, a colorful altar called an *ofrenda* is constructed at a certain section of the house where pictures of departed relatives or esteemed people are placed along with votive candles and an *incensario*, an incense burner made with sage and copal. An arch over the altar made of reed or pliable plastic is covered with marigolds. The marigold, *caléndula* or *cempasúchil*, is the flower of the dead. It is believed that with its strong fragrance and bright orange color, the flower will help the spirits find their way home. Along with the pictures, items are placed on the altar that describe a person's life, such as a guitar, a toy, or a piece of clothing. The year that the Tejano singer Selena died, *altares* throughout Mexico and the United States were built in her memory. In Texas, one family decorated an altar with a pair of large earrings, a can of Coca-Cola, and a What-A-Burger hamburger, all of which she loved. You may want to make an altar for someone special such as a deceased *abuelito* or *abuelita*. This is a unique way to connect your children with the memory of their *antepasados*.

On the altar, one can also find colored *calaveras*, skulls, with the names of the *fallecidos*, the deceased, written on the foreheads, along with chocolate coffins. Along the altar, families place colorful *calaveras*, *esqueletos*, skeletons, and bright flowers made of tissue paper. They add papier mâché masks and *papel picado*, paper cutouts, with beautiful geometric designs. An *ofrenda* would not be complete without *pan de muerto*, a big round loaf of bread that is sometimes shaped like a person. Following is the recipe for making this delicious treat. Parents and children can have fun decorating the bread with sprinkles of colored sugar or with skulls made of icing.

▼▼▼▼▼▼▼▼▼▼▼▼▼▼▼▼▼▼▼▼▼▼

Pan de Muerto

½	cup butter
½	cup milk
½	cup water
5	cups flour
2	packages (¼ ounce each) active dry yeast

1   teaspoon salt
1   tablespoon whole aniseed
½   cup sugar
4   eggs
1   egg lightly beaten with 1 tablespoon water, for glaze

Icing

4   tablespoons unsalted butter
½   cup sugar

In a saucepan heat butter, milk, and water until very warm. In a large bowl, combine 4 cups flour, yeast, salt, aniseed, and sugar. Beat in warm liquid until well mixed. Add the eggs and 1 cup flour and beat until dough is soft but not sticky, adding more flour if necessary. Turn dough onto a lightly-floured board and knead until smooth and elastic, about ten minutes. Place in a lightly greased bowl, cover, and set aside until double in bulk.

Turn dough out onto a lightly-floured board, punch down, and form into one or two round loaves or shapes resembling people or skulls. If making round loaves, reserve enough dough to roll into a rope and shape a skull in the center of the loaf. Place loaves on lightly-greased baking sheets, cover, and set aside in a warm place to rise for 1 hour.

Preheat oven to 350°F. Brush loaves with egg-and-water glaze and bake 30 to 40 minutes, or until lightly brown. You can also have your child decorate the bread after it is cool with icing made by mixing 4 tablespoons of butter that has been melted with ½ cup sugar.

People celebrate *El Día de los Muertos* in different ways throughout the United States. The gathering at the cemetery, *el camposanto* or *pan-teón*, is perhaps the most elaborate ritual. In Hispanic communities across America, these gatherings can become organized community events that involve the church or they can be private family affairs. Take your children to the cemetery on November 1 to pray for the *angelitos*, the little children, who died. Clean their graves and tomb-stones and lay out fresh flowers and candles at the grave. As in Aztec times, graves can be decorated with white flowers for children and yel-low marigolds for adults. Sometimes, marigold petals are shaped into crosses on the graves. On November 2, take your family to the ceme-tery to pray, sing, and eat the favorite foods of the deceased adults and talk about how special their lives were. In Mexico and Central America, you'll find cemeteries crowded with families holding all-night vigils for the dead. El *Día de los Muertos* is an occasion for bringing together friends and family members, young and old, to instill a sense of culture, spirituality, and continuity.

In some communities, especially along the Mexican border, elaborate events with large groups of people are common on *Día de los Muertos*. Participants meet in front of the cemetery wearing papier mâché masks and carrying musical instruments like rattles, drums, and guitars, as well as incense burners and large wreaths covered with marigolds, represent- ing the relatives who have died. Marchers dress as skeletons, wear col- orful masks, and carry an arch of altar flowers. Sometimes, they carry a coffin with a fake skeleton that pops up and waves as if mocking death. Facing the north, they pray for the *ancianos*, the elderly; to the west, they honor *las mujeres*; to the south they pray for all the *angelitos*, the young children and infants; and to the east they pray for *los hombres*, especially the men, fathers, sons, and grandfathers who have died in wars. *Mariachis* can also be found in cemeteries serenading the spirits of the dead. A person blows a *concha*, a conch shell, in honor of the spir- its. Then the people scatter marigold petals from the cemetery all the way to the altar at home. Once the families get home, they hang a wreath of marigolds on the wall and take part in a prayer and great feast, in remembrance of the departed. Masses are also held for the dead, and, as in ancient times, the *Matachines* and *Concheros* perform ritual dances wearing bright colorful costumes with feathered headdresses and bells around their ankles. Perhaps you can convince your church to organize such an event for your community.

EASTER—*DÍA DE PASCUA*

The Easter season in some parts of Latin America begins with a week of carnivals, parades, music, costumes, fireworks, and lots of food before the commencement of the forty-day Lenten period, known in Spanish as the *Cuaresma*. During Lent, which starts with the *cenizas* (ashes) on Ash Wednesday, people over twelve years of age offer penance by giving up something they like such as candy, meat, soda, TV, or videos. People may go into a semifast, excluding the traditional lenten foods of *nopali- tos* and *albóndigas*. Many families participate in the traditional Good Friday and Easter Sunday Masses to commemorate Christ's death and resurrection. This is also the time when children, dressed in white, make their *Primera Comunión*, and children and adults get dressed up in their Sunday best.

I recall that my mother used to spend weeks sewing our beautiful Easter dresses when we were children. With our petticoats, hats, and gloves, we felt pretty special that day. If you attend church on Easter Sunday, make it a grand occasion for your children by decking them out in their Sunday best. They will remember it and you surely will with those special snapshots that you will treasure forever.

For many Hispanics in Texas, the Easter Sunday festivities begin after church, with a family picnic complete with barbecue, potato salad, and traditional bread pudding, or *capirotada*. We also have the traditional Easter egg hunt for the children and a confetti egg battle among the adults and older children. Weeks prior to Easter Sunday, we collect whole eggshells to make these confetti eggs, known as *cascarones*. If you are cooking or baking with eggs, punch a small hole in the top and drain the contents through the opening, rather than cracking the egg in two. Rinse out the eggshells and let them dry. The eggshells are dyed in different pastel colors. The shells are then filled with confetti and sealed with a piece of colored tissue paper glued at the top to keep the confetti from spilling out. Some *cascarones* become works of art with *papel de china* (cut tissue paper), ribbons, feathers, and tinsel. Some feature very elaborate multicolor geometric art designs; others resemble human heads, people, or animals and are given as gifts or displayed as Hispanic folk art.

However, the real purpose of making and breaking *los cascarones* is that it is a delightful fun-filled tradition. Nothing can match the laughter and surprise of the "victim" of a *cascarón* attack. In our family, adults and children chase each other around the yard trying to gently break the confetti-filled eggs on each other's heads. There is so much laughter and excitement for young and old alike. We celebrate this joyous occasion of the Resurrection of the Lord with the extended family in a gathering that always includes laughing, talking, eating, and playing games.

It would not be Easter without *capirotada*, the traditional Mexican bread pudding. While the traditional *capirotada* mostly has the bread, cheese, raisins, apples, and peanuts, my aunt Lupe loves to add more ingredients to make it sweeter. Some cooks use three kinds of nuts: peanuts, almonds, and pecans. *Piloncillo*, or unrefined sugar, comes in cone or bar form and can be found in most supermarkets' ethnic food sections. You can make the *capirotada* as sweet as you desire by adding whatever ingredients your child can help you cut up or throw in. Both of you can put each of the layers together or you can take turns. Following is the *capirotada* recipe that has been used in the Rodriguez family for generations.

Capirotada
Mexican Bread Pudding

1   *piloncillo*, or 1½ cups brown sugar
2   cups boiling water
¼   teaspoon ground cinnamon, or 1 cinnamon stick
½   cup raisins
6   slices bread, toasted
1   cup grated cheddar cheese
½   cup crushed pineapple
½   cup peeled, cored, and thinly sliced apples
½   cup finely chopped pecans
½   cup sliced banana
½   cup coconut

Preheat oven to 350°F. Place *piloncillo*, boiling water, cinnamon, and raisins in a small saucepan and set over low heat, stirring, until sugar has melted; remove raisins and set aside. Place one layer of bread on the bottom of a 9-inch by 13-inch glass pan. Sprinkle with one-half the cheese, pineapples, apples, pecans, bananas, coconut, and reserved raisins. Pour half of the sugar mixture over the ingredients and then repeat the fruit, nut, and sugar-mixture layers. Bake uncovered for 20 minutes, or until bread is moist and top is slightly brown. Can be served hot or cold.

New Year's Eve

New Year's is another day that brings family and friends together to ring out the old year and bring in the new one with fun, laughter, and excitement. Some people have their traditions of throwing out a pail of water, making sure their house is clean, or going to parties on New Year's Eve. But for us, with the extended family, it is a day of praying, making resolutions, and having a celebration with music, fireworks, food, and games. When we return home from a very joyous and exhausting day, my family kneels down in front of the Christmas tree. Holding hands, we pray and thank God for His blessings during the prior year and ask Him to protect us, guide us in the coming year, and help us improve.

Instead of trying to describe the day, I have included an excerpt of a short essay that my oldest son, Sal, wrote for an English class recalling how his family spent New Year's Eve the year that he was twelve years old. For a twelve-year-old he remembers the excitement of family and friends coming together and experiencing what the Lord represents: love, peace, and joy. His teacher wrote on my son's paper, "Sal, this is such a heartwarming story. It makes your reader realize what family is really all about, and that you realize how special it was to grow up the way you did."

As a twelve-year-old there was nothing I looked forward to more than New Year's Eve. I enjoyed the food, family, fun, and fireworks, but most important, although I did not know it at the time, what I really held dear to my heart was the tradition. Every event that transpired that day was passed down from earlier generations. What I felt as a child, which I could only describe as a little lump in my throat and a tingling in my heart, was actually pride. I was proud of myself, my family, and my culture.

The morning of New Year's Eve is one of chaos and disorder for my family. "Salvador Julián Rodríguez. Get out of bed and put these things in the car," Mother yells as I am stretching in my bed. "Steven and Vanessa, turn off the TV and help!" My father would always get his camera and film together. He loved to take pictures, and it was not unusual for him to take six or seven rolls of film on any family gathering.

By about four or five, we are on our way to Grandma's. Her house was located deep in the West Side of San Antonio. One thing I noticed about that part of town was that there were so many dogs. Some would sit in the middle of the road and wouldn't move, so we had to drive around them. Others would attack our car.

"Hey, look who is here!" everyone said at the same time. We were always the last ones to show up to any family gathering. So that meant I had to go around and say "hi" to everyone in the house, all aunts, uncles, and cousins. There must have been over fifty people crowded into the small three-bedroom house, but somehow, everyone seemed comfortable.

After all the formalities were taken care of, all the boys and men went outside to play a game of football. Since we had enough players to make two full teams and since the yard was so small, we played in the street. The touchdowns were from one mailbox to another and every player had their own cheering section when they scored, either their wives or girlfriends, or their mothers and sisters. Someone always happened to get hurt somehow, and that usually meant that the game was over.

More than twenty tired and exhausted men went straight to the kitchen. There was every kind of Mexican food imaginable. There was *pan dulce*, *polvorones*, *bizcochitos*, *enchiladas*, *tamales*, rice and beans, *caldo* or *menudo*, *chalupas*, and much more. But the thing my grandmother prided herself on the most were her *buñuelos*. She had a family recipe that had been passed down for many generations. There were rows and rows of *buñuelos* stacked about twenty high. So after everyone stuffed themselves, we all went outside. Out came the guitars, maracas, *claves*, and trumpets and on came the Mexican music. All my uncles would play the instruments and sing, while the kids and wives just sat and listened. It sounded wonderful. The music continued until it got dark.

Then it was time for the fireworks. Before fireworks were banned, we all loaded up in a couple of cars and went to the outskirts of town to buy every firework imaginable, from "black cats" and sparklers to the "midnight specials." If you have ever been around San Antonio's West Side on New Year's, you would think we were in the middle of a war zone. It seemed like every house tried to outdo their neighbors. BOOM!! I could feel my heart stop beating for a couple of seconds, when my Uncle Ramiro, a Vietnam veteran, exploded his homemade cherry bombs. At exactly twelve midnight my dad would take out the trumpet again and play "Auld Lang Syne" as loud and clear as he could, and everyone sang along, kissing and hugging each other. I paused from lighting the firecrackers for a brief moment and just looked around at everyone. I would hear the music and the fireworks, the singing, and I felt, just for an instant, that everything in the world was perfect.

Buñuelos and *menudo* are a must in many Hispanic homes on New Year's Eve. Following is my mother-in-law's favorite recipe for the delicious *buñuelos* that we longed for each New Year's Eve. The trick is to make them very thin and to have the oil very hot. Get your children involved by putting them in charge of the cinnamon sugar mixture. As mentioned earlier with the tamales, the *dicho Una vez al año no hace daño*, *una vez al mes*, *tal vez* applies to the *menudo* as well as to the tamales. Both are extremely fattening, but, oh, so good, and very much a part of our cultural traditions. The aroma of a pot of *menudo*, with all its spices, can be smelled coming out of many homes as you drive down the barrios during New Year's Eve.

Buñuelos

3 cups flour
1 teaspoon salt
¼ cup (½ stick) butter
¼ cup sugar
1 tablespoon ground cinnamon
2 eggs, lightly beaten
3 cinnamon sticks
1 cup water
4 to 5 cups vegetable oil, for frying
½ cup sugar mixed with 2 teaspoons ground cinnamon, for dusting

In a large bowl, sift together flour and salt. Cut butter into flour until mixture resembles coarse crumbs. Add sugar, ground cinnamon, and eggs and stir to mix. Boil cinnamon sticks in water for 10 minutes. Stir 5 to 6 tablespoons of the cinnamon water into flour mixture a little at a time and beat until dough forms. Turn dough onto a lightly-floured board and knead until firm and moist but not sticky, adding more flour or cinnamon water if necessary. Cover dough with a damp cloth and let stand for 20 to 30 minutes.

Turn dough onto a lightly-floured board and form into 12 balls, each 2 inches in diameter. Flatten each ball until 3 inches in diameter. (To prevent bubbles from forming, some people let the *buñuelos* rest for another 20 minutes.) With a rolling pin, roll out each flattened ball until it is extremely thin and almost transparent. (Tears in the dough will probably appear; don't worry about them.)

Pour oil to a depth of 1 inch into a large skillet. *Buñuelos* need to be fried in very hot oil, 360 to 375°F. Use a candy thermometer or test to see if oil is hot enough by putting a small piece of dough into the oil. If the dough puffs up, it is ready. Lift the rolled dough from the board very carefully without tearing it further and slowly slide it into the hot oil. Cook 10 to 15 seconds on each side, or until golden brown. Remove from oil with tongs or a long fork and let drain a few seconds on several layer of paper toweling. Dust with sugar-cinnamon mixture. (You can create an assembly line with friends and family to finish your batch of *buñuelos*. My sister-in-law Dolores Garza gave me this recipe. She recalls when her grandmother used to stretch the *buñuelos* on her kneee to get them extremely transparent.) Makes 12 *buñuelos*.

Menudo

2   pounds of honeycomb tripe, washed and cut into 1-inch squares.
2   pounds pork hocks, shoulder, or leg, cut into 2-inch pieces (optional)
2   to 3 pig's feet (optional)
    Water
1   to 2 teaspoons salt
2   onions, chopped
3   garlic cloves, chopped
2   tablespoons cayenne
2   tablespoons oregano
2   tablespoons paprika
1   teaspoon black pepper
1½ cups white *pozoles* or 1 28- to 30-ounce can of hominy, drained
    Slices of lemon or lime
    Warm corn tortillas

Place tripe, pork, and pig's feet in a large Dutch oven and add water to cover the ingredients by about four inches. Bring to a boil over high heat. Add salt; reduce heat and cook for 1½ hours. Add one-half of the chopped onion and all the garlic, cayenne, oregano, paprika, and black pepper. Cook another hour, or until the meat is tender. Add *pozoles* 30 minutes before *menudo* is done. Add additional water during cooking if needed to maintain enough liquid for soup. Taste for salt and add if necessary. Serve hot with remaining chopped onion, lemon or lime slices, and warm *tortillas*. Easily serves 6 to 8.

RELIGIOUS CELEBRATIONS CENTERED ON *NUESTROS NIÑOS*

BAUTISMO—THE BAPTISM

A baptism is an occasion for celebrating an important religious milestone in a child's life. *Compadres*, either relatives or good friends of the parents, are chosen by the parents to baptize the child before family and community. Usually *compadres* are selected because they are well liked by the parents and are good spiritual role models for the child. They become the children's *padrinos*, who traditionally purchase the child's christening outfit as well as the candle that should be lit every year to renew the sacrament of the *bautismo*. They stand next to the parents at the church ceremony. After the *bautismo*, there is a meal at the home for the *padrinos*, relatives, and special friends.

In Puerto Rico, *bautismos* are celebrated with *capias* or mementos pinned to the clothes of the guests. They could be made with a coin glued to a ribbon bearing the child's name. In Mexico, a *padrino* will toss coins to neighborhood children outside the church. Both of these traditions symbolize the hope for a child's financial security.

Padrinos are an important part of the parents' and child's social support system. They accept the great honor of being the child's religious sponsors to help strengthen the child's spiritual growth. But they also serve a larger purpose to help the child feel loved and special. In the early years of a child's life, the *padrinos* will shower their godchild, the *ahijado*, with a present on his birthday and a special basket on Easter. In some cases, when the *compadres* do not have children of their own, the godchild receives everything from clothes to vacations. Sometimes *padrinos* even help pay for a *quinceañera*, a college education, or a wedding. Through difficult times, the *padrinos* can intervene and mediate when parents have problems rearing their child. They understand that should both of the parents die and if no one from the extended family can assume the responsibility of rearing the child, the *padrinos* will be able to meet that responsibility until the child is old enough to care for himself or herself.

Do you have *padrinos* for your children? Or perhaps you yourself are a *padrino?* Being a *padrino* requires two-way communication, which means being in close contact with your *compadres* so that they can get to know and love your children and support them in their spiritual and moral development. The benefits of maintaining this cultural tradition are just as important for you as they are for your children. If you are someone's *padrino*, take your role seriously. Keep in close contact with your *ahijado*, and become his or her greatest friend and mentor.

PRIMERA COMUNIÓN–THE FIRST COMMUNION

La Primera Comunión, the first time a child receives the Eucharist, is celebrated during the Lenten season, usually when young children are in the second grade. In some parts of Mexico, the First Communion is celebrated on December 8, the day of the Immaculate Conception. Boys and girls traditionally wear white suits, although this tradition is changing in some churches. My boys wore white suits and my daughter wore a beautiful white satin embroidered dress with a long white veil and white gloves. She looked like a miniature Madonna. Many Hispanic homes have pictures of their children kneeling on a pew, holding the rosaries and rosary books that were given to them by their *padrinos*. The *padrinos* vow to guide them and support their religious growth. Just as with the *bautismo*, the *padrinos* remember the *ahijados* during special holidays and on their birthdays.

Quinceañera—The Fifteenth-Birthday Celebration

The *quinceañera* is a very special event for a fifteen-year-old Hispanic girl. It is the day when she "comes of age" and when her "rite of passage" from childhood into adulthood takes place. Through a special Mass and celebration, a girl publicly establishes her relationship with her parents, her community, and her Creator. Aside from the pomp and circumstance, the most meaningful aspect of the *quinceañera* is the church ceremony, during which parents express their affection toward their daughter and she in turn reflects on her relationship with her parents, God, and the Virgin Mary. She reads scripture, renews her baptismal vows, and reaffirms her devotion to God and to *la Virgen*. One of the most captivating moments of the ceremony is when the *debutante* and her godparents present fifteen fresh roses to a statue of *la Virgen de Guadalupe* while the "Ave Maria" is being sung. The young girl is presented by her sponsors with gifts that have special significance, such as a cross necklace, earrings, ring, Bible, crown, rosary, and her "last doll," which is usually wearing the identical dress and crown as the honoree. She may also be presented with items that represent her interests, such as a basketball if she likes sports and books if she wants to be a schoolteacher.

An invitation to the *quinceañera* often includes a picture of the *debutante* as a child and as a young woman of *quince años*. It is yet another occasion to bring the extended family and friends together to celebrate, dance, and capture one of the most important days of a girl's life with memorable photos. Some *quinceañeras* are elaborate affairs with ice sculptures, balloons, multilayered birthday cakes, stretch limousines, large portraits of the *quinceañera*, videos or slide presentations of the fifteen-year-old, carousels, and fancy *capias*, or gifts of remembrance for the guests. Let's not forget the music, food, hall, and church. This event may cost as much as a wedding and is paid for by parents and sometimes sponsors, who are usually *compadres* and members of the extended family.

The *debutante* has a court of honor, which can consist of her own escort, *el chambelán de honor*, and fourteen female friends or relatives dressed in matching gowns, all of whom are escorted by young men in tuxedos. The girls are called *damas* (ladies) and the boys are called *chambelanes*, which means lords (they are often called *escortes* or *galánes*, as well). Sometimes there are little girls called princesses who throw rose petals along the church aisle. The *quinceañera* court sometimes leaves the church in limousines or a special trolley. This is one day when the young woman is treated royally and made to feel very important. She becomes *una princesa* for the night as she marches alone or with her escort through a decorated archway made of flowers, balloons, or ribbons attached to long-stemmed roses held by the court. She goes to the center of the dance floor and a tiara of rhinestones is placed on her head. She promenades and greets people and in a show of grace, she bows all the way to the floor. In some celebrations, the *debutante* is then escorted to an elaborately decorated high-back chair where the father kneels in front of his daughter and changes her shoes from flats to her first pair of high-heel shoes, carried on a satin pillow by the mother. The *debutante* then stands up and dances the first dance of the evening, *La Muñequita*, *La Quinceañera*, or a waltz, with her father. The father dances, then hands her over to her brothers and then to her prince charming, *el chambelán de honor*. They continue the waltz along with the rest of the court. At the end of the waltz, the court switches to a Latin beat such as a salsa, polka, or merengue.

Sometime in the evening, the lights are dimmed and the fifteen boys hold a decorated lighted candle for the *debutante* to make 15 wishes. A toast, or *brindis*, is made by the father, grandfather, *padrino*, or an older brother. Then the *mariachis* or a *trio* enter singing "*Las Mañanitas*." There is usually not a dry eye in the house when the birthday girl dances the traditional song, "*La Muñequita*," with her father. As the audience listens to the words, they admire the affection between father and daughter and they reflect how fast the years have passed, as his *muñequita* goes from *la cuna to la escuela* to become *una señorita*.

La Muñequita

*Llegaste tú, mi bien, llenando de ilusión
mi corazón, también el de mamita.
Con gusto celebré y a todos les conté
Dijeron qué bonita.*

Los días pasaron ya, creciste un poco más
Y ahora estás dormida en tu cunita.
Por nombre al bautizar, les dije llevará
por nombre muñequita.

Los años han pasado, ya recuerdo estos momentos
que fueron en mi vida de una gran illusión.

Muy pronto partirás a la escuela a estudiar,
Y cumplirás del destino nacida
Y todos al pasar con gusto te dirán,
qué linda, qué bonita.

Y cuando vayas ya a la universidad,
Preguntarán, ¿Quién es la señorita?
Y tu contestarás por gusto de papá,
me llamo muñequita.

Quinceañeras do not have to be lavish to be meaningful. I did not have a quinceañera because we could not afford one since there were eight children in the family. But my two eldest sisters were fortunate to have a modest quinceañera with madrinas, a tiara, and lots of friends, family, music, and food.

I cannot wait for my daughter to turn fifteen, when she will have the opportunity to celebrate in a special way. Some parents begin to prepare for the quinceañera at least two to three years in advance, saving money and making decorations. Planning a quinceañera can be a wonderful way for mother, father, and daughter to explore their bicultural experience by adding elements of both cultures—for example, choosing a mix of traditional Latin and modern music or a combination of Hispanic and American foods. It is a time to renew her baptismal vows, to learn social graces, and to learn about her culture, including dancing to Latin music.

Do not be surprised if your daughter tells you that she does not want to have a quinceañera if she has friends that do not celebrate their fifteenth birthday in this manner or if she doesn't like to be the center of attention. Some of my nieces did not have a quinceañera. Instead, they wanted the money the parents would have spent on a celebration to buy a car or go to Europe. Many Hispanics opt for a "Sweet Sixteen" party instead. Others share the spotlight with a sibling or other friends. One of my friends told me that she did not want a quinceañera because her friends were not having one and she did not think the whole Hispanic "cultural thing" was very cool. But when she grew older and went to *la universidad* she became aware of her ethnicity and her cultural roots. She would get so upset when she visited her aunts' homes and saw the lovely pictures of her cousins proudly displayed in their *quinceañera* dresses. Now my friend wishes she had had a *quinceañera* and wants to make sure her daughters have a glorious fifteenth birthday—the Latina way.

The most important suggestion to help encourage your daughter to have a *quinceañera* is to begin early. When your daughter is young, take her to *quinceañeras*, have her serve in other *quince años* celebrations, either as a member of the court as a princess or as a *dama* when she is older. Get her books on the subject, like Mary D. Lankford's, entitled *Quinceañera: A Latina's Journey to Womanhood*, Sister Angela Erevia's *Quince Años Celebrando una Tradición*, and Michele Salcedo's *Quinceañera*. Also, make sure that your daughter associates with friends whose parents are intending to have a *quince* celebration. If your older daughter had one, you stand a better chance with the younger ones. Brothers can also help. Steven stood in numerous *quinceañeras* as a *chambelán* and would tell Vanessa every time how he couldn't wait for her special day when she would be the "belle of the ball."

OTHER CELEBRATIONS

EL DÍA DE LA MADRE—MOTHER'S DAY

Like all cultures, mothers in the Hispanic world are honored, loved, and bestowed the ultimate *respeto*. On Mother's Day, the entire family comes together to show gratitude for the many sacrifices and abundant love that a mother shows throughout the year.

The day starts for many lucky Hispanic mothers *en la madrugada*, in the wee hours of the morning, with a *serenata*. In San Antonio and in many Latin American communities, a group of *mariachis* serenade the mothers at their windows or front porches. My husband, who is a musician with a *mariachi* outfit, used to join other musicians to sing *"Las Mañanitas"* to *las madrecitas queridas*. This tradition originated in Spain, where men used to serenade women outside their windows. In spite of the fact that my husband had to fight off dogs in the barrio to get to the porch or window, he continued to do so for many years because he was so moved when he witnessed the *lágrimas de gusto en las caritas de las viejitas*, the tears of joy in the faces of the little old women, when he began to strum the guitar or play his trumpet.

Usually older children who paid for the *mariachis* would congregate at a certain hour at the mother's home to give her *besitos y abrazos* and to tell her how much she is loved and appreciated. Sometimes the mothers would come out to the porch when the *mariachis* arrived or would invite them inside the house for *un cafecito*. Other times, depending on the hour, the mothers would just turn the lights on and off or appear briefly at the window as a sign of appreciation for such songs as "O Madre Querida," "Canto a la Madre," and "Las Mañanitas" that so warmly touch any woman's heart and soul. When my husband and the *mariachis* came to my house to serenade me, my children would run to my side, hug, and kiss me, as did my husband. There is no way that a Latina mother will not get emotional when she hears these classic Mother's Day songs:

O Madre Querida

O Madre Querida, O Madre Adorada
Que Dios te bendiga, aquí en tu morada
Que Dios te conserve mil años de vida
Feliz y dichosa, O Madre Querida

Si estás dormidita, escucha este canto
Que todos tus hijos convierten en llanto
Tú que por tus hijos vives implorando
En ti, Madrecita, vivimos pensando

Recibe el cariño de todos tus hijos
Que nunca en la vida podrán olvidarte
Hoy, Día de las Madres, venimos a darte
Perfumadas flores para consolarte.

O Madre Querida, O Madre Adorada
Que Dios te bendiga aquí en tu morada
Tu nombre es (María)* y no hallan que darte
Se sienten dichosos al felicitarte.

*insert name

Canto a la Madre

Madre querida en este día,
Las Mañanitas quiero cantar.
Recibe, madre, mil bendiciones,
Que Dios del cielo te mandará.

En este día todos tus hijos,
aquí reunidos estamos ya.
Trajimos flores de primavera
y todas ellas te adornarán.

Madre querida, despierta madre
Si estás dormida, despierta ya.
Que desde el cielo una corona
Hecha de estrellas te adornará.

Todos los campos ya florecieron
Y sus aromas te brindarán.
Mientras que un coro de pajarillos
Alegremente te cantarán.

Madre querida, despierta madre
Si estás dormida, despierta ya.
Que desde el cielo una corona
Hecha de estrellas te adornará.

Las Mañanitas

Éstas son las mañanitas que cantaba el Rey David
Hoy que es Día de las Madres*
te las cantamos así.

Despierta mi bien, despierta, mira que ya amaneció.
Ya los pajarillos cantan, la luna ya se metió.

Qué linda está la mañana, en que vengo a saludarte.
Venimos todos con gusto y placer a felicitarte.
El día en que tú naciste, nacieron todas las flores

Y en la pila de bautismo, cantaron los ruiseñores.
Ya viene amaneciendo, ya la luz del día nos dió.
Levántate de mañana, mira que ya amaneció.

*For birthday use *"de tu cumpleaños"* or *"de tu Santo"*

CUMPLEAÑOS Y PIÑATAS—BIRTHDAYS AND PIÑATAS

Hispanic birthdays are often multigenerational celebrations filled with food, presents, songs, and *familia. Primos,* together with *tías* and *abuelitos,* join friends around the cake to sing *"Las Mañanitas,"* followed by the song "Happy Birthday" to the special birthday child. One of the high points of the day is when the children get to break the piñata, a papier mâché figure stuffed with candy. The two best-known types of piñatas come from Mexico and Cuba, and can be made at home or bought at specialty shops.

The Cuban piñata is different from the Mexican piñata in size, structure, and in the methods used to extract the candy from inside. The Cuban piñata is usually about the size of a three-foot-square basket with a platform that is adorned with a scene depicting children's heroes and characters, such as Winnie the Pooh and Barney. The main difference between the two piñatas is that the Cuban one is not broken. At the bottom of the beautiful work of art is a rectangular container that is filled with candy. Colorful ribbons hang from the bottom and each child pulls a ribbon that opens the container to bring the candies down. The main part of the piñata remains intact so that it can be used again.

The Mexican piñata was brought to the New World by the Spanish missionaries to help convert the indigenous children to Christianity. The first adobe piñatas were shaped into devil figures or into figures with seven cones representing the seven cardinal sins, which the children would symbolically reject each time they hit the piñata. As the children broke the piñata, they were showered with fruits and nuts that would signify the grace that comes with rejecting Satan. With time, the piñatas changed from a religious symbol to one used for entertainment during *Las Posadas* and *Los Pastores* and at birthday parties. The traditional star evolved into shapes of animals and then to popular characters like Mickey Mouse. Making a Mexican piñata can be a wonderful way to engage your children in the preparation for the party as well as a way to connect them with their culture. If you live in or near a large Latino community, you can also purchase piñatas ready to be filled with trinkets and candies.

Instructions for Making a Piñata

Make a sticky paste in a large bowl by mixing two parts water for every one part of flour. Take some newspapers and tear them into many strips. Dip each strip into the bowl of paste and remove the excess paste by sliding strip between two fingers. Cover an inflated balloon—the larger the better—with the strips four to five layers thick. When the paste dries, deflate the balloon and make a hole in the top of the shell. Make a loop of twine at the top of the shell and hold it in place with masking tape. Cover the tape with the remaining strips of paper and paste.

The base of the piñata can be transformed into a star or a character, like Mickey Mouse, with some creative use of newspaper. Cement two ears and a tail made from several layers of paper onto the base of the balloon for the Mickey Mouse piñata, or three to five cones made of newspaper (or cardboard) to make the points for a star. (You can make any animal by rolling several pieces of paper for the feet, hands, tail, or trunk). Decorate the piñata with strips of colorful crepe paper or tissue paper. Use black, white, and red paper to make the Mickey Mouse and any brightly colored paper for the star.

For any piñata, cut folded tissue paper into two-inch strips, and then cut into the folded part ½ inch from the edge to make a fringe, leaving the top part uncut. Unfold the tissue paper and turn it to the reverse side to make folded looped fringes that will be glued one strip at a time until the piñata is completely covered. If you use crepe paper, cut the folded part in two and spread the strip of fringe crepe paper. Use the blade of a pair of scissors to curl the fringe. Glue the uncut parts of the strip to the piñata one at a time, covering it completely with the curls going either up or down. For the star piñata, glue six long, thin strips of tissue paper through the ends of each of the cones.

Both Cuban and Mexican piñatas are a great deal of fun for the children. They provide lasting impressions, wonderful memories, and many good treats. However, for the Mexican piñata, the fun lasts longer and the children are more actively involved. Putting a Mexican piñata together can be as much fun as tearing it apart. Buy a matching stick or decorate an old broomstick in the same colors as the piñata. Simply cut a hole at the top of the figurine and fill the piñata with candy. You can also add coins and confetti. Use a long rope to hang the piñata on the branch of a tree and tie a second one to the piñata to pull it away as a child tries to break it while the other children shout or sing, "*dale, dale, dale.*" You may or may not want to blindfold the older children who take a whack at the piñata, but beware that you will have a horde of screaming children piled on top of each other once the *piñata* is shattered and the candy comes out. To make the event even more fun, you may want to teach your children and their guests the popular song that usually accompanies each child's turn:

Dale, dale, dale,
no pierdas el tino
mide la distancia
que hay en el camino.

Que si no le das
de un palo te tiro.
Que si no le das
de un palo te tiro.
Dale, dale, dale.

Chapter III

Hispanic Role Models

Nuestras Estrellas

Brillantes

You may have heard about geniuses in physics, medicine, or chemistry who discovered or invented something that advanced our understanding of medicine, science, or our physical world. Many marvel at those individuals whose talents can create beautiful literary masterpieces or those who demonstrate shrewd diplomatic skills or outstanding bravery to bring about peace in the world. Then there are individuals who are blessed with the knowledge and skill to be able to explore different planets or create beautiful music. Just as the European world produced a Beethoven, Michelangelo, Einstein, and Pasteur, the Hispanics of the Old and New World have also nurtured exceptionally brilliant individuals.

Consider the wide range of fields in which Hispanics have excelled. The world of music and entertainment has such stars as Desi Arnaz, Edward James Olmos, Jennifer López, Anthony Quinn, Raul Julia, Jimmy Smits, Julio Iglesias, Paul Rodriguez, Vicki Carr, Gloria Estefan, Andy Garcia, Rosie Pérez, Celia Cruz, Cristina Saralegui, and Jon Secada to name but a few. Hispanic playwright Luis Valdez produced *Zoot Suit* and *La Bamba*. Your child could be another Rafael Méndez, the first trumpeter to play a solo performance at Carnegie Hall, famous cellist Pablo Casals, or Evelyn Cisneros, the prima ballerina of the San Francisco Ballet who danced at the White House. He could have operatic talents like opera singer Plácido Domingo, composer Daniel Catán, and violinist and world-renowned conductor Jorge Mester. Linda Ronstadt, a Hispanic performer who has achieved many platinum and gold albums and was invited to sing at President Carter's inauguration, credits her father for influencing her musical career. Her album "*Canciones de Mi Padre*" was a tribute to her father as well as to her culture. Latinos boast a good share of entertainers, but Rita Moreno stands out for having won all four major industry awards: the Oscar, Emmy, Tony, and Grammy and Geraldo Rivera for winning ten Emmy awards.

We have Hispanic artists of yesteryear like Diego Rivera, Pablo Picasso, Frida Kahlo, Salvador Dali, Goya, and El Greco. We also have more current artists like Jesse Treviño, whose paintings have been presented to Prince Charles and Hillary Rodham Clinton, and Manuel Acosta whose portrait of César Chávez graced the cover of *Time* magazine. Hispanic fashion couturiers like Carolina Herrera, Paloma Picasso, Oscar de la Renta, and Adolfo have made their mark in life through their unique, exquisite designs. All of these men and women are among the many Hispanics who cultivated their God-given talents and abilities and became shining role models for our Hispanic children.

MacArthur award winners Sandra Cisneros and Ruth Behar stand out in the world of letters, along with other Hispanic writers like Julia Álvarez, Rudolfo A. Anaya, Hispanic Heritage Award winner Luis Rodriguez, and philosopher George Santayana.

Athletes like golfers Lee Trevino, Chi Chi Rodriguez, and Nancy Lopez and jockeys Ángel Cordero and Jorge Velásquez proved that Latinos could be champions in sports. Other outstanding Hispanic sports figures include professional football coach Tom Flores, Pro Football Hall of Famer Anthony Munoz, Vince Lombardi winner Tony Casillas, boxers Oscar de La Hoya and Julio Caesar Chávez, and gold Olympic medal winners Pablo Morales and Trent Dimas. Baseball legend Roberto Clemente showed that with hard work and determination Latinos could be heroes as well as Hall of Famers. Even in our lifetime, we witnessed the historic 1998 baseball season during which Sammy Sosa of the Chicago Cubs from the Dominican Republic, hit 66 home runs and surpassed Roger Maris's 1961 record of 61 home runs in a single season. This was an incredible year for baseball and for Latinos. Sammy Sosa and Mark McGwire raced to beat Maris's record and Sammy Sosa and Juan Gonzalez of Puerto Rico both won the Most Valuable Player award for the National and American Leagues respectively.

Those who have worked to give Latinos a stronger voice in the political arena and beyond include Joseph Marion Hernández, who was the first U.S. Hispanic Congressman in 1822, and Octaviano A. Larrazolo, who was the first Hispanic U.S. Senator in 1928. Those leaders opened the way for others like Henry B. González and Edward R. Roybal. The first Hispanics who served in cabinet positions include Lauro Cavazos, Henry G. Cisneros, Federico F. Peña, and most recently Bill Richardson. Antonia C. Novello served as the U.S.'s first Hispanic Surgeon General in 1990. Costa Rican born Franklin Chang-Diaz, who spoke in Spanish from outer space in 1986, was the first Hispanic astronaut in the United States. He was followed by Sydney Guitierrez and Ellen Ochoa, who became the first Latina astronaut in 1993. John Ortega and Philip Bazaar were the first Hispanics to receive the Medal of Honor for fighting in the Civil War. Thirty-eight Hispanic Americans, including most recently Cleto Rodriguez, Roy Benavidez, Euripides Rubion, and Hector Santiago-Colon received Congressional Medals of Honor. The first and only Hispanic four-star general in the U.S. Army is General Richard E. Cavazos.

We have so many champions who have assumed leadership roles to improve the quality of life of Hispanics. Migrant farmworker leaders César Chávez and Dolores Huenta, American GI Forum founder Dr. Hector Pérez García, poet José Martí, and journalist Rubén Salazar were activists who brought about a social consciousness. Reies López Tijerina, Rodolfo "Corky" Gonzáles, and José Ángel Gutiérrez were the leaders of the Chicano movement and brought about ethnic pride in the 1960s. Dr. Blandina Cárdenas, Antonia Hernández, and Raul Yzaguirre have labored tirelessly on education, social, and civil rights issues for Hispanics as has Antoñia Pantoja who founded the Aspira organization. Willie Velásquez, through the organization he founded, Southwest Voter and Education Project, was responsible for increasing the number of Hispanic voters, which in turn has increased the number of Hispanic politicians. We are very proud of Arturo Madrid, Mario Obledo, and Dr. Manuel Berriozabal, who received awards from President Clinton: Madrid as the founding president of the Texas Rivera Center; Obledo for helping establish the Mexican American Legal Defense and Educational Fund (MALDEF); and Berriozabal for implementing Texas Prep Program, a national model in math and science.

Eugenio María de Hostos and George I. Sánchez were among our great educators. Dr. José A. Cárdenas and Dr. Gloria Zamora were the early champions of bilingual education for Hispanics. Community organizer Ernesto Cortez has been recognized with the MacArthur and the Heinz Awards. In business, we have champions like Roberto Goízueta, Chairman and CEO of Coca-Cola, and Solomon Trujullo, President and CEO of U.S. West.

Latinos around the world have been recognized with Nobel Prizes, Pulitzer Prizes, or Congressional Medals of Honor. To begin with, in 1906 Santiago Ramón y Cajal from Spain, known as the "father of neuroscience," won the Nobel Prize in Medicine for his work in the structure of the nervous system. His work has provided the foundation of modern neuroanatomy and has inspired the current interest in brain functioning. In 1959, Dr. Severo Ochoa of Spain won the Nobel Prize in Medicine and Physiology for the discovery of RNA, one of the chemical building blocks of life. In 1968, Luis Alvarez of the United States, a physicist, received the Nobel Prize for creating the hydrogen bubble chamber. The Argentinean César Milstein and Venezuelan Baruj Benaceraf were also given this highest of honors for their work in immunology. Another Argentinean, Luis Federico Leloir, received the Nobel Prize in Chemistry. In 1995, Mario J. Molina of the U.S., who recognized the dangers of man-made chemicals to the earth's ozone layer, also won a Nobel Prize in Chemistry. Hispanics who won Nobel Prizes in literature include Octavio Paz from Mexico, Gabriel García Márquez from Columbia, and Miguel Ángel Asturias from Guatemala. Multiple winners of this distinguished honor in literature from one country include Pablo Neruda and Gabriela Mistal from Chile and Juan Ramón Jiménez, Camilo José Cela, and Vicente Alexandre from Spain. There have been at least five Hispanic Nobel Peace Prize winners. Among them are Guatemalan author Rigoberta Menchú, Óscar Arias of Costa Rica, and Alfonso García Robles of Mexico. Multiple winners from Argentina include Adolfo Pérez Esquivel and Carlos Saavedra Lamas. Oscar Hijuelos, a Puerto Rican, won the 1990 Pulitzer Prize for his novel *The Mambo Kings Play Songs of Love.*

Each child at some point in his life develops goals or dreams about what he would like to achieve in life. For an innocent, young mind, nothing seems too impossible to attain. From sports heroes to television and movie favorites, role models emerge to fascinate the impressionable child. Every Hispanic child should learn about the outstanding accomplishments and contributions that have already been made by other Hispanics, like those listed above. She can then relate to that role model and her dream will not seem so impossible to reach.

My husband was interested in math and science as a young man, and he was supported and encouraged by his parents to go into this field. But as the first member of his family to get a college degree, he had no one to talk to about pursuing a career in engineering. Today many organizations have been formed by professional Hispanics in various fields, like engineering, medicine, and law, to fill this void, inspire Hispanic youth to enter those careers, and to serve as mentors. Some of these organizations are National Hispanic Medical Association, Society of Hispanic Engineers (SHPE), Society of Mexican American Scientists and Engineers (MAES), Hispanic Nurses Association, National Society of Hispanic MBAs, Hispanic Dental Association, Hispanic Lawyers Association, National Association of Hispanic Publications, National Association of Hispanic Journalists, U.S. Hispanic Chamber of Commerce, National Hispanic Business Association, National Coalition of Hispanic Health and Human Services Organizations, Hispanic American Association (HAA) of Dancers, and the Hispanic Communications Association (HCA).

Clearly, Hispanics have demonstrated excellence across a range of fields. I mention them here, along with a list of professional organizations, to illustrate the possibilities that await your *niños*. Reading about any of these individuals either at the library or on the Internet or contacting these organizations may uncover a wealth of information and inspiration. It will also give you insight into how Hispanic men and women have been able to apply their talents, many times against the odds, to succeed and make the world a better place without forgetting who they are.

Part Two

Basic Developmental Needs of Children

Chapter IV

Our Children Are Unique and Special

*Como los Dedos
de la Mano*

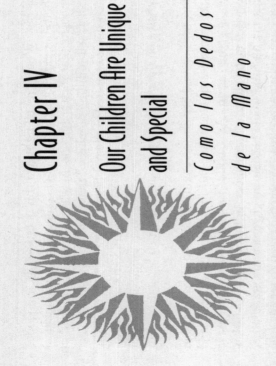

My mother-in-law, who raised eight children, used to hold up her hand and say, "*Mira mis dedos*, look at my fingers. Do you see how they are all different? My fingers are just like each of my children." From a complex set of DNA and fingerprints to a unique personality and body structure, every child is born with abilities, interests, talents, and a *carácter* that sets him apart from everyone else on the planet. The purpose of this section is to help you as a parent to recognize those differences and that you should understand, accept, and nurture them, and not bemoan or fear them.

When my mother-in-law passed those words on to me, she had already noticed that her children were exhibiting certain unique qualities that, with some guidance and support, would take each one in a certain direction. "I am going to have a doctor, a lawyer, an engineer, and a teacher," she declared to her neighbors. In fact, one of her children did become a medical doctor, another became a teacher, and two of her children became engineers. The only thing that she did not produce was a lawyer, but she was blessed with a college counselor and two federal employees instead. How did these accomplishments happen? Was it the high aspirations and expectations that she passed on to her children, or was it that she really noticed that each one had unique gifts that she was able to draw out? When I asked *mi suegra* this question, she responded that it was both her expectations and her encouragement. As an educator, I first thought that such achievement was what we in the field of education call a "self-fulfilling prophecy," that children eventually react to or become what is expected of them. I began to understand what she meant as I became aware of and supported my own children's unique talents, interests, and temperaments. I, too, made such predictions about my children based on their own unique qualities, which became evident early on.

Long before my husband became an engineer, he used to have a keen interest in the mysteries of electricity and in taking things apart and putting them together again. As a child, he constructed homemade radios and rewired many electrical appliances. Just as my mother-in-law predicted that my husband would become an engineer, my grandfather predicted that I would be a schoolteacher when he used to see me line up all the dolls in the house in a make-believe classroom. "*Ahí viene la maestra*," he would say. "Here comes the teacher." The acknowledgment and encouragement of these two people played an influential role in our future vocations. Can you recall what interested you as a child? How did your parents encourage you or support you to become who you are today? Can you identify the uniqueness in your own children and the interests they are displaying? How you respond will make a difference. As parents, we need to appreciate and respect the uniqueness in our children's temperament, interests, and inborn abilities through patience, support, and encouragement.

UNIQUE IN PERSONALITY

A child's personality will surface early. My mother used to tell me that I was "*bien risueña y bien lista*," very friendly and astute. I was a true extrovert, always smiling, friendly, and talkative, even to strangers. My strong character and leadership qualities were manifested early in life. I have often been told that I am very opinionated, creative, and strong-willed as well as a risk-taker, analyzer, and organizer. These qualities were cultivated over the years through a series of activities and positions of leadership, from safety patrol officer and columnist of the school newspaper to officer of clubs, cheerleader, and high school Sweetheart Queen. In college, I was elected Miss Fiesta, queen of the San Antonio Night Parade, which allowed me to represent my city at various out-of-town parades, including the Tournament of Roses parade in California. Being from the barrio, I never attended cotillion schools, yet I learned my p's and q's by observing others. In those days, my motto was *Cuando en Roma, haz como los romanos*, when in Rome do as the Romans. The character each person is born with is further shaped by countless experiences.

All individuals have distinct dispositions and personalities. My children's individual personalities became evident from the time they emerged from the womb. During the birth of my first son, I was able to watch Salvador Julián Rodríguez enter the world, quietly looking about with his huge dark eyes, curiously observing every detail of his surroundings. His eyes immediately stopped their wandering when they met mine, as though he was programmed to recognize a human face. At that moment, with deep emotion, he quietly began to cry. Since birth, Sal has always been soft-spoken and sensitive. From the moment your child enters the world, observe his first gestures and movements, touch him, and immediately hold him close to you. You will learn a great deal about his personality, and as you caress and hold him close, you will begin to develop a strong parent-child relationship that will be essential for future social relationships.

As a child, Sal generally tried to avoid problems, confrontations, and disharmony by keeping his emotions to himself, never being rude or outwardly disrespectful. As he got older, he reacted to conflict through passive-aggressive means, never expressing his true feelings. For example, one day when he was about seven, I was admonishing him for not wanting to practice his piano lessons. As I spoke, he quietly listened to me, but then slowly put his thumbs into his ears and tuned me out.

For a so-called "type A" extrovert personality parent like me, someone who is very active, aggressive, and more controlling than others, it is very difficult, *sumamente difícil*, to rear a child who marches to the beat of a different drummer. Are you an extrovert? Is your child an introvert? If you and your child are opposite in personality it can really be a challenge. If the answers to these questions are yes, you have found out that one has to be *very* patient, understanding, and flexible. As an extrovert growing up, I needed firm discipline from my mother and grandfather. You may find disciplining a child like Sal to be like walking on eggshells, never quite knowing when you have entered the child's discomfort zone and always being afraid that if you say or do the wrong things, your relationship will be negatively affected forever. With this type of personality, you may have to be firm but calm. Talk to your child in a low, rational voice as you explain and reason with him. Children learn best when you logically point out the *porqués* or the "whys" of things. Avoid using a high-pitched voice, negative body language, or threats. They do not work. All children need clear limits with firm consequences. There will come a time, as your child grows older, when you will have to let go, as I did, and let him learn from his mistakes.

One year, although he scored in the ninety-ninth percentile on a standardized test at school, Sal was on the brink of repeating a grade because he refused to turn in his homework. I attributed his lack of motivation to a mismatched personality between my son and his assertive teacher, who was not very flexible. *El agua y el aceite no se revuelven*, and she and Sal were like water and oil that do not mix well. She shared my strong personality, but she did not learn along the way to relax and be more sensitive to Sal's needs. She was strict and demanded that children assume responsibility for their actions. In not too many words, she told me *"que lo estaba mimando,"* that I was spoiling him.

Generally speaking, Hispanic mothers tend to do too much for their children, especially for their boys. As I stated earlier, our children are at the core of our existence. We are constantly driven by the idea that we must do just about everything for our children. This is true, especially for our boys, although we know that doing too much is not good for them. This may cause a cultural clash with teachers who sometimes demand independence and responsibility at a much earlier age than some Hispanic mothers are used to. As the *dicho* goes, *Si chocamos nos rompemos*, if we crash, we destroy ourselves. I felt that it was up to me as a parent to try to work together with the teacher to prevent a complete disaster.

I recall what Sal's teacher told me when we met for a teacher's conference, "If you do not do something about his attitude and behavior now that he is twelve years old, Sal will become dependent on you for the rest of his life." *¡Ni lo mande Dios!* That was all the motivation I needed to work with her to help Sal understand that he had to be responsible and face the cold, cruel facts; that is, that not all people would cater to his unique, sensitive personality. Sal was given two choices: either we would keep after him to turn in his homework, or we would not pester him to turn it in and he would take the consequences. He chose the latter. Together my husband and I signed a contract with him and his teacher agreeing that we would not nag him anymore and that he would be held accountable for his actions. His teacher remained firm and demanding, and Sal tested the limits.

It is hard for any parent to watch their child head in the wrong direction, especially after you have tried everything to modify his behavior.

Although he scored beyond the high school level on the standardized tests that year, Sal repeated the seventh grade. As the *dicho* goes, *El error sólo es fracaso cuando no se convierte en experiencia*, an error is a failure if one does not learn from it. He learned a valuable lesson the hard way. But I never had to remind him to be responsible for turning in his homework again. He learned that his actions hurt him more than it hurt his teacher (or parents), as he watched his friends move on to the next grade without him.

It was important, though, that my husband and I support him during this unpleasant learning experience. It would have been so easy for me to force him to complete his assignments, but *no hubiera aprendido*, he would not have learned. We demonstrated our unconditional love, which was not based on his grades or his accomplishments, or what others thought of me as an educator or as an "expert" in parent education. It was more important that he learn that he needed to be responsible for his own actions and that part of growing up meant learning from mistakes.

You may see much of yourself or your spouse in your children. I see many of my husband's traits when I think of how my son loves to spend hours in solitude, fishing, camping, boating, or just meditating. Also, they are similar in the way they react to things, like commitments, schedules, and chores. Sal embodied the old adage *De tal palo, tal astilla*, like father, like son. Each has his own clock and will do certain things according to when he wants to do them. This can be upsetting when chores are left undone or when Sal would get out of practicing his piano lessons. Sometimes my husband and I had different expectations about household chores and discipline. We did not always agree on the boundaries that we set for our children. Yet, it is so important that you and your husband compromise and at least agree on the big issues, as we did.

Sal's piano teacher used to get upset with him because she knew that he had a good ear for music and a talent for playing the piano, but she could not get him to practice. Still, at the recitals, he was *¡fantástico!* He came through like a master pianist, just as my husband predicted. My husband felt that if Sal truly had a love for music, we would not have to force him to practice.

Expose your children to as many activities as possible so that those things that really interest them will surface. You can use behavior modification up to a certain point, such as giving rewards and privileges for desirable behavior, but you should realize the limits of that approach. I felt six years of piano lessons was plenty of time for establishing a good foundation. I told my son, "Sal, when you do not want to take piano lessons anymore, just let me know." He immediately responded, "I DO NOT WANT TO TAKE PIANO LESSONS ANYMORE!" I got the message loud and clear and we stopped the lessons. But a short while after his strong declaration, Sal returned now and then to the piano and played for the enjoyment of it. He was able to do this with a solid foundation from years of practice and I knew that if he wanted to continue his lessons he would let me know.

Just because children exhibit a talent in a certain field does not necessarily mean that they have a strong interest in it. You never know which interest will surface. If you push your children to get involved in an activity, even if they like it, a hobby can turn into work for them, and they can grow to hate it. All you can do is expose your children to things and see what clicks and be ready to quit when they send you a message that they have had enough. Sal tried gymnastics, sports, arts and crafts, and several musical instruments but was not very excited.

In contrast, when it came to computers, electrical equipment, and water sports, Sal radiated! This was the same feeling that my husband had when he first held his *trompeta*, his beloved trumpet. He would not let it go. My mother-in-law never had to tell him to practice. In fact, he had to practice outside the house because she could not stand the loud noise. This reminds me of the son of an Avance graduate who one day heard someone practicing the piano in the barrio. The boy ran home and told his mother and father that he wanted to learn to play the piano, and they scraped the money together to buy him one. He practiced every moment he could and looked forward to the piano lessons from the man who first introduced him to it, the same person he'd heard practicing.

Similarly, the first time Sal ever laid his hands on a computer, he never wanted to leave it. By the age of four, he was much better at working on computers than I was. I was so frustrated when his interest and ability were not matched with an appropriate curriculum in middle school. Still, his school was not able to quench his thirst for learning. But because the school insisted that all children go through a prescribed set of curricula together, Sal became extremely bored. I tried to get him into an advanced class in computers, but the computer teacher responded by saying, "not until he meets the requirements of this introductory class." Meanwhile, Sal refused to communicate his feelings. His teacher and principal refused to listen when I tried to tell them that he was already into programming software while the rest of the class was learning basic computer skills. Later, Sal got into trouble with his teacher because he obtained access to his computer and tried to figure out a new software program without permission. He knew the rules and the consequences, but he was so driven to master the new software that he was willing to face the consequences. Finally, in high school, Sal's ninth grade teacher recognized his talents and abilities and not only put him in honors classes, but asked him to help teach a computer class. He excelled!

This experience made me realize that parents need to work closely with the school and insist that their *niños* be challenged and supported academically. Parents and teachers should work together to help children progress developmentally and help them reach their potential. As an educator, I learned that schools have to meet children's developmental needs and work with them from that point on. Teachers must assess where each child is in the educational continuum. They must communicate with and support the parents, who know their children best. Parents must also do their part to support teachers by reinforcing and augmenting the curriculum at home. In this way, parents and teachers become educational partners. Together they nurture children's interests and talents. If this partnership does not occur, parents should take advantage of the avenues they have by lodging their complaints with the principal or a member of their local school board. When all else fails, it is ultimately up to you to make sure that your children do not fall behind developmentally. You might consider supplementing the school's curriculum by enrolling your children in private weekend enrichment programs or making your home as enriching and stimulating as possible.

Since he was young, Sal has been very curious and analytical, like his father, always trying to take things apart and put them together again. I do not know how many electrical appliances he experimented on to figure out how they worked. It was then that I realized what my mother-in-law was referring to when she described "*los dedos de la mano*." I knew that I would have an engineer in the family, too. This idea was constantly being reinforced through the years. As early as the third grade, when Sal was in a school for gifted and talented children, the headmaster of the school also predicted that he would be an engineer. "He is such a dreamer and is always trying to figure things out. Children like Sal do not like a structured environment or anyone pushing them. They need time and space," he said.

If you notice that your young children have an interest in becoming future engineers, doctors, astronauts, or scientists, support them at home by providing safe objects like Tinker Toys, blocks, and model airplanes. Encourage your young child to play with sand or water and all kinds of containers. With your supervision, allow your older child to construct things or take things apart using old appliances, lumber, hammers, and nails. Sal built several forts with his brother and sister and he helped his father build a bed in the shape of a car. One Halloween he helped his father make his own robot costume that lit up.

Computers are now more than ever a major part of our lives. It is critical that you expose your child to computers, for we are in the information age, when everyone will soon be required to operate a computer in the workplace, regardless of the job. But it is also important to make sure that you surround them with all kinds of books that will open their minds to the wonders and fascinating things around them.

Sal never deviated from his love of math, science, and computers, regardless of setbacks. He was nominated by his congressman and senator to the Naval Academy, the U.S. Air Force Academy, the U.S. Military Academy, and the Merchant Marines. He chose the Naval Academy and had taken and passed all the requirements, except for the physical. Before he could take his physical, he broke his leg playing high school football. Needless to say, Sal had to change his plans and decided to go to Texas A&M to study engineering and computer science. Sal wanted to join the Aggies (the A&M team) despite the fact that both his father and I graduated from the rival school, and were Longhorns from the University of Texas at Austin. Again, Sal wanted to be different and unique.

What if your child is the energetic, expressive extrovert who is less difficult to draw out? In fact, what if he is a handful? My middle child, Steven René Rodríguez, was the antithesis of Sal in telling others how he felt. He was a little more daring, much more aggressive, active, and out of bounds. *¡Bien bárbaro!* How does a mother deal with such an unmanageable child?

Even before birth, Steven managed to get his way. While still in my womb, he would wake me up in the middle of the night, *dándome unas patadítas tan fuertes,* sometimes kicking so hard that he would literally make me roll over to my left side. At birth, Steven came out with a bang! *¡Me dio un buen susto!* When he was born he was a very purplish color so I became terrified because I thought he was having problems breathing. But he was that color because he was about to let out a gigantic *grito,* to let everyone know that he was angry that he had been disturbed from his warm, cozy slumber. As an infant, Steven would wake up from his short naps, suddenly roll over, grab the crib pad and take great pleasure in tossing it back and forth, up and down until it was almost in shreds.

For many years, that child, *lleno de energía,* did not change. When he was young, he was a bundle of raw energy, curious, adventurous, and driving me crazy. I did not think he, nor I, would survive past his sixth birthday. Steven has always been an expressive, determined person, questioning everyone and fighting for his rights and the rights of others. He has to have *la palabra final*, the last word. He always has opinions and can build a good case on issues he believes in. As he was growing up, I knew more than I wanted to know and I always knew what was on *his* mind!

This type of child is not always trying to make his parents go crazy. Steven could fluctuate from one extreme emotion to another. At one time he could be the sweetest, funniest, and most sensitive person and then at another time be the opposite. If he wanted attention, all he'd have to do was lovingly say, "Mama, scratch my back," and he would get that warm human touch that he desired. Give Steven a microphone and he would act, sing, and recite without being told. He was always the center of attention as the clown, entertainer, and self-proclaimed leader. The right side of his brain, which controls creativity and expression, was always at work as he pursued his talent in drawing, exploring, and experimenting. There is never a boring moment when the Stevens of the world are around. They always impress you with their talents.

As parents, we must support and love all our children, but especially these *caranchitos*, these *diablitos*, until we can transform them into *angelitos*. All they need is our unconditional love, acceptance, guidance, and lots of patience. Your strong-willed children need to know that you will always be there for them. With the right kind of direction, they will probably turn out to be very successful entrepreneurs, lawyers, or great community leaders—even the President of the United States, especially if you tell them that it is possible. You do not want to kill the driving spirit that makes them so determined. We just have to channel it in the right direction and be ever so vigilant, knowing where they are and what they are doing.

I had many unforgettable and frightening moments with Steven. Have you ever lost your child in the mall or grocery store for a few minutes? Those minutes seem like an eternity! Shortly before he was two years of age, Steven went exploring in the neighborhood with his dog Buffy, and we could not find him for three hours! Can you imagine what I went through? A young mother at the time, I remember my shaky knees became so weak from despair and fear that I fell to the ground crying. I thought I would never see him again. We had police officers, firefighters, and all of our relatives looking for him. Finally, my sister-in-law Lupe spotted Buffy, who led her to Steven, six houses from where we lived, playing inside the garage of a vacant house. He had no idea what all the commotion was about and marveled when everyone rejoiced and kissed him. I went through a thousand deaths with this child. When he was three, we went camping in Colorado. One moment he was by my side. The next, he was following a chipmunk deep into the woods. It seemed that Steven needed a leash the first six years of life.

These children are a challenge to any parent. As I said, I am an extrovert and Steven is one, too, and he was overwhelming for me many times. I can imagine what it would have been like for parents who had the opposite personality. Don't despair. The trick is to keep them *busy*! My husband and I knew that we had to release some of that excess energy. We enrolled Steven in swimming lessons when he was nine months of age and karate lessons at three. He has always been competitive and an achiever, striving for excellence. Your child, boy or girl, may surprise you with their competitive spirit. When Steven was three, we attended a fair at the YMCA where he had just won several ribbons in a swimming competition. We were leaving the grounds when he stopped the whole family to watch a breakdance competition. Immediately Steven wanted to compete. My husband was reluctant to let him because the other competitors, who were much older, wore costumes and had practiced their routines for weeks, but I convinced him to let Steven try. Steven studied the kids' movements as they practiced their breakdance routine and in the short time that he spent observing, he learned to moon walk and spin on his head. He entered the contest and came home with the first prize trophy.

Again, it is important that you know where your active children are at all hours of the day—and night. Make sure your babysitter is also extra-vigilant, for these kinds of children are often in a make-believe world, fantasizing and role-playing. Like the day Steven wanted to be a Ninja. My husband and I were in Puerto Rico on a business trip that doubled as an anniversary get-away, and we had hired a babysitter to stay at the house with the children. One night, eight-year-old Steven snuck outside wearing his black karate uniform, his face and hands painted black. He hid under one of the many cars that were parked on our property for a Beastie Boys concert that was going on adjacent to our home. He wanted to see what all the *borlete* was about. We received a call that night from the babysitter, who told us that a police officer had just brought Steven in handcuffs to the front door. The police officer could have shot Steven as he crept around in the darkness. We immediately returned home! If you have a child like mine, childproof the house throughout, and pay special attention to doors, windows, and gates. The idea isn't to make your child a prisoner, of course, but to deter your niño from letting his *curiosidad* get the best of him.

The nuns at Steven's Catholic elementary school told us that they would do a lot of praying for him after he left the school. Years later, they would ask me, "How is Steven?"—followed always by a "pobrecitos" look as though they felt sorry for my husband and me. I would respond, "Ya verán, you'll see. One day Steven will become a great leader. I have faith in my special son."

The prayers must have worked, for as Steven got into middle school, he really did mature and became calmer and more self-controlled. Football also helped him, and it or any physical sports activity might help your niños con mucha energía. Football had everything Steven needed: excitement, adventure, competition, prestige, and a sense of belonging. And the coaches really worked him out! In order to play football he had to maintain his grades and he could not get into trouble. Football taught him the meaning of cooperation and sportsmanship. It boosted his confidence, courage, strength, and self-image.

Many Hispanics are below average in height, bien chaparritos—Steven was one of them. What do you do to help your children if others make fun of them because of height? We gave Steven some ammunition to fight back, dichos, dichos y cuentos. Although Steven was shorter in size than many of his teammates, Steven used to respond to anyone who tried to put him down because of his height with the dicho, "Like a chile piquín, soy chiquito pero picoso," I'm little, but hot, like the chile piquín! We also told him the Mexican folktale of the race between the cocky horse and the small bee, in which the bee won the race by perching itself on the tip of the horse's nose. "What counts is not your height, but your astuteness, agility, and how dedicated and committed you are to something," Steven would say. Because of his attitude, I think he has the makings of a good lawyer, politician, or community leader. His version of a common law of physics for force is: force = mass x acceleration + ganas.

Later, as a starter on the high school varsity defensive team, standing five feet six inches tall, with a one-hundred-fifty-pound frame, his strong drive and determination enabled him to tackle huge, six-foot, two hundred-pound players. Pumping iron every day helped. He was determined to be like the character in the movie Rudy, a story about a pint-sized football player who finally gets to play college football at Notre Dame through perseverance and hard work. Steven was always playing against the odds. For the people who told him he would never be a varsity football player because of his height, he proved que el que quiere, puede and proved that más hace el que quiere, que el que puede. He not only played in the starting lineup, but he was captain of the team that won district.

Grades for some of your children will come easy. Others, like Steven, have to work harder. Do not compare your children. They are all different and march to the beat of a different drummer. She may need you to help her more with homework and tests than others do. We spent many days going over spelling lists or history questions with Steven. Many times teachers tried to discourage him from taking honor classes, thinking he couldn't handle them. As parents, you should be there to support your children and make sure that they get the opportunities that they need to get a good education. Although he was smart and managed to make A's and B's, there was usually one C that would eventually keep him from making the honor roll many times. But he showed the teachers that he could handle the honors math classes. Steven loved logic and analytical problem solving, which he used shrewdly and skillfully to achieve his goals.

Children who are extremely spirited and full of energy need firmness, consistent rules, and vigilance from parents until they are able to be more self-disciplined. I could not give Steven any slack for many years. While my husband and I agreed that we would not use corporal punishment as a form of discipline, I have to admit that on a few occasions Steven did things that were *fuera de los límites*, beyond the limits, things that could physically hurt him and others. Raising Steven, I often recall my mother's famous words, "*Vas a pagar todas las que debes con este muchacho*," you will pay all that you owe with this boy. I could not complain too much because my mother tolerated my expressive and curious behavior. She was strong and very strict, but never killed the driving spirit that eventually helped me become a community leader later in life. I, like my mother, tried to use all my resources and strengths to keep my children safe and on the right path while maintaining their unique personalities.

If you have a child like Steven, you can probably draw some comfort from knowing that you are not alone in the episodes that you have had to go through. While *nos salen canas*, we get gray hair, with the incredible things they do, they can also give us many joyous memories. Enjoy their radiant spirit; eventually they grow up and you will later laugh at the things that made you cry.

Each of your children is so different. I have given you a description of two distinct personalities that perhaps you recognize as a parent. Here is the third, the obstinate child. As with my two previous deliveries, the actual birth of my last child, Gloria Vanessa Rodriguez, gave me a sign of what was to come and the kind of personality she would possess. Even before she was born, she was different from the boys. From the time I entered the hospital, the boys were delivered in under an hour, with Sal being delivered in forty-five minutes and Steven in thirty minutes. When my water broke, I knew that I would have Vanessa in the elevator. I warned the nurses that I would have the baby in less than thirty minutes. After all that *borlote*, it took me twelve long hours to deliver Vanessa. Three different women came in and out of the waiting room to have their babies, *y yo, nada. ¡Qué vergüenza!* After the doctor had to induce labor, we began to think that this was a sign of what was to come: Vanessa would forever be unpredictable and *terca*.

With only Vanessa's head out, the doctor prematurely concluded that she was a boy because her facial appearance looked just like Steven's. She fooled the doctor. She turned out to be the most beautiful girl, pink as the roses that my husband gave me. Throughout life, Vanessa continues to be unpredictable. She has an expansive personality that includes many interests and abilities. She is bright, strong-willed, friendly, and empathetic. She is shy, but very aggressive and very competitive. These traits have helped her excel in different sports, particularly in basketball, which she has played fervently since preschool. My husband was her coach and enrolled her in every basketball league he could to help her develop her interest.

While Vanessa's interest in math, science, and sports matched her brothers', she in contrast appeared to have a more caring and nurturing personality. Many times Vanessa would beat me to the medicine cabinet to retrieve cough medicine or Band-Aids when the boys got sick or hurt. She also paid considerable attention to ailing animals. Perhaps it was her natural maternal instincts that made her that way, for these traits were less prevalent in the boys' behavior.

Do you have a girl who is the youngest and has been raised with nothing but brothers? If you do, you will probably find that this has made her strong and assertive, just to be able to defend herself. Yet, did you still see a feminine nurturing side in her, regardless of whether she turned out to be a tomboy? Did you ever think about whether girls are naturally different from boys?

Vanessa's play was always different from the boys'. Her imaginative play was more down-to-earth. She would line up the dolls and become a teacher or a doctor, just as I did when I was a young girl. Whether it was teaching or performing an "operation" on her brothers, the neighborhood children, or small cousins, Vanessa showed her love for children and her ability to reach even the most *terco*, or stubborn, children.

I hear parents in the barrio say that their boys are *"puros hombres,"* and while I generally do not like using this label, I definitely saw a difference in my children's play. My boys' play never demonstrated the nurturing behavior that I saw in Vanessa's. While she gently played with her dolls and took care of them, Steven would take off the clothes, hair, and arms or use them as if they were footballs. I found that although I bought male and female dolls for all my children and tried to de-emphasize gender-role stereotypes, sometimes the differences manifested themselves on their own.

Carol Gilligan's book *In a Different Voice* confirms these differences. She cites research that found sex differences in the child's play during recess and in physical education classes. Boys were found to play out of doors more often than girls do. They play more often in large and age-heterogeneous groups and play competitive games more often, and their games last longer than girls' games. The games last longer not only because their games are more complicated and require more organizational skills, but because when disputes occur the boys resolve their problems more effectively than girls. When the girls have a dispute, they end the game because they are more concerned with maintaining a relationship than winning. Girls' games involve smaller, more intimate groups, cooperating and taking turns, mostly in private places. Gilligan states that in little girls, intimacy goes along with identity, as she comes to know herself through her relationships with others. Boys get their identity by their particular position in the world, their abilities, their beliefs, and their physical characteristics.

In her book *Your Child's Growing Mind*, learning theorist Jane M. Healy cites research that found that the majority of girls talk, read, and write earlier than boys and score better on tests that measure verbal skills, including reading, writing, grammar, and spelling. Girls are generally better in fine motor coordination (using their hands for intricate tasks) and mathematical calculation. Girls are thought to be more sensitive to facial expressions and to cues in the environment, which some researchers believe makes them more intuitive. Girls are known to be different from boys in that they seek other people's opinion before they act. Have you found this to be true with your girls? Most boys, according to Healy, are better in spatial skills, mathematical reasoning, abstract thinking, and large body movements. Some research studies claim that boys do better at solving mazes than girls, and by the tenth grade, they generally surpass girls in math.

Perhaps these differences can, to some extent, be traced to how adults treat their children. Hispanics are just like other ethnic groups, in that many times we expect different things of girls than of boys. When we do this, we are giving nonverbal messages to girls that can ultimately affect their self-image and behavior. Do you treat your boys differently from your girls? In Vanessa's case, my husband and I have tried very hard to demand and expect as much from her as we have from the boys, which is why I think she has remained aggressive and competitive. Her assertive nature would not allow us to treat her any differently, for she would immediately say, "What about the boys!" or "Wait a minute, are we being sexist here?"

If you're the parent of a girl, let her know that she deserves an equal chance in a competitive world. Give her plenty of experiences and opportunities to observe many types of role models. At the same time, help your boys become more nurturing and sensitive by asking them to be more helpful, empathetic, and understanding. They need to understand how they affect others and to be open to other people's point of view. When Sal's teacher told me that I was babying him, I became more aware of my actions and tried very hard not to let him manipulate me to do things for him. I felt myself going against the grain in a culture where mothers tend to do more for *los hombrecitos*. Still, my husband and I had to make a strong effort to be fair and equal to all our children.

Vanessa's kind, nurturing personality won her many friends, but it has also gotten her into trouble. For example, when she was in kindergarten, her teacher would tell me, *"Vanessa es muy metiche,* Vanessa is very nosy. She takes it upon herself to see who needs help. She is out of her chair too much, talking to her neighbors too much, and not listening to me enough. I know that she means well and the children like her a lot, but as a teacher, I want her to stay in her seat and mind her own business!" Being *metiche* and sociable was the subject of many parent-teacher conferences up until middle school. It would bring Vanessa both praise and punishment. As for the children, they regarded her as a leader, and sought her out as a resource and a companion. At home she also assumed the bossy role, telling everyone what he or she needed to do. Her leadership skills surfaced as early as kindergarten, when the other children elected her class leader. As parents, we should reinforce and support these leadership qualities, as well as teach them more positive social skills. We should help them understand how their behavior affects others, including the teacher.

Even though some research indicates that boys perform better than girls in math, Vanessa demonstrated strong analytical and math skills, but she also had a natural sense of creativity, which she expressed through her cartoon drawings and model figures. She was always conscientious about her grades and was on the honor roll every year before middle school. I never had to remind her to do her homework and her assignments were always on time, as well as neat and orderly, at least up until the age of twelve.

If you did not notice the difference between your boys and girls when they were young, you will surely see it when they approach twelve years of age. Something happened to Vanessa when she turned twelve. Perhaps it was her hormones or the move from a small Catholic school to a larger public school that brought out a stronger and somewhat rebellious personality. She just about turned into a complete stranger. Vanessa had always been almost perfect: sweet, kind, and respectful, always doing what she was supposed to do and never getting into real trouble (except when Steven was behind it). She was daddy and mommy's *princesa.* But when she turned twelve, she became a person we just did not recognize. Just as her birth was unpredictable, I was not expecting such an abrupt change in personality. I did not see it as abruptly in my boys. I am forewarning you, parents, *"cuidado con esas listas y calladitas, pueden saltar a picarte."* If you feel that you have the perfect child, the perfect *princesita,* brace yourself. Some children seem to begin the tumultuous teenage years with few early eruptions.

Vanessa, like many preteens, wanted very much to please and to be like others. So, if her best friends were not making good grades, she did not want to be labeled the "smart one" or "the nerd." She was very self-conscious about her appearance, especially when she wore braces, and did not want to be different from the others. As her appearance changed to "fit in," so did her attitude, self-respect, and how she related to others. She wore her brother's large shirts and at the same time became argumentative, defiant, rude, insensitive, and disrespectful—a typical teenager, a few years before her time, though.

Again, parenthood has its ups and downs and peaks and valleys. It is not easy being a parent of a preteen. As a Hispanic parent, it is so difficult to deal with self-centeredness and disrespect that will surface.

One cold winter morning, for example, I woke up early to make Vanessa some warm cereal before she headed off to school. She came downstairs in shorts and said, "I don't want to eat." Shocked at her summer clothes, I instructed Vanessa to go back to her room and put on something warm. She responded with words she had never used before. "Oh mother, go back to sleep," she said as she went out the door, leaving me completely flabbergasted. *"¿Qué pasó?"* What happened? I thought. Why was she so disrespectful? Should I run after her or let her freeze? Before I could decide, she was on the school bus.

For traditional Hispanic mothers who value *respeto,* dealing with this kind of behavior can require *un esfuerzo tremendo.* On the one hand, I wanted her to show me respect, but on the other, I knew I had taught her to question things and to assert herself. When she had an opinion, she became unyielding. Vanessa felt so much pressure to conform. Clearly, the values that she had been taught were being tested during this critical period. What does one do during these episodes?

This experience taught me that some personalities are more vulnerable to peer pressure than others. As parents, we need to be very patient, supportive, and attentive to what they do and say. We must also be aware of the people with whom our children associate, for each one of them can have a tremendous influence on our children. As the saying goes, *Dime con quién andas y te diré quién eres*. Tell me who you hang around with and I will tell you who you are. Our children can easily pick up things they hear and see from those they associate with. If your child seems drawn to or actually joins up with the wrong crowd, do not try to handle it yourself; work with the school personnel. Perhaps they can counsel your child, let you observe a class if they are concerned about the children they are associating with, or maybe you can serve as a chaperone at school activities. Get to know the parents of the children in your children's class, and most important at this age, keep your children busy in school, church, and community activities where they can meet a variety of friends.

I had to work in partnership with the school to do something about Vanessa's changing behavior. Her teachers sensed that she was beginning to feel overwhelmed at trying to belong to a group of girls who had different values than hers. All children have to deal with peer pressure, and as parents we must help them cope with it. Peer pressure made Vanessa change outwardly, but inside, she was still yearning to be herself. The foundation that was set when she was young was in conflict with her need to belong and to please.

Eventually, Vanessa willingly returned to the small Catholic school that she had attended from prekindergarten to the third grade. The classes were smaller and I knew the children and the families with whom she was associating. She went back to an environment that reinforced the values she had grown up with. I saw a transformation in her appearance as she began to associate with friends who had similar values and as she went back to wearing uniforms. She took pride in the way she looked and her behavior reverted, most of the time, to the compassionate and helpful person she has always been. *¡Gracias a Dios!*

In this chapter, I have shared with you three separate personalities in an attempt to demonstrate how distinctive children can be, even in the same family. I have put forth some strategies that parents can use to bring out the best in those personalities. As parents, we should not show favoritism toward one child, nor compare them with their siblings, *porque cada quien es como Dios lo hizo*. Every one of your children is unique and special, *como los dedos de la mano*.

UNIQUE IN PHYSICAL CHARACTERISTICS

Children are also different and unique in the physical characteristics that are passed from one generation to the next. Hispanics come in all shapes, shades, and sizes. Indian, European, African, and Asian blood have added many dimensions to how we see ourselves. Even within a single family, the physical distinctiveness of each child can be profound.

For example, in my parents' families, you will find straight, naturally wavy, and "Afro" hair. You will find persons who have extremely fair skin as well as those with olive complexions and dark skin. You will find *ojitos chinitos y negros* and big, round blue, brown, or green eyes. On my husband's side of the family, there are seven children with green eyes and one with dark brown eyes.

All children deserve to be accepted and respected. I have heard Hispanics say of one another's children, *"ay, pobrecito, salió morenito,"* as though dark skin were a misfortune or a curse. One day my daughter told me that other children were calling her names at school because of the shape of her *chinito* eyes. Children's self-esteem is shaped and reinforced by the parents' verbal and body language. The child who is dubbed *morenito, chinito,* or *negrito,* all of which are often used affectionately as terms of endearment by you or by others, must know by your words and actions that she is loved and admired as much as her other siblings. We need to remind our children that they are beautiful, different, and special and that we love them all the same.

UNIQUE IN INTELLIGENCE

Each of your children, like mine, has distinctive strengths and capabilities, each is born with certain tendencies and preferences, and each possesses a great potential waiting to be tapped and cultivated. As the *dicho* goes, *El que nace para tamal, del cielo le caen las hojas*, each person is endowed with a set of personality traits and unique innate abilities. Howard Gardner, a Harvard neuropsychologist, refers to these abilities as multiple intelligences. According to Gardner, everyone is capable of demonstrating knowledge in nine ways. He explains that, in varying degrees, every person possesses all of these intelligences. They are:

1. linguistic, or a talent with language (especially writers, poets)
2. logical-mathematical, the ability to solve problems, for example, through reasoning and deduction and to figure out patterns (scientists, engineers)
3. spatial, the ability to visualize a physical picture of an object or environment and navigate or design (architects, chess players, artists)
4. musical, the ability to orchestrate and produce rhythm and song (composers, singers)
5. bodily-kinesthetic, using one's body to express oneself, create, or find a solution to a problem (athletes, dancers)
6. interpersonal, possessing an understanding of other human beings, their thoughts and emotions (teachers, politicians)
7. intrapersonal, knowing one's inner self, one's feelings and how they affect behavior, knowing how to solve problems or survive in difficult situations (strategists, military analysts)
8. naturalist, one who loves and appreciates nature (environmentalists)
9. spiritual, a connection to "other-worldly" aspects of life (religion, philosophy, and hypothesizing)

A child may be endowed with both logical-mathematical and linguistic intelligence. He may be a computer whiz or a gifted writer. A child with a keen ability to solve problems through associations and relationships is a child with good intrapersonal skills. What about your children, what are their intellectual strengths? What do they really like to do? Your son or daughter may excel in bodily-kinesthetic intelligence as a dancer or athlete. They may be a combination of these. Gardner stresses that multiple intelligences do not cancel each other out. To be good at math and drawing does not mean one is necessarily poor at maneuvering a basketball, as we found out with Vanessa. A child who associates well with people and has a special talent for negotiating to get what he wants, possesses strong interpersonal skills.

The phrase *cada cabeza es un mundo* reminds us that each person's experiences, thoughts, and abilities are different and unique. Understanding that children possess a variety of innate abilities may help parents support and nurture their children's individuality. It has taken a lot of critical observing and attentive listening to recognize the gifts that each one of my children possesses. It will take parents, teachers, coaches, relatives, and friends to bring out their innate gifts. Unfortunately, too many schools in the U.S. are designed for children who are strong only in language and logic, those skills that are said to emerge from the left side of the brain. We need to support and value the creative artist, those who are musically inclined, and those who think "outside the box."

Many schools today are striving to do a better job of recognizing budding talents and nurturing them with an eye to our culture, but as parents we must work with our children's teachers to help them recognize the strengths, patterns of interest, and uniqueness of *nuestros niños*. Nurture these strengths at home so those teachers can reinforce them in class.

Each year a select number of children are chosen to participate in gifted and talented programs in schools around the country. As a member of the Presidential Commission on Educational Excellence for Hispanic Americans, I can confirm that Hispanic children are disproportionately underrepresented in these programs. As a parent, it is your responsibility to inquire about these programs and to ensure that your children are not excluded and that they participate in them. Magnet schools are designed to cater to children's different talents and interests. Enroll your children in classes that will help them develop their talents. My brother was ten years old when my mother realized that he had an affinity for and talent in art. She enrolled him in art correspondence classes. By the time he was eleven years old, his religious and cultural paintings were displayed throughout his school.

If your children like to take things apart, allow them to experiment and explore with old radios and discarded electronic equipment (but make sure there is no danger of electrocution by unplugging the objects while they are experimenting). If your children are inclined toward music, get them instruments, enroll them in music lessons, encourage them to sing, or take them to dance classes. Make that special effort to help your children achieve their destinies. You play an important role in what your children will become by providing a stimulating environment for them.

UNIQUE IN LEARNING STYLES

Children also differ from one another depending upon which side of the brain is more dominant, the left side or the right. Left-brain dominant children like to take things apart with their minds, while right-brain dominant children like to see the "big picture." The left-brainer is someone who appreciates detail and is good at writing and listening. I think of the way Sal excels at writing and using rapidly changing fine motor skills when he uses the computer, works on challenging video games, or demonstrates his agility at the piano keyboard. His learning style is more like a left-brainer. This is not to say that a left-brainer will not excel at other things, as Sal's talent in football, soccer, and baseball have demonstrated. A left-brainer may possess a very analytical, logical mind, but will only do one thing at a time and must follow a sequential order. Do you have a left-brainer in your house? Watch how your children go about solving problems. For example, when Sal was exposed to something new, like the time he started his fish aquarium, he had to analyze and learn everything about the process. First he started his freshwater aquarium, and then methodically he advanced to a saltwater aquarium.

While left-brainers may be stronger in the facts and formulas of mathematics, right-brainers are good at mathematical word problems, geometry, charts, maps, and graphs. Right-brainers are more intuitive and creative. They are people who are called visionary and learn by doing and creating. Like Steven, they may excel at art or drama with their powerful burst of creativity. They are affected by sensory images, especially if it involves interacting with people. When Sal read, he was fascinated by words, whereas Steven, the right-brainer, was more interested in relationships and the meaning behind the story. Sal liked routine and Steven liked novelty and excitement. Right-brainers march to the beat of a different drummer—with their unique rhythms and sounds.

I know Sal can be categorized as a left-brainer and Steven as a right-brainer, but labeling Vanessa was not so easy. Her natural abilities make her strong in both sides of the brain. She is good at math, personal relationships, and creativity. She is very much like her father, who is an engineer, a musician, and a poet.

How would you classify yourself or your children? As parents, we must be patient, understanding, and supportive of our children's unique learning styles and their strengths. At the same time, we must provide a variety of experiences to stimulate and balance both sides of the brain (we'll explore this in depth in the following chapter). Although children are born with certain tendencies and patterns, ultimately their immediate environment will be the determining factor in reaching their potential, shaping their personality, and developing their abilities, talents, and interests.

NATURE VERSUS NURTURE

Are some people naturally born with more potential or intellectual capacity than others, or is it the environment that makes the difference? Some years ago, I was fortunate to meet astronaut Franklin Chang-Díaz at the NASA Space Center, where he addressed a gathering of scientists and mathematicians. I was invited to speak at that conference to discuss ways to enlarge the pool of Hispanic children entering the fields of engineering and science. My topic was the importance of early childhood stimulation and the role of parents as the first teachers. During the question-and-answer period I asked Dr. Chang-Díaz the question, "Why did you become an astronaut? Who motivated you to follow that dream?" After pondering the questions for a moment, he emphatically credited his mother for the direction he took in life. I could have stood up on the chair and shouted, "YES! Give me five!" He told the group that as a boy, he was always curious about the moon and the stars, and his mother would go to the library and get him all the books she could find on the subject. She brought home huge empty furniture boxes, put them together, and encouraged him to pretend the structure was a spaceship. This enabled him to dream that someday he could become an astronaut. His dream became a reality thanks to his genes and to the people in his environment who encouraged him.

Selena, the beloved Tejano singer, is another example of what can happen to children with the right kind of parental support. Her parents recognized her singing ability when she was just a small girl and cultivated her talent through encouragement and support. They taught her to sing in Spanish and stressed the importance of her bicultural experience. Because of her loving and supportive environment, the late Selena's talents flourished and she became a super performer. For generations, there has been a great debate between the so-called "nature/nurture" theorists who dispute whether heredity or environment determines one's intellectual potential and personality. My view is that a person is genetically prewired with a predetermined potential, intellectual capacity, and temperament, but this fact does not guarantee that one's potential, capacity, or personality traits will be fully developed, if the environment is not a favorable one.

The child will be affected by environmental influences positively or negatively before and after birth. For example, the behavior of a pregnant mother who does not eat well, who uses alcohol or drugs or exposes herself to viral infection before giving birth, can be the cause of forms of epilepsy, mental retardation, autism, and schizophrenia in her newborn.

Too often children's development suffers because of preventable hearing and vision problems, accidents, or treatable disorders like dyslexia. It is important that children receive annual physicals and get immunization shots. If they don't, their poor health might negate their inborn abilities. Sometimes children's learning and development is stunted because they need eyeglasses, because they are hungry, or because they grow up in an environment of violence and fear.

Some people still think that it is futile to try to change a person's nature. They might use the *dicho Lavar puercos con jabón, es perder tiempo y jabón*, washing pigs with soap is a waste of time and soap. Many others do not agree. Genetics and the environment work together and affect a person's temperament and personality. One influences the other. For example, parents can modify a child's out-of-bounds, potentially dangerous behavior by restricting his environment somewhat until he learns to moderate his own behavior, as my husband and I had to do with Steven. At the same time, parents can channel their child's excess energy and determined personality in a positive manner to help her fine-tune leadership qualities, for instance. Never doubt that you, as a parent, have the ability to bring out the best in your children. Sal outgrew his shy personality as we encouraged him to become involved in sports and other activities that required him to relate to people. His peers elected him president of his high school class and vice president of the student council. All this gave him self-confidence. Many great leaders and successful CEOs who were naturally shy have met the challenge and succeeded in positions that were generally reserved for extroverts.

Parents can alter their child's destiny by changing her environment. If parents recognize that their child *va por el mal camino*, is heading in the wrong direction, as we saw with Vanessa, they can alter their child's environment by removing negative influences and ultimately changing her behavior and her future. Many children who are not supervised or taught morals, values, or limits become delinquent. In addition, children who are abused and not shown love will find it difficult to be kind and compassionate.

You as a parent can reverse or accelerate linguistic, cognitive, or motor development depending upon the environment you provide. Research has found that children deprived of affection and intellectual stimulation during early childhood, including infancy, can be seriously impaired intellectually, socially, and emotionally. Children who have less intellectual potential but who are motivated and work hard can achieve more than children with more intellectual potential but who are not as motivated to achieve. Therefore, "nurture," or the environment, plays just as important a role as "nature," or heredity, in one's development and achievements. In any event, there's no question that after birth, children must have a continuously rich, nurturing, and stimulating environment if they are to reach their potential.

AGES AND STAGES: YOUR CHILD IS NORMAL AND PREDICTABLE

Though every child is different and unique, all of them, regardless of race, class, gender, or personality will go through predictable and normal patterns of growth and development. These are the so-called "ages and stages," the phases in a child's development. They include typical behaviors and characteristics that have been observed in most children at each age, yet not all children fit them exactly. Each stage is based on averages. This means that approximately 50 percent of children are at the same stage at a particular age, while 25 percent are ahead in their development and 25 percent have not yet reached the stage. Even though children develop at different rates, the sequence of development is the same for all children.

Experts in child development say growth patterns are characterized by periods of good behavior followed by periods of bad behavior, referred to, respectfully, as *equilibrium* and *disequilibrium*. When children are struggling to accomplish a new developmental task such as walking, but have not fully mastered it, they enter a disequilibrium state and become anxious, frightened, sensitive, and irritable. They may have temper tantrums or suffer from eating or sleep disorders. As he learns new skills, a child may regress temporarily to a state of dependency again, clinging to the mother's skirts or leg.

They enter a state of disequilibrium when they have not quite mastered a skill that is necessary for learning a more advanced one. For example, a child who has entered the imaginary play stage but who has not developed his language sufficiently will get very frustrated. A child who wants to run but has not mastered his walking will get very irritated. When children try to learn many things at the same time, such as walking, talking, stacking, and riding a tricycle, it is understandable that they may become overwhelmed and behave *terriblemente*. They will become scared, clingy, and dependent and use all of their energy to understand and cope with what is happening. It is important that parents understand and express comfort and support to their children. They need to help them resolve their problems and master their skills. Remain close to your children and spend extra time with them during this period, to bring about a greater sense of security.

When they finally master the skill, they will feel better, and will again enter the state of equilibrium. They are the *angelitos*, the little angels, who command the center of attention as they demonstrate their newly acquired *talentos*. When they are in disequilibrium, *¡mucho cuidado!* Watch out, because they will be determined to master the skill, regardless of who gets in the way.

The period of two years to two-and-a-half years is the peak of disequilibrium, which we call the terrible twos. There is definitely a swinging back and forth of good and bad behavior. But be assured that the negative stage will be followed by a more pleasant stage. Just as parents are enjoying their children, another period of disequilibrium begins and the parents have to brace themselves again.

While all children go through the same sequential stages of development, they are perceived and dealt with differently from culture to culture. One of the worst insults that a Hispanic person could hurl at a parent is to call his unruly child *un hijo malcriado*, a badly reared or spoiled child. Often this judgment is made without a clear understanding of the normal developmental processes that all children go through. Without this knowledge, parents may experience a great deal of embarrassment and anger when their child becomes more assertive and *terco*. But after learning the whys and hows of development, they will be more patient and understanding when the child enters the disequilibrium stage. They will know that this undesirable behavior is temporary and that the good behavior is just around the corner.

Chapter V

Helping Your Children Develop Intellectually

Cada Cabeza Es un Mundo

THE NATURAL DRIVE TO LEARN: ¿QUÉ? ¿POR QUÉ? ¿CÓMO?

Nuestros niños, like all children, have an innate drive and need to learn and to grow intellectually. They have a natural desire to explore, experiment, and master their environment and their bodies. Children need to feel that they are competent and that they can accomplish things. From the moment they are born, they are active learners; they absorb information and try to make sense of the world using their senses of seeing, hearing, touching, smelling, and tasting. As children encounter new information in their environment, their natural curiosity makes them ask questions like, "What is it? How does it work? What does it do?" This curiosity forces them to question, poke, and search until they discover, understand, or find a solution. Everything to a young child is a sense of awe and wonder. *Es una aventura.*

The uncontrollable *urgencia y presión para aprender*, which all children are born with, is what fosters intelligence. What is intelligence? It is what happens in the mind: the acquisition of knowledge and language and the development of fine and large motor (muscle) skills. It is the ability to think, perceive, and remember. It includes the ability to understand, solve problems, reason, plan, judge, invent, and create. A person who is intelligent is someone who is "smart," or *listo*, as we say in Spanish. *Tiene buena cabeza*. However, every child's mind is its own unique world. As the *dicho* reminds us, *cada cabeza es un mundo*. Every child's mind can be thought of as a rich storehouse of lights, or *focos*, that are associated with his unique learning experiences.

The children who continuously build on those experiences have an advantage because they produce knowledge and knowledge is power, *saber es poder*. Parents can either help their children harness this power or they can extinguish it. If parents do not understand that the children have a natural quest for knowledge, the child's actions can be seen as *travesuras* and he will be labeled *grosero, rebelde*, or *malcriado*, rude, rebellious, or spoiled. Consequently, this natural curiosity can cause parents great frustration and anger and make them want to *gritar*. It is not easy for you to keep up with your child's boundless energy and his need to learn. But the more you understand what is behind his actions, the more patient and understanding you will be.

How did your children manifest their natural curiosity and need to learn? My own children displayed their natural curiosity in many ways. Most memorable were the lessons they learned as they sat in their high chairs as toddlers. They loved to toss the spoon to the floor again and again. A frustrated parent might respond with "*¡Ay Dios mío! ¿Qué hace este niño?*" each time she has to bend down to pick up the spoon and wash it off. However, when she considers how much can be learned by a child from this simple act, such as the unique sounds it makes or the principles of gravity, then she may not mind the extra effort. When my children became absorbed in this activity, I would make the lesson more powerful by saying, "*¡Oh! ¡Oh! ¿Dónde está?*" each time the spoon fell to the floor. I imagined that they wondered where the spoon went and probably asked themselves why it fell down and not up.

Another example of children's insatiable curiosity involves the milk that inevitably winds up on the floor during every meal. After my children threw the cup of milk on the floor, they demanded that I fill it again. As soon as I did, they immediately dropped the cup again. Though scenes like these can sometimes cause any parent to become exasperated, we have to remind ourselves that our children are experimenting with the concept of cause and effect. They are asking themselves, "*¿Qué va a pasar?* What will happen? Will I produce the same result if I push it again?" Sometimes your children test this cause-and-effect hypothesis on their siblings when they pinch, bite, or hit them, just to be amused at the responses and reactions they caused. As you correct this type of behavior, your children are learning the limits and parameters behind his or her natural curiosity.

Children have a tremendous need to repeat things. I remember a young child in the Avance neighborhood who entertained himself by putting a rock through the gaps of a chain link fence. He put the rock through the hole, walked to the other side to put the same stone through it again, and then repeated this action many times. He was learning about the concept of "through" while developing the skill of eye-hand coordination. Sometimes parents' patience can be tested when their children go about the world gaining essential skills, if the parents do not understand the importance of their children's need to learn.

Have you ever wondered whether your children are determined to break or destroy everything in the house as they go from the television knob to the toilet handle, radio dial, light switch, and every other movable object in the house? Here again, you must have *paciencia*, and remember that your *niños* acquire information when they act on the environment and over their bodies. They need to have a sense of control over their world around them. They need to think, *Yo lo hice que pasara*, I made this happen. Supporting this process of discovery and experimentation can enable your children to invent, create, or do something outstanding that could someday change the world. The foundation for learning must be set by parents who demonstrate patience and can provide essential information that children need to make sense of their world and create their own *mundo* of thoughts and experiences. As your children's first teacher, you need to label, reinforce, correct, and build on what they already know.

Curiosity can be hard work for children. Each day they wake up with a great deal of energy, enthusiasm, and wonder, thinking to themselves about the *aventuras* they have yet to encounter. If you have seen toddlers at play, they love taking things in and out of drawers. They also love climbing and getting into things. Vanessa loved taking the clothes out from the drawer and climbing the bookshelf. *¡Caramba!* She was determined to reach the top several times. *¡Qué sustos pasé!* I had to put a barrier in front of the shelf or help her reach her goal through support and guidance. What adventures have your children had with the toilet paper? Both Vanessa and Steven, at about the same age, discovered they could drag the toilet paper around the house until it disappeared from the roll. Vanessa used it to drape herself like a mummy. Steven put it all in the toilet and was ready to flush it when I stopped him. Your children may do the funniest, most creative, and interesting things, not only with things like toilet paper, but also with toothpaste and with the water in the commode to name but a few. Bathrooms are a great source of wonder and discovery, but they can also be hazardous traps when razor blades, cleansers, and pills are accessible to the inquisitive child. It is important that you childproof your house to prevent your children from harming themselves.

Children's learning can be messy. If you are a very neat person who expects everything to be *en su propio lugar*, in its proper place, you may be distressed when your toddler discovers your pantry or kitchen cabinets. He will nest and bang pots and pans together. He will stack and line the cans and roll them all over the kitchen floor. You may even find him covered with *harina*, flour, or find a trail of salt he made along the kitchen floor. While it can be disturbing for you to clean up the mess, it is important to realize that children are practicing and learning eye-hand coordination, mathematical principles, cause and effect, sounds, and textures. What an episode we had when Sal, who was less than a year old, became fascinated with the color red, which he discovered in a bowl of spaghetti sauce. He rubbed the sauce all over his shirt, arms, legs, and face and topped it off by placing the bowl with the remaining spaghetti on his head. *¡Qué espectáculo!* What a sight!

Have your children had any experiences with mud, such as pretending to make and eat mud *tortillas* or *taquitos*? How about building castles or making *animalitos* or *monitos* out of mud? One hot summer day when Steven was playing outside with the water hose, he delighted in how good the mud felt as it oozed through his fingers. He took the water hose and made a huge mud puddle right at the base of the slide that he was playing on. Then he took off all his clothes and, *totalmente desnudo*, he slid right into the puddle he had created. As I came out of the house *riéndome a carcajadas* with the camera in my hand, this mud-covered monster came at me *como si me iba a comer*, as though he were going to devour me. You should always have a camera ready for special "Kodak moments" like these. To this day, we look at those priceless pictures and laugh, reminiscing over the many incredible things they did! You can expect to have many of your own marvelous episodes, during which your children do crazy and unbelievable things as they go about *explorando y descubriendo su mundo*.

Children have no schedule and no commitments when it comes to discovering, experimenting, and learning. *Cuando andas de prisa*, the day that you need to get somewhere in a hurry, will be the day that your children will want to observe the smallest beetle or follow jumping *chapulines*, grasshoppers, through long blades of grass. Our picnics were usually interrupted when we had to look frantically for Steven, who was with us one moment and gone the next as he went out chasing after chipmunks and squirrels. *Necesitaba mucha paciencia y fortaleza*, I needed all the patience and strength I could muster just to keep up with Steven's immense curiosity. We think we won't survive, but somehow we do, especially if we understand their love for learning.

Children's *curiosidad* needs to be supported, not stifled. If parents scream at their children, constantly tell them "no," or spank their hand every time they are curious, that natural drive to learn will diminish. Once you realize that children will be naturally curious and find their way into everything, you will learn to be more vigilant and childproof your home thoroughly inside and outside. You should create a safe, stimulating, and enriching *ambiente* to satisfy the most determined curious mind.

Children also have a strong drive to master and control their bodies through the development of the so-called large motor skills, the use of the large muscles. They use these *músculos grandes* to walk, run, hop, throw, ride tricycles, and climb trees. Their fine motor skills, or use of the smaller hand muscles, are used for such things as writing, cutting, pasting, and playing with clay. For some children gifted in athletics, the large motor skills will coordinate with their visual skills to help them one day win a track meet or break an Olympic world record. Those with strong kinesthetic skills combine fine motor skills with their visual or auditory skills, to become surgeons or violinists.

As your children develop language skills, expect to be bombarded with millions of questions: "*¿Qué es esto?* What is this?" As they get older, they will enter the "*¿Por qué?*" stage, the time when "hows" and "whys" are abundant. How does it work? How did you do that? Why is *abuelita* sad? Why is the sky blue? What keeps the moon from falling? Why does the ice melt? What makes the lightbulb burn brightly? Your children need you to try to answer their countless questions. If you do not have an answer to an inquiry, *está bien*. If your child is old enough, suggest that you find out the answer together using the encyclopedia, dictionary, resource books, or the Internet. Explore answers at the library, museum, or planetarium. Get a tutor or speak to your child's teachers or caretakers about her growing curiosity. Stimulate your children's thinking and satisfy their quest for knowledge. Helping your children reach their fullest potential will require a great deal of patience, energy, understanding, and a commitment on your part to help them learn and grow.

There is much that your children are expected to know before they enter school. As their first teacher, you must know what you need to do to get them ready for school. For example, children are expected to know their full names, as well as the names of basic colors and shapes like a triangle, square, circle, and rectangle. They should be familiar with putting puzzles together. They should have had enough experiences drawing and scribbling with large crayons, chalk, or pencils. They should be able to draw a man or a woman with a great deal of detail, including the parts of the face, hair, neck, fingers, and clothing. Some very smart children will even draw a ring, a hat, or spurs on the boots. They must be able to count at least ten concrete things, tie their shoes, button, snap, color, cut, paste, sit quietly for a short period, listen, and follow instructions. Perhaps most important, they must be able to express their basic needs in either English or Spanish. By the age of three, the average child has a vocabulary of 1,000 words. By four, this storehouse of words grows to 1,500 words, and by five, most children have acquired about 2,000 words. I can't overemphasize the importance of talking to your children. The more you talk the more words they will know.

As a first-grade schoolteacher, I was very concerned that children were entering my school at the age of six *con muy pocas experiencias, conocimientos, y habilidades,* with very few stimulating experiences, knowledge, and skills. From a survey that I administered to the parents of my students, I learned that the parents did not know what was expected of them during their children's early years, nor did they see themselves as teachers of their children. For example, many parents believed that learning began between five and seven years of age.

This discovery led me to think that perhaps they might not have talked with their children enough or allowed them to play freely during the most critical years. Perhaps they failed to support their children's innate drive to learn or they failed to answer their many questions. Since many of the children in my first grade class could not hold a pencil or draw a circle, I knew that their parents or caretakers had not provided them with simple tools like crayons and colors. When asked to draw a man, some of the children drew two lines on a circle that wasn't completely enclosed. Some schools categorize children as "blue birds," "black birds," or other labels according to the drawings they make or the level of knowledge they have at the time they enter school.

The Latino children that were assigned to me had been erroneously labeled "slow learners," "mentally retarded," and even "vegetables" by the teachers. These children were smart, healthy children, but some lacked essential *experiencias, conocimientos, y habilidades* before they entered school. They required more time and assistance than the school was able or willing to provide. Because they were so far behind when they entered school, they had been set aside for the first half of the year and ignored. Under such circumstances, they were destined to fail. When I was assigned as a bilingual teacher to these students late in the school year, I was told simply to do "whatever I could" to help them. I later received another group of children who'd been similarly mistreated. *¡Basta!* I thought to myself. Enough!

Frustrated, I felt I could not continue as a teacher knowing that there were so many children entering school so ill-prepared and that parents did not know what was expected of them before their children entered school. I knew also that the gap between those who entered school *preparados* and those who didn't would only widen. I wanted to do something to solve this problem. I decided to leave my teaching career to help parents understand the importance of the first four years of life and guide them in becoming the best parents and teachers they could become. I wanted parents to provide a stimulating, enriching environment for their children so that when their little ones entered school, they would be among the "blue birds," *los listos*, the ones who would succeed. And with that as my motivation, Avance came into existence.

At Avance parenting classes, parents make puppets out of socks or hobbyhorses out of old broomsticks, socks, and yarn. They make colorful nesting containers from cans of different sizes covered with colorful contact paper. They also make books, dolls, sponge cutouts, and other intellectually stimulating toys. During the nine-month program, they are exposed to many experiences. We take the parents and children to the library to check out books, to the supermarket to teach them what a child can learn in an ordinary grocery aisle, or to places like the airport where they learn about how systems work. Just as some children lacked experiences, I discovered, so did their mothers. Some of the mothers that attended the program did not have simple experiences like coloring, cutting, and pasting. One day, during an Avance field trip to a department store to see the Christmas display, I was taken aback when a mother hesitated to get on an escalator because she had never been on one. The mother was probably asking herself, *"¿Qué es esto?"* Many parents were able to recapture what they had missed as they made inexpensive yet stimulating toys for their children and as they participated with their children on outings.

Since 1973, Avance has helped tens of thousands of parents with young children build that strong foundation for learning. Parents are not born knowing how to do this. As I have said many times, effective parenting is a skill that must be learned, regardless of a parent's social and economic circumstances. Whether in the barrio or in the suburbs, one will find parents who provide stimulating experiences for their children and those who do not.

As a domestic worker, my mother-in-law used to observe what a middle-class Anglo mother did with her children daily and applied it to her own children. She bought her children puzzles, checkers, chess, and board games. She took them to places like museums, beaches, and parks. She talked and read to them constantly. My mother-in-law belonged to a comic book club that would supply an array of adventure and science fiction comic books, which helped her children to read. She also made use of a set of encyclopedias she bought and was very active in school functions. She always had wood around so that her children would construct things, like forts or cages for all the animals she allowed the children to have. My mother also knew the importance of a stimulating environment from her own mother and from nurses who would make home visits after the birth of each of her children. They would provide her with information on child growth and development. We had *trompos*, *boleros*, and *loterío*, Mexican bingo, as well as dolls, books, puzzles, crayons, markers, coloring books, paper dolls, and board games. My mother would give us scraps of material, needles, and thread so that we could make clothes for our dolls. I still recall the hula-hoops, jacks, and *canicas* (marbles) of every size, color, and design that we used to entertain ourselves. The vacant yard adjacent to our house became a jungle for us and the streets became baseball fields.

When I was growing up in the barrio, a thirteen-year-old assumed a great deal of responsibilities. At that age, my older sister Julia was expected to take us on outings. She was like our mother duck and we were her ducklings in tow at parks and museums. At the Japanese Sunken Gardens in San Antonio, my siblings and I used to spend afternoons walking through trails and near ponds filled with beautiful orange-colored fish swimming amidst the green lily pads. We explored the base of a majestic waterfall and climbed up a winding path to what seemed, to a young child, like the top of the world. We also looked forward to rolling down the small grassy knoll, exhilarated by laughter and excitement.

My childhood was full of pleasant and educational experiences. We were so blessed to have *tíos* who took us to the family farm when we were young. Those impressive experiences we had milking a cow or a goat, gathering eggs, or just gazing at the night sky full of stars with the sounds of crickets in the background are imbedded in my mind and my soul. Even when we did not leave home there was always plenty to do. All the children in the barrio used to come together to play several versions of tag we called "*La Les*," "*Los Colores*," and "*La Roña*." We played the Spanish version of London Bridge, called "*La Víbora de La Mar*," "*Las Escondidas*," hide and seek, and circle games like "*Naranja Dulce*." We played the most complicated jump-rope games. By the time we entered school, my sisters and I had many experiences and concepts, many *focos* that lit up each time we had a new experience that would later help us succeed in school and in life.

Do you remember playing these games? Many of my friends do remember, yet somehow they did not pass these down to their children. It is not too late for your children. Teach them these games if you know them. If you don't know them, go to a school supply store for bilingual teachers, or if you visit Mexico, buy some children's tapes or CDs by Cepellín, CriCri, and Orozco who sing traditional *juegos y rondas*. Niños catalog also has records and CDs to help you. You, too, can create these kinds of illuminating experiences and a solid learning foundation for your children. In doing so, you can help them develop their intellectual capacity as well as expose them to their rich Hispanic culture. As your children's primary teacher, you play a vital role providing a rich environment, where your children can learn and grow. You are the primary person responsible for building that solid foundation for *éxito* in school and in life. The following are important topics about learning that will help you enhance your child's intellectual development.

WHEN LEARNING BEGINS: *LA INTELIGENCIA COMIENZA DENTRO DE LA MATRIZ*

Children begin learning in the womb, where they are able to listen and perceive. If you are pregnant, do you communicate with your child in the womb? I recall that my daughter used to move to the rhythm of soft classical music in the last trimester of my pregnancy as though she could appreciate one musical piece over another. As I talked to each of our children while they were in the womb, they seemed to respond to my voice. Researchers have found that infants, two to three days after birth, will respond more to a familiar song or voice they heard when they were in the womb over others. They can also differentiate between smells up to sixteen days after birth. While you are pregnant, you can begin to stimulate your child's environment with soft music and fragrant scents. *No tengas vergüenza*, don't be shy about talking and singing to your baby. *¡Anímate!* You and your husband should carry on your own *pláticas* with your child as you softly caress your tummy. Both of you can start establishing a warm relationship with your infant even before you can see and touch him.

FOUNDATION FOR LEARNING: THE CRITICAL PERIOD— *EL TIEMPO CRÍTICO*

The first four years of life are considered the most critical years for learning. If a child learns many things during the first four years of life, he will have *un base sólido* on which to build in the future. All new knowledge must be connected to previous knowledge. *De un éxito, nacen otros éxitos.* Learning is a process that builds on itself. If the foundation is too narrow or weak, then his future learning capacity will be stifled by those limited experiences that he acquired early in life.

According to learning theorist Benjamin Bloom, half of all the knowledge a child acquires from birth to seventeen will be learned by age four. During the first three years of life, there is rapid language development and learning. Values, morals, and self-esteem begin to surface by age three. Even the development of certain functions, such as vision, can be impeded depending on what happens during the first few months of life. For example, a child born with cataracts on both eyes will be permanently impaired if the cataracts are not removed until after six months of age. The visual connections in the brain are tentative and need stimulation from the environment to remain active. If they do not receive appropriate stimulation during this critical period of development, these systems will cease to function or will not function as well as they could. *Lo que se aprende en la cuna, siempre dura,* what is learned in the crib lasts forever. All future social relations are also related to the bonding that a child receives from his mother during the first months of life.

THE PHENOMENAL HUMAN BRAIN: *¡EL CEREBRO FENOMENAL!*

Did you know that providing a stimulating environment could also affect the size, weight, chemical composition, and neurological structures of your child's brain? A baby is born with some one hundred billion neurons in the brain, all that he will ever have in a lifetime. Immediately after birth, with the proper stimulation, the brain develops trillions of synapses, or connections, between these neurons to organize them into the different facets of intelligence. Some of these connections group together to form such basic functions as hearing, seeing, walking, and talking. In order to survive, these synapses need to be stimulated by sights, smells, sounds, tastes, and touch. If there are no experiences to strengthen these networks, the synapses begin to die off. In contrast, the more experiences one has, the stronger the connections. The opposite is also true. Negative experiences, or the absence of stimulating experiences, can have harmful and long-lasting effects. While some of these negative effects can change, they may require costly therapy and extensive intervention by school, health, and mental health officials trying to remedy the problems.

The release of the Carnegie Corporation's groundbreaking 1994 "Starting Points Report" emphasized the importance of the brain on development during the first three years of life. As a member of the task force that produced the report, I was amazed at the public's reaction to information that many of us in the education and child development fields have known for decades. When I attended college in the 1960s and '70s at Our Lady of the Lake University, we learned about extensive research on the brain that had been conducted on animals. For instance, in one experiment, a group of rats was allowed to play with a variety of toys and encouraged to figure out mazes while rats in another group were not allowed to have anything to play with in their environment. Later, researchers killed the rats, examined the brains of one group, and compared them with the brains of the other group. The study showed that the brains of those that were allowed to play and explore were larger and heavier and produced 25 percent more synapses among their brain cells, or neurons. Rats that were allowed to play and be more active had larger and heavier cortical tissue than those that had little stimulation. Rats in the group that were allowed to have stimulating objects and activities had 15 percent more neurons than rats that were left in barren cages. Such studies indicate that the weight of the brain can double during the first year of life as the child is exposed to many experiences.

With new brain imaging technology called positron emission tomography (PET) scans that allows close examination of brain activity, we can now see the same results and effects of brain stimulation in children. Studies show that most of the brain's development occurs outside the womb and that it has a direct relationship to the experiences a child acquires from the external environment. The more stimulation the child receives, the more synapses and the heavier the brain. Harry Chugani and his colleagues from Michigan Children's Hospital, using PET scans, were able to demonstrate remarkable findings regarding brain activity in the cerebral cortex of the brain, which includes complex cognitive functions, like language and spatial orientation. From birth to one year, this area of the brain hardly shows any activity, but right after one year of age it explodes with activity. By three years of age, the brain shows two and a half times the brain activity of an adult. Most of the synapses are produced the first three years of life and remain very dense until about ten years of age. Then, the density begins to gradually decline to about five hundred trillion during late adolescence, thereafter remaining steady.

Although the weight of such an organ may not seem to mean too much on its own, the difference can be seen very clearly in the everyday observations of children. I saw the transformation in a few "failure to thrive" cases after the parents of thin, sad, and lethargic children who had been referred to Avance began to apply what they learned on their children. They learned the importance of talking, cuddling, and touching their children in addition to providing a healthy and nutritious environment. After the proper stimulation and care, their children began to gain weight, thrive, and even smile. Research conducted on Romanian orphans who were virtually ignored by their caretakers showed that many died because of this deprivation. Their physical needs, such as food and water, were met, but because they were not spoken to, touched, or stimulated in any major way, their development deteriorated.

In the Avance parenting curriculum, we teach a lesson on the brain that includes a drawing depicting all the parts of the brain and their major functions. I used to joke with the Avance mothers that the more stimulating and enriching environment they provided for their children, the longer those branches in the brain (dendrites) would grow *hasta que les salían por los oídos*, until they grow out of their children's ears. The mothers got the message. I did not have to quiz them on all the scientific terms (neurons, dendrites, axons, and synapses) or the exact electrical and chemical processes through which learning takes place in the brain. They simply learned that with more stimulation the child's brain structure, weight, size, and chemical composition changed. They realized that, ultimately, the quality of an individual's thoughts, behavior, and ability would also be affected by the environment the parents provided, especially during the critical formative years.

In a study of Avance families funded by Carnegie Corporation of New York, we found significant differences in the home environment of children who attended Avance compared with those who did not. The Avance mothers provide a more nurturing, organized, stimulating, and responsive home environment. The environment is structured so that their children can learn, explore, and experiment. They have more developmentally appropriate toys, which they make themselves. They interact with their children using language that promotes learning, and they praise them more. They encourage and support their children's learning and are actively involved in reading and talking to them as well as teaching and playing with them. The mothers change their attitudes toward physical punishment. They begin to see themselves as teachers as they learn more about child growth and development and how to make use of the resources in their communities.

CONCEPTS: *FOCOS E IDEAS*

All intelligence is built on *conceptos*, ideas or pictures in the mind that organize and unite everything that a child learns from his environment. Close your eyes. Imagine the concept of a cat. What kind of picture do you have in your mind when you think of a cat? I might have imagined something a little different from you, but we both have a general idea of what a cat is. A concept is like a *canasta*, a basket, in which things with similar properties are put together. For example, the concept of a "cat" can be defined as the basket that contains the characteristics that describe cats, from the sounds they make to their fur, long tail, and whiskers. By seeing a variety of cats, the child learns that cats come in different colors, shapes, and sizes. These experiences sharpen his concept of cats.

If a child sees a small furry animal that looks like a cat, but does not have long whiskers and does not say "meow" and barks instead, he gets confused. There is a discrepancy between what he knew about cats and what he sees in this new *animalito*. Consequently, this experience motivates him to learn a new concept for "dog." After this experience, your child sees another animal that looks like the first dog, but is much larger and has different kinds of ears. This animal also says "woof," and has four legs, a tail, and soft hair. Because the child has learned some characteristics that pertain to dogs, he realizes that it still has some of the same properties. With many more experiences, he broadens and refines his concept of "dog." He will add more information to the "*canasta*," or concept of "dog," or he will realize that he will have to create a new concept because the new information doesn't quite fit with the old. As your *niño* grows older, the categories become broader and his thinking becomes more precise, more logical, and more abstract. The child organizes his world and his experiences through concepts, which will enable him to acquire higher intellectual skills, such as planning, analyzing, creating, and solving.

In a bilingual and bicultural world, a child will go through the same processes in both languages. Initially while she is attempting to learn the concept, she may mislabel the concept by combining one part of the word in one language with another part from another language. For example, when I first learned the concept "broom," I used to call it "*esc-room*," combining the beginning of the Spanish word "*escoba*" with the ending of the English word "broom." With enough experiences listening and repeating these words, the bilingual child will eventually drop words like "*chequear*," "*chusiar*," "*mistiar*," "*dostear*," and "*parquiar*," unless, of course, that is what she hears in her environment and it becomes the acceptable way of speaking instead of *revisar, elegir, extrañar, sacudir, y estacionar*. Children have the ability to learn many concepts and to learn different labels for each concept in more than one language. They will have the ability to switch from one language to the next, depending on the appropriate signal that the brain receives in a particular situation. As I will discuss in more depth later in this chapter, children can learn many languages, especially if they are exposed to them often when they are young.

LEARNING ENVIRONMENT: *EL AMBIENTE PARA APRENDER*

As I have said before, everything that a child learns is based on knowledge that he has already gleaned from his early experiences. Let me reiterate that all knowledge must be connected and related, otherwise it will be forgotten. As *nuestros niños* learn, they move from the simple to the complex, from the concrete to the abstract, and from the general to the specific. For example, they will learn to put things through a hole before they can sew. They will learn the concept of ball before they learn the concept of "soccer." They will learn the concept of "dogs" before they learn about poodles. They will learn the concept of "kiss" or "hug" before they learn about the meaning of love. A child will learn best when there is a slight difference between the new information and what he already knows. The new concept must not be too new or too familiar. Remember the example of the cat and the way a child will recall its characteristics when he encounters another kind of animal for the first time. If an activity is too familiar, or if he has already mastered it, he will become bored. If it is totally different from anything he already knows, he could easily pass it up or ignore it. If it is too much too soon, he will not even try to figure it out. It is a challenge for parents to provide the right kind of stimulating environment for their children to bring about maximum learning. The key is to watch and see if your child is responding and seems interested in what you are trying to teach.

Learning is also very much affected by how your child feels. As I stated earlier, your *niña* will not be able to learn if she is hungry, scared, sad, nervous, stressed, or angry. If a child feels threatened or *llena de emoción*, full of emotions, the bottom part of the brain, the cerebellum, sends a "flight or fight" message to the nervous system. She will resist or desire to flee an emotional situation, preventing any learning from taking place. Many children experience learning problems when the parents are in the middle of a divorce, when they or someone else in the family are being abused, or when they witness violence in the neighborhood. Children who are overstimulated and forced to go from one lesson to the next without any control over what is happening are sometimes so exhausted that they cannot think or process information. They must have control over their environment. We as parents must read their cues to keep that natural thirst for learning alive.

The best learning environment is established when children feel happy, secure, and well rested. They can learn better if they have a fairly clean, organized, and secure environment. Learning also comes about if the learning experience is attached to positive feelings. A love for reading can be fostered by sharing a storybook with your child as he snuggles next to you and you caress and fondly embrace him. The child will associate this pleasant experience with reading. At the same time he is also establishing a strong relationship with his parents that will last a lifetime.

In a bilingual, bicultural world, where warm and colorful images and close human contact abound, there are no limits to what Latino children can learn and the skills they can acquire with the proper stimulation. They have the ability to develop their inborn talents and interests and to discover and eventually create unimaginable things. With the right kind of stimulation, they will have the ability to think, solve problems, judge right from wrong, and create the kind of world they would like to live in. It is critical that you develop and maintain a strong relationship with your *niños* if you want them to become responsible, self-confident, and moral individuals. As children get older, their learning is largely dependent on how they feel about themselves and others.

Learning also comes about through modeling. If children see someone they admire smoking, drinking, or taking drugs, they will want to do likewise. On the other hand, if parents, relatives, or celebrities they admire demonstrate good manners and positive values, children will grow to emulate them. If your children see you reading, they may want to read too. As the *dicho* illustrates, *El que bien vive, bien cría*, he who lives well, raises (his children) well. As parents, we have to teach and live what we desire for our children. Everything your child is exposed to, including television programs, music, and new friends, can positively or negatively affect his development.

REINFORCEMENTS AND PUNISHMENTS: ¡PÓRTATE BIEN! DULCES, SONRISAS Y CASTIGOS

While a child possesses a natural drive to learn, sometimes his need to discover or withdraw can be directed or influenced by reinforcers. Reinforcers work in training animals to do all kinds of tricks. They can also work on children. A *sonrisa*, a pat, or a wink are all reinforcers that will strengthen behavior. Reinforcers are things that a child likes or desires and can be used to get your child to do what you want him to do. They can include an occasional treat, watching TV, or a trip to the zoo or a movie. "When you put your toys away, we will go buy *pan dulce* or ice cream" is one example of how reinforcers are used. Another is rewarding your child for making good grades by taking her to the park. Unfortunately, behavior modification, as this approach is called, does not always work unless you use the right kind of reinforcer. Reinforcers do not have to be expensive or things that you do not approve of. A word of caution: sometimes reinforcers can backfire and kill the natural drive to learn. Children can lose the desire to do something good for the mere satisfaction one gets from learning or mastering a skill. It is more important that your children feel good when they do something positive rather than simply try to please *mamá* or collect their reward. While you should praise and reward good behavior, ultimately children have to develop a *conciencia* and a positive feeling about doing the right thing, even when you are not present to give them rewards or praise.

Still, positive reinforcers are better than *castigos*. Punishment (that causes physical pain) can extinguish a child's natural drive to learn and can cause *resentimiento*. An example that I already mentioned is spanking a child's hand every time he wants to touch something. In lab experiments with animals, researchers found that rats that were given electrical shocks every time they behaved a certain way eventually eliminated that particular behavior. But if the shocks continued regardless of what they did, the rats would give up altogether.

However, as you will learn in the chapter on the emotional needs of children, negative attention is better than no attention at all. No one likes to be ignored. If a child wants to learn something and his questions are ignored, he will give up. If he is ignored, he may prefer *castigos* to your silence. The parents' lack of responsiveness and attention may drive their young ones to tear their sister's homework or break a window. My mother knew exactly how to maneuver my strong-willed personality in positive ways. She knew that spanking did not produce the results she wanted, so she would ignore me long enough to get my attention so that I would do what she wanted me to do. Then she immediately (and consistently) rewarded me. She would, for example, make a cake, hug me, or give me a warm smile. Those were the rewards that I wanted and enjoyed.

I am not saying that children's curiosity and actions cannot have limits. You must set limits for the child's safety and healthy development. You can alter children's out-of-bounds and potentially dangerous curiosity by restricting their *ambiente* somewhat until they learn to moderate their own behavior. More will be said about this in the section on discipline.

NIÑOS ACTIVOS: LEARNING THROUGH THE SENSES AND MOTOR ACTIVITY—BIRTH TO TWENTY-FOUR MONTHS

Children are born with the ability to see, hear, taste, feel, and smell, all of which enable them to take in information from the world around them. From the moment of birth, they can focus on objects up to thirteen inches away. They enjoy gazing, especially at human faces as well as bright and contrasting colors. When they are born, babies use reflex actions, such as sucking, grasping, and reaching. They want to bring everything into their mouths, from their thumb to your chin. Tiny infants naturally want to take off. If you put your infant on a hard surface, his legs automatically move as if to walk or run, but the rest of his body can't. These reflex actions are all programmed in the brain at the time of birth along with the innate drive to explore and learn. From these rudimentary reflexes, they begin to discover the world around them. As children grow, they practice these reflexes until they learn to control them, then they learn to adapt and coordinate them. Their actions become more deliberate and purposeful and their knowledge gets more refined and organized.

A young child is constantly acting on her environment by using her senses, grabbing, pushing, shaking, throwing, and the like. Almost everything goes into a young infant's mouth to see what it tastes like. She swings her tiny arms at the mobiles and tries to grab objects. As she learns to control her body, she begins to act on the environment intentionally. She is attracted to novel things, and will use all the inborn tools that she has at her disposal to actively learn about them using *los cinco sentidos.*

Children are very active learners, *son muy activos.* They have to act on the environment in order to learn from it. For instance, one day at an Avance parenting class, a mother was holding her six-month-old baby. I gave the child a beautiful red rose, without thorns, to illustrate to the mothers how children learn through the senses. Just as I had predicted, as soon as the child saw the rose, he grabbed it. He touched its soft petals, smelled it, and then shook it to see if it made a sound. Inevitably, he put some of the petals into his mouth. He then continued to feel the texture as he tore the petals apart.

Try observing your child at play. Record what he does. On another day, I watched my son react to a new tire swing that my husband and I had just put up in the backyard in the same inquisitive manner. When Sal, who was about six years old, first saw the tire swing, he ran to it, smelled it, and touched it. He tried to lift the tire to see how heavy it was. He lay on it one way, turned around and lay on it the other way. He stood on it, put his head through the tire hole, pushed it and allowed it to bump him. After Sal learned all he could from being actively involved with the tire swing, he enjoyed it and swung for the pleasure of it. His head went as far back as he could take it as he pumped himself higher and higher. When that got old, he tried several times to jump off the swing and land on his feet. He was so proud that he had mastered every aspect of the swing he could think of. The fascinating thing was that all of these activities happened in less than an hour.

Children have a need to explore and experiment with a variety of things. They need to feel their bodies in space. A wonderful family project would be to build a playground structure in your backyard. You can enlist the help of professionals or, if you're handy, there are simple structures you can build or assemble yourself. I took a class on building playgrounds from Dr. Joe Frost at the University of Austin and my husband and I built one in our backyard. Our children's playground included a slide, a fireman's pole, a wobbly bridge, an enclosed room with windows of different shapes, and a sandbox. Our children spent hours running, climbing, swinging, sliding, laughing, *and learning! Los niños aprenden cuando juegan.* They had several forts throughout our large backyard and a trail on which they would take their go-cart. They had all kinds of animals. Mowing the lawn was an adventure when we attached a small trailer to the riding mower and filled it with the fresh cut-grass. Neighborhood friends and *primos y primas* liked to come to my children's birthday parties because there were so many exciting things that they could enjoy, like the piñatas, clowns, magicians, and hay rides.

A child who is not allowed to explore and experiment and who is made instead to be *quieto,* quiet, is being deprived of learning. While infant swings are emotionally soothing and help establish balance in babies, they, like playpens, can sometimes become very restrictive. Television can prevent children from being active learners. Children need real-life experiences that will help them absorb information through the senses and connect it to as many parts of the brain as possible. As children grow older, parents need to control television watching, video, and computer games while encouraging their children to play freely. I remember how often my mother used to say to us, *"váyanse para afuera a jugar,"* go outside to play. She might have said that out of frustration *cuando la poníamos de nervios,* got on her nerves, but she also knew the importance of play and exercise for the development of the body and mind.

Birth to twenty-four months is a time when children learn through the senses and through physical contact with concrete objects. The stimulation they receive needs to be the appropriate kind of stimulation. Bright colors, contours, and different geometric designs—all of which are found in Hispanic folk art—provide children the right kind of backdrop. Babies can become mesmerized staring at polka dots or black geometric designs against a white background. They respond to high-pitched voices and soft noise. Decorate your child's room with bright and contrasting colors. Mothers at Avance make beautiful wall designs by tracing pictures from coloring books of flowers, animals, or other objects onto poster boards that they color and laminate. They also make colorful *Ojo de Dios* mobiles of yarn, sticks, and jar lids. You and your child can make an *Ojo de Dios* design by alternating different shades of yarn to create a rainbow of colors. Following are instructions for making a beautiful, colorful *Ojo de Dios.* Your child will enjoy seeing the multi-colored pattern—the same design that his ancestors used to make many generations ago.

Ojo de Dios

You'll need two wooden sticks or dowels, 24 inches long, and at least two different colored lengths of yarn. Position the two sticks to form a cross. Select one color of yarn. Tie one end to either stick, near the center where the sticks meet. Bring the yarn up and around both sticks to make an "X", crisscrossing the center several times, until the sticks are securely tied. Holding the crossed sticks in one hand, use your free hand to start weaving the Ojo de Dios pattern. Weave the yarn over and behind the first stick and then behind, over, and then behind the next stick again. Then bring yarn behind, over and behind the next stick. Repeat same procedure with last stick. Repeat the weaving by going around all four sticks as many times as you want. You can tie different colors together. Start your new color by tying the new length of yarn to the first one (trim away any excess), and repeat the weaving process as desired until you have a design that you like (or you run out of yarn). You can create your design by determining how many times you change colors or by adding beads as it is wound around the sticks. Stop weaving when you reach the last inch of the sticks. Tie off the yarn by securely knotting it to the end of either stick, and trim excess.

You can make four pom-poms to add to the end of each stick by wrapping yarn around your hand 20 times, leaving the end of the yarn long enough to tie to the ends of each stick. Slip off the loop, and tie it in the middle with a separate 3-inch piece of yarn. Cut the loops and trim excess. With the longer piece, tie pom-poms to the end of each stick. You can use sticks of any length, and from one to as many colors of yarn as you like.

Bright beautiful *mariposas* and colorful flowers also provide a variety of images in any household. It is important to change the child's view periodically. Hispanic folk arts, from tapestries to *papel picado* (tissue paper cut into beautiful designs), can truly fascinate a young mind and make perfect exhilarating room decors. Besides putting up beautiful and interesting things for the baby to see, you can also turn on soft, soothing music. As parents, we must know how much is appropriate stimulation, otherwise we may end up *con un niño necio y enojadísimo*, or a cranky and angry child. If overstimulated, children fall asleep, withdraw, or have a tantrum.

BEING RESPONSIVE TO YOUR CHILD'S NEEDS: *¿QUÉ QUIERE, MI HIJO?*

During this period, children believe that if they do not see an object, it does not exist: *fuera de vista, fuera de mente*, out of sight, out of mind. They assume that everything is attached to them. At about eight months, children acquire "object permanence," the belief that objects or things continue to exist even if they do not see them. By two years of age, children master object permanence and are able to anticipate the relationship between actions and future consequences. A child can anticipate that her *mamá* will return when she walks out of the room or that an object will continue to exist even when it is not in full view. This is a critical milestone in learning, for it signals the moment when memory, mental thought, and language merge. During this period, your child begins to think that her actions cause certain effects, without having to "act" them out. If I do this, the child thinks, then this will happen. She begins to realize that she is a separate being and that people and things exist apart from her. It is a time when *muchos focos se prenden o se están encendiendo*, the child's brain lights up with all kinds of new knowledge.

It is important that you are responsive to your children's feelings and to their physical, emotional, social, and learning needs. If your daughter is crying because she is hungry, *dale de comer*. If your son cries because he senses that you are leaving, *asegúralo*, tell him that you are coming back. Make sure that his environment is as familiar as possible by choosing a babysitter with whom he feels comfortable. If she wants a toy, *dáselo*. If he is bored, *habla o juega con él*. If you do not do these things, your child will learn that it does not matter what he does, *se dará por vencido*. He will give up because he cannot bring about a desired effect or change in his environment. He will inevitably stop trying if people ignore him. (In cases of severe child neglect, children will become lethargic and refuse to eat, and some eventually die.) Neglecting your children's need to learn and to have a stimulating environment may affect their future learning potential and their future social relationships. Through your responsiveness and attentiveness, you are supporting their well-being, teaching them to trust you and others and to feel a sense of *seguridad*.

The earliest forms of communication through which this foundation is set occur when the child gazes into your eyes and you try to guess what she needs: "*¿Tienes hambre, mi hija?*" Are you hungry, my daughter? "*Te ves tan triste, ¿qué quieres, mi amor?*" You look so sad, what do you want, my love? "*¿Quieres tu tetera?*" Do you want your bottle? "*¿Quieres que te levante?*" Do you want me to pick you up? When you respond to your child's needs, you are communicating with her. You are getting the message that she is trying to convey. If you respond to her needs, then she will gain the necessary confidence that will help her become an active learner. Make contact with your child and read her facial expressions. If your baby sticks out her tongue or blows bubbles, imitate her. You will find that the baby will then imitate you in return. Not only is the child learning, but she is also sending you messages. There is a *dicho* that says *La mejor palabra es la que no se dice*, sometimes the best words are those that are not spoken. This bit of wisdom applies to these earlier months when the basic forms of communication begin. When your children make a sound and you try to repeat it, you are communicating. The first "coos" will transfer to words, sentences, and later to *cuentos*, or stories. Your children will come to realize how communication is a reciprocal, synchronized action *entre dos o más personas*, that involves everything from gestures to words and body language.

LEARNING THROUGH PLAY

Young children have an innate need to *jugar*. For them, play is not only fun, *es serio*, it is serious business. Children learn from all those joyful play activities. From the moment they discover that they have hands and feet, they will spend much of their waking hours *jugando* with them and learning what they can do with them. It will not take long before hands and feet go into their mouths. They soon realize that their mouths and other vocal organs produce sounds and they spend their time entertaining themselves and others with these new *descubrimientos*. When your child gurgles, coos, and babbles, he is not only playing, he is creating basic sounds, tones, and pitches that will eventually lead to the construction of words and sentences.

During the first months of life, a mother and father are their children's favorite play partners. Many child development experts describe this time as a give-and-take between parents and children. When your *niño* coos or smiles and you coo and smile back, he is not only having fun, he is learning to trust you, establishing *confianza*, and developing an important relationship that will help him relate to others later. Another interplay happens when your young infant imitates the different sounds, gestures, and expressions that you make. For example, I sometimes made a sound like "ba ba" to my child and he would imitate the sound. Then I would change the sound to "da da" and he would repeat that sound, too. I would tell him, "*Ojitos, mi hijito*" (squinting my eyes), and he would squint his eyes. If I said, "*Dame un besito*," he would oblige by throwing me some baby kisses. If I asked him to say "bye bye," he would wave. If I stuck out my tongue or blew bubbles, he would do likewise.

Another thing that each of my children loved was when I poked their tummies as I sang rhymes like, *Pin Marín de Don Pingüé, Cúcara Mácara, Títere Fue Él*. With the last stanza, I would blow on or tickle their tummies. Sometimes I would say, "*Te voy a hacer cosquillitas*," I am going to tickle you, and they would laugh even before I touched them. A very young child knows how to warn us when he has had enough. He is able to regulate the appropriate amount of stimulation he can take by turning away and gazing at something else. After a short break, he may want to resume the play. We, as parents, must respond to those cues.

Studies have linked high IQ tests scores and academic achievement in reading and math with the presence of interesting and challenging play materials that children use in the home especially during and after the first year of life. *Juguetes*, such as rattles, mobiles, and soft, stuffed animals, will motivate them to manipulate their physical environment. Play materials like sand, water, puzzles, and blocks help children learn *conceptos* such as shapes, numbers, and skills, like eye-hand coordination. Playing with balls, tricycles, and jump ropes helps children develop motor skills. Dolls, miniature play furniture, and play clothes create an imaginary world for them to explore.

When your child is old enough, give her toys and objects of different colors, sizes, and textures that she can manipulate. When she begins to crawl, your child will need plenty of space to explore and experiment. However, as she becomes older, stronger *y más activa*, you must child-proof the house and be more attentive to where she is and what she is doing, for she will wander about finding interesting things she has not yet discovered. Ordinary things around the house will satisfy her interests as she goes around turning things on and off, moving them in and out, or passing one object through another or into another.

Music is often a powerful medium for play. Even *en la cuna*, children respond to rhythmic sounds. Stores sell records and CDs with the sound of the mother's heartbeat that some parents, especially mothers of premature babies, play to remind their babies of the warm gentle comfort of the womb. Provide your children with play drums, maracas, and miniature xylophones so that they can begin to develop an ear for music. Try to combine music with bath time and you will have *un bebito muy contento*, a very happy baby, though most of the water will wind up on the floor. As a baby, my brother Eddie would make me play his favorite song, "Soldier, Soldier Won't You Marry Me," constantly and each time he would get carried away dancing to the music. Likewise, when I was a young girl, I used to become the center of attention moving my shoulders back and forth every time the song "*Mambo, Qué Rico el Mambo*" was played. Children love to move to the sounds and rhythm of music. In the Hispanic world, you will see little children in the middle of the dance floor during wedding cele-brations moving to the beat of the music. Many parents enroll their children in folkloric dance classes at a very young age if they see that their children have an interest in dancing. While music can be used to energize children's creativity, soft music can also calm them after a day of exhausting play.

Whether listening to the English lullaby "Hush Little Baby" or "*Señora Santa Ana*" or "*A la Rurru Niño*," children love to be rocked to lullabies. Just as my grandmother sang "*Señora Santa Ana*" to my mother, who in turn sang it to us, my children will probably share this melody with their children. To this day, that song produces positive emotions for my children and me. (See more lullabies in the next chap-ter). If you do not know "*Señora Santa Ana*," ask an older person from Mexico if he knows the melody to this very popular lullaby. You can also find adaptations of it as part of "*A la Rorro Niño*" on the *Juegos Infantiles* cassette and CDs by Tish Hinojosa and Jose Luis Orozco that are mentioned in the Resources Guide. Sing it to your baby and you will be starting a tradition that will continue through the generations. "*A la Rurru Niño*" has the same melody as "*Señora Santa Ana*."

Señora Santa Ana

Señora Santa Ana, ¿Por qué llora el niño?
Por una manzana que se le ha perdido.

Iremos al huerto, cortaremos dos,
una para el niño y otra para Dios.

Manzanita de oro, si yo te encontrara
se la diera al niño para que callara.

Santa Margarita, carita de luna,
méceme este niño que tengo en la cuna

Duérmese mi niño, Duérmese mi sol,
duérmese, pedazo de mi corazón.

María lavaba, San José tendía
eran los pañales que el niño tenía.

A la Rurru Niño

A la rurru niño, a la rurru ya,
duérmase mi niño y duérmase ya.

Este niño lindo, que nació de día,
Quiere que lo lleven a pasear de día.

Este niño lindo que nació de noche,
Quiere que lo lleven a pasear en coche.

Very young children also love "pat-a-cake" and different kinds of hand games. Through these games, they acquire language skills, develop their musical abilities, and forge a close relationship with you. The following are favorite traditional Spanish and English hand games that have delighted children for generations. Get on the floor with your child and play these traditional hand games. If you do not know the melody, make one up. Try to act out the words, such as moving your fingers slowly when you say dedos, and then moving your fingers very fast when —you say Que gire, que gire, como un girasol.

Qué Linda Manita

Qué linda manita que tiene el bebé.
Qué linda, qué mona, qué bonita es.
Pequeños deditos, rayitos de sol.
Que gire, que gire, como un girasol.

Las Ojitas

Las ojitas, las ojitas
De los árboles se caen
Viene el viento, y las levanta
Y se ponen a cantar.

Repeat with the word *bailar* at the end. Child waves hands in the air and brings the hands down when mother says "caen," then she brings them back up again.

Pon Pon Pon

Poke the palm of the child's hand while you recite this rhyme.

Pon pon pon la manita en el bordón.
Dame un veinte para el jabón
Para lavar el pantalón de tu tío Simón.

Pat-a-Cake

Pat-a-cake, pat-a-cake, baker's man.
Bake me a cake as fast as you can.
Pat it, roll it, and mark it with a B,
and put it in the oven for baby and me.

Papitas

Papitas, papitas
Para mamá.
Las quemaditas,
Para papá.

Another version, favoring the father instead of the mother:

Papas

Papas 'y papas para papá,
papas y papas para mamá;
las calientitas para papá,
las quemaditas para mamá.

Así Palmadas Damos

Así palmadas damos
Clap, clap, clap.
Así los pies movemos
Trap, trap, trap.
A bailar, a cantar
En buen orden, y con paz.

La Pequeña Araña

La pequeña araña, subió, subió y subió.
Calló la lluvia, y se la llevó.
Salió el sol, y todo lo secó.
Y la pequeñita araña subió, subió, subió.

Itsy, Bitsy Spider

This is the English counterpart of "La Pequeña Araña," also known as "Eensy, Weensy Spider."

Itsy, bitsy spider went up the waterspout.
Down came the rain and washed the spider out.
Out came the sun and dried up all the rain.
And the itsy, bitsy spider went up the spout again.

My children loved the following hand game called "La Viejita," which was similar to "This Little Piggy Went to Market." To play it, you begin by tickling the palm of the child's hand. As you recite the line referring to the *leñita*, you pretend to cut off each of the fingers as though you were sawing branches for firewood. Then when you come to the part *llover*, to rain, tickle the palm again. Crawl up the child's arm, pretending that you are the *viejita* running so that she would be able to *meterse en su casita*, and then tickle your child's armpit. My kids used to make me repeat this game over and over again. They loved the anticipation of what they knew would happen at the end of the rhyme.

La Viejita

Había una viejita
que cortaba su leñita,
y comenzó a llover,
y no hallaba dónde correr,
y se metió en su casita.

This Little Piggy Went to Market

This little piggy went to market.
This little piggy stayed home.
This little piggy had roast beef.
This little piggy had none.
This little piggy cried wee wee wee all the way home.

Your child starts to learn at a very young age that her actions cause certain effects. She is able to tell herself, "If I do this, then this happens." Jack-in-the-boxes and toy telephones are very popular at this stage. Through them, children cause a response to an action, either a burst from a box or a voice on the telephone. It makes them feel good to see the reaction. They are learning that they can have some control over aspects of the world. As you learned earlier, children before eight months of age will generally not get as upset when you leave the room. After this age, however, they know that you and objects exist even if not visible. This is a great time to play "Peekaboo." With a small blanket, you can entertain your child, saying, "Peekaboo," or *"Te veo,"* I see you. During this game, my children used to cover their *caritas* with their hands, pretending to hide, and I would go along with it saying, *"¿Dónde está mi hijito(a)?* Where is my child?" until they would bring their hands down. When I said, *"Allí está mi hijito(a),* There you are," they would always burst out laughing.

EL MUNDO DE FANTASÍA: DRAMATIC AND IMAGINARY PLAY —
TWO TO FIVE YEARS

During this time, the child's play consists of a world of make-believe. Children act out relationships by playing games like *comadritas,* playing house, or *la escuelita,* school. They can imagine they are *el médico* or *un policía.* Allow your children enough time in their imaginary or pretend play. Give them the props they will need such as hats, clothes, blocks, dolls, trucks, dishes, miniature tools, and plastic household appliances. After your child has observed you for two years, you may see everything that you do and say acted out in their play. Beware! *Lo que no puedes ver en tu huerto ha de crecer.* They imitate you going to the office or arguing with your spouse or a sales attendant. This is why you have to be careful about what you say and do. In their play, children will act out things that stir strong emotions, like getting their *vacunas,* vaccinations, or being taken to daycare or preschool, or *mami y papi peleándose,* mommy and daddy fighting.

A designated section of my children's room served as their "imaginary corner." It was stocked with different hats, clothes, household items, and Halloween costumes. By watching a child at play, you can almost see the brain at work. They think aloud as they try to solve problems or as they construct buildings out of blocks. They will continue to play with something until they learn all its properties and how it works. Then they move on to something else that fascinates them or just gives them pleasure.

As the child is playing and learning concepts, parents should take the opportunity to join the process and introduce labels to the objects of actions that they are involved in. Remember the Avance child who was placing the rock through the holes in the fence? This activity offered an excellent opportunity for his mother to say, "Oh, I see you are putting the rock *through* the hole." Parents need to be around their children when they are creating and exploring. Do not interrupt your children's play, just facilitate it. Enhance it with a safe and enriching *ambiente.* Intervene at the right time and respond to them, like when your *niño* needs help or when he needs the label, use appropriate words for the corresponding concepts and actions. For example, as he is playing with blocks and *carritos,* tell him, "That *car is going around* the building. *Where is the blue car going?*" Stress the words "car," "around," and "blue."

Children need a variety of activities and materials with which to explore and experiment when at play. When they are outdoors, for example, provide them with water, sand, buckets, shovels, sieves, funnels, and containers of different sizes and watch what happens. Through discovery, children will learn math skills such as volume and weight. They will learn the meaning of "more than," "less than," "equal to," and "half." This kind of play is laying the foundation for your children to be strong in math and science later.

Give them blocks so that they can construct buildings, bridges, houses, and towers. Not only will they learn some aspect of math, physics, and architecture, they will have fun creating objects. Children also need to be outdoors to run, ride, climb, swing, roll, jump, slide, and walk. Build or buy balance beams and or a backyard playground structure as was discussed earlier. Buy them toys with wheels, jump ropes, and chalk. Take them on hikes and on picnics. They need opportunities to explore their world and master their bodies.

Toward the end of this stage, children are able to sort by categories: animals, fruit, shape, color, and size. They can do puzzles and create things with modeling clay. Give your children crayons, pencils, and lots of paper and encourage them to draw, scribble, connect dots, and trace lines. Put butcher paper all around the room so that they can scribble on the paper and not on your walls. Give them art supplies, *pero cuidado*. Let me warn you to put newspaper all around the floor during their bursts of artistic expression and make sure the future Diego Riveras wear old clothes as they work. As they get older, keep encouraging your children to express their creativity by giving them paper to draw on. Vanessa was fascinated with cartoon characters. She began sketching them from the newspaper. Since I knew she had an interest in drawing, I bought her an easel, paint, colored chalk, and lots of drawing paper, so that she would have them available whenever she wanted to draw. As I displayed her masterpieces, she was motivated to continue drawing. Her friends discovered her artistic talent and she soon began creating drawings for them. Make sure you have plenty of materials that can be used to create pieces of art, such as scissors, markers, glue, construction and tissue paper, feathers, rhinestones, buttons, stickers, streamers, pipe cleaners, etc. Organize a family art project to make hats, drawings, boats, or horns. This can be lots of fun!

If your child has an interest in music, this is the period in which she will try to imitate certain melodies and learn repetitive songs, such as *Acitrón de Fandango*. In addition, this is a perfect time to teach children rhymes, songs, and games that will help them learn numbers, days of the week, and parts of the body. The following are a few traditional rhymes, songs, and games, some that I sang to the children at school and to my own at home. You may want to try them with your child. You can find recordings of these songs by some of the artists mentioned in the Resource List at the back of the book.) You may find these or other children's songs in Spanish that your children will love. My children still remember the CriCri albums that I used to play for them, especially "El Ratón Vaquero." Your child, living in a bilingual world, can learn the numbers in both English and Spanish through these songs and rhymes.

Acitrón de un fandango

Acitrón de un fandango
Sango Sango Sango
Savaré
Savaré que va pasando
Con su triqui triqui trán.

Matarili-rili-rón

This game is about a boy (B) who is trying to marry the daughters of a woman named Ambo Gato (M). The mother asks the boy a series of questions, including what his profession will be. He names several professions until he says the one she accepts (*cancionero*, *engeniero*, etc.). She agrees to the marriage and all the children say the last line together. The daughter then goes to the boy.

The boy and the girl he marries go to where the mother and daughters are asking or responding to a question. The daughters and mother go to the boy's side chanting the question or responding. They both say it once going and repeat it as they go backwards to the original place. The game ends when the mother is left by herself.

B: Ambo Gato, *Matarili rili rón*
M: ¿Qué quería usted? *Matarili rili rón*
B: Yo quería un paje, *Matarili rili rón*

M: ¿Qué oficio le pondremos? *Matarili rili rón*
B: Le pondremos (carpintero). *Matarili rili rón*

M: *Ese oficio no me agrada. Matarili rili rón*
B: *Le pondremos (cancionero). Matarili rili rón*
M: *Ese oficio sí me agrada. Matarili rili rón*
All: *Celebramos todos juntos, Matarili rili rón*

Un Elefante

To play this game use several elephant cutouts with a different number on each. Use the corresponding numbered elephant as you recite the rhyme. The song is also sung replacing *balanceaba* with *columpeaba*.

Un elefante se balanceaba (columpeaba)
sobre la tela de una araña.
Como veía que resistía,
Fue a llamar a otro elefante.

Dos elefantes se balanceaban (columpeaban)
sobre la tela de una araña.
Como veían que resistía,
fueron a llamar a otro elefante.

Tres elefantes...etc.
Cuatro elefantes...etc.

El Barquito

Count your fingers as you say the numbers.

Había una vez un barco, chiquitito. (Repeat twice.)
Tan chiquitito, tan chiquitito, que no podía navegar.

Pasaron una, dos, tres, cuatro, cinco, seis, siete semanas. (Repeat twice.)
Y el barquito, el barquito, no podía navegar.

Y si la historia no les parece larga. (Repeat twice.)
Volveremos, volveremos, volveremos a empezar.

Zapatito

Zapatito blanco, zapatito azul
Dime, ¿cuántos años tienes tú?
Seis. Uno, dos, tres, cuatro, cinco, seis.

One, Two, Buckle My Shoe

One, two, buckle my shoe
Three, four, shut the door
Five, six, pick up sticks
Seven, eight, lay them straight
Nine, ten, a big fat hen.

Los Diez Perritos

Yo tenía diez perritos, uno se murió en la nieve. Nada más me quedan
    nueve, nueve, nueve.
De los nueve que quedaban, uno se fue a comer bizcocho. Nada más me
    quedan ocho, ocho, ocho.
De los ocho que quedaban, uno se subió en un cohete. Nada más me
    quedan siete, siete, siete.
De los siete que quedaban, uno se comió cien pies. Nada más me quedan
    seis, seis, seis.
De los seis que quedaban, uno se mató de un brinco. Nada más me quedan
    cinco, cinco, cinco.
De los cinco que quedaban, uno se perdió en el tiatro. Nada más me
    quedan cuatro, cuatro, cuatro.
De los cuatro que quedaban, uno se lo llevó Andrés. Nada más me quedan
    tres, tres, tres.
De los tres que quedaban, uno se murió de tos. Nada más me quedan dos,
    dos, dos.
De los dos que quedaban, uno se lo llevó Bruno. Nada más me queda uno,
    uno, uno.
Del uno que quedaba, se fue con Bruno y me queso sin ninguno.
Aquí se acaba el cuento de los perros que perdí.
Y si usted no lo ha entendido, se lo vuelvo a repetir.

¿A Qué Hora?

A la una, miro la luna.
A las dos, miro el reloj.
A las tres, no me ves.
A las cuatro, miro el sapo.
A las cinco, pego un brinco.
A las seis, tarde es.
A las siete, sale un cohete.
A las ocho, como un bizcocho.
A las nueve, voy a la nieve.
A las diez, comienzo otra vez.

The Days of the Week

Lunes y martes, miércoles y jueves, viernes y sábado—
domingo es la semana.

CHILD CARE: ¿QUIÉN CUIDARÁ A MI NIÑO?

You have to go back to work, but who will care for your baby? You may have to take your child to a daycare facility. Child care plays an important part of your young *niño's* cognitive growth and development. Daycare or preschool centers can be places where children will spend a great deal of time learning and playing. Today, many parents are finding it difficult to find a quality child care center that is good for their children. Hispanics are no exception. It is a given among many Latinos that there is no better babysitter than *la abuelita* or a member of the extended family to care for the children, especially when they are very young. Many people, however, are not fortunate to have those family members around. Even if you do not work, you may want to give your child an opportunity to play with other children, especially after they are three years of age. It is up to you to find the kind of child care that fits your needs and budget. You want it to be a place where you feel comfortable leaving your *niño precioso* in the care of someone you can trust who will provide a safe environment that will be conducive to learning.

Once you have decided on a child care arrangement that meets your standards, prepare your *niño* to be away from you for a few hours and ease him gradually into his new surroundings. Talk to him about the new place he'll attend every day. Read him books and stories about children who are experiencing similar feelings. Visit the school a few hours a day. Let the teacher get to know him. On his first day, make sure that it is not a stressful day for you or him. If possible, stay in the child care center with him for part of the day for two or three days. These activities should help him make the transition.

You may consider it important for the center to expose him to your culture through foods, songs, games, and language. If they are not willing or equipped to do so, perhaps the center would allow you to bring some items that reflect your culture such as tapes of Spanish songs and Hispanic folk art. Show the teacher or the students how to make a piñata, an *Ojo de Dios*, *cascarones*, or an *altar for El Día de Los Muertos*. Describe the cultural significance of the celebration. Make a traditional dish like *arroz con habichuelas* or *buñuelos*. Share some of your cultural beliefs and practices with the class. You could shed light on the many beautiful aspects of our cultural heritage with your child's classmates in ways that are more than just "show-and-tell."

Even those who have managed to hold on to their first choice for child care—*la familia*—face sacrifices and compromises. My sister Rosa Linda gave up her job to care for her grandchildren at her home. She strongly believes that no one else could give her *nietos* the love and care that she could give them, and she loves doing it at the same time. She considers it an investment of her time in establishing a relationship with her grandchildren. My mother-in-law and my mother took care of my children, a fact that made life easier for me.

Such arrangements can, of course, have disadvantages when "*la Doña*" has a different concept of rearing children. *Cuando los abuelos entran por la puerta, la disciplina sale por la ventana*. I felt, however, that the connection that my children had with their grandmothers was worth my overlooking certain things, like letting the kids get away with things, the *dulces* they would give them, or the occasional *piedritas*, or comments my mother-in-law would make about how she stayed at home to take care of her children. Whether your child's caretaker is a relative or not, it is important that you feel comfortable with your child care arrangement. To this day, my children recall the wonderful adventures they had with *abuelita Dolores*, who would take them on picnics and to the theme park. My daughter Vanessa was very appreciative of *abuelita Lucy*, who picked her up at school one day when she was ill and gave her *caldito* and *té*. *La comadre* becomes like a member of the family when it comes to child care. Vanessa got to know her godmother Carmen very well the mornings she drove her to school. Our family got to know her son, Adam, very well by driving him home from school.

Regardless of which child care arrangement I had, there were times when the school holidays or a babysitter's vacation meant I had to call on someone else. A good strategy is to keep a list of various people you can depend on, beginning with the extended family, *comadres*, neighbors, and others who may be willing to fill in.

LANGUAGE DEVELOPMENT: *APRENDIENDO A HABLAR*

The way children develop language is one of the most fascinating aspects of their growth. When you hear your child cooing at about three months, he makes the sounds that are included in all languages throughout the world, whether it be German, Spanish, English, or Japanese. All children have the ability to learn all of these sounds. According to psychologist James Deese, at six months of age, a child gradually begins to differentiate and favor some sounds over others. Over time, she will drop the sounds that she does not hear from her environment and practice only those that she does hear. If the Spanish-speaking child hears the word *"perro,"* she will continue to practice rolling her "rr's." If she is raised in a bilingual environment, she will also hear and continue to say the English sounds such as "th," "sh," "ch," and the twelve vowel sounds, some of which are not found in the Spanish language. However, sounds like the "ch," as in the German word "Bach," will drop if the child does not continue to hear them. Exposing children to a broad range of sounds very early in life may facilitate her ability to become multilingual. The English-speaking child will learn forty-five basic sounds that can be made from the twenty-six letters of the English alphabet and the Spanish-speaking child will learn the twenty-two to twenty-four sounds of the Spanish alphabet.

The child will practice her sounds by cooing, chuckling, and gurgling. At six months, the child babbles as she puts the consonant-vowel sounds together to make sounds like "ma," "ta," and "pa." She practices making a variety of sounds, and tries to explore how the different parts of the mouth work to produce these sounds. Repeat the babbles that your child makes. Smile and hug her when she repeats the sounds that you make.

It is important that you talk to and with your children. Use what is called "parentese" or "motherese," the affectionate language that parents

use when they speak with infants. Hispanic mothers know these soothing words as *cariños*. This kind of language makes it easier for the baby
to find, understand, and recognize your words. Mothers naturally try to
connect with their babies by making eye contact, slowing down their
speech, and using a high-pitched voice. They pause between sentences
to emphasize the sounds of important words. The sentences in "parentese" are short and simple. There is a lot of repetition and many questions embedded in their speech. As you look into your child's eyes, smile
at him and softly raise your voice to a singsong, high-pitched tone as you
say things like: "Hiiiii. How's my precious doooing? Did you have a good
naaaap? Yeaaaaa! You diiiiid have a good nap. You are soooo cute. Give
mama a biiiiiig smile." Whether in English or Spanish, "parentese"
sounds very much the same:—"¡Ay qué liiiinda, mi hijita! ¡Qué chuuuula!
¿Dormiste bastante? Dale un besiiiiito a mamaciá. Mamá quiere muuuuucho
a su angeliiiito. Dame una sonrisa. Ay, qué precioooosa, mi luna de miel."
After conversing with your baby in this manner, she will be hooked and
will become very attentive and receptive to whatever you want to teach.
Keep in mind that "parentese," which can continue up to the third year,
is very different from baby talk, which distorts the pronunciation of
words. It is important that you pronounce words precisely. Even if your
child says "teta," "bibi," or "baba," you must repeat the words in the correct form by saying "tetera," "biberón," or "bottle."

Receptive and Expressive Language: *Entender y Hablar*

All children go through two kinds of languages: first the receptive and
then the expressive languages. Both are building blocks for communication. During the first year of life, *nuestros niños* can understand what you
are saying, but they generally are not able to express it. This is called
receptive language. For example, when you ask a ten-month-old to give
you a ball and he gives it to you, he is showing you *que entiende*.
Expressive language means that he can verbalize what he wants.
Expressive language is learned in stages. The first stage begins with coos
and babbles, one-syllable consonant-vowel sounds, like "ma," "ta," and
"pa." It is important to talk and read to your child even before he can
say his *primera palabra*. The child's first expressive word appears at
approximately one year of age, and grows rapidly if you continue to label
and talk to him. At around eighteen months of age, the child will combine two-word sentences consisting of the subject and the verb. This is

Language Development Milestones

Age	Milestone
2 months	babbling begins
3 months	cooing begins, two-syllable nonspeech
4 months	baby makes sounds with four to five syllables
6–9 months	lalling (intonation patterns with jargon speech)
9 months	vocalization syllables; can do pat-a-cake, bye-bye
9 months–1 year	echolalia; child displays a variety of pitches
12 months	follows simple commands, says one word
14 months	child can say three words
16–18 months	child can say 5–25 words; recognizes pictures; responds to commands
18–24 months	child has vocabulary of 200–300 words
24 months	two-word sentences begin ("car go"); child pulls you toward something and shows it to you; uses words and suffixes such as *in*, *on*, *ing*, *I*, and *it*
24–30 months	child has vocabulary of 400 words; my, me and mine, you
30–33 months	asks what, where, why, who, how questions; uses words like *he*, *she*, *we*, *your*, *yours*
3 years	3–4 word utterance; child has vocabulary of 1,000 words; dramatic play; has trouble with *s*, *z*, *r*, and *l*; asks when questions; uses words like *its*, *our*, *him*, *myself*, *yourself*, *ours*, *their*, *theirs*, and *under*
4 years	child has vocabulary of 1,500 words; uses words and phrases like *herself*, *himself*, *itself*, *ourselves*, *yourselves*, *themselves*, *behind*, *in back of*, *in front of*, *above*, *below*, and *at the bottom of*; retells stories
5 years	child has vocabulary of 2,000 words; begins using logical thought

called telegraphic speech. He leaves out articles, prepositions, verb endings, or auxiliary verbs. For example he may say "dog eat," "me eat," "me up," "ball up," "more juice," "big dog," "big baby," or "big truck." At age two, his vocabulary increases from about 200 to 300 words. At three, he knows about 1,000 words. At four, he has acquired 1,500, and at five, he has reached 2,000 words. You help the list grow by following your niño's interests and labeling what he is interested in. If he points to an object, dile la palabra. Whatever he is interested in (ball, pelota, dog, perrito), describe it. Children will talk to themselves as they go about experimenting and practicing with new words. Give them new words to use through nursery rhymes, chants, and games.

EXPLOSION IN LANGUAGE DEVELOPMENT: ¡MÍO! ME DO IT— TWO TO SEVEN YEARS

Have you been amazed at how your child's language explodes once he is approaching the end of his second birthday? Your child has had plenty of time jugando, explorando, experimentando, tocando, oyendo, y observando. He has created many images and numerous concepts, and understands the meaning of quite a few words. Now his verbal language is ready to explode. He can now label concepts that represent images and words. He can visualize pictures, memorize, and recognize words. You wanted your child to speak, but now you wonder how to make him take a breather.

When your two-year-old child tells you "Me do it," even if you think they can't, let them try. They may surprise you. When children turn two years of age, they enter the "mío," or "nine" and "me," stage. They sometimes say their name in place of the word "me." They will let you know that everything is "mío" or "mine." They believe they can do anything and that everything is theirs. In a family video of my son Steven reciting nursery rhymes, a two-year-old Vanessa could be heard chiming, "Me too! Me do it. I can do it." After Steven recited "Jack and Jill," she wanted to do it also, and she immediately followed him with: "Jack and Jill, went up the hill to get aaaaawa (water). Fell down. Broke crown. Jill...af...af er." Then Vanessa rolled on the ground to show me that Jill tumbled. She had a strong mental concept of how the story unfolded and in what order, but she expressed some of the labels for the concepts in English and some in Spanish; also, when she did not have words for some of the concepts she showed me through her actions.

At this age, children continue telegraphic speech, making up two- to three-word sentences. They have problems pronouncing sounds with the letters *s*, *z*, *r*, or *l*. You will hear sentences like "I wuv you," "I wun fast," "Give me thum," "Give me thith," "*Dame etho*," "*Vatho de agua*."

After telegraphic speech, your child will add articles (a, an, the), prepositions (in, on), pronouns (he, she), plurals, and possessive forms. He will also begin using irregular verbs and contractions. At about five years of age, your child uses the future tense. His sentences include tag questions, where he makes an affirmative statement and then wants a reaffirmation by asking a tag question. For example, "Daddy is home, isn't he?" "*¿Está lloviendo, verdad?*" Children have learned that a pronoun has to match its object in person, number, and gender. From this point on, children's sentences get longer and more complex as they combine two thoughts and then two independent ideas into one sentence, for example, "I want water," and "I want to watch TV."

By the age of five, the child will almost have mastered the language structure needed for life. A child will learn language naturally by listening, through trial and error, experimenting, and practicing. He will make mistakes trying to apply the rules he learns, such as when he says "foots" and "mouses." *No le hagas burla*, don't make fun of him when he does this. Simply correct him by giving him the proper word. Children learn the complexity of the rules and the structure of language by listening to language spoken around them. The more you speak with your child, the greater his language and thinking ability. If you point things out to him, he will remember them better. Language helps children understand, think, and solve problems as they develop intellectually.

Keep in mind as you watch your child go through this process that although it may not appear that she is learning, she is acquiring "receptive language," that is, the language she understands but is not yet able to verbalize. When you say, "get me the bottle," and she gets it, you know she understands what "get" and "bottle" mean. She knows that you want her to give it to you, not to someone else. Children need to hear the same words many times to comprehend what they mean.

If the child points to something, stress the word that goes with the object by saying it and asking her to repeat it. Even if she refuses, make sure she hears the label. Her verbal language will grow very rapidly at two to three years of age if you begin talking to her from the beginning of life. Studies have shown that children who are spoken to frequently will develop a broader vocabulary and will eventually score better on intelligence tests later in life. So, label, label, label! Talk, talk, talk! Read, read, read! The only way your *niña* will learn to speak is if she hears you speak.

After you label, pause a while and allow your child to respond. Reinforce whatever sound comes out of her mouth, and repeat the word in a complete sentence. "Yes, *mi hija*, that is a ball, a big red ball," or "*Sí, mi hija, ésa es una pelota, una pelota roja y grande.*" Use the same word in different sentences. Put signs on familiar objects so that the child can begin to associate the spoken word with the written word. Think aloud about what you are doing so that the child can learn new words: "Ay, *tengo que tener cuidado porque me puedo cortar. I have to be careful because I can cut myself.*"

As you go about your daily routine, take your child with you. Label and describe the objects you use and explain what you are doing: "*Los vasos van aquí y los platos acá.* The glasses go here and the plates go there." As you are feeding your child, say things like: "Eat your peas. The peas are green." Stress the words *peas* and *green* and encourage her to repeat words. When you are folding clothes, talk aloud about what you are doing: "The towels go here. The shirts go there." Ask her questions: "What is this? This is a towel." Say *towel* and allow her to respond. "What color is this towel? Blue." Let her repeat the word. "Blue." It is like your blue shirt." If the child says, "blue," repeat it in a complete sentence: "Yes, the towel is blue, it is a blue towel. Find me something else in the room that is blue. You are so smart for getting the blue ball. What color is this?" Wait for a response. Hug her, and say, "Yes, you are right. It is blue. It is a big blue ball. What is this? This is daddy's *shirt*." You can repeat the process. The child will learn many vocabulary words as well as grammatical structure and rules. The formula is simple. Label, and then ask your child to repeat words. Pause and wait for a response. Reward with a smile or a hug. Repeat and elaborate.

In Spanish, the formula is the same. "*¿Quieres una manzana? Di manzana.*" Pause. Wait for a response. "*Sí, muy bien, manzana. Esta manzana está dulce. Esta manzana es roja y redonda. Di manzana otra vez.*" Pause. Wait for a response. "*Ay, qué chula, mi hija.*" Give a smile or hug. Use the same word *manzana* in other situations: "*Voy a hacer ensalada de manzana. Dame una manzana. Vamos a cortar la manzana.*"

HABLANDO EN DOS IDIOMAS: THE BENEFITS OF BILINGUALISM

Today many Hispanic parents wrestle with the decision of whether or not to teach their children to be bilingual. "Will they have trouble learning two languages?" they ask. "Will they confront discrimination in school and society if they speak Spanish?" "Why should my child be bilingual?" No doubt, questions like these are very important, but they can sometimes overwhelm parents who are exposed to misinformation that overshadows the many benefits of being bilingual. I cannot stress enough to my children as well as to you the importance of knowing two or more languages. Being bilingual is one of the greatest assets a person can have.

Saber es poder, and that refers to knowing two languages *porque el que habla dos idiomas vale por dos*. Today, half of the world's population is at least bilingual. Many people know several languages. You should remind your child, as he grows older, that a person who is multilingual will be able to communicate with more people and be understood in different settings. Children who speak two or more languages will be able to communicate with their non-English-speaking relatives and will be better able to appreciate and value their culture and themselves. They will have a greater self-esteem as they are able to respond to people who expect them to speak the language because of their Spanish surname or their physical characteristics. They will be able to make more friends. Language is part of a person's culture, identity, and sense of belonging. In addition, they can build a greater mental storehouse of literature, music, and memories. When our young children become adults, they will comprise the largest ethnic group in our country. Therefore, if they are going to become leaders, they will have to know Spanish in order to relate to and understand a greater number of people. Knowledge is power, and the persons who understand and are able to communicate with more people will have the power.

In today's global market, those who speak two languages are valuable resources. Because the Hispanic population is growing so rapidly, many service jobs in the health, social service, education, entertainment, marketing, and business fields will require their employees to be bilingual. Even today, I find myself translating and interpreting for people whenever I am at airports, hospitals, department stores, hotels, and restaurants. I do not mind doing it, but I try to make a point that bilingual personnel are needed to better serve the customer. "It was fortunate I was around this time," I say. Bilingual people are highly sought after for their dual linguistic knowledge. Even in the schools there is such a great shortage of bilingual teachers that more than 250,000 bilingual teachers are needed nationally. In California school districts representatives are having to go to Spanish-speaking countries to fill the teacher shortage.

If entrepreneurs want to serve their customers effectively and compete in today's world, they will need to have more bilingual employees.

Bilingual schoolteachers, bilingual telephone operators, and bilingual telemarketers are paid more for their bilingual skills. Children who know *dos idiomas* will be able to take on supervisory positions because of their ability to communicate, solve problems, and market in two languages. Accompanying the language is an understanding of the cultural nuances among Hispanic Spanish speakers that can also be of great advantage. For example, in Latin America, making a sales pitch to a Spanish speaker may require more than a clever way with words. It may require an understanding of customs, traditions, beliefs, and preferences, all of which can vary between ethnic groups.

Although some of us may value bilingualism, many Hispanic parents, myself included, are guilty of not being persistent and consistent in speaking to our children in Spanish. We have denied our children the full, rich heritage that they deserve by not being tenacious about keeping Spanish an ever present aspect of our homes. It has not been easy for Hispanics who live in a society where the speaking of Spanish is rejected and there is an insistence on speaking "English Only." This has had a negative impact on our children's desire to learn and a parent's willingness to teach their native language. Some assumptions about bilingualism have impeded parents from giving their children *su herencia*, their heritage, and the gift of being able to live in two worlds.

Myths About Bilingualism

Society is filled with exaggerated and negative ideas about bilingualism. Among these beliefs:

- Bilingualism is harmful to children since they cannot learn either language well
- Being bilingual can result in prolonged and permanent delays in language development
- Bilingualism confuses children
- Mixing languages is bad and signifies that children have not learned to communicate
- If you want to teach children to become bilingual, it is best to do it when they are older
- Children have a capacity to learn only one language well
- If you teach your children Spanish first, they will learn English with an accent

- There is no use in speaking to your children in Spanish if they are not interested in learning the language
- The only way Hispanic children can succeed in America is to speak English only
- Children must speak English only or they will not be accepted in this society

These are myths that have been challenged by experts as well as by experience, time and again. Being bilingual is not harmful for children. It does not confuse them. There are no permanent delays in learning or in language development due to being bilingual. In fact, children are capable of learning many languages if they have the opportunity to be exposed to them, especially during the critical period for language development. By the age of eight, a child is considered an adult as far as language is concerned. What this means is that children under the age of eight are better able to learn many languages with the appropriate accent. Children at this young age are like sponges, able to acquire many languages. If we do not make a concerted effort to help our children become bilingual, time will pass so rapidly that *nuestros niños* will lose a great opportunity to learn *su idioma*. Although you cannot pressure them to learn Spanish, you have to find a way to make it part of your daily conversations.

Your child needs rich, varied, and continuous experiences with languages. It is a challenge for parents to help children learn a language that they do not hear as often. It is up to us to expose them to the Spanish language, even if it appears that they are not interested. It should not alarm you to hear your child mixing the languages at first. Eventually he will differentiate between the two. A bilingual child may regress or slow his language development down while he is learning another language, but this is temporary. Eventually he will catch up and perform equally well in both languages. Given a rich, constant, and varied experience with both languages, he will become fluent in both. Many non-Hispanic, nonminority parents are realizing the importance of knowing two languages and are doing all they can to help their children become bilingual. Unfortunately, by the third generation many Hispanics in the United States lose their most important cultural asset. Today, one-third of Hispanics know Spanish only, one-third know English only, and one-third know both languages. If you are a fluent or even semifluent Spanish-speaker, then you have a natural facility for teaching your children to be bilingual. All you need is the will, *sólo las ganas*, to teach them this valuable tool.

TIPS TO HELP YOUR CHILDREN BECOME BILINGUAL: *AYÚDALES A LLEGAR A SER BILINGÜES*

There are many reasons why it is important for your children to be bilingual. How do you do it when there is so much pressure from outside to deny our children to speak two languages? First, ignore people who try to discourage you from helping your child to become bilingual. Tell them you know otherwise when they give you some myths about being bilingual. Stay focussed and determined.

What if your children feel the pressure not to learn and tell you they are not interested? Exposing your children to the language means doing so even if they seem to resist your efforts. Remember that receptive language comes before expressive language. As long as you speak to them in both languages beginning when they are young, you are setting the foundation for when they get older and realize the importance of being bilingual. Even if they complain that they do not want to hear the language, continue to speak to them in Spanish. They will thank you later. As with anything, learning Spanish is something that your child must grow into and feel a need for. Perhaps you live in a Spanish-speaking community where there are other children who speak the language. If you can manage it, take vacation trips to Mexico, Puerto Rico, South and Central America, or Spain to give your children an opportunity to practice the language. Let your children stay with Spanish-speaking relatives for an extended period so that they can experience an environment in which they are compelled to use the language in order to communicate. When I was in college, I went to Mexico for several weeks and I remember that it took me a couple of days to loosen my tongue and sound like a native speaker. How quickly I advanced from the first days when I was called a *pocha*, an American Hispanic who had forgotten her roots to sounding almost like a native speaker.

The only way children will be able to learn two languages is if both are spoken naturally and if both produce equal pleasure, feedback, and rewards. Reflect on the natural process described earlier through which a child learns to speak any language. The same principles apply when learning two or more languages. Children need to hear words associated with objects, persons, or actions many times. In the normal course of interaction, the parents must say the words they want their children to learn and encourage the child to repeat them. When the child finally attempts to speak words, the parent should repeat the words, elaborate, and reward the child again for his efforts. *Enseñando se aprende.* If you can do this in both languages, you will be helping your child to learn both languages.

The child has a natural need to communicate, to understand, and to be understood. If the mother speaks only one language, and the child wants to interact with her, then the child will have a strong desire to learn that language in order to communicate. You must begin by teaching your child the language in which you feel more proficient. If it is Spanish, talk to him in Spanish. If it is English, begin teaching your child the language as you learn Spanish and ask those family members who are more fluent to help you introduce it. Some of my Hispanic relatives, colleagues, and friends have taught their children to become bilingual by dividing the task with their spouses. One parent would speak entirely in Spanish to the children, while the other parent would speak entirely in English. Other parents teach their children first in one language and then, several years later, they will introduce the other language. Since they know that their children will learn the English language through television, friends in the neighborhood, or in school, they will teach their children Spanish first and then English. Both of these are acceptable methods. Sometimes both parents speak Spanish only and will teach the oldest child Spanish first. After she learns English in school, the child will probably speak to her siblings in English and to her parents in Spanish. In that way, the oldest child becomes a kind of bridge to help pass on the language within a family and becomes a role model.

Learning a new label for a word is not as difficult as learning its concept, or meaning. Once the concept is learned, a person can learn different labels for the same concept. For example, *manzana* is just another label for apple, just as there are many names we use to refer to our daughters. I call my daughter *mi hijita, mi corazón, mi princesa*. A car can be called a *carro* or a *coche*, depending on whom you speak with. There can be many labels for the same concept. When I was a teacher, I found that children who came from Mexico knowing many concepts in Spanish made the transition to the English language with greater ease than the group of Spanish-speaking children born in the United States who had fewer concepts in both languages because they were not spoken to in either language enough. While the group from Mexico was learning a new label, the group born in the United States was still learning concepts, which take much longer to learn. From these experiences, I realized how important it is to communicate with your child first in the language that you feel most comfortable using and that you have a greater command of. Once the child has a good foundation in one language, then she can learn a new label for the same concept later. If you do this before your child reaches age five and no later than age eight, your child can become bilingual more easily.

However, in many Hispanic homes today in the United States, children have learned concepts in both languages, but they are verbal in English because it has been the dominant language in the home. Even if your child speaks only in English, continue to speak to him in Spanish. Help him acquire the receptive language, so that he can at least understand the language. The important thing is to start early. Teaching your child nursery rhymes, riddles, songs, games, and folk stories in Spanish will help him appreciate and learn the Spanish language. Following are some that you could teach your children. The instructions might help you recollect the fun games you played *en tu país cuando joven*. Share them with your children. If you do not know how to play them, ask first-generation Hispanics if they or their parents remember.

Juegos—Games

Los Pollitos

One of the children role-plays the part of the mother hen and the rest of them are the chicks who walk around the hen in a circle with their elbows moving up and down. The children stop while the mother feeds them. Then the children sit down and close their eyes and the mother hen goes around hugging them. There is a variation in *"les da la comida y les busca abrigo."*

Los pollitos dicen, *"pío, pío, pío"*
cuando tienen hambre, cuando tienen frío.

La gallina busca el maíz y el trigo,
les da de comer y les busca abrigo (or les da la comida y les presta abrigo)

Bajo sus dos alas acurrucaditos
hasta el otro día duermen los pollitos.

Arroz con Leche

Start with a boy in the middle and girls in a surrounding circle. The boy selects a girl and trades places when she says "Yo soy la Señorita...." The girls selects another boy and the game starts all over again with the boy selecting a girl, etc. Instead of *sociedad*, some say *capital*.

Arroz con leche. Me quiero casar.
Con una señorita de la sociedad (capital)
Que sepa coser. Que sepa bordar.
Que sepa lo mismo jugar y cantar.
Con ésta sí. Con ésta no. Con esta muchacha me casaré yo.

Arroz con leche. Me quiero casar.
Con una muchacha de la sociedad.
Que sepa barrer. Que sepa trapear, asear la cocina, lavar y planchar.
Con ésta sí. Con ésta no. Con esta muchacha me casaré yo.

Yo soy la Señorita. La hija del Rey.
Me quiero casar y no encuentro con quién:
Contigo sí. Contigo no. Contigo, mi vida, me casaré yo.

Los Colores

Children sit in a circle. Every child picks a different color. Then Child A, who has not heard the colors, goes to the circle and says to the group, "*Quiero un listón* (ribbon)." They ask her, "*¿De qué color?*" Child A tries to guess the color once. When she guesses someone's color, that child, Child B, gets up and is asked by Child A, "*¿Cuánto cuesta?*" How much? Child B answers a number, "*Cinco,*" and puts out her hand to get that many slaps. When Child B is caught, she is brought back to the circle and after her. When Child B is caught, she is brought back to the circle and does not get a color. If she is not caught, she goes back to her position and picks a new color. The process is repeated until children get tired or choose another game.

La Muñeca
Mexican Version

This song is used when jumping rope.

Tengo una muñeca vestida de azul,
Zapatitos blancos, delantal de tul.
La saqué al paseo y se me constipó,
la tengo en la cama con mucho dolor.
Esta mañanita me dijo el doctor

que le diera jarabe con un tenedor.
Dos y dos son cuatro,
Cuatro y dos son seis,
Seis y dos son ocho
y ocho, diez y seis.
Brinca las tablitas, yo ya las brinqué,
bríncalas de nuevo, yo ya me cansé.

La Muñeca

SPANISH VERSION

Tengo una muñeca vestida de azul,
Con su camisita y su canesú.
La saqué a paseo, se me constipó,
la metí en la cama con mucho dolor.
Una mañanita le llamé al doctor,
que le dé jarabe con un tenedor.
Dos y dos son cuatro,
Cuatro y dos son seis,
Seis y dos son ocho
y ocho, diez y seis,
y ocho, veinticuatro
y ocho, trienta y dos,
Ánima bendita, me arrodillo yo.

Brinca la Tablita

In this game, a circle of girls surrounds a girl rocking a baby, and then she acts out the things that the group tells her to do: *lavar, planchar,* etc. During most of the song the girls in the circle are kneeling down. When it comes to *Brinca la Tablita,* they jump up, hop forward and backward. Another girl then gets in the middle, and the process is repeated until everyone takes a turn.

Brinca la tablita, yo ya la brinqué.
Bríncala de vuelta, yo ya me cansé.

Lava la ropita, yo ya la lavé.
Lávala de vuelta, yo ya me mojé.

Dos y dos son cuatro, y cuatro y dos son seis,
Seis y dos son ocho, y ocho, diez y seis.

Plancha la ropita, yo ya la planché
Plánchala de vuelta, yo ya me quemé.

Dos y dos son cuatro, y cuatro y dos son seis,
Seis y dos son ocho, y ocho, diez y seis.

Osito, Osito

This is a song that is sung when children jump rope. Each child has a stone. They drop the stone when they say *"tira,"* pick it up when they say *"levanta,"* turn around when they say *"date,"* and exit when they say *"salte."*

Osito, osito, tira la piedrita.
Osito, osito, levanta la piedrita.
Osito, osito, date una vuelta
Y salte para afuera.

Juan Pirulero

Several children draw lots to be Juan Pirulero, who is to pretend to play a clarinet at the beginning of the game. Juan Pirulero assigns each child an instrument to "play" like *la guitarra, los tambores, órgano, marimba, el bajo, bandolín,* or *acordeó,* or tasks to do like washing dishes, typing, driving a car, ironing, painting, etc. Juan Pirulero sings the song twice, pretending he is playing the clarinet. Then he stops and says, "Y *ahora le tocar al órgano,"* etc., and Juan Pirulero imitates the actions of one of the children, who, in turn, is to copy him playing a clarinet. Then Juan Pirulero begins to sing the song again; the first child goes back to his original action if Juan Pirulero selects another instrument or action; otherwise he continues that action. Again he sings the song twice, stops, and imitates the actions of another child. When he mentions the drums (*tambores*), everyone sings *la, la, la,* etc., to the tune of Juan Pirulero. If the child cannot keep up with the changes, he has to pay the price that Juan Pirulero deems funny, like to pretend to be a gorilla or a cat, etc. This can be a very funny and confusing game.

Adivinanzas: Riddles

Adivinanzas are clever ways to use descriptive words to guess certain objects. The answers appear in parentheses at the end of each adivinanza.

Blanca es de pequeña,
la adornan con verdes lazos,
lloro con ella de ver
que la hacen mil pedazos.
(la cebolla)

Negro por fuera,
verde por dentro
y con hueso de aguacate adentro.
(aguacate)

Adivina, adivinanza,
qué tiene el rey en la panza.
(el ombligo)

Doce señoritas en un corredor;
todas tienen medias, pero zapatitos
no.
(las horas)

Una vieja flaca
y la escurre la manteca.
(una vela)

Adivina, adivinanza,
qué se pela por la panza.
(la naranja)

Colorín, colorado,
chiquito, pero bravo.
(el chile)

Allá en el llano
está uno sin sombrero.
Tiene barbas, tiene dientes,
y no es un caballero.
(el elote)

Oro no es.
Plata no es.
Abre las cortinas
y verás lo que es.
(el plátano)

¿Qué le dijo la luna al sol?
(Tan grande y no te dejan que
salgas de noche.)

Una vieja
flaca y seca
que arrastra
las tripas.
(aguja e hilo)

A simpler version of this game is for Juan Pirulero to tell one child at a time which instrument to play or action to do, and at the end everyone plays her instrument or does her actions at the same time.

Éste es el juego de Juan Pirulero.
Que cada quien atienda a su juego.
Éste es el juego de Juan Pirulero.
Que cada quien atienda a su juego.
Y ahora le toca a tocar la guitarra—

(Repeat and change instruments—*y ahora al órgano—a los tambores; a la marimba, al bajo, al bandolín, al acordeó,* etc.)

When Juan Pirulero calls out the drums, *tamboras,* all the children sing along with him.

Lalalalalalalala, lalalalalalalala. Lalalalalalalala, lalalalalalalala.

Traditional Song

Allá en el Rancho Grande

Allá en el rancho grande, allá donde vivía
Había una rancherita que alegre me decía, que alegre me decía.

Te voy a hacer tus calzones, como los que usa el ranchero.
Te los comienzo de lana y te los acabo de cuero.

Cuentos: Stories

There are many special *cuentos* that have been handed down through the generations, but one of the favorite ghost stories among Latinos is *La Llorona,* which is told in many versions and has been around since the time of the Aztecs.

La Llorona

La Llorona, the weeping woman, is a *cuento,* about a mother who falls into a deep depression after her husband abandons her and her two young children. The husband lives across the river from her. The woman is so overwhelmed with grief, she drowns her two young children in the river that separates her from her husband. When she comes to her senses, she goes crazy realizing what she has done. "*¿Dónde están mis hijos?*" she wails. When told to children, the legend warns them to be in bed early and out of the street, or the *llorona* will get them. As the legend goes, one day a young boy who did not believe in the *llorona* went to the river where she is said to wander. He saw the ghost and heard the wailing cries of the mother who was still looking for her children. *La Llorona* grabbed him, thinking that he was one of her children, but the bells of the church rang and she let him go. The son ran home terrified, and told his mother what he had seen and heard. At first, the mother did not believe him, until she saw *La Llorona's* bloody fingerprints on the child's shirt.

La Chupacabra

La Chupacabra is becoming as popular a scary tale as *La Llorona*. *La Chupacabra* is a little gray or green lizardlike creature with big monster eyes and a spiny back that walks on two legs. It got its name from sucking most of the blood from Puerto Rican goats, and leaving two puncture wounds in their necks. *La Chupacabra* was first "spotted" in Puerto Rico in 1994 and is said to have migrated to the United States and South America. The legend has it that he now is sucking the blood and organs of animals such as dogs and sheep, leaving the puncture holes as his calling card. He has appeared to several humans, walking, flying, and hopping like a kangaroo, and his height has ranged from three to six feet tall. There are some who believe that this creature is an alien.

MIS EXPERENCIAS SIENDO BILINGÜE: FIGHTING BATTLES TO MAINTAIN THE SPANISH LANGUAGE

Think back for a moment to how Spanish may have manifested itself in your life. As I reminisce, I think of how different my world at home was from that of the school that I attended. Like many Hispanics my age, I think of how the school system did everything possible to have me reject my dominant language. Yet in spite of the agony and pain, I was able to maintain my Spanish language.

During the first six years of my life, I spoke mostly Spanish but could understand English somewhat. Although I occasionally combined both languages, I was able to communicate with everyone around me because everyone spoke in the same manner. I knew, however, that if I spoke to my mother or grandfather I would have to do it solely in Spanish, because that was the only language they knew. After I entered school, I experienced culture shock when teachers did not allow the children in my elementary school to communicate in the language they knew best. At that time, schools believed in the immersion method of learning the English language, and the usage of the Spanish language was to be eliminated entirely. The *golpes* that I suffered on my hand and the humiliation of having my nose in a chalk circle against the blackboard every time a teacher heard me speaking Spanish made it very difficult for me to learn. When they spoke to me entirely in English, I could not understand what they were trying to teach me. We were being forced to learn a language and subject content in an unnatural and punitive manner. Those traumatic experiences as a child affected me for quite a long time. I felt very uncomfortable speaking Spanish in public for fear that I was doing something wrong. While many of us managed to learn English and retain the Spanish language, it was at a great emotional cost! I was held back in the first year I entered school, either because of my lack of knowledge of the English language at that time or because of my emotional trauma, since I literally jumped out the window of the classroom to look for my older sister. School was a scary place for a child who felt rejected because of the language she spoke.

Many Hispanics tried to prevent their children from experiencing the same trauma by keeping them from speaking Spanish altogether even though English was not their dominant language. Others felt that by knowing only English, their children would have the best chance to succeed in school and in the United States. They did not realize that their children could absorb both languages if they were exposed to them, especially when still young. Some Hispanic parents would send their children to school speaking only Spanish and would ask the school officials to speak only in English, not realizing that teaching a child first in his native language made it easier for them to learn the English language, without the emotional scars.

Like many Hispanics of my generation, I tested out of Spanish courses when I was in college but refused to get credit. I felt that I needed to get the formal instruction in my native language that I never had. I also had a need to continue my knowledge of the language, since it seemed to have been sidetracked when I entered school. Over the years, I have made a special effort to increase my vocabulary and have had the opportunity to practice speaking Spanish with the Avance families and with the Spanish media. When I am holding a formal conversation in my professional field or on a familiar subject, I speak Spanish with confidence.

Throughout my life, I have mixed the languages with ease. When I speak to a friend or relative who knows both languages, I find myself mixing. When I am upset, tired, worried, or nervous about something, I find myself wanting to speak in Spanish. When my husband and I did not want our young children to understand what we were saying, we would speak in Spanish. Of course, this did not work very well after the children became more familiar with the language.

Do you see that the language you use frequently has a great deal to do with the context of a conversation? It may vary with the person one is addressing, age, sex, occupation, social and economic status, country of origin, ethnicity, and the subject matter being discussed. Whenever my grandfather or my mother would ask me a question, I responded in a more formal, respectful Spanish with words like "Mándeme" and "Usted" as opposed to the "qué" and "tú" that I would use with my friends. I may speak English at a professional meeting, Spanish on an interview with a local Spanish television station or to my mother at home, and a mixture of both to my siblings and Hispanic friends. If I see a cute baby, I will want to make gestures in Spanish like, "Ay, qué chulo!" If I am angry with Steven, I change his name to "¡Esteban!" Then, of course, there are those emotional words, especially when one is angry, frustrated, and exasperated, that are more appropriate en nuestra lengua. They include words and phrases like "¡Se sale!" (describing someone who did something bad, unfair, or just plain dumb) and "¡Tonto!" or "¡Bobo!" (describing someone who lacks common sense). Even if I am around English-speaking people, if I hear something very upsetting the first words out of my mouth are, "¡Ay mamá!" or "¡Ay, Dios mío!" in Spanish, instead of "Oh, my God" in English. These Spanish words are so emotionally laden that they tend to be the ones we cling to, even if we do not maintain Spanish as our primary language.

My mother, who spoke only Spanish, felt very helpless in trying to teach us English. How she wanted us to succeed and not suffer the humiliation. She had a great desire to speak English and demanded that we speak to her in English as we were learning it ourselves. Of course, since we were not dominant in the English language right away, she learned it mocho, partially in English and Spanish. When my mother spoke to a Hispanic teacher, she forced herself to speak in English, even if the teacher was bilingual, and even after the rules in the school changed. She, too, must have been as affected as her children. She was determined to learn English. When members of the Jehovah's Witness church came to the house to leave her some literature, my mother wanted it in English, when she could have had it in Spanish. She mastered the language by reading and later evangelizing to others in English with her English-speaking "sisters" or friends from the church. With all her determination and hard work, it took her many years to learn the language. However, when she speaks to her children, especially about emotional things, she reverts to her native tongue, occasionally mixing the languages because she knows that we understand her.

As my children became school-aged, they did not want to speak Spanish when they were in school because their friends didn't speak the language. We realized that we were hurting our children if we did not make an effort to speak Spanish to them, but for a long time whenever we did, they rejected it. In spite of this, we were persistent in ensuring that our children acquired the accent, vocabulary words, and the receptive language. We continued to speak Spanish occasionally at home even if our children responded in English, for we knew that eventually when they got older and wanted to know more about their roots, they would have a foundation to build on. I had already taught them nursery rhymes, games, and songs in Spanish. We had many records, tapes, and books in Spanish for them to use, and when they grew up, they listened to Tejano music. I read to them in Spanish and then translated to English. We used to play Mexican *lotería*, a kind of bingo, in Spanish. I had everything around the house labeled in both English and Spanish. I watched *telenovelas* in Spanish, scheduled trips to Mexico, and took my children to bilingual plays in an effort to have them be bilingual. We had several "How to Learn Spanish" tapes and, when they got older, acquired interactive computer compact disks (CDs) in Spanish that were very effective in giving them instant feedback. These strategies and continuous formal instruction in Spanish at school helped them eventually learn to speak the Spanish language, to a certain degree. To this day, all three of my children continue to take formal Spanish courses.

Three things had a significant impact on my children's desire to embrace the Spanish language (and as a result, other parts of our culture). The first was a trip the family took to Europe, where my children were exposed to very young boys and girls who spoke two to seven languages with ease. They realized that it was possible to learn two languages and that knowing two or more languages was an asset. Reassessing the opportunity they had at home of learning a second language, they began to ask my husband and me what certain words meant in Spanish, and I saw them making an extra effort in practicing the language with us and with their friends. The other great motivating factor came with the advent of Tejano music and popular artists such as Selena. Our children knew all of her songs in Spanish. When they saw that their non-Spanish-speaking Anglo friends liked her music and were singing her songs, they became even more motivated to learn Spanish. They felt proud that they sounded as though they had spoken *español* all their lives, since they had a perfect Spanish accent. But sometimes I questioned whether they knew what they were singing. Steven, the most proficient Spanish speaker of my children, had a Spanish-speaking babysitter when he was very young. I also took him when he was three and four years of age to a summer recreation program in the barrio for children of mixed ages. He quickly picked up the language and all of its social nuances. He would come home, swinging his head forward and his arms from side to side saying, *"¿Qué pasó, bato?"* From the barrio, Steven's interest in the Spanish language grew as he learned to listen to it everywhere: at his school and his *abuelita's* house, on television and the radio, in restaurants and the neighborhood.

My children mixed the languages as Vanessa did when she substituted *"agua"* for water when she recited "Jack and Jill." The word that helped her to learn the concept for water was the first word that came out of her mouth. Whenever her babysitter or I used to ask her, *"¿Quieres agua?"* she would respond with the word *"agua"* when she wanted water. Then I would repeat, "Do you want water? *¿Quieres agua?"* Eventually she differentiated between the languages.

I believe now that the schools and society could have worked together with families like mine and encouraged us to become proficient in both languages. Instead, for many years there existed an attitude that people who live in this country should speak English only. Hispanics should stand firm and defend our *derechos* to speak two languages. Even if Spanish is the only language spoken in the home, research demonstrates that children will adopt the dominant language, English, because they are exposed to it everywhere, from television to the schoolyard.

Contrary to the opinions of some people, Hispanics in this country are eager to learn the English language in order to get jobs and to communicate with others. It is critical to learn English just to be able to read such things as medical prescriptions, traffic signs, and instructions. Avance parents who take English classes do so for all of these reasons as well as to help their children with their homework. When there is a need to communicate and be understood, people are driven to learn English. But that does not mean they should not value and maintain the Spanish language. Expose your children to *"Plaza Sésamo"* and to children's songs by CriCri,

Tatiana, Orozco, and Cepellin. Do whatever you can to help your children become bilingual. One day they will be appreciative you did.

The Chicano Movement of the 1960s and early 1970s, like other movements during the civil rights era, infused pride in Hispanics in knowing the Spanish language and in their culture. Today, however, government policies like the English Only movement and the stigma associated with immigrants have forced some Hispanics to reject their native language, because of fear of being humiliated. Some parents feel that because of their own negative experiences associated with their knowledge of the Spanish language, they do not want their children to learn Spanish. Many were led to believe that speaking Spanish is bad, and they do not want their children to suffer. They have to realize that today with bilingual education, children can maintain their language and culture while they make a transition to the English language. They will no longer be like many of us who were trying to learn the English language at the same time we were trying to learn basic skills and content in a foreign language. Parents should encourage their children to participate in bilingual programs that value both languages equally. They should support bilingual education and consider it essential for *nuestra gente*.

Still, as effective as a bilingual program can be, it is important to remember that schools only build on the foundation that parents have already established in the home. Children must enter school full of rich experiences in both languages. Also, if you want to encourage bilingualism, you must make an effort to speak both languages to your child. Each experience reinforces the other.

Body Language: *La Ceja, los Brazos, y el Pie*

In any culture, body language is considered another form of communication. We speak through words and gestures. Parents learn about children's needs and feelings by reading their body language and vice versa. For example, when *la ceja*, the eyebrow, goes up or when you press your lips together, a child knows that you are angry. When you tap your foot and cross your arms, you may be saying that you want your child to hurry. Children know when people are angry, upset, tense, or happy based on body language.

There are a few subtle cultural differences between the body language of English and Spanish speakers. For example, many English speakers immediately establish eye contact when they begin talking to someone. If you do not look at them directly, they may think that you are sending a message that you are either trying to avoid something or you are not being forthright. But some traditional Hispanics have been taught that eye-to-eye contact is disrespectful or rude. For example, if they are speaking to their grandparents, they may not want to display disrespect by looking at them straight in the eyes.

In addition, Hispanics love to touch. We cherish *abrazos*, and abundant *besos*. Psychologist S. M. Jourard once observed the behavior of couples seated in cafés around the world. He found that in a single hour, Puerto Ricans touched 180 times, while people in Florida touched 110 times, white middle-class people in Florida touched only twice in an hour, and Londoners in a similar situation did not touch at all. The study illustrates the cultural differences that can affect communication.

Many Hispanics are accustomed to keeping a closer distance when speaking to one another. I have found that in conversations with people, sometimes I take one step forward and the person I am speaking to moves two steps back. Even a weak handshake and smiling too much are considered inappropriate among many Anglos. Because we are trying to teach our children to live in a bicultural society, as they get older, we should help them become aware of the differences between the body languages of the two cultures. Although we do not want them to lose their cultural values or change their personalities, in certain circumstances, we want them to learn to be flexible and be ready to adapt to new situations.

READING: *AYÚDALE A TU NIÑO A LEER*

Reading should be a continuous process from the first days of life. My children had many books, some made at home, others purchased, or borrowed from the library. When they were very young, they had alphabet books, nursery rhyme books, and picture books that popped up when they were opened. Children love all kinds of books, big and small, cloth, board, or plastic. You can find *Beauty and the Beast* (*La Bella y la Bestia*), *The Lion King* (*El Rey León*), and *Snow White* (*La Blancanieves*) in both languages. To children reading becomes an adventure taken with their eyes, ears, hands, and, if done with love, their hearts.

Schedule at least fifteen minutes each day to read to your young child. Sit next to him when you are reading so that he is close enough to study each page. Talk about the objects and activities in the book as your child points to them. As you read, hug him, stroke his hair or arm, smile, and keep eye contact with him as you examine his reactions to the story. Say things like, "What do you think will happen next?" or "How did the *osito* feel when the chair broke?" After I finished reading a story to my children, I would end it with "*Colorín, colorado, este cuento se ha acabado,*" and I would give them a hug. This warm, pleasant experience will be associated with a love of reading.

Teach your child to go from the front of the book to the back. Make sure that your child turns the pages from right to left and that when you read, he sees that you are proceeding from top to bottom and from left to right. After watching you do it, he will want to take over. Let your child turn the pages and point to what interests him. Whatever he points to (cat, ball, beetle), label and describe it. Give him time to repeat what you said. Compare what is in the book to concrete objects in his environment. Name the letters and illustrate them with wooden or magnetic letters. Ask questions about the different activities in the book, the theme, and how the story unfolds. Ask him to tell you the story or to recite the rhyme. Whenever you read to your child, you are telling him that reading is important and enjoyable. Try to keep newspapers, magazines, encyclopedias, and reference books around your home so that you can answer his many questions. Have fun with your child as he learns to communicate and to read. The more words and concepts he learns, the more he will be able to think and acquire greater competence intellectually.

Take your child periodically to the library. There is now a larger selection of wonderful bilingual books available in almost every public library. Check out both Spanish and English children's books. There are many wonderful children's books in Spanish where each of the pages could be beautifully framed. See the Resource List at the back of the book for some books and the addresses and phone numbers of the publishing companies. A large section of one of the floors of the San Antonio Public Library, for instance, is devoted to the Latino collection, consisting of hundreds of books written by and about Latinos. If your *biblioteca* does not have one, request that the librarian establish one. Our collection came about because a group of dynamic Latino women requested—no, demanded—that we have one in our city, which is 60 percent Hispanic.

As your child grows, continue to read to him and encourage him to tell you more and more about each story. Cover the illustrations and ask him to create his own image to describe a story. Show him a picture in the story and ask him to guess what the written words say about the picture. As you read a section of the story, ask him to tell you about the characters, the theme, and the setting. Read a section of the story and ask him questions to see if he understood what you read. "Where was the boy at the beginning of the story? Where is he now?" If you read a book like one from the *Curious George* series, you could ask him, "What is this book about? Is it about a cat? No, this book is about a monkey. What kind of monkey was George? He was a very curious monkey. He wanted to know everything." If you read a bilingual book like *The Bossy Gallito, El Gallo de Bodas: A Traditional Cuban Folktale* by Lucia M. Gonzalez, you could say, "*Este libro es del gallito mandón*, the bossy rooster. What kind of a rooster was he? Yes, he was a very bossy rooster. He ordered everyone around." After you have read your child's favorite book many times, he will be able to tell you what happened next or tell you part of a sentence or section from the story. He may be able to tell you the entire sequence of the story without ever looking at the words. Pretending to read only motivates him more to experience the real thing.

Reading is about connecting a group of letters with corresponding sounds to a particular meaning. A child will not be able to comprehend something he reads if he has not had enough experiences interacting with others and with the world around him to fill his imagination. Those experiences that allowed him to acquire language and form concepts will now be very useful in helping him to understand what he is reading. All those experiences observing small details and discriminating between similar objects will now help him to decipher between the "b" and the "d" and the "p" and the "q."

At about two and three years of age, most children learn to recognize letters. Name the letters in the book and use plastic, wooden, or magnetic letters to illustrate them. Write the letter on a piece of paper. Write words he says so that he can learn the association between written words and thoughts. There are many children's alphabet books in English and in Spanish that you can use to teach your children the uppercase (capital) letters and lowercase letters. By age four or five, most children have learned the letters and are ready to connect words with objects or activities. When my children were young, I used flash cards with the names of many objects around the house. I used capital and small letters so that they would realize that there were two sets of letters. My children had a toy with slots carved out in the shape of letters, which they used to fill with matching letters. They had letters made of plastic, wood, felt, and some that were magnetic, which they used to make words on a magnetic board or on the refrigerator door.

Some of the rhymes that my children knew in English and Spanish taught them the names of letters and the sounds that animals make. One such rhyme in English is the classic "Old MacDonald," which teaches children about the sounds that animals make. Below are Spanish verses and songs that teach children about words, sounds, and the creatures of the world.

Old MacDonald

Old MacDonald had a farm. E I E I O.
And on this farm he had a cow. E I E I O.
With a moo moo here and a moo moo there. Here a moo. There a
moo, everywhere a moo moo.
Old MacDonald had a farm. E I E I O.

(Repeat with cat, dog, horse, duck, etc.)

Los Pollitos

Los pollitos dicen, "pío, pío, pío,"
Cuando tienen hambre, cuando tienen frío
La gallina busca el maíz y el trigo,
Les da de comer y les busca abrigo.

El Sapito Glo-Glo Glo

Nadie sabe dónde vive.
Nadie sabe dónde vive.
Pero todos lo escuchamos
Al sapito: Glo, glo, glo.

Los Tres Cochinitos

Los tres cochinitos están en la cama.
Muchos besitos les dio su mamá.
Y calientitos todos en pijama.
Dentro de un rato los tres roncaron: oink, oink, oink.

De Colores

De colores, de colores se visten los campos en la primavera.
De colores, de colores son los pajarillos que vienen de afuera.
De colores, de colores el arcoíris que vemos lucir.
Y por eso los grandes amores de muchos colores me gustan a mí.
Y por eso los grandes amores de muchos colores me gustan a mí.

Canta el gallo, canta el gallo con el quiri, quiri, quiri, quiri.
La gallina, la gallina con el cara, cara, cara, cara.
Los pollitos, los pollitos con el pío, pío, pío, pí.
Los pollitos, los pollitos con el pío, pío, pío, pí.
Y por eso los grandes amores de muchos colores me gustan a mí.
Y por eso los grandes amores de muchos colores me gustan a mí.

I used to remind my children that just as animals on Old MacDonald's farm and the *pollitos*, *sapitos*, and *cochinitos* in the Spanish rhymes and *el gallo*, *la gallina*, and *los pollitos* in "*De Colores*" make certain sounds, the letters do also. When they showed an interest in playing school or just playing with the letters, I took the lesson to the next step by teaching them the names and sounds of the letters. I taught my children the sounds of the letters in Spanish first because the sounds in Spanish do not vary, as they do in English. Once they learned the process of putting the sounds together phonetically in Spanish, they could transfer that same process to English.

The rhymes and chants that my children learned and the times that I encouraged them to listen to soft music or the crickets and crackling of wood during a campout helped them to acquire good listening skills. In teaching my children to read in Spanish and English, I used the same approach that I had used with my first-grade students. I began with the vowels in Spanish, saying: "*La A en español suena como el sonido* 'Ahh,'" the Spanish A makes the sound 'Ahh,'" and I showed them a picture of a woman screaming because she saw a spider. "*¡Ahh, araña!*" I continued with the letter E: "*La E en español suena como el sonido* 'Ehh,'" the letter E makes the sound 'Ehh,'" and I held up a picture of a man who could not hear while I cupped my hand over my ear saying, "Ehh?" The letter "I" came with a picture of a squirrel that made the sound of "Iiiii," which I demonstrated by putting my hands together and pretending to be a squirrel. The letter "O" stood for the sound a cowboy makes as he tries to stop the horse: "Ooooh, *caballo*," and the letter "U" made the sound of a train. "Oooo Oooo," I said as I pulled the imaginary whistle chord of a train. I ended the lesson with a chant that I learned as a child:

A, E, I, O, U, *el burro sabe más que tú*.
A, E, I, O, U, the donkey knows more than you,
to which we all replied, "Oh, no he does not!"

Once the children learned the vowel sounds, we continued the lesson with the consonants. I connected each of the vowels with the letters M, N, C, T, D, S, and P first to make simple words they knew like *mamá*, *papá, cama, toma, dedo, sopa*. It was easy for them to understand the process of reading when they learned to put the words together phonetically in Spanish. Then I introduced them to the English vowel sounds. I compared the two vowel sounds in English and Spanish. I asked them to watch my mouth so that they could learn that different sounds were produced based on how I opened my mouth. I began with the short "A" in English by making the sound "Aaa," as in Aaapple. I continued with the rest of the sounds: "Eeeehh," as in egg; "Iiiihh," as in Indian; "Ohhhh," as in orange, and "Uhhh," as in umbrella, trying to act out examples for each (some suggestions are given below). Then I combined those sounds with the similar consonant sounds that they already knew in Spanish, stressing the vowel sound.

M A D	Mad. I am so mad (make an angry face).	A, Aaa, Aaa. Apple.
C A T	Cat. The cat goes meow (make meow sound).	A, Aaa, Aaa. Apple.
S A T	Sat. I sat down (sit down).	A, Aaa, Aaa. Apple.
F A N	Fan. I fan myself (do it).	A, Aaa, Aaa. Apple.
F A T	Fat. I am very fat (exaggerate fatness).	A, Aaa, Aaa. Apple.

P E N	Pen. We write with a pen.	E, Eeeehh, Eeeehh. Egg.
P E T	Pet. A dog is a pet.	E, Eeeehh, Eeeehh. Egg.
G E T	Get. Get the ball.	E, Eeeehh, Eeeehh. Egg.
R E D	Red. This is red.	E, Eeeehh, Eeeehh. Egg.
N E T	Net. Something used to catch a fish.	E, Eeeehh, Eeeehh. Egg.

K I S S	Kiss. Give me a kiss.	I. Iiihh, Iiiihh. Indian.
S I T	Sit. I sit down.	I. Iiiihh, Iiiihh. Indian.
F I N	Fin. The fish has a fin.	I. Iiiihh, Iiiihh. Indian.
H I T	Hit. Do not hit anybody.	I. Iiiihh, Iiiihh. Indian.
M I T T	Mitt. You catch a ball with a mitt.	I. Iiiihh, Iiiihh. Indian.

M O P	Mop. I mop the floor.	O, Ohhhh, Ohhhh. Orange.
T O P	Top. The top spins.	O, Ohhhh, Ohhhh. Orange.
S O N	Son. You are my son.	O, Ohhhh, Ohhhh. Orange.
P O T	Pot. He cooks in a pot.	O, Ohhhh, Ohhhh. Orange.
C O T	Cot. I sleep on a small cot.	O, Ohhhh, Ohhhh. Orange.

S U N	Sun. The sun shines brightly.	U, Uhhh, Uhhh. Umbrella.
C U T	Cut. I cut my finger.	U, Uhhh, Uhhh. Umbrella.
N U T	Nut. Squirrels eat nuts.	U, Uhhh, Uhhh. Umbrella.
C U P	Cup. Baby drinks milk from a cup.	U, Uhhh, Uhhh. Umbrella.
P U P	Pup. A pup is a small dog.	U, Uhhh, Uhhh. Umbrella.

It was easy to teach words with regular long vowel sounds like "go," "so," and "no," until I came to words like "to," "put," and "do." I told my children that they had to learn certain words by sight. We repeated them several times. Then we came to words with the silent "e," as in "came," and double "oo" as in "too." When we came to the words "seat" and "pear," I explained how they had different sounds and they just had to memorize them. I then continued teaching them all the consonants, including blends like *bl*, *st*, and *gr*, moving the process along. I usually stopped teaching them to read at this point, but continued to help my children when they asked me to explain a particular word. Based on the context of the story, they could now decipher many words on their own. Although my children knew the process of reading and could decode the simplest words, I had to continue to stress the importance of comprehension—understanding the meaning of the words. If the child does not have a strong vocabulary or has not had enough experiences learning about his world, he may not be able to comprehend what he is reading. I used to create silly pictures to teach my children how to read short sentences. For example, there was the "fat man in a hat." (Dr. Seuss books are ideal for this kind of reading exercise.) Simple books and nursery rhymes in both English and Spanish that children can memorize will help children learn to read as well.

If you follow some of these teaching techniques, you will send your children to school with a good foundation in reading. It is important that we make reading fun, instead of a chore. A child's brain will be most ready for reading around his sixth year, but for some children reading starts as early as four or as late as seven. You need to read your child's cues to know when he's ready, otherwise he may feel overwhelmed.

My son Sal started reading simple books at the age of four. He always had a great love for books and a great thirst for reading. He was constantly surrounded with library books or ones we gave him for his birthdays, and the encyclopedia. He had favorite stories that I read repeatedly. Some children, like Vanessa, used reading as a game. She took on the role of "teacher" to her dolls, cousins, and neighbors and became *la maestra* as she read to them. Steven also enjoyed reading, but only if I scratched his back as I read to him. Although each of your children may approach reading differently, most of them can read phonetically by the time they enter kindergarten.

My sister-in-law's children, all of whom were in gifted-and-talented classes, were very advanced readers before they started school. When her children were four and five years of age, she established a routine of going to the library and getting books that interested them. She taught them to listen very carefully to several things: the title of the book, author, main characters, and plot. Then she would ask them questions.

Her children learned to be very attentive and could readily comprehend what their mother read. She would ask them what happened first, second, and third. In doing all of these things, she was teaching them that words have meaning, that stories have a certain structure, and that they could one day write their own books.

As your children get older, play games of "Round Robin," during which you take turns reading pages from a book. Children will really acquire a love for reading if you spend quality time taking turns reading with them. Let them experience the joy of deciphering words and images on paper. Sometimes after an outing ask your children to tell you what they saw that day and give them a marker to create a story on butcher paper or easel paper. When I did this, I would give each story a title and would write their names down as the authors of the work. Then I would let them read the stories and would praise them for their efforts. I would never get upset if they made mistakes in their sentence structure. I knew that mistakes were part of the learning process. On other days, you can make birthday and Christmas cards, play Scrabble, and write poems, all of which will help them sharpen their reading and writing skills.

I sometimes think of the kind of rich, stimulating experiences my husband and I provided for our children, and compare them to those of children who did not have someone to read to them, were not allowed to write or scribble, were not taught songs or rhymes, and rarely were taken on outings. There is a marked difference between the children who have had these experiences before they entered school and those who haven't. They know more, speak more, and are more prepared to meet with academic success. Though not impossible, it is very hard for children to catch up if they do not have these experiences when they are young. Those children whose parents lay the proper foundation will continue to grow and develop and build on that foundation.

EXPANDING THEIR WORLD: *DEL MUNDO CONCRETO AL MUNDO LÓGICO*—AGES SIX TO ELEVEN

A child in this stage learns to use logic to solve problems, but he is generally limited to concrete objects and events instead of abstract ideas. He does a lot of reflecting. Now he is able to learn broader categories of things, such as people, food, fruit, trees, birds, and animals. He can order objects and events in a series and draw relationships between things. He is able to recognize properties such as physical mass at age seven. At age nine, he can grasp the concept of volume and weight, even if the container he is studying changes in shape and size. At nine years, a child can remember and repeat four to five numbers consecutively. He practices what he has learned and refines and increases the number of concepts.

During these ages, it is good to expose your children to many activities that can broaden their worldview. This is the stage in which they learn to develop their interests and innate talents. Encourage them to get involved in activities they like to do. Have them start a collection of stamps, cars, baseball cards, or coins. Buy them telescopes and chemistry sets. Crossword puzzles, for example, may grab their interest and help them to increase their vocabulary.

Take your children to children's museums and take them on vacations that will help them learn about different people, cultures, and places. If you have an opportunity to take your children to a place like Washington, D.C., do it. There are many free educational museums like the National Museum of Natural History, the National Air and Space Museum, the National Museum of American Art, and the Holocaust Museum. The Smithsonian puts out a resource guide that describes the works of Latinos in its collections as well as programs designed by Latinos. Explore American history at the Jefferson and Lincoln Memorials, the White House, the United States Capitol building, and many other important landmarks. Have them learn how money is made at the State Treasury. Have them attend a play. Closer to home, you can take your niños to your local museums, botanical gardens, to the beach, mountains, lake, or local parks.

Help your children research their roots. Take them to La Basílica de La Virgen Guadalupe, to the Pyramid of the Sun at Teotihuacán in Mexico, or to the Mayan ruins of Chichén Itzá, Uxmal, and Palenque. There are other fabulous museums in Mexico City where your children can learn a lot about their culture. The Machu Picchu ruins in Peru would be another magnificent sight to behold. In Granada, Spain, they can learn about the Moorish influence on the Hispanic culture by visiting the Alhambra Palace, built in 1238. Take them on a tour of the Southwest to visit Native American reservations. This is the time in their life where a trip to the Caribbean islands to snorkel would be not only enjoyable, but educational.

Allow them to be creative. Encourage your children to demonstrate their talents by encouraging them to write and perform their own plays with the help of a video camera. My children created several plays. Steven usually was the director. Some of his productions were musicals in which my children and their playmates dressed up as rock stars. Sometimes the productions were dramas in which the actors kidnapped Vanessa. Other times they were staging a "bank robbery." One day I came home from work and the kids grabbed my hand and sat me down to view their latest production. I was flabbergasted when I saw the videotape of fifteen-year-old Sal, who did not yet have a driver's license, driving the family truck on a slow trip down our long driveway. The camera zoomed from Sal in the front seat to the back of the truck, where ten-year-old Steven was hanging on to the edge of the bed, feet dragging, as he dramatized his escape in the "getaway truck." I screamed to my husband, "¡SALVADOR, *mira lo que hicieron tus niños!*" The kids told me not to worry. They had the approval of their twenty-one-year-old cousin, Lisa, who was babysitting. She, in fact, was the one who was doing the filming. Despite such scares, we encouraged our children to be creative and to pursue the outer reaches of their imaginations, with some necessary precautions.

This is an appropriate time to buy your child female dolls, perhaps the Rosalba or Josefina dolls, that come with the accompanying English and Spanish books. To purchase these Latina dolls, refer to the Resource List in the back of the book. Rosalba is available from the Niños catalog. The Josefina doll and book series is available from the Pleasant Company American Girls Collection catalog. Rosalba is a Puerto Rican girl who explores New York with her *abuela* in the book *Abuela* by Arthur Dorrios. In the book *Isla* by the same author, she tours the island of Puerto Rico with her *abuela*. Josefina Montoya is a nine-year-old Mexican-American girl in Northern New Mexico in 1824 at the time of the opening of the Santa Fe Trail. Some of her books written by Valerie Tripp include *Happy Birthday, Josefina; Josefina: A Springtime Story; Josefina Saves the Day: A Summer Story; and Changes for Josefina* (Pleasant Co., $5.95). Your daughter could spend countless hours playing with the accessories that can also be found in the catalog, such as furniture, dishes, artificial food, animals, and cooking utensils, as well as a complete wardrobe.

During this period, children play games where they learn to follow rules. Children have graduated from pat-a-cake to board and card games to sports. Through sports, children at this stage can learn rules, fair play, and teamwork. How I looked forward to the family's weekly outings to watch our children play baseball, soccer, football, or basketball. Our children expected us to be there not only for moral support, but to videotape and take pictures.

Children, both girls and boys, need to be encouraged to participate in organized competitive sports as well as cooperative games. There are many games for children at this age that provide important lessons about cooperating, following rules, and making decisions. The following are more traditional Spanish games that many Hispanic parents learned as children. I taught some of them to my first-grade students in my class. As you read them you will discover how much they can contribute to your older child's playtime experience. If you are in Mexico, stop by a music store and purchase cassettes, such as *Juegos Infantiles* and *Juegos y Rondas*, that contain the music to some of these games. You can also order some of Jose Luis Orozco's cassettes by calling (510) 527-5539.

Naranja Dulce

This game is usually played by girls, but boys can join in, too, and be the soldier. Children stand in a circle holding hands and singing. A child who is pretending to be a soldier going to war stands inside the circle. The children walk around the child in the middle chanting *Naranja Dulce*. After the line, "*Dame un abrazo que yo te pido*," the soldier selects a girl, hugs her, and takes her to the center. The first child (boy) leaves the circle and remains outside. The second child becomes the soldier and stands in the middle of the circle. Children continue to go around the circle and repeat the song until all but the last two children are outside the circle.

Naranja dulce, limón partido,
Dame un abrazo que yo te pido.
Si fueran falsos mis juramentos
En otros tiempo, se olvidarán. (Repeat entire stanza.)

¡Tocan la marcha! Mi pecho llora,
Adiós, Señora, yo ya me voy
A mi casita de Solology. A comer tacos y no le doy. (Repeat.)

La Víbora de la Mar
MEXICAN VERSION

The following traditional game is the Spanish version of London Bridge. It involves two people; one is the *sandía* and the other is the *melón*, holding hands, facing each other with their arms raised to form an "underwater cave." The serpent, which is made up of a train of children, will go through the cave singing the following song:

*A la víbora, víbora de la mar, de la mar
por aquí pueden pasar,
los de adelante corren mucho,
y los de atrás se quedarán.
¡Tras, tras, tras, tras!*

*Una mejicana que fruta vendía
Ciruela, chabacano, melón o sandía
Una mejicana que fruta vendía
Ciruela, chabacano, melón o sandía*

*Verbena, verbena, jardín de matatena.
Verbena, verbena, jardín de matatena.
Campanita de oro, déjame pasar
con todos mis hijos ¡menos él de atrás!
¡Tras, tras, tras, tras!*

The child under the arch is trapped, tossed back and forth, and asked to choose *melón o sandía.*

*Será melón. Será sandía.
Será la vieja del otro día,…día,…día,… día,… día.*

When I was a child, this game included a tug-of-war. The child who is caught is taken to the side away from the other children and asked to choose *melón* or *sandía.* Depending on his choice, he goes behind the line of one of the two children forming the arch. The song continues until all the children have been caught and are placed behind either of the two children forming the arch. Then there is a tug-of-war where the children hold each other at the waist. Whichever side pulls the hardest and makes the other team cross the line wins, or if one team falls down, the other wins. Some people call the winners *los angelitos,* the angels, and the losers are *los diablos,* the devils. In the past, this game ended with everyone on the ground laughing.

La Víbora de la Mar
PUERTO RICAN VERSION

Two children leading:

*La víbora, víbora del amor,
De aquí podéis pasar,*

Others: Por aquí yo pasaré.
               Y una niña dejaré.

Two children: ¿Y esa niña cuál será,
               la de adelante o la de atrás?

Others: La de adelante corre mucho
               y la de atrás se quedará.

Two girls: Pásame, sí, pásame, ya,
               por la puerta de Alcántara.

In another version of *La Víbora de la Mar*, the person who is caught takes the place of either *melón o sandía*, the players forming the arch, so that he or she can then join the other children in becoming part of the serpent. The rules to this game are similar to the first version, where the two children forming the arch are a color, a fruit, gold, or silver. The two sides hold each other at the waist and the game ends with a tug-of-war.

A la Rueda de San Miguel

A child stands at the center of a circle of children holding hands. The circle moves clockwise as the children recite the rhyme. When they come to the part of the rhyme that says, "*que se voltee,*" the child in the center names a child from the circle, and together they all say the child's name followed by "*de burro.*" That child who is picked turns around and faces outside the circle while still holding the others' hands. The song is repeated, and the game continues until all the children have turned around. In another version of the game, the speed increases with each repetition. The game starts again after everyone falls down from the velocity.

A la rueda, rueda, de San Miguel, San Miguel
todos traen su caja de miel
A lo maduro, a lo maduro,
que se volte
(Juan)* de burro.

*insert name

Doña Blanca

Children form a circle with *Doña Blanca* in the center and the *Jicotillo* (hornet) outside the circle. After the children in the circle sing the song twice, the *Jicotillo* tries to break through the circle to catch *Doña Blanca*. After she gets caught, she chooses a new *Jicotillo* who becomes *Doña Blanca*.

Doña Blanca está cubierta
con pilares de oro y plata.
Romperemos un pilar
Para ver a Doña Blanca. (Repeat)
¡Quién es ese Jicotillo
Que anda en pos de Doña Blanca?
¡Yo soy ése, Jicotillo
que anda en pos de Doña Blanca!

La Raspa

This Mexican folkloric dance is played in partners. In this dance, children hold hands. Sometimes the boy clasps his hands behind him and the girl holds her skirt at two points at the left and right. As they recite the lyrics, each child places the right foot in front, heel on the floor, swaying to the right. Then, with a hop, they switch to the left foot, heel on the floor, swaying their body to the left, and then they repeat the step with the right foot. Each child completes these steps with the beat *da dun, da dun, da dun.* For example: *La ras pa, la, bailó* (right foot, left foot, right foot) *un viejo, bigo tón* (left foot, right foot, left foot). They repeat the sequence with the next two sentences: *y en medio, del, salón—se le cae (cayó), el pan talón.* When the song comes to "*¡Ay Mamá pégale a María!*" each pair of children skips around in a circle, connected by arms that are interlocked at the elbow, first with the right arm in one direction with the first *¡Ay Mamá pégale a María!*, then with the left in the other direction with the second *¡Ay Mamá pégale a María!*, then switches back to the right with the third line and then to the left, with *Porque trajo la leche fría.* The children hold hands again and repeat the steps from the beginning one more time.

La raspa la bailó
Un viejo bigotón
Y en medio del salón,
Se le cayó el pantalón.

¡Ay Mamá, pégale a María!
¡Ay Mamá, pégale a María!
¡Ay Mamá, pégale a María!
Porque trajo la leche fría.

(Repeat once from the beginning.)

¡Que Llueva! El Chicote

This is a game in which the players walk in a line holding each other at the shoulders, while everyone looks up at the sky except the leader. The leader tries to get the rest to fall down by pulling them in different directions. When the line falls, the second person in line takes over and the first person goes to the end of the line.

¡Que llueva! ¡Que llueva!
la virgen de la cueva,
los pájarillos cantan,
las nubes se levantan.

¡A que sí! ¡A que no!
¡Que caiga el chaparrón!
¡A que sí! ¡A que no!
Le canta el labrador.

Pin Marín

Pin Marín is a verse that is traditionally used to select a person in a game. The person that you point to last when the verse ends is the one you want on your team or the one who has to be "it." The rhyme goes: Pin Marín de Don Pífuel, cácara, mácara, títere fue él.

La Campana

This game involves two children whose arms are linked with a third child between them and each takes turns swinging that person like a bell.

San Serafín

In this game children form a semi-circle and follow the directions and movements of the leader; very much like Simon Says. Children can also go around in a circle skipping and stopping to do the action that the leader calls out.

San Serafín del Monte,
San Serafín Cordero,
Yo, como buen Cristiano,
me hincaré (sentaré, acostaré, rascaré, pararé, brincaré, reiré).

GETTING YOUR CHILD READY FOR SCHOOL: ¿ESTÁ LISTO?

Preparing your child for school involves much more than buying school supplies and shopping for shoes. If your child has rich, stimulating experiences at home, if she has opportunities to play, talk, listen, sing, explore, experiment, read, and write, as mentioned throughout this chapter, she will be ready to meet with success in the classroom. In some schools, children are given a series of tests that are used to categorize them and place them into groups. Very often, these groupings are classified as the "average" class, the "below average," and the more accelerated group, or as mentioned earlier, "black birds" and "blue birds." Children develop at different rates, but no child should be denied a stimulating educational program where they can develop to their maximum capacity. Your role as first teacher includes preparing your children before they enter school. Here are some things to remember:

- From the moment of birth, talk to your child and teach her things. Carry on two-way dialogues.
- Make sure your child has enough stimulating experiences before school, such as drawing, cutting, playing with clay, identifying the parts of the body, reading, and going on outings, among other activities.
- Make sure that her physical and nutritional needs are met. Send your child to school with a good night's rest and a healthy breakfast.

- Let her know that she is loved and help her feel secure and confident.

- Be sure that she has had previous experiences being with other groups of children, so that her first day of school will not be totally foreign and frightening.

HIGH EXPECTATIONS: ALL YOU NEED ARE GANAS Y ESPERANZA

One of the most important things that you can give your children is the ability to believe in themselves. You must have high expectations, aspirations, hopes, and dreams for your children. Let them know that you believe they can succeed, that they are smart and that they can, with determination and hard work, become anything they want to be, whether it be a doctor, an astronaut, or even the president of the United States. As the movie *Stand and Deliver* points out, all it takes is *ganas*, a deep-seated desire to succeed at anything.

From the survey I administered to the parents of the children I taught, I found that many mothers expected their children to go to school only as far as the seventh grade. They did not expect their children to achieve more than they had attained. If parents have low expectations, they can bring about what is known as the "self-fulfilling prophecy." This means that if someone believes that a child will only accomplish up to a certain level, then he starts following that course because he starts believing it. The opposite can also be true. If the significant people in a child's life believe that he can succeed and often tell him so, then he will believe it as well. Although my mother had only a third-grade education, she had hopes, dreams, and high aspirations for all of her children. I recall that she would tell my sisters and me that we could meet and marry a prince and eventually become queens. My mother made me believe in myself, in my capabilities, and in my worth as a human being. Therefore, I believed that I could achieve anything that I set out to do. Well, I did in fact meet Prince Charles when he came to Avance and I twice became queen of my high school and college. I also married my prince charming who treated me with kindness and respect. Unfortunately, some research studies have shown that some teachers have lower expectations of Hispanic Americans, African Americans, and Native Americans than they do for whites and Asian Americans, and this can be reflected in how they relate to those children. Therefore, it is important that you send them to school knowing that they have value and that they are loved.

Though parents can help teachers become aware of their negative attitudes and their effects on students, they must first make sure that their child goes to school believing he can succeed. Your words and actions must be persuasive so that your child can be strong enough to overcome the pressures that may come from those who may prejudge his potential. Get to know your child's teachers so that your presence will send the message that you care and are concerned about how your child is treated.

Getting Organized and Prepared: *Ayúdale que Sea Organizado y Preparado*

Un lugar para todo, y todo en su lugar. Preparing for school means helping your children to organize their possessions, time, and learning environment. Get them prepared. Make sure that your children have all the materials they need to function in school. These include notebooks, dividers, paper, pens, pencils, dictionaries, poster boards, and for older children, a typewriter or computer. While a computer may mean a large investment, it has now become an essential tool for children. A computer is far more important than purchasing a television set for your children. Make sure that your children take the responsibility to complete the things they need to do, from their homework to a science or research project. Assign a special place in the house where your children can do their homework or where they can just relax and read books. You can provide an inviting environment by playing soft music or keeping noise to a minimum while they are reading and learning. Also, help your children organize their time so that they can balance their homework, chores, and after-school and weekend activities.

Homework: *Ayúdale con la Tarea*

Make sure your children get into a routine of finishing their homework assignments before they turn the television set on or before they start to play. You can help them go over vocabulary words, multiplication tables, or quiz questions. Check their work and take them to the library to learn how to use reference materials. Help your children learn how to memorize facts better. One method that I used to help my children learn formulas, concepts, or lists of names was through mnemonics. They simply memorized the first letter of each word and then created a new word from those letters, which helped them recall a series of facts better. In Hispanic families, as in many cultures, older siblings play a big role in helping the younger ones succeed in school. Do not underestimate the potential of *los hermanos mayores*, older brothers or sisters, to teach the younger ones how the system works and what to expect from certain teachers. They can model appropriate study habits and can be excellent tutors. These are habits, however, that must be formed early. While you or the older siblings can provide support, make sure that you do not wind up doing their homework for them. Children need to learn that there are consequences if they do not turn in assignments on time or if they refuse to do them altogether. Making good grades and succeeding in school mainly boils down to turning in their homework assignments correctly and studying for tests. If they try to cut corners or slack off, they will see it in their grades.

Television: *Controla y Apaga la Televisión*

Monitor the programs and length of time that your children are allowed to watch television. Encourage them to watch educational programs like *Plaza Sésamo* or *Sesame Street*, *Barney*, the *Puzzle Place*, or the Discovery and History Channels. Television should be limited to no more than two hours a day on weekdays. If the TV stays on all day it can prevent kids from doing their homework or from acquiring good listening skills, as well as decrease the likelihood that they will be exposed to more concrete and active experiences.

Before seven years of age, children cannot distinguish between fantasy and reality and are often affected by what they watch on TV, videos, movies, and advertisements. Children who are allowed to watch violence on TV learn to solve their problems in an aggressive manner and become less sensitive to people's feelings. At this age, young children watching violence on TV can become more fearful of the world around them. Parents should set limits and parameters on television watching. You should always explain why you do not approve of programs your children are watching. You should encourage and be part of other activities with your children besides watching television, such as playing dominoes, cards, or board games. Generally, as a rule, the television should remain off during school days, as should video, computer games, and telephones. Yet as they get older it becomes more of a challenge for parents.

ENRICHMENT AND SUPPLEMENTAL PROGRAMS: *EXCELENCIA EN LA EDUCACIÓN*

As a member of the College Board's Educational Excellence for All Students Task Force, we have discussed strategies for helping Hispanics, Blacks, and Native Americans achieve educational excellence in school, score higher on their SAT tests, and ultimately do well in college. Sending children to enrichment courses and Saturday academies that can enhance their knowledge in math, science, and problem-solving are but a few ways. It is important that you get your children ready to take algebra in middle school, for that will enable them to take essential college preparatory classes such as advanced algebra, geometry, chemistry, and physics later in high school. As parents, you should make sure that your children's middle school offers algebra courses, and that they enroll. With attacks on Affirmative Action, it is getting harder for our children to enter the colleges of their choice. We advocate and assist them in establishing a good foundation by taking supplementary classes in math, science, English, computers, and even test-taking when they are young so that they will be able to compete. My son once took a weekend class on building a miniature rocket ship. Other children attend summer academies sponsored by NASA or do diverse activities such as exploring archeological or geological sites. They are learning while they are having fun. Enrichment programs just about run the gamut, and can include music, art, dance, gymnastics, or whatever talents your children possess. If we help our children develop their interests and talents, they will do well in life.

Schools offer special programs for the gifted and talented. Unfortunately, Hispanic children are too often excluded from gifted and talented programs and disproportionately placed in special education classes for children who are behind and who have special needs. As a parent, you can insist that your children have every opportunity to participate in these enriching programs. Your children deserve and have a right to be included. Also, understand that if the school is trying to deny your child participation in these courses, you have recourses that you can take. I knew a young Hispanic girl who had an IQ of 170 and was denied entrance to an accelerated class, even after her father had her tested at his own expense. He took the matter to the school superintendent and finally to the local school board to get his daughter into the school's advanced programs. She later graduated with honors from an Ivy League university. This example illustrates why parents have to advocate for their children and demand that they be treated fairly and given equal access to a quality education.

Question teachers and administrators if your children are categorized and labeled or not placed in a program appropriate to their potential and needs. While so-called "resource programs" or "special education" programs are good for special-needs children who have some kind of disability, too many Hispanic children are often inappropriately put into these classes without adequate testing. If your child has a learning disorder, like dyslexia, the school should provide special support. If he does not know English well, it is important that he be placed in a bilingual program that uses his language to make the transition to English and to help him learn the other subjects like math and science in his native language until he learns English. If he starts school academically behind, get actively involved in his schooling. Tutor him yourself, find other tutors, or enroll him in special programs that can help him catch up. When our children are placed in special classes, which happens too often, eventually they can drop out of school altogether. Today, almost half of Hispanic youth drop out of school. Of those who graduate, only 10 percent of Hispanics go on to finish college. Parents play a vital role in changing these troubling statistics from before a child enters school and continues throughout his formal education.

Becoming Partners in the Education Process: *Compañeros en la Educación*

As I mentioned earlier, parents should get to know their child's teacher. It is crucial that you let each of them know that you care and are very concerned about your child's educational achievement. Attend Open Houses and parent-teacher conferences and volunteer for special activities and events. Become partners in the education process. Tell your child's teachers that you expect them to let you know about any problems or concerns immediately after they arise so that you want to help your child deal with any academic or behavioral problems. Doing so will make teachers think twice before they "track" your children, give up on them, treat them unfairly, affect their self-confidence, or damage their self-esteem. I used to tell my children's teacher straight out at the beginning, "My children are very special to me and I want to do what I can to help them succeed in school. Let me know what I can do to help you help them succeed in school." These are statements all parents should feel comfortable saying to those who share the responsibility of educating *nuestros niños*.

When I was working on my Ph.D., I was appalled to hear a college professor in a language course tell my class that Hispanic mothers do not speak to their children and that we as teachers had to respect this silence as part of the culture. As the only Hispanic in the class, I informed the professor that my mother spoke to me a great deal, as do many Hispanic parents I know. "Even if it were true," I said, "which it isn't, as educators, don't you think that it is important to teach parents about their important role as teachers, especially when it comes to language acquisition and learning? Don't you think we should help parents help their children, especially during the critical period when language and learning is most easily acquired?" She responded by saying, "I am quoting this book." (The book was written by an Anglo, who knew little about our culture. It was then that I realized how important it was for Hispanics to write and speak out about our culture and write about our special needs.)

Afterward, a student in the class, who was a teacher by profession, thanked me for my comments. She told me that for the same reasons given to her by our misinformed professor, she had missed opportunities to tell Hispanic parents what they needed to do to help their children in class. She said, "I feel so bad because some Hispanic parents have come to me and asked me if there was anything they could do to help their children. I hesitated to tell them because of what this professor had taught us. I knew better, but I wanted to respect their culture. I am glad that you spoke up." For my class project, which was going to determine a major part of our grade, I took some videotapes of Avance mothers, all Latinas, playing with their children and talking and teaching them concepts with toys they had made in class. I wanted to make a point that at Avance, we teach Hispanic parents the importance of speaking to their children, especially when they are very young, and to let the students see that Hispanic mothers do in fact speak to their children. The students graded each other's work, which was the basis for the project grade. Although I received A's from the students, I received a B in the course. Oh well, ¡Hice mi punto! I had to make my point regardless of the consequences. Planteé las cuestiones y dejé en claro las respuestas. I asked the questions and I made it obvious and clear what the answers were.

Again, I can't stress enough the importance of getting to know your children's teacher. Hispanics, like many groups, respect authority figures, especially our children's teachers. We need to be sensitive to the fact, however, that some teachers, quite frankly, are not qualified for the teaching profession. While most teachers are dedicated and talented, some of them can hurt our children by their lack of concern or sensitivity. When I was a first-grade teacher, one of my colleagues forced three Hispanic children to eat on the floor during lunch as punishment for passing food from one tray to the other. That same teacher threw one of my former students against a wall, causing her to fall into a wastebasket, only because she would go to my classroom to read to me after school. I complained to the principal and then made the little girl's parents aware of what had happened to their daughter. I told them that they should go to the school to advocate for their child, because what the teacher did was wrong. What the teacher did was inappropriate behavior. I was surprised when her father tried to give me excuses for not wanting to go. He told me, "*Mi esposa y yo nunca hemos entrado a la escuela. No hablamos inglés. No tenemos ropa apropriada para ir a la escuela.*" He explained that he and his wife had never gone to the school, they did not speak English, and they did not have the "proper clothes" to go to the school. I explained to the father that it did not matter how he expressed himself or what he wore, but what was most important was that he show up to defend his daughter. He agreed to go. I was so proud of him when he filed a complaint against the teacher the next day. Many years later, when she was in high school, this man's daughter called to tell me she would never forget the day that her father and I came to her aid. Again, let me reiterate, while there are many good teachers, there are some, unfortunately, who are not, and should not be teaching. Therefore, make it a point to know your children's teachers.

It is important that you get involved in your child's education and know what is happening in the school. Each day, when your child comes home from school, ask him to tell you one good thing and one bad thing that happened to him in school. One day when I asked my son this question, I was shocked at his response. Sal's teacher, I discovered, had been keeping him in the hall during class for two weeks without my knowledge. The school year had just started. I describe how I dealt with this situation in the section on Discrimination. Teacher training programs should help teachers become aware of their hidden biases, because their prejudices may surface and negatively affect *nuestros niños.*

PEER PRESSURE NOT TO SUCCEED: *DIME CON QUIÉN ANDAS, Y TE DIRÉ QUIÉN ERES*

You may have grown up hearing this *dicho,* Tell me who you hang around with, and I will tell you who you are. Your parents knew that you would be positively or negatively influenced by the company you keep. In the *dichos Acompáñate con los buenos y serás uno de ellos*, If you hang around with good people, you will be like them, and *El que anda entre la miel, algo se le pega*, your parents desired that you hang around with good people so that something good would stick. But when they said, *El que anda por malos caminos, levanta malos polvos*, they were telling you that your attitudes and performance were going to be negatively influenced by those around you that they did not approve of.

Throughout the ages, parents have desired that their children have friends who possess the values they want for them. One value that parents hold dear in the United States is academic achievement. However, research shows that some Hispanic and African-American youth resist doing well academically because of peer pressure. They have the erroneous belief that only nonminority white children are to do well in school and if they strive to succeed, their Hispanic friends might think that they are rejecting them in order to fit in with the "Anglo crowd." You need to assure your children and their friends that they are just as smart as any other child and that they have the potential to do well. Invite your children's friends to come to your house more often so that you can, in a subtle way, encourage and help their friends to succeed in school, also.

One way to combat the effects of negative peer pressure is to ask a successful person whom you know and respect to become your child's mentor. They don't need to spend more than a few hours a month to make an impression on your *niño*. If the chemistry is right, your child will aspire to be like that person and will learn more about what it takes to become successful. Maggie Comer, the single mother of well-known Yale psychiatrist James Comer, used to launder a medical doctor's shirts in exchange for the doctor's agreement to mentor her son. The young Comer hung around the doctor's office and simply talked to him about life. And what a difference it made! You, too, can find an appropriate mentor for your children to help them succeed. In Chapter Three, I mentioned many professional organizations that stand ready to help your children.

Nuestros niños need role models who value education, beginning with you. If your child sees you reading and making an effort to continue your own education, you will be teaching her the value of learning and of academic achievement. Take her with you to the college campus library if you are attending college. While the values you tried to impart at home will be challenged, they will probably not be changed by negative peer pressure if you maintain a positive relationship with your children, if they receive guidance from mentors, and if they continue to hear the words of wisdom that have guided Hispanics through the ages.

CONFLICT IN TEACHING AND LEARNING STYLES

In an often cited study of Hispanic children, two well-known researchers, Manuel Ramírez and Alfred Castañeda, concluded that Hispanic children reared according to traditional principles such as respect for authority displayed what has been called "field-dependent" cognitive styles. Traditional Hispanic societies, they said, adhere to certain characteristics:

1. A belief in the role of supernatural forces in the creation of the universe. What this means is that religion, faith, and spiritual beliefs still very strongly influence the way Hispanic families see themselves and others.

2. An identification of self in relation to family, tribe, religion, ethnic or racial group. We value and are loyal to family, community, and to our ethnic group.

3. A loyalty to hierarchical social structures in which the authority is designated by age, birthright, or position in the family or group. From a very young age the child shows respect to those in authority, whether it is the *abuelito*, mother, father, or older brother. While the father is "*el quien manda*," he is assigned a lesser role when his mother enters the room. The honor and respect that she commands from all may then shift to her husband when he walks into the room.

"Field-sensitive or field-dependent cognitive [learning or thinking] styles," as Ramírez and Castañeda explain it, are characterized by a strong connection to interpersonal relationships. According to this theory, learning requires a high degree of personal interaction and involvement in communication. "Field-dependent" children prefer social rewards and have a tendency to focus on the global aspect of ideas and problems. Generally speaking, traditional Hispanics are very sensitive people. Body language and cues are as important as words. We care about how people feel and how they are going to be affected by what we say and do.

Manuel Ramírez, who also studied the dynamics of classrooms in which Mexican-American students were taught by non-Hispanic teachers, found that most teachers displayed more impersonal tendencies than their students. Other studies showed that some teachers perceived students who mirrored their own style more favorably and gave better grades to these students than to students whose learning style was different.

Schultz, Florio, and Erickson in their 1980 research study found different teaching styles between Hispanic teachers and Anglo teachers. In the Anglo teacher classroom, the children were "encouraged to work independently, individual achievement was rewarded by the adult, a slight distance was maintained in the teacher-child relationship, and competition among the children was utilized to motivate success." In contrast, the Hispanic teachers "called the children by pet names, often hugging and kissing them and holding them on their laps during lessons." These teachers encouraged the children to appreciate each other's achievements and the class was less competitive.

Parents must be aware that conflicts in learning and teaching styles between Hispanic students with traditional values and non-Hispanic teachers may hinder their child's success. Traditional classrooms designed with chairs arranged in straight rows in which children are rewarded for being competitive, individualistic, and aggressive may conflict with a child raised in an environment that reinforces cooperation, respect, group loyalty, and sensitivity. Hispanic children in such situations may feel rejected and can eventually perceive themselves in negative terms, which leads to low self-esteem. It is important that children have teachers that they can relate to and identify with in the classroom.

Young people who are reared in nontraditional cultures referred to as "field independent" may prefer an impersonal, formal style in communicating with others. Field independent people rely heavily on sophisticated information systems. Their communication tends to be more technical, less dependent on personal ties, and more dependent on procedures for working through systems. The world of a field independent person is characterized by (1) a perspective of the universe as a creation of natural forces which can be rationally explained by science; (2) an identity that is more individualistic and supersedes loyalty to family, community, group, or religion; and (3) social institutions organized according to principles of democracy and egalitarianism.

Eventually we should try to have our children be bilingual, bicultural, and bi-cognitive. In the United States, some Hispanics have felt pressure to choose one set of values over the other so that their children can succeed in school and in life. You play an important role in helping your children to value themselves and their culture, family, and ethnicity. You need to make your children aware of the differences between languages, values, and cognitive styles by helping them understand that they are unique and special. As Latinos we are different because we will be able to possess two cultures to fulfill our lives, and depending on the situation, we can switch from one culture to the other or combine them. Similarly, our children should grow up learning to operate in two cultures. *Nuestros niños* do not need to reject their language, values, culture, or cultural styles to succeed in school or to be part of mainstream America. On the contrary, Hispanic values will enable our children to succeed in a multicultural environment where divisions are sometimes too common and cooperation is in short supply. Our Hispanic values and worldview should be reinforced in our children. I believe that this world would be a better place if more people possessed values shared by Hispanics like respect, cooperation, sensitivity, and reverence for family, community, and spirituality.

We need to teach our children to respect diversity and to respect each person's beliefs, even if they are different from our own. It is also important that our children watch us associate with different ethnic groups and with traditional and nontraditional Hispanics. We must teach our children to be flexible and adaptable to different people in different situations. We need to help them be socially competent and be able to function well in many social settings.

Just as parents can help a child accommodate in a traditional classroom environment, schools should try harder to accommodate the needs of Hispanics. Teacher-training programs must prepare educators to respond to Hispanics' needs, communicate with our children in a sensitive, interpersonal manner, and participate in group activities. In the classroom, too often knowledge is introduced without being connected to the child's background and culture. In learning, it is critical that all new information be connected to previous knowledge or experiences. Class lessons should include cultural activities and images with which children can identify.

Volunteer to assist in teaching the Hispanic culture by singing a song or playing an instrument, teaching a game, cooking, or doing a craft. Schools should also realize the importance of the *familia*—parents, grandparents, extended family, and the community—and make them feel welcome in the schools. They should have programs in which family members can come to watch their children participate. As a schoolteacher, I helped to make inexpensive and colorful costumes for the children in my class to wear when they performed "La Raspa" and other traditional Hispanic songs and dances at PTA meetings. We sent out personal invitations to family members so that they could watch their children perform. Never before had so many parents attended a PTA meeting, which also included the children's *abuelitos, tíos, y tías*.

Sometimes our children will be punished because of cultural differences. Remember the episode in which my colleague made three Hispanic children eat on the floor because they were sharing their food? This could have been attributed to a culture clash between the value of sharing and "taking care of number one." As one of eight children in the family, I always shared my food with my siblings. Children should not be humiliated or rejected for their values and beliefs.

Knowing how to behave and to respect authority is ingrained in our culture. Parents want their children to be *bien educados*, a trait that has more to do with manners and knowing how to behave. *"Pórtate bien"* a Hispanic parent tells her child as he heads to school. For the child this may mean respect the teacher and do not look at her directly and do not ask questions, which are exactly the opposite of what the field-independent teacher expects from children.

Hispanic parents should understand that our children live in two worlds that do not have to be mutually exclusive. While there may be differences between the values taught at home and those in schools, one is not better than the other; both incorporate important virtues. Although Hispanic children are taught the value of respect for elders and for authority, this does not mean that they should not be allowed to express their opinions. Our country is built on the premise that people have the right to question and to express their beliefs. This is true for parents as well as for children. That is why we have to encourage our children to think, judge, analyze, question, and express their opinions. When our children say, "It's not fair, I want to say what I think," let them do it. I used to tell my children, "Yes, you can express your opinions, but it is important that you do it in a respectful manner. I will be more receptive to what you have to say if you say it in a polite way. Convince me, give me a good reason, and build a good case for why I should change my mind and do what you desire." Needless to say, I did not have to prod Steven, the "lawyer," from having his say. He always had a position and would hold steadfast to his beliefs. On numerous occasions, our children have convinced my husband and me to change our minds on certain issues.

Sometimes people who are not familiar with our culture may misinterpret our silence, kindness, and friendliness as a sign of weakness. Parents need to prepare their children to associate with people who are not able to leave their own cultural world and be accepting of different cultural styles. I once told my children of an incident in which I had to change my facial expression and tone of voice in order to more effectively communicate with a person who began to get too assertive and rude. When I did, the person realized that strength does not always come from being aggressive. However, I was able to adapt to the situation and adjust my communication style to a more formal and more assertive one so that the person would alter her behavior. As Hispanics, we must help our children to be able to move in and out of both worlds.

Like parents, schools have a role in preparing children to live in a harmonious, peaceful, and democratic world, as well as to prepare them for the world of work. For many years, schools have prepared children for the labor force by encouraging individualistic, competitive, and aggressive behavior. However, in business, working cooperatively in groups, as they do in Japan, for example, can be just as profitable. Sensitivity to others, positive interpersonal skills, and teamwork are essential leadership qualities. We want our children to be proud of the beautiful cultural values that they bring to the school and take with them into the world of work.

SYMBOLS AND LOGIC: *DE OPINIONES A VALORES—* 11 YEARS OLD TO ADULT

The last phase of cognitive development is when knowledge is acquired and structured symbolically and logically. During this stage, a child is able to handle abstract concepts such as hypotheses, theories, judgment, and more complex mathematical functions. He has become more critical about situations and is able to consider various outcomes before they happen. By isolating different aspects of the problem, he can then come up with the best solution or course of action. By adolescence, children are able to analyze political and philosophical positions as well as social conditions around them.

They have an opinion for everything. This stage marks a time when children really begin expressing their points of view and ideals. All of a sudden, you will hear your child tell you that you are wearing the wrong kind of clothes or that your car is too old and the wrong color. They are so concerned about what others think that they may demand that you leave them two blocks away from school so as not to risk being seen "dropped off" by their mothers or in that old clunker. At my house, we used this assertiveness to encourage our children to examine social issues. We would ask them their thoughts about policies on immigration, the "English Only" movement, Affirmative Action, bilingual education, welfare reform, and other current topics that affect Hispanics. At this age, children like to plan, judge, and solve problems. This is the perfect time for them to get involved in church and youth activities and to do community service. Through these activities, they will begin to develop leadership skills as they get involved in planning, organizing, and delegating.

Children during this period will begin to challenge your values and beliefs. I remember being confronted by questions that began with, "What if...," or "What would you do if I..." Some of the things my children came up with were totally against the values that we had taught them. It seemed that they were testing my husband and me to see if we really believed in and practiced what we preached.

After you have made sure that your children know where you stand on certain issues, you should help your children clarify their values. Keep probing to see how they feel about different issues and circumstances. What would they do if they were in a certain situation? What are their beliefs in certain areas? Issues such as sex, drugs, smoking, alcoholism, guns, and discrimination need to be discussed openly. According to recent behavioral studies, 31 percent of young people aged ten to fourteen years are drinking and 23 percent of eight graders have tried marijuana. According to the Texas Hispanic Youth Health Assessment conducted by Avance and released in 1998, 15 percent of Hispanic youth in grades nine to twelve smoke. The average age that children begin smoking is 12.7 years. In the area of sex, 45 percent of Hispanics under the age of seventeen reported having sex, and yet only 45 percent used condoms during their most recent sexual experience. In the same survey, Hispanics were more likely to use crack and freebase cocaine in grades nine to twelve than any other ethnic groups at that age, and 9.4 percent of Hispanic eighth-graders used inhalants one month before the survey was administered, also higher than any other ethnic group.

Indeed the study underscored the need for parents to be vigilant and society to support parents in providing mentors, more positive activities, and educational and mental health services for their children. You need to let your children know where you stand on these issues and why. Talk to them about the effects that television and uncontrolled access to the Internet have on sexual behavior. Tell them why you have to monitor their television viewing, and install controlling devices on the television and on your computer. Stage role-playing sessions on how they would handle a particular situation, such as what they would do if they were offered drugs, encouraged to have sex, or to join a gang. They can practice how they would respond if confronted with numerous difficult situations. The consequences of making bad choices can have devastating consequences. Some popular board games like Life and Scruples are good at helping children think about making the right choices in life. These games really made my children think about their values and the consequences of their actions. Research tells us that the best predictor for children saying no to drugs, drinking, sex, and gangs is if they have a strong relationship with the family. As parents, we need to be very vigilant during these inquisitive and risk-taking years. Set the limits and keep repeating what you feel is right and wrong so that eventually that inner voice in your child's head will take over and make the right choices.

This is a challenging time for parents, but it should also be a pleasurable, joyful time as we watch our children move closer to adulthood and settle into their own identities. As your children begin to approach twelve years of age, you can expect to be questioned about what you did when you were their age. Sometimes your responses may spark an uproarious argument. It can be tough, especially for Hispanics who really value *respeto*. Building a strong moral foundation and a healthy parent-child relationship will help you continue to be firm in your convictions while learning to be flexible and yet understanding. You will hear things like, "Nobody does this," or "Everybody does that." I used to respond to my children by saying, "Yes, but you are not just *anybody*. You are *special*, and that is why I am telling you to do this (or not to do that), because I care." After I would give them reasons why, I would end it with: "*¡Punto final!*" Case closed! Many times, they already knew the answer, but they wanted to test the consistency of my answers.

As they mature in their logical and analytical thinking, children begin to work at self-control and develop morals and values that they will take with them through life. I find myself repeating my mother's words when I say "*¡Esteban, no te descompongas!*" Don't lose control! Sometimes, when he's wrestling with an issue or problem, I catch him saying to himself, "*No te descompongas, Esteban.*" The rewards of parenthood are to have each of your children grow to become responsible, self-controlled, morally competent, and compassionate individuals. They will eventually do what they have come to learn is the right thing to do. During this stage, children will find themselves at a critical fork in the road.

Everything that you as a responsible parent do for each of your *niños*, to prepare and provide the right kind of learning and nurturing environment during the first twelve years of life, will enable them to take the right path to academic success and proper social functioning. You are the first teacher and there will never be a more important teacher in the life of your children than you. The time, energy, and resources that you provide for each of your children will influence the kind of student, parent, worker, and citizen they will become in the future. Your love, commitment, and effort will bear much fruit for generations to come.

Chapter VI

Social and Emotional Needs of Children

El Niño Bien Educado/Amor a Manos Llenas.

El árbol que crece torcido, nunca su tronco endereza. When a tree grows crooked, no one will ever be able to straighten its trunk. I often think of this *dicho* when I consider the impact of the first years of life on the social and emotional development of a child. How parents interact with their young child, how they teach, love, guide, set limits will have a big influence on her self-esteem, character, behavior, and interpersonal skills later. As the child gets older, these attributes are harder to change.

Socialization is the process by which a child learns to interact with other human beings appropriately within a group in different circumstances. Socialization begins in the home and within the family and continues with institutions in the community. The process begins with the development of bonding between parent and child, an attachment through which a child learns *confianza y seguridad,* trust and security. Parents have the primary responsibility to teach their children to become socially competent. Parents lay the foundation for the child's capacity to behave in socially acceptable ways as they teach appropriate behaviors and help their children control disruptive or overly impulsive behavior. Being self-disciplined, putting off gratification, and regulating emotions are important skills necessary for social interaction and social functioning. To be well socialized is to know how to handle setbacks, to communicate effectively, and, ultimately, to show concern for the welfare of others. While institutions like the church, schools, media, and the community at large have a responsibility to reinforce good morals, values, and good social conduct, parents are the primary socializing agents. From the home, parents provide the essential foundation necessary to help their child function successfully *desde la cuna hasta la comunidad*, from the crib to the community.

As mentioned before, Harvard psychologist Howard Gardner states that children are born with multiple intelligences. One of those intelligences is the natural gift of interpersonal skills, the ability to understand people, to discern and respond to their feelings and needs. This gift can be divided into four categories: leadership skills, social analysis skills, personal connection skills, and conflict-resolution skills.

1. A good leader is one who can influence others to do what she wants. She can organize groups of people and motivate them to get things done.

2. Children with good social analysis skills can detect and have insights into people's feelings, motivations, and concerns, a process of building rapport between people.

3. Children who have the ability to nurture relationships and keep friends are those who can empathize and connect with the feelings and concerns of others. They are good at reading social signals such as facial expressions and body language.

4. Children with good negotiating and mediating skills are those who can prevent or resolve conflicts.

But children's inherent social graces may not be able to flourish if their environment does not nurture their development.

A child's social competence is directly linked to her emotional development and vice versa. Her behavior is a reflection of how she feels, her ability to understand, manage, and communicate her feelings as well as interpret and relate to the feelings of others. Even if a child is not endowed with natural social graces, he can learn these social interpersonal skills. Similarly, those children who are naturally outgoing will not always demonstrate these social abilities if they are reared in an environment where they are not emotionally nurtured.

Psychiatrist Stanley Greenspan describes six stages of emotional development in his book *First Feelings: Milestones in the Emotional Development of Your Baby and Child*. Each stage overlaps and builds on the other to create a child who will be better able to relate to different people in different situations. By knowing these stages, you can identify where your child is and assist him along these major milestones. I will present them with a Latino perspective. It will take parents a great deal of patience, understanding, energy, and love to properly guide their child from birth to maturity. It becomes more demanding if they have a child exhibiting extreme traits, for example, the very active and assertive or the very shy and quiet. Successful rearing in these cases will require parents' imagination, resourcefulness, and creativity to mold their children into *niños bien educados*—children who are respectful, considerate, compassionate, and self-disciplined, as well as personable, resilient, adaptable, and self-confident.

GREENSPAN'S STAGES OF EMOTIONAL DEVELOPMENT

STAGE ONE: *CALMADO PARA APRENDER—SELF-REGULATION AND INTEREST IN THE WORLD—BIRTH TO THREE MONTHS*

The first stage of Greenspan's emotional development pertains to the child's ability to regulate his feelings and to become calm and relaxed immediately after birth. After having been in the perfect environment of the womb, where all his needs were automatically met, the baby is abruptly plunged into a world full of noise, sights, tastes, and smells. It is a place where he is now dependent on others for his basic needs. Overwhelmed, the baby's immediate reaction is to tense up and cry. The role of the mother is to calm him down and help him regulate his intense emotions so that he will want to observe and learn what is around him. He has to learn to control what T. Berry Brazelton and Bertrand G. Cramer call his "input and output systems." They must learn in those earliest moments to disregard distracting noises and yet absorb other sensations around them. As they do this, they learn to control muscles, heartbeat, breathing, and reflexes.

The mother plays an important role in making this happen before and after birth. Research shows that a baby can tell the difference between sounds inside and outside the womb and can identify its mother's voice seven days after birth. The relationship with his mother began before he ever saw her. Through her soft, gentle touch and soothing sounds, she can help the newborn make a transition from a protective, warm womb to a safe, secure, loving world.

The role of the father is very important during this time as well. Not only is it important for the father to love and support the mother so that she can perform her maternal role, but he also needs to foster an attachment to the baby by holding, talking, and loving him. When a father talks to the baby in the womb and attends Lamaze classes and prenatal doctor's visits with his wife, he demonstrates that he, too, wants to be intimately involved with his infant, even before birth.

All future relationships are rooted in the interactions that begin with the first person the child meets right out of the womb. Babies have a need to be touched and to be spoken to in a soft caring voice. The studies mentioned earlier of young children in orphanages underscore what can happen when physical needs for things like food, clothing, and shelter are met, but emotional nourishment that comes from talking and touching is not. These children did not develop well, and some even died because they lacked the human touch, *el calor*, the warmth of a person.

Immediately after birth, a mother can establish a bond with her young infant by putting him affectionately to her breast, caressing him and looking into his eyes, smiling, and welcoming him to his exciting new world. Allow your baby to observe his surroundings in the delivery room. Talk to him until his head turns to you and your eyes meet. The baby will recognize your voice, snuggle in your arms, mold his soft body next to yours and then instantly take to your breast, feeling secure in his new environment.

Many years ago, anthropologist David Landy observed that mothers in a Puerto Rican village would swaddle their babies in a cloth hammock called a *coy* and keep them nearby at all times after birth. This provided maximum bonding for baby and mother. Today, whether in a sterile delivery room or in a more relaxed birthing room, mothers can still make the most of the immediate period right after birth to bond with their *bebés*. In the Puerto Rican village that Landy studied, and indeed throughout Latin America, Hispanic mothers have observed the *cuarentena*, the forty days of seclusion that a mother experiences after giving birth. During these crucial days, a new mother is relieved of her duties so that she can rest and bond with her new child while allowing her body to heal. Today, mothers do not observe the *cuarentena* the way Hispanic women did in the past. Yet, this tradition still emphasizes the importance of allowing as much time as possible during the first weeks after giving birth to interact with the child and to help him learn about his body and the world around him.

The first couple of weeks of interacting with the child are crucial in helping him regulate his emotions. Once calm, he becomes attentive to the parents' cues and then uses his facial expressions, vocalizations, hands, feet, or body to bring about a response from his mother. According to Brazelton and Cramer, this rhythmic synchronized reciprocal action between parent and child produces a child's first social smile at the end of the second month. It is a give-and-take-process, where the mother receives cues from the child and then responds with a set of behaviors that continue the exchange. The baby's eyes light up as he coos, smiles, and delights in what the mother does. He then waits for the mother to respond with similar gestures that show her pleasure. When the child turns away, he is telling the mother, *"Ya me cansé,"* I have had enough.

During this first stage, hold your baby in a semiupright position, ten to twelve inches away from your face. Talk to him affectionately using *cariños.* Expose him to a stimulating and enriching environment with bright, sharply contrasting colors, soft, gentle sounds, sweet smells, and slow-moving objects. A baby will have an attention span that will last only a few minutes at a time after birth and then twenty to thirty minutes after two to three weeks. Using the sounds and images of your culture, whether through brightly colored folk art or gentle rhythms of traditional music, you can help your child use his five senses. He can then absorb, respond to, and interact with the different aspects of his surroundings. Children need the right kind of stimulation, not too noisy or too bright. As I mentioned earlier, if an environment is too stimulating, an infant will tune it out or get very upset and cry. Activities that a child might enjoy when he is in a quiet but in an alert state are imitative behaviors, such as making *ojitos* (opening and closing his eyes) or making *burbujas,* bubbles. He will imitate you when you stick out your tongue or open and close your mouth. If both parents are actively involved with their child from the beginning of life, they will both have the opportunity to feel reaffirmed and gratified in knowing that they were successfully influencing their child's development.

STAGE TWO: *ENAMORÁNDOSE*—FALLING IN LOVE— TWO TO SEVEN MONTHS

The second of Greenspan's stages is called "falling in love." This is the stage when an infant radiates and glows at the mere sight of her mother or other caregivers, such as a father or babysitter. This reaction reflects her love as well as her sense of *confianza y seguridad*, competence and security. By the third or fourth month, the child needs to form an attachment to the mother and the mother needs to form an attachment to the child, otherwise, the parent-child relationship and future interpersonal relationships are at risk. When a child's face lights up at the sight of his *mami*, it reaffirms that a healthy and harmonious bond between the parent and child exists.

All children are born with a range of emotions. Even as *recién nacidos*, newborns, they can experience joy, excitement, and satisfaction, as well as sadness, anger, pain, and disappointment. Children will cry when they are scared, hungry, sleepy, or when they have *cólico o empacho*, colic or indigestion. From the baby's first healthy *grito*, or cry, as she emerges from the womb to the heartwarming gazes that follow you around *la cuna*, she is sending social signals to those around her. She may be telling parents that she needs to be fed or diapered, that she wants to be turned over, or *que simplemente quiere que la arrulles en los brazos*, that she simply wants to be cradled in your arms. Through the simple actions of feeding, changing, burping, and rocking, the mother helps the child feel competent in expressing her needs. She establishes a loving relationship with her child that produces beaming smiles and continuous reinforcement of her role as a nurturing, competent parent. As a parent bonds with a child, she makes a very deep, instinctive commitment to continue to nurture the child and be concerned for her welfare.

A parent cannot possibly spoil an infant at this young age with too much attention. Babies need you to smile, cuddle, kiss, caress, and speak to them in a soft and gentle voice. Of all the things in the environment that a child will see, hear, and smell, she becomes most attracted to the individual *que le da mucho cariño*, the one who lovingly responds to her needs and desires. Through this interactive process, during which a mother and child take turns responding to and stimulating each other, *el amor brota*, love emerges. When you shower your baby with *cariños*, with warm *abrazos*, and the sweet words of affection that seem to flow from a Latin mother's lips like: "*¡Ay qué linda, mi amorcito!*" Oh, how gorgeous my love! she can't help but fall in love with you. *Cuando la arrullas*, when you rock her to sleep with the sweet sounds of traditional lullabies, you are touching *su corazón y alma*, her heart and soul. Very popular lullabies that have already been mentioned in Chapter Five are "*Señora Santa Ana*" and "*A la Rurru Niño*." The following lullaby, *A la Rorro Niño*, found in *Juegos Infantiles* by Yolanda de Campo y Conjunto de Carlos Oropeza, was arranged by Tío Nando and interpreted by Evangelina Elizondo. This song is an adaptation of "*Señora Santa Ana*" and "A la Rurru Niño." Tish Hinojosa did the same in her tape called *Cada Niño*. Even you can create your own lullaby by combining parts of one lullaby and adding your own creativity.

A La Rorro Niño

Duérmete mi niño, duérmete mi amor.
Duérmete pedazo de mi corazón.
Este niño lindo, que nació de noche,
Quiere que lo lleven a pasear en coche.

Señora Santa Ana, ¿Por qué llora el niño?
Por una manzana que se la ha perdido.
Yo le daré una. Yo le daré dos.
Una para el niño, y otra para vos.
Sh sh sh.

Duérmete Mi Niño

The lyrics to another popular Puerto Rican lullaby illustrate the warm bonds of affection that mothers build with their little ones through their words:

Duérmete, mi niño, duérmete, mi sol,
duérmete, pedazo de mi corazón
Este niño lindo, se quiere dormir
háganle la cama, en el toronjil
Y de cabecera, pónganle un jazmín
para que se duerma como un serafín.

Sleep my child, sleep, my sunshine,
Sleep, little piece of my heart
This beautiful child wants to sleep
Make his bed in the orange grove
And on his pillow, place a jasmine
So he can sleep like a cherub.

Many mothers, myself included, have put their babies to sleep with the traditional English lullaby "Hush, Little Baby," even though the words are not as loving as the Spanish ones above.

Hush Little Baby

Hush, little baby, don't say a word,
Papa's going to buy you a mockingbird.
And if that mockingbird won't sing,
Papa's going to buy you a diamond ring.
If that diamond ring turns to brass,
Papa's going to buy you a looking glass.
If that looking glass gets broke,
Papa's going to buy you a billy goat.
If that billy goat won't pull,
Papa's going to buy you a cart and bull.
If that cart and bull turns over,
Papa's going to buy you a dog named Rover.
If that dog named Rover won't bark,
Papa's going to buy you a horse and cart.
If that horse and cart fall down,
You'll still be the sweetest baby in town!

Amparo Ortiz, a mother from Colombia, used to sing the following
two songs to her children to put them to bed:

Niñito Jesús, sal del copón
Da un brinquito y ven a mi corazón.
Ángel de la guardia, mi dulce compañía,
No me desampares, ni de noche ni de día.
Hasta que me ponga en paz y alegría
Con todos los Santos, Jesús, y María.

Baby Jesus, come out of the chalice
Take a jump and come into my heart.
Guardian Angel, my sweet companion
Don't leave me, neither by night nor day
Until I am in peace and happy
With all the Saints, Jesus, and Mary.

Antón Tiruliruliru

Duérmete, niño chiquito
Que la noche viene ya,

Cierra pronto tus ojitos,
Que el viento te arrullará.

Jesús al pesebre
Vamos a adorar,
Antón Tirulirula
Antón Tiruliruliru

Duérmete, niño chiquito.
Que la madre velará,
Cierra pronto tus ojitos,
Porque la entristecerás.

When Hispanics describe the affection that a parent feels for a child, some call it *amor a manos llenas*, two hands full of love, the maximum that a person can hold. Although we parents have many unique terms to describe our love, like when we refer to our loved ones as *mi vida, mi cielo, mi alma, mi corazón, y mi luna de miel*, we can also show our love in countless other ways. Everyday scenarios present parents with opportunities to fulfill emotional needs, beginning in the crib and continuing throughout adolescence. Dr. Urie Bronfenbrenner of Cornell University once said that each child needs to have at least one person to be *absolutamente loco*, extremely crazy, about him. An infant feels *la expresión de cariño*, the expression of love, by the special things that are said or done for him, like providing relief to sore gums or caressing *el cabello suave*, the soft hair on his little head, after a bath or holding him on your lap when you read. We as parents cannot take for granted that our children know that we love them. We must say it constantly and continue to show our love *con palabras y acciones*, with words and actions. *Las acciones afectuosas*, the kind acts that we do for our children, will continue when we celebrate their *cumpleaños* or when we celebrate our *tradiciones*, such as *la Navidad, Día de los Tres Reyes*, and *Día de Pascuas*. These events will stay with them always. As the years go on, your love for your *niños* will be demonstrated by the nights you stay up making Halloween costumes, that special dress, or caring for them when they are sick. When a mother and father, *con su amor tierno*, with their tender love, take care of sensitive itchy skin, a nasty cold, or a bothersome gas bubble, they turn cranky babies into *niños agradecidos*, who show their thanks with smiles de *oreja a oreja*, from ear to ear.

My husband and I loved watching our children play sports, participate in their school plays, or at recitals. Spending such special moments with your children is the best way to demonstrate your love for them. Listen to them. Ask them questions. Look into their *ojitos lindos*, their lovely eyes, as they speak.

A child will not be able to give something she does not have. If she has not received *el amor*, she cannot give it to others. It is very difficult to treat someone with affection or to be kind and considerate if one has not experienced these acts from others. But if a child is loved, cared for, and nurtured, then it will be easy for her later in life to return love to you and to others. Love is reciprocal and contagious. You can experience *el cariño del niño*, not only with the joyous giggles that erupt from a game of Peekaboo or *el caballito*, but also with *un abrazo bien fuerte*, a big bear hug. You will see your child's *agradecimiento* and appreciation when she gives you wildflowers con *un besito cariñoso*. Her intense and emotional feelings can also be felt as she gently caresses your face, *cuando te acaricia la cara suavemente*. You will see it when she turns to look at you con *una sonrisa gozosa* right before she hits the grand slam homerun or when her sparkling eyes meet yours right after a piano recital. It has been said that the eyes are the windows to the soul. Children who feel loved radiate confidence, happiness, and a zest for life. They feel a sense of *seguridad y confianza and compasión y alegría* that will enable them to reach out to others con *cariño*.

One of the most beautiful symbols of the lasting bonds of affection in Hispanic families is the care and attention that children devote to their parents when they are elderly and frail. Because of the strong *cariño* that Hispanic parents gave their children when they were young, it is reciprocated when they become adults. In many Hispanic families, you will find a grandparent living with one or more generations of kin. It is generally not a common practice to place our elderly parents in nursing homes.

Folktales are a way of reinforcing behaviors we value and want repeated. The folktale "*La Nuera*," "The Daughter-in-Law," in Paulette Atencio's *Cuentos from My Childhood*, illustrates how the cycle of reciprocal love continues from one generation to the next. In the story, a young child teaches his parents about the importance of upholding their promise to take care of their parents in their older age. When the mother wants her father-in-law out of the house, the boy gives his mother and father a vision of how he, in turn, plans to treat them when they get older by building a bed for them made of an old cot and tattered blankets. Then he sets two cracked wooden bowls on an old table. At this, the parents remember the *dicho*, "*Joven eres y viejo serás, según lo hiciste, así lo verás*," Young you are and old you will be, what you've done will be done to you, which makes them cry and ask the grandfather for forgiveness for wanting him out of the house. They vow never to treat him *sin respeto* again, for they found out that there is some truth to the *dicho, Si respetas a tus mayores, te respetan tus menores.*

My mother and uncle took turns caring for my grandfather Papayo in their homes when he got older until his death. I admire Latinos who, *con ternura y cariño,* with tenderness, hold their aging *mamitas* by the arm as they take them places or when they make a big *borlote* for them on their birthdays and Mother's Day. I would take my mother on some of my out-of-town business trips. I will never forget one trip, in particular, to New York. My mother and I laughed so hard as we held on to each other to keep from falling as we skidded on the icy sidewalks, mesmerized by the beautiful holiday decorations and by the soft snowflakes that gently fell on us. Now that my *mamá* is approaching her eighties, all of her daughters take turns taking her out to eat, shopping, or to search for bargains at her favorite pastime—garage sales. Once a year I take time to have a garage sale at my house where she is able to sell everything she has bought at other garage sales for three times what she paid. Her continuous presence in our children's lives has enriched our families as she constantly imparts words of wisdom regarding their behavior or their respect for God. Our strong bond comes from the early interactions and the loving acts that my mother imparted throughout my youth.

STAGE THREE: *HÁBLAME*—DEVELOPING COMMUNICATION— THREE TO TEN MONTHS

This is the stage when interaction with the human world becomes more purposeful. After a child establishes his *primer amor verdadero,* first true love, he can now become interested in establishing relationships with others. During this stage, you continue to play an important role in teaching him the process of communication, where the child and the parent take turns speaking and listening. This is the period of reciprocal interaction, when you and he will repeat each other's sounds, figure out respective cues, and learn that a certain action or expression produces a reaction. Try to be responsive to his signals by following his interest.

As human beings, children also have a broad range of *emociones,* from *felicidad,* pride, and *orgullo* to sadness, *celos,* and anger. Children will experience these and many other emotions throughout their lives. By three months, children begin to experiment with a variety of emotions and they are somewhat capable of calming themselves down. During this stage, a child begins to realize that his mother will not be able to respond to all his needs all of the time. When you do not read your child's cues correctly or don't give him what he wants, he will let you know it through his emotional weapons, like screaming, or exploding into *corajes or rabietas*.

The home is the training ground for teaching our children how to deal effectively with negative feelings and learn to behave so that they will not to be labeled as *malcriados*. It is in the home where they will begin to control their emotions. Children must experiment with emotions in a safe and loving environment if they are to know how to respond to them in future social settings. Do not deny your children your love and attention when they are exploring their feelings. Do not be overprotective, overcontrolling, or passive at these times. When your *niño* gets into his sibling's possessions, divert his attention to something more interesting or to an activity that will produce joy through movement.

Hispanics label someone *grosero*, *malcriado*, *o mal educado* if he lacks the proper social skills to interact well with people. This deficiency can be traced to the first months of life, when his emotional cues and his desire to communicate were left unanswered. This has great implications for working parents of young infants, as they must not only make time to interact intimately with their children, but also make sure that their children are in a quality child care center with warm, nurturing caregivers who will communicate affectionately with your child. Someone must take the time to effectively interact with your child, help him experience the joy of communication, and learn that he can have an impact in the world.

As stated earlier, children whose smiles, requests, and demands are consistently ignored will eventually give up and cease to interact with others. Even if you and your child's other caregivers are not always correctly reading your child's signals, or responding to his cues, as long as you do it most of the time, he will learn that he can have an effect on people. Not all babies have the same emotional needs. For a baby who is very active and emotional, it is important that a parent spend the time needed to calm him down and get his attention before interaction begins. Eventually the child will be able to regulate his own emotions. For the child that is *tímido y reservado*, shy and reserved, it will take more creativity to draw him out of his shell. A child needs to *enamorarse*, fall in love, with someone who will spark emotions of joy, satisfaction, and excitement. This person must respond to his feelings of sadness, disappointment, and pain. In Chapter Five, I included games, rhymes, and strategies that will help you spend precious moments with your child during this very important period. Remember that the rules in general are simple: talk to your children, play with them, and love them.

STAGE FOUR: EL SURGIMIENTO DE UNA CONCIENCIA DE SÍ MISMO— THE EMERGENCE OF AN ORGANIZED SENSE OF SELF—NINE TO EIGHTEEN MONTHS

This is the stage when behavior becomes organized. During this stage, the child's behavior becomes more complex and organized, more deliberate and "out-of-bounds." This is a very trying period as children realize that they are separate, unique individuals who are distinct from other people and objects. By eight months of age, the child enters the "separation anxiety" stage as she realizes that her mother is separate from her and becomes anxious when she is not there. She may cry the moment her *mami* is out of sight. Before this stage, the "out of sight, out of mind" principle applies.

Throughout this period, a child will have a great need to explore and experiment. This is the time when she is very expressive. If your child is angry, she will not only cry, she will hit, throw, whine, and kick. Her love is not only expressed with glowing smiles, it emerges with hugs, kisses, and gentle pinches. She begins to understand that her caregivers have different roles and that they have authority. This is an important time for Hispanic parents to divide responsibilities and time with the child so that she does not simply identify *mami* alone as the nurse, cook, playmate, and chauffeur. Both parents can take care of hurts with *un beso* or with the loving rhyme *Sana, sana, colita de rana, si no sana ahora, sanará mañana*. Through observation, your child also learns that things have different functions as well. Rattling of *las llaves*, rattling the keys, means "let's go," and the ringing of the *teléfono* means someone is wanting to talk on the other end. If she brings a diaper, it means she needs to be changed, or if she brings a bottle, she is telling you she is hungry. All of these observations will be used in getting her needs met and in her imaginary play later.

In this stage, a child learns to connect small units of feelings and social behavior into larger, complicated, orchestrated patterns. Through this more organized behavior, she will initiate activities on her own, create things, and express herself in unique ways. She begins to detach from her parents to explore her surroundings, as long as she can maintain a sense of *seguridad* from her parents by being able to see and hear them close by. During this time, a child can figure out how to get her parents to do what she wants by combining her motor skills with other senses, like when she points to an object that excites her. Her lack of mastery will produce frustration and anger. On the other hand, her ability to master things such as walking, stacking, or being understood will produce pride, satisfaction, and a sense of confidence.

Children at this age can drive their parents crazy as they explore a repertoire of emotions. At times, they are sweet, kind, and playful, and at other times angry and *necios*. Making children happy is important, but not at the expense of their safety, well-being, and development. Children's "out-of-bounds" behavior needs to be controlled. Parents must set the limits and the boundaries on what they consider appropriate behavior. They must immediately and consistently express their displeasure at what they consider unacceptable. Remember what curiosity did to the *gato*? Be ever vigilant of their whereabouts during their daily exploits in and out of the house.

If you want to keep your child from engaging in negative behavior, use Greenspan's "eyeball-to-eyeball" technique. Look your child straight in the eye with an air of *disgusto*, displeasure. Tell her "no" in a firm way and shake your head. Lower your head, purse your lips together and raise one eyebrow. When a mother *levanta la ceja* and looks a child straight in the eye, it gets her attention. Be firm and consistent. Eventually your child will get the idea that you are serious and you intend to control her behavior if she can't.

Each of Greenspan's stages builds on the previous ones. So that limits can be more readily set by regulating your child's emotions, calm her down, get her attention, and help her focus on your signals while maintaining an emotional attachment. Your child will accept your rules and values easier if they are presented in an atmosphere of love and security. Even if she gets upset when you place limits on television or you make her go to bed at a certain time, she can remain emotionally attached to you if you work at keeping that relationship strong. After she has calmed down, try to reconcile with her and then try to maintain the doors of communication open to keep the relationship strong.

Use parentese, the soft parental language, to communicate that you empathize with your child's hurt feelings. Be understanding and empathetic regarding her feelings. Mirror her feelings by expressing what you think she is feeling: "Oh, you are so upset because you don't want to take a bath. I know you'd rather play, but all of us have to take a bath every day. Where is your *patito*? Let's get your *patito*. He wants to play with you." "We do not tear books. Books are for reading, and we must take care of books. We cannot read a book if it is torn. Let's tape it up."

In families where emotions are not nurtured, children and parents can fall into *mal humor*, a pouting and silent mood, which communicates that one is hurt by another's actions. This resentment can build up and explode in other unacceptable ways. It is up to the mature parent to help the child cool down, reengage her, and turn the negative situation into a positive one by *acariciándola*, cuddling, or distracting her. Your child will be more receptive to what you want her to do or will become more independent and curious if your relationship with her remains strong and if she senses love and security.

According to Greenspan, limit-setting should begin by eight months. By twelve to thirteen months of age, your child should acknowledge your *autoridad* and begin to accept the boundaries you set. Children need to live in an organized world. They need to be told the functions of things and the reasons you want them to behave in a certain manner. Even if they do not understand all of your words, they will interpret your displeasure by your tone of voice and expressions. You should not only give orders like *"¡no!" "¡quieto!" "¡no seas malo!" "¡pórtate bien!" "¡calma!" "¡tranquilo!"* and *"¡silencio!"* but you should also provide the *porques* of things like, "It hurts when you hit someone," "Daddy is trying to sleep," and "Beds are for sleeping, not for jumping on." Setting limits, though, does not mean using physical force or spanking.

Some parents begin to set limits much too late. They may think that under the age of one, children are not capable of understanding what adults are saying when they speak. Many Hispanic parents at Avance used to say, *"Los niños no entienden a esa edad."* Children don't understand at that age. They didn't realize they were missing a golden opportunity. It is easier to shape children's behavior at a young age because they accept and respect you as an authority figure and because they love you as the person who fulfills their needs. They will accept anything you say without question. Some parents begin to set limits years later, when it is more difficult and may be too late in many circumstances.

Parents must determine what they consider appropriate and inappropriate behavior. They need to be ready to teach their children when and where certain emotions are appropriate and the times and places they are not. For example, you may tell your son: "Expressing your excitement by screaming and running is okay outside the house, in your bedroom, or in the playroom, but not in any other room." "Playing with action figures or punching a bag to vent your anger is fine, but it is not okay to hit your brother or sister." Give your child an alternative: "Instead of hitting and screaming, why don't you tell me what is bothering you." The time and effort that is spent in teaching, guiding, and setting limits will bear fruit later in the development of a socially competent individual, *un niño bien educado.* You are setting the foundation for future social interactions and for how your child should behave in a social setting. Be empathetic and supportive, as you help your child organize his world into a safe, peaceful, caring and orderly one.

STAGE FIVE: *PRODUCIENDO IMÁGENES MENTALES*—CREATING EMOTIONAL IDEAS—EIGHTEEN TO THIRTY-SIX MONTHS

In this stage, the child grows from playing with concrete actions and physical sensations to expressing feelings and exploring interactions through pretend play, which includes language, gesturing, and spatial relationships. He will be better able to communicate his emotions because he now has labels for them, like, "I am mad" and "I want ice cream." He will be able to remember the warm feelings he has toward his *mami* and eagerly waits for her to walk through the door. He wants the ball, even when he cannot see it, because he remembers the joy it brings when he plays with it. He will hesitate taking *la empanadita* his *mami* told him not to eat until after supper, because he has a mental picture of how his mother looks when she is angry.

This is the stage when a child discovers imaginary play. The two-year-old will first play by himself or next to another child, each in his own imaginary world. By the age of three, children are less egocentric and are able to play with other children. A child's imaginative play prepares him for different roles and relationships. Through play, he explores his world, tests its limits, and discovers his talents and interests. He role-plays the way objects work, and practices emotions that he observes and combines them into patterns. Hispanic children can learn gender roles this way. While playing house, a boy learns to help his "*esposa*" to cook and to rock the baby. He takes the bottle and gently gives it to the "*bebé*" as he rocks it to sleep. Another scenario can also appear during imaginary play. If a child takes a doll and screams at it or spanks it, he may be acting out what he sees at home or how he is feeling. If your *marido* is detached from the family, and doesn't get involved in child rearing, your child may act out those same actions in his play and in real life. Words and actions he has heard from his mother and father, television, or the neighbor's house can be repeated and acted out in his imaginary play. Observe your child at play. You may be surprised at what you see.

You can expand your child's play into more complicated scenarios and help describe the emotions he is expressing and the characteristics and functions of objects. You can join him in his play to show him how to rock, feed, and interact with the baby, and teach him language and other behaviors that you want him to learn. Hispanic boys can benefit from a model of *"un hombre noble,"* which allows for an open expression of *sentimientos,* or feelings, and self-control. You can acknowledge and respond to transmitted gestures by rocking, humming, caressing, or stroking, demonstrating an understanding of the emotions conveyed by the child. You can help him express his fears and concerns using words instead of hitting, kicking, or throwing things.

Your child can also learn to deal with her fears and anxieties through play, as she takes the role of the doctor who tries to calm and comfort her patient or as she deals with her feeling about *mami* going back to work. You can help her resolve some of her concerns that emerge from her play by "becoming" one of the characters in her game. Through play, you can also help her practice setting limits by, for example, using a stuffed animal to "tell" another stuffed animal what kinds of behavior to use in different situations. But be aware that some children are naturally more aggressive than others and they need to be given opportunities to show their anger through play. If they don't, it will surface in more undesirable behavior later.

Through play, a child begins to create patterns and images with toys or with other objects about persons and things and their characteristics and functions. Blocks can become people, houses, roads, or animals that he has seen in the past. Through play, he learns how his body operates in space and how to identify and understand different kinds of emotions. He describes sensory characteristics of how the person or things feel, smell, sound, and look. His play, language, and conceptual development grow from a simple fragmented form to a more complex story, with patterns and organized themes. He can have one player perform many activities or many characters performing one activity like playing *comadritas* or *la escuelita.* My son Steven would separate his *monitos* into two teams and play football. Vanessa would play school with her dolls. Sal would be the conductor of all the stuffed animals that he lined up in rows.

This can also be a very difficult period for your child and for you. After realizing that he is a separate individual, he starts to assert his autonomy. As we saw in Chapter Five, "Me do it!" and "Mine!" are words that are commonly heard among two-year-olds. Just as he has no control over his bladder or bowel movements, the young child has no control over his emotions. He is very impulsive and says "no!" to everything you want him to do. He does not know how to share, and may try to carry all of his possessions around with him so that no one else will even look at them. Because of his inability to communicate his feelings, he is very impulsive, ready to scream, scratch, and bite if he feels threatened. This is normal behavior for toddlers. During this period of a child's development, he is not very sociable with other children. He especially may not get along with his brothers and sisters, who are competing for *juguetes*, toys, food, and even his mother's *tiempo y atención*, time and attention.

It is a very difficult time for the parent of a two-year-old, but con *paciencia se gana el cielo*. One must be patient and reassuring, as the child's language expands tremendously and as his motor skills develop at the same time. During this time, a child may experience a great deal of anxiety, frustration, and fear in learning new skills. Parents must help their children grow intellectually, linguistically, and physically by supporting them during this period of disequilibrium. They must spend a great deal of time with their *niños* to bring them back to a state of security that will allow them to advance developmentally. The more a child's language and motor skills develop, the better he will be able to communicate his needs, and the happier he will become. Every child has a need to succeed and achieve. With every small accomplishment *y gran éxito*, he gains a confidence that is demonstrated with *una cara orgullosa*, a beaming, proud, and happy face. Acknowledge that you are proud of your child by kissing and hugging him, and clapping when he accomplishes a goal. Tell him, "*Mi hijito*, you must feel so proud that you were able to do it all by yourself."

A child will continue to need assurances that you understand what he is feeling. Some children regress developmentally when they are trying to master new things. You may have to go back to previous steps to help your child feel a sense of security. Sometimes you can change a child from being a *llorón* or *cabezudo*, a weeper or stubborn child, by showing him that you understand his feelings. Continue to mirror his feelings with comments like, "I know that you feel sad that your doggy is gone. *Pobre perrito*, I will take you in the car to look for him." "I know that you are angry because *Juanito* broke your toy." Children who become insecure and clingy can be encouraged to play near you at first, but then gradually urged to play away from you by assuring them that you are nearby. Say, "*Mami* is not going away. *Mami* is right here cooking. You can play in the other room and hear me sing." If your child is having *corajes*, or temper tantrums, you can set the limits and apply the punishment, but reengage with him later and say, "Are you feeling better now? Are you ready to come and play with me?" When he joins you again, hold and cuddle him.

You play an important role in helping your child progress along the continuum of play to more complex activities that will lead her to the next developmental stage. Remember from the chapter on cognitive development that a game of *Papitas Papitas*, Pat-a-Cake, can advance to a game of *La Víbora de la Mar*, as a child's thinking, linguistic, and motor skills become more complex. By experimenting using many emotions in her pretend play, she will be able to transfer what she learned in her make-believe world to her real world, where the ability to express one's emotional ideas is critical in becoming socially competent.

Stage Six: *Pensamiento Emocional*–Emotional Thinking: The Basis for Fantasy, Reality, and Self-Esteem– Thirty to Forty-Five Months

This is the time when your child begins to develop a sense of his individuality and when his self-esteem really begins to take shape. You may see your child looking at himself in the mirror a great deal, noticing the features that may make him different from other children. Help him draw pictures of himself using colors and details that reflect his uniqueness. Remind him how handsome he is. Children's self-esteem comes from the first interactions and opinions of family members. Be sure to say positive things to your child because negative comments, like "*estás feo*," "*don't be stupid*," or "*no seas un bobo*," make a child feel worthless and he may begin to act out these behaviors once he identifies himself with them. Praise your child when he does something well.

Help him feel good about who he is. This will prepare him for the cruelties children sometimes inflict on each other. Your child may come home in tears saying, "*Mami*, Juan told me that I have big ears" or "The kids call me *negro*." It is important that you help your child accept himself, his talents and abilities. Even if your child perceives he has faults or if he has a physical handicap, if the significant people in his life tell him that he is special, handsome, and important, he is more likely to believe them and ignore negative remarks from children. In the movie *Forest Gump*, the role of the main character's mother, who constantly encouraged him despite how others saw his handicap, illustrates the importance of this support in the development of a child's positive self-concept. Children are influenced by what a parent says, so it is important that you fill your conversations with positive comments that build them up, not diminish them.

This is the stage of emotional logical thinking. The child begins to think in a more complex manner by combining many ideas, feelings, and experiences into themes and patterns that present a more realistic portrayal of life. She is now able to organize and manipulate her ideas into a cause and effect understanding of her emotions. Like intellectual development, emotional and social development is fostered through relationships, as well as by patterns and connections that are formed in the brain. At this stage, your child can start differentiating between things that are real and unreal.

By the age of three, your child is able to play with other children. At this stage, her imagination runs wild. For example, the doctor, teacher, policeman, fireman, and astronaut are all characters whose roles are played out in a child's fantasy world. This is the time when parents should observe what interests their children, then provide the appropriate props for them to use, as well as books on subjects that fascinate them most, as astronaut Chang-Díaz's mother did for him.

During the next three years, children will ask *un millón de preguntas*, a million questions. They try to make sense of their world and test the limits of their social, emotional, and physical environments. They are very observant and are always trying to figure out how to get what they want. They are beginning to know about cause and effect. A young child who gently holds her parent's cheek, gives him *un beso*, and expresses her love will most likely get what she wants. A child who screams and kicks will soon find out that this kind of behavior will not produce desirable results.

This is the beginning of moral consciousness. It is a time when a child visualizes what will happen if she does something she is not supposed to do. She is now able to differentiate between her feelings and those of others. During this period, a child will listen to her parents and obey the rules, because she doesn't want to be punished or because she wants to be rewarded. She will understand that certain actions produce short-term rewards or certain punishments. Nevertheless, she *will* do things that she knows she isn't supposed to, but is more careful not to get caught. She will look around to see if the parent is nearby or she will hide behind her back the *galleta* that she knows she is not supposed to eat before dinner. But when you find her right in the act of getting the cookie, she gives you that guilty look. If she were older, the mother would probably tell her, I know you have it, *porque cuando digo que la mula es parda es porque traes los pelos en la mano*, the child was caught with the evidence in her hand. It is important that you keep a strong, positive relationship with your children. At the same time, teach them what is correct or unacceptable behavior and the values you want them to acquire. As you do this, children will develop a sense of right and wrong. It is critical that parents set the rules, values, and standards of behavior between three and eight years of age, and do it in a loving, consistent, and rational manner.

At this stage, a child is able to recognize other points of view and becomes more empathetic. She begins to develop shame and guilt, as she realizes the impact of her behavior on others. She begins to control her impulses, because she now knows that certain actions can cause disappointment or fulfillment and that consequences are real. This will force her to plan and behave differently. She becomes more focused, more tolerant, more determined to achieve desired goals.

During this stage, a child begins to organize her world by time (today, tomorrow, or next week). She begins to learn to wait for things. She can anticipate what will happen in the future when her mother says, "Wait until *papi* comes home" or "You can have a candy *later*." She will learn that current actions can be related to previous behavior when she hears her father or mother say, "You are not going to play with your brother for thirty minutes because you hit him, and we do not hit or hurt people."

When your child gets angry, help her learn how to control and regulate her anger. Balance empathy and compassion with a stern voice in setting limits. Stay in control and show her that you can control your emotions most of the time. *Levanta una ceja*, raise an eyebrow and use the approach Stanley Greenspan calls the "eyeball-to-eyeball" technique, when you look at the child straight in the eye, until she calms down and regains control. Use a firm voice, or perhaps distract her from what she is angry about. Make clear what the punishment will be for the infraction, such as denying privileges like watching cartoons the next morning, or sending her to her room for a "time-out" until she calms down. Tell her that you still love her and communicate the reasons behind your displeasure. Allow her to express herself. If you do not try to reengage with her, resentment and rebellion may build up. These will then resurface through passive aggression later, in the form of power play and through displaced anger.

Children will always try to pit one parent against the other. Parents need to be united in the way they socialize their children. It is crucial for a mother and father to agree on the values and rules they want for their children, as well as to adhere to and enforce them. When parents do not agree, there is no mutual support and consistency in the rearing of their children. A parent may use the child to get even with a spouse by forming an alliance with the child. This kind of action may ultimately lead to the breakup of the family. This then places a heavy burden of guilt on the child who is caught *en medio de uno y el otro*, in between. Sometimes even when spouses are united and both disapprove of the child's conduct, one spouse can relate to the child's emotions through empathy and sympathy, trying to restate in a rational manner the reasons behind their action. The parent who is outside the dispute can serve as the mediator and be the source of security for the child as well as the one to help keep the family in harmony.

THE IMPORTANCE OF BALANCE FOR SOCIAL AND EMOTIONAL DEVELOPMENT—*EL ÁRBOL QUE CRECE TORCIDO, NUNCA SU TRONCO ENDEREZA*

The parents' role in emotional and social development is critical during these first years of life. Like the tree that needs a strong, straight trunk with deep roots, your child needs guidance when she is young, to give her proper direction in the future. During the first four years of life, parents need to lay the essential foundation for the development of a healthy character that will help their children function later in society. Through countless interactions with their parents, children can develop a sense of trust, love, positive self-esteem, self-control, and compassion that will help them later in life. By administering a healthy combination of discipline and love, children will test their limits and learn to control their emotions and behavior.

Our goal as parents is to help our children become socially and emotionally competent individuals. In a bicultural world, this involves attaining a delicate balance between two forces that are often in competition with each other. All children need to establish a balance between being independent, assertive, self-disciplined, and competitive and being adaptable, interdependent, compassionate, and empathetic. Hispanic children who grow up in traditional environments may face the added pressure of social messages that reinforce only some of these qualities. There must be a balance between *ahogando*, smothering our children with attention, and not giving them any attention, between making them do everything themselves and doing everything for them. We must find a middle ground between setting harsh, rigid limits and no limits, and between not encouraging them to succeed and being overdemanding.

Sometimes parents try to avoid *rabietas*, or temper tantrums, by catering to their children's every wish, without teaching them to have self-control or to develop a consciousness of right or wrong. They may find later on that their children will make wrong decisions with devastating consequences, such as choosing to associate with the wrong crowd or taking drugs, because they didn't know how to regulate their desires by considering the consequences of their acts. They may not see how someone else's actions affect them or how their actions affect others until it is too late. Some children who had a chance at a productive life are in prison today because they were in the wrong place at the wrong time with people who manipulated them. They were like Juan Bobo, the Puerto Rican literary character who is depicted as lazy and not very smart, unable to make wise decisions and proper judgments because he cannot connect actions with future consequences. Their lack of prudence and courage make them prime targets for abuse at the hands of others. The *dicho* that says, *El camarón que se duerme, se lo lleva la corriente*, the shrimp that goes to sleep will be taken away by the current, describes what happens to children who lack strength of character to navigate through life because their parents were very permissive. The *dicho Detrás de la desconfianza está la seguridad* counsels children about the security that comes with being cautious and knowing that there are limits and consequences to their actions.

Children who are used to getting everything they want when they are young grow up believing that the world owes them whatever they desire. They may steal or bully others for what they want, without ever thinking they did anything wrong. They may not care whom they hurt, because they care only about themselves. I have seen good kids get into trouble because they never stopped to think how their actions would not only hurt them, but would bring great pain to their parents, drain the parents' finances, and destroy the family's stability and happiness. Children need to see relationships between actions and consequences.

While children need love and attention, parents need to know that giving too much love and attention can be just as harmful as not giving enough. When we hover over our children or try to do everything for them, they will not be able to think, discover, and learn for themselves. Children are not perfect. They will make mistakes, but they will need space to learn from those mistakes. Remember the *dicho El error sólo es fracaso cuando no se convierte en experiencia*. Help them discover their talents and potential. Parents who are too demanding and controlling can make their children feel anxious, guilty, and insecure. They may feel they cannot possibly meet their *padre's* high standards and expectations. Parents who are overprotective and overindulgent can produce arrogant, egotistical, and unkind children who will be rejected by their peers and may not be able to function independently or sustain intimate relationships.

On the other side of the spectrum, if parents are not responsive enough to their children's needs during these critical formative years, the repercussions for development can also be very serious. Children will sometimes be driven to misbehave out of anger or rebellion. Children need rules and limits as much as they need love and attention. They need firm, fair, and consistent discipline from loving parents.

While it is crucial always to give unconditional love and attention to children, after eight months of age they must also learn to deal with frustration, rejection, and disappointment that comes from not getting everything they desire. Sometimes when parents want everything to be "Norman Rockwell" perfect every day, their children will not be able to handle the real world, *que no es siempre perfecto*, that is not always perfect, and where things happen that are beyond their control. I have known children from very stable families who have attempted suicide because they did not know how to accept rejection from their first girlfriend, admonishment from a strong teacher, or from a personal failure.

After the age of three, children must be exposed to other children to learn effective social skills. We cannot shelter them from negative emotions. Some of the parents at Avance, like many Hispanic parents, tended to keep their children *encerrados*, away from the negative influence of others. By arranging supervised playtime for their child so that they can interact with other children, parents can learn the benefits to be gained from these interactions. If children learn to deal with intense emotions when they are young, within the context of a supportive, safe environment of the home, a trusted friend's home, or a child care center, they will learn that these emotions are part of normal life. If they experience such emotions as rejection, failure, and frustration when they are young, they will be better able to cope with them in the future.

As I have noted before, children who never experience love cannot return something they do not have. If they are victims of abuse and neglect, they can be programmed to abuse their own children later and to transfer a great deal of anger, resentment, and pain to others. These are the ones who will hurt and manipulate the weaker ones without feeling any remorse. Children need a balance of love, attention, understanding, success, limits, and rules.

ATTENTION: ¡MÍRAME!

When parents do not respond to their infant's cues, their children are negatively affected by this rejection. If they do not get the social and emotional attention they seek and need, they may first become disappointed and frustrated, and then ultimately withdraw to a self-protective state such as playing with their hands or sucking their thumb. They become *introvertido*, withdrawn within a shell of insecurity that keeps them from people. Like the children in the orphanage study previously mentioned, whose physical needs were met but whose emotional needs to be touched and stimulated were denied, a child may not develop well under such circumstances.

Parents need to be aware that sometimes the type of attention they give their children is affected by their own emotional state. In some families, a child can become the victim of a mother who is depressed, anxious, or under a great deal of stress due to such things as spousal abuse, community violence, or financial problems. The mother does not have the energy to interact with her child, demonstrate her *cariño*, or give her child the attention he needs. If she was a victim of child abuse, she may either abuse her own children or try to overcompensate by giving them too much attention as they grow older. Sometimes a mother does not want to become attached to her child because the child reminds her of a husband who abandoned her, a father who abused her, or a child who died. Sometimes the resentment that female siblings feel toward the *varones* for not being expected to do much around the house can be redirected to their male children later. It may be necessary for mothers or fathers to get counseling from professional mental health services to confront ill feelings and resolve the inner conflicts that can produce anxiety and anger before it adversely affects their *niños*. Parents must try to be physically and mentally strong, for how they feel may determine how they behave.

Parents have three options in dealing with children: they can provide positive attention, negative attention, or no attention at all. Children have such a great need to be acknowledged and not ignored that they will try to get it any way they can, even if it means negative attention. Although it is best to give your children positive attention most of the time, children will be driven to behave in a way that will provoke *castigos* if they feel it is the only way to get attention. Unfortunately, many parents fall into the trap of reinforcing and rewarding bad behavior by only responding to children who break the rules. A parent should ignore undesirable behavior that she wants extinguished, but only if it will not cause her child or others harm, such as a temper tantrum. Instead, she should be like a detective searching for good behavior to reward, like when she puts her toys away and helps to empty the dishwasher. Through praise and positive attention, a mother reinforces the desired behavior she wants repeated. If a child gets positive attention, she does not have to behave badly to get her *mami* to take notice.

Rewards can be as simple as a smile, a pat, or a few kind words: "You and your brother are playing so well"; "Thank you for helping me set the table, I really needed help"; "That's right, *todo tiene su lugar y todo en su lugar*"; "You did a good job in putting the toys where they belong"; "Look how handsome you look with your hair so nicely combed"; "I like the way you smell when you take a bath"; "Oh, *mi hijito*, that is a nice house you built"; "Thank you for being quiet while I was trying to put the baby to sleep."

An important tip to remember is to share activities with your children from time to time, like reading a book together or drawing a picture so that you can give them the attention that they need. Spend quality one-to-one time with each of your children. Too often parents leave their children in front of the television for hours and completely ignore them while they do what they have to do around the house. A parent can be so busy that the whole day goes by without his spending at least thirty minutes of quality time with his child. Turn off the television. Put away the newspaper. Look at your child and interact with him. Otherwise, the next time you interact, it may be to hand down a punishment.

In many Hispanic families, expressing certain kinds of emotions does not come easily, and in some households, it is even frowned upon. Parents may not readily show praise to a child for fear that he will become *un niño mimado*, a spoiled child, or *un niño orgulloso que se cree mucho*, a child who is arrogant and thinks he is better than others. Many Hispanic parents create a healthy balance between giving praise and doing whatever it takes to keep their children *humildes*. In my family, my mother always used to say, *"Ay qué bonitas están mis hijas"*; but the moment she thought her words were getting to our heads, she would immediately say, *"No se chiflen,"* don't get spoiled, or *"No se descompongan."* She used to say that although she was very proud of our accomplishments, it did not look right to boast about them all the time. She subscribed to the *dicho* that says, *Alabanza en boca propia es vituperio*, self-praise is a disgrace. On the one hand she wanted us to be competitive, to win and to prove that we were just as good as anyone else; but, at the same time, she did not want us to display that we thought that we were better than everybody else.

She believed and taught us just as the Aztec parents taught their children that there had to be a balance. *Todo con moderación*, everything in moderation. As the saying about the candle goes, *Ni tanto que queme al santo, ni tanto que no lo alumbre*, Don't put the candle so close to the saint that it will burn it, nor so far away that it will not give it light. A parent who smothers her children with praise and gives them everything they want runs the risk of killing their spirits or of having the children grow up to become *chiflado*, spoiled, or mean and selfish. *Todo el que a su hijo consiente, va engordando un serpiente*, Those who pamper a child will feed the serpent whose *mañas* can strike at any time. While the ideal is to have balance, it is better to err *slightly* on the side of giving too much than not giving enough. So give your children attention and acknowledge their existence, their talents, and their successes but remember the importance of balance.

THE NEED TO SUCCEED: *EL DESEO DE APRENDER*

Every child has a need to achieve, develop, learn, and discover, as discussed in the last chapter. She has an innate drive to create, invent, and experiment, and to feel a sense of competence. She yearns to master things, and control her environment. She also has a need to discover who she is, her strengths, limitations, and potential. Children take on new explorations every chance they get because of the euphoria and satisfaction that comes with having an impact on their environment. While your child may like your words of praise, she is persistent and determined to accomplish her goals because her *logros*, or accomplishments, make her feel confident and competent. Your *cariños* are important to acknowledge her efforts, but your role is also to provide a stimulating environment in which she will become challenged and self-motivated. Children need to feel that you are there to give them the support to try something new. They need you to be there when they fail, not only as an emotional cushion, but to help them cope with and learn from their failures.

When your children do something well, immediately praise them. Emphasize their achievements and recognize their *nuevos talentos*. When they create, build, and invent things, display their work on the refrigerator for everyone to see. When one of your children accomplishes a major milestone, like walking or eating by himself, bring the family together to clap for him and give him a hug. Ask him how he feels. When my children would feed or bathe the dog I would say, "Great job! You are being so responsible. Buffy sure is lucky to have someone who loves him and takes care of him." They all loved the recognition and acknowledgment. When they were not successful at something, I encouraged them to try again, and I would support them trying not to be intrusive, *entremetida o metiche*. Parents need to be careful not to push their children beyond their limits or to drive their children to excel in order to meet their own aspirations. You have to respect your child's individuality, help him discover his own interests, and help him reach his unique potential.

Parents must have realistic expectations of how much their children can do, based on their stage of development and on their interests. Occasionally, I would give my children a hint at how to solve a puzzle, a gesture that wasn't always appreciated. Sometimes parents must wait until the task is complete, a process that may seem *insoportable* at first. Other times a suggestion at the right time is welcomed.

Some things were very difficult for my children to do, and they needed assistance to keep them from becoming *frustrados*. So I would break the task that I wanted them to accomplish into parts. For example, when they were trying to put their socks on, eat by themselves, go to the potty, or get along with their siblings. I praised or rewarded them for each step that got them closer to the desired goal. If you want your child to put his *calcetines* on by himself, you need to reward him for simply getting the sock onto his *deditos del pie*. Say to him, "I knew that you could do that. Boy, you are getting to be a big boy, you almost can put your socks on all by yourself." Later you can encourage him to go a little futher, maybe taking the sock up to his heel. Say "You're almost there, *mi hijito*. You were able to pull that sock a little more up to your heel. That's good. Next time you will be able to do it all by yourself." When he finally does finish the task without help, reward him again with a smile and a hug. Ask him how he feels now that he can do it all by himself. He has to internalize the good feeling he gets when he finally achieves his goal.

After the sock, try teaching him the difference between the right shoe and the left shoe. Then challenge him to learn how to tie a shoelace. When he masters this task, you can tell him to put his shoes and socks on, and all the steps will fall into place automatically. My husband and I were there to support and encourage *nuestros niños* as much as we could, when they took their first steps by themselves, built a tower out of blocks, or rode their bicycle.

We gradually encouraged them to be brave and venture out on their own, beginning with the terrifying, insecure times when *nuestros niños* wrapped their arms around our legs or when they wouldn't let go of my skirt. We have to help them to take risks, support them when they fail, and help them learn from their mistakes. Children need to experience success to feel that they are competent. With each conquest, they realize that they can master their environment. It is not healthy to deny children the freedom to express their true feelings. You must encourage them to think of different ways to solve a problem. Let them make decisions on things that affect them. Give them chores and responsibilities; remain firm in your expectations and don't take on their responsibilities. Parents hurt their children when they do not teach them about the consequences of not being responsible. The best way to help your children to learn about responsibility is to allow them to make decisions and then hold them accountable for them. Parents have a right to disagree and exercise veto power on the "big" decisions that may be harmful to their children. But it is important that they encourage their children to make decisions and to gain a sense of responsibility. Ask them questions like, "Which shirt do you want me to buy you?" or "Here is the money, would you please pay for the movie?"

UNDERSTANDING YOUR *NIÑO—COMPRENDER A TU NIÑO*

Children need to feel that they are understood. Before a child can speak, her parents can only guess what is causing her pain by the signals she gives. She may kick and scream to let you know what she desires. The person with whom she bonded and who took care of her needs will also help her to be understood and to understand.

As a child gets older and interacts with the world outside of the family, his feelings will be greatly affected by the words and actions of others. He will need to have parents who show they understand what he is going through. Parents will need to provide support to help him deal with set-backs, failures, and rejection. Explaining emotions in words is not easy for any child, whether he is naturally expressive or not. He may decide not to share his feelings. Again, parents have to be like detectives. They have to figure out what is bothering the child who comes home *de mal humor*, with drooping shoulders, or with a definite temper ready to explode at the slightest provocation. You know that he is upset when he slams the door, or pushes the furniture to the side. Tell him that you understand his anger by mirroring his feelings. Say to him, "You really are upset! Would you like to talk about it?" or "It seems like someone did or said something that got you very upset, would you like to discuss it?"

Things like losing a game, not making a team, not being accepted or liked by someone, or being bullied are all issues that parents will have to help their child cope with. Yet, you cannot solve the problems for them. As your child gets older, she must come up with her own solutions. If she is not being invited to a party, it may be because of her own attitude and offensive behavior, which only she can change. Your attitude as a parent is just as critical as the advice you give. Taking time out to listen, pay attention and ask and answer questions tells children that they are important, that you care and that you understand. Once this rapport is established, you can lovingly suggest alternative or corrective behavior.

The opposite is true as well. Parents with a negative attitude can adversely affect their children. Harsh comments produce feelings of inadequacy, unworthiness, helplessness, and low self-esteem. They make children unnaturally shy, defensive, or mean. A poor self-image will be very difficult to change when a child grows older, and he may choose to associate with others who validate his negative self-image. Harsh words and actions will also provoke children to anger, passive aggression, dangerous behavior, lack of motivation, and procrastination. Making fun of our children or overreacting when something goes wrong will make them give up and refuse to try again, but constructive criticism is actually helpful, if done in a sensitive, loving way.

A SENSE OF BELONGING: *LA FAMILIA, LOS AMIGOS, Y LA RELIGIÓN*

There is a *dicho* that says, *Lo que viene del mar, al mar vuelve*, That which belongs to the sea returns to it. This bit of wisdom reminds me of the comfort that comes with a sense of belonging, which every person craves. All children need to feel secure by belonging to something larger than themselves in order to experience self-worth.

First, they need to feel part of a family that validates, accepts, and values them and shows concern about their welfare. They need a family that will help them experience joy through memorable experiences. From the beginning of time, people have had a need to belong to a clan or a large extended family that will protect, nurture, and support them. As Hispanics, our strong connection to *la familia*, the extended family, and the community can serve to give *nuestros niños* the sense of security that all humans long for.

La familia (which we'll explore more in Chapter Eight) becomes a haven, where children can "let their hair down" and where they can grow and develop. When children experience rejection and pain, they can always turn to family for affirmation, replenishment, and assistance. Within the family, children are to be loved, accepted unconditionally, and treated equally. When they aren't, children will let you know it by actions or words, "O *todos hijos, o todos entenados*," Either we are all children or we are all stepchildren.

Our traditions and beliefs connect *nuestros niños* to their ancestors and make them feel part of a continuum of life. As children grow older, it is also important to help them feel a connection to the world outside the family by getting them involved in groups such as the Boy or Girl Scouts, Boys' and Girls' Clubs, church youth groups, school clubs, and sports team. It is necessary that they develop relationships, get a sense of belonging and validation that extends beyond the immediate family. Spirituality has been found to be a protective factor against stress and depression.

Unfortunately, some children do not have an association to family, friends, and religion; they may feel completely ignored and isolated. Even if the parents are together, they may not always be there for their children. The children are given material things, but not the time, attention, and energy needed to feel a sense of *familia*. Money cannot buy love and respect from our children. Sometimes it is difficult for some parents to meet their responsibilities to care for and respond to their children's needs. They may be alcoholic parents, parents who work long hours without making an effort to connect with their children, immature parents, depressed parents, or parents who were neglected and abused themselves. Children's self-confidence and self-esteem will be negatively affected if they feel that they have been abandoned physically or emotionally. This can be true for some children of divorced parents. Even if the parents *pierden el amor*, fall out of love with their spouses, they cannot abandon their responsibilities to love, nurture, and protect their children. If they do not receive a sense of belonging, acceptance, and love from the family and other institutions, such children will seek to find it outside the family, perhaps from a gang.

Hispanic parents sometimes find it difficult to let go of their children when they become adults. Many times they want them nearby so that they can have more control over them, a feeling that is true for both boys and girls. They may be afraid that *"algo terrible"* would happen to them alone in a strange city without the family to help. My mother believed that her children were different and each needed to be guided differently. Some children needed more guidance than others. Beginning with the early years, parents must give all of their children sufficient freedom within safe enough limits to allow them to explore, experiment, make decisions, and take risks in order to grow and develop well. Even if our children are away from the house, at school, camp, or college, our early interactions with them should establish the security to feel comfortable dealing with others and being away from the family.

SIBLING RIVALRY—DE RIVALIDAD A HERMANDAD

Dos gatos en un costal, no juntos pueden estar. If you have more than one child, you can anticipate that there will be sibling rivalry. Since the time of Cain and Abel, and Joseph and his many jealous brothers, siblings have fallen out of blissful harmony. *Nuestros niños van a pelear, atormentarse, argüir, molestar y a burlarse unos a otro.* At some point, they may wish the *niño* had never been born. They chase each other around the house, *gritándose y riéndose a la misma vez,* screaming and laughing at the same time.

I have heard my *angelitos* say about and to each other, "Mom, look at what she did. Do something!" They have screamed "He started it!" "I had the controller first!" "He gets all the privileges!" "You never make her do anything!" "Mommy likes me more than you," "He touched me!" and "Don't touch my daddy! He loves me more!" Some parents sometimes just want to throw their hands up and cry out of frustration and fear that one day their *niños* will kill each other. Sibling rivalry can drive parents crazy! I have heard mothers say: "My children are *bárbaros, son terribles y carunchos.* What am I going to do with them?" Well, you cannot give your children away. They are here to stay. And most likely, you will not have *un ataque de nervios* nor will your children kill each other.

You must remain calm and try to understand why your children behave the way they do.

There are many reasons why children appear to be *egoístas*, or selfish and mean, and why they seem to be constantly at war with their brothers and sisters. They may be feeling *enojados o irritables* because they are hungry, sleepy, or tired. The cause may lie in something they ate, like sugar or food with artificial coloring, which may make them very active. They may be *celosos* of what the other accomplished or possesses. Perhaps they are what some Hispanic mothers call *chipi*, jealous of the arrival of a newborn sibling. They may demand all of the parents' attention or fear losing it with the new arrival. Sometimes pent-up resentment or aggression against someone bigger is redirected to the weaker or more defenseless sibling who is *más débil*. It may seem that children now and then just want to fight to create some needed excitement or because they are curious about what will happen if they pinch their brothers or scribble on a sibling's drawing.

Sometimes without realizing it, we as parents can be the cause of sibling rivalry when we inadvertently designate *"el hijo favorito, el consentido,"* the favorite child. That child receives more attention, while the others may be ignored or rejected. Hispanic parents may highlight their children's flaws when they use names like *llorona or tonto* or they refer to the child they consider the cutest or smartest as *el chulo or el más listo*. The subtle derogatory remarks may produce deep emotional scars that can affect sibling relationships for years. This resentment may subconsciously be transferred to other people later.

When young girls, as *las mujercitas*, are made to take care of their brothers, cook for them, iron their shirts, or clean up after them, they may later direct this resentment not only toward their male siblings, but to their own male children as well. The reverse can also occur in boys who are not allowed to express their emotions. They are called *chillones o viejas*, hiding their feelings at all cost. They, too, may feel resentment against their sisters, who can freely express their emotions. They may also be told to be the "man of the house," which is expecting too much from them and more than they can handle. If they do not meet people's expectations, they begin to question their sexuality. Every child needs to experience love and attention. He must be made to feel special, competent, and wanted. Parents should have high but realistic expectations for all their children based on their interests and talents.

There are other factors that provoke *los corajes*, or tension between brothers and sisters. A child's personality, the birth order of siblings, age, gender, and environment all have an influence on behavior and could bring about *competencia y rencor*, competition and animosity. Very often, the first-born child tends to be assertive and self-confident. Some studies suggest that the oldest child is likely to be the most successful among his siblings. Many leaders and executives are first-born children. This may be the result of the attention, time, energy, and high expectations they received from their parents.

If the other children were given the same kind of attention, they too could blossom. Unfortunately, some parents have to spread their limited time and energy among several children. My mother, who had eight children, used to say that after three children, it becomes impossible to maintain that special one-to-one attention with only two parents. She believed that it was important to teach the older children to take on some of the nurturing responsibilities. My mother-in-law used to pair up her children *tomados de la mano*, hand in hand, when they went on outings. My mother expected the older children to help the younger ones with their homework. Sometimes in large Hispanic homes, it may be the younger ones who are better equipped to reach their potential because of the help they receive from the older siblings.

In the Latino culture, the eldest boy and girl tend to have more privileges, a fact that can bring about *celos*. This is particularly true when parents tell the younger ones not to question their older sibling's or older son's authority. In many families, the middle child always has to fight for attention. This can cause them to be more *agresivos y manipuladores*, aggressive and manipulative. Sibling rivalry tends to be more intense between children who are between one-and-a-half and three years apart and between children of the same gender. The younger children tend to be more protected by parents and are regarded as *chiflados o mimados* by their siblings. A girl may have a special relationship with her mother or have *papi* wrapped around her finger. She may be called *la consentida*, the pampered one.

Sibling rivalry is part of the normal course of development. It is a necessary side effect of a child's struggle for autonomy and his need to search deep within himself to discover who he is and what he can get away with. Children must be encouraged to discover the wide range of emotions they possess, from love, kindness, and excitement to aggression, resentment, and jealousy. You should guide them to express their feelings and solve their own problems in the safe and secure confines of the home. It is in the home where they will first be able to control their *corajes* and *deseos impulsivos*. Sibling rivalry, if guided by limits, rules, and unconditional love, actually can help children learn to have self-control, to defend and assert themselves in a world where obstacles await. Sibling rivalry, within a safe and loving context, can be the vehicle that will prepare children to live in society.

By establishing a warm, loving, and orderly home, where everyone looks out for each other's well-being, parents can encourage their children to love one another, share, and empathize. Older siblings can serve as role models for the younger ones; they can encourage, challenge, teach, and inspire. With time, they will learn that enduring lesson of every Latino home: *los hermanos se deben amar cuidar y apoyar uno al otro*.

Children who do not have siblings can be at an advantage emotionally and intellectually with the parents' undivided attention. On the other hand, they may have fewer opportunities to be challenged socially, unless their parents periodically arrange for them to be around other children. The parent of an only child can still impart the same values of compassion, consideration, cooperation, and empathy as he comes into contact with others. This may be at relatives' and neighbors' homes, child care centers, sports events, church camps, and Boys' Clubs. By "adopting" a family in need of help, or serving in a soup kitchen, parents can teach their child the joy of giving to others.

The parents' role is to help their child control his emotions and impulses, to provide love, to listen, understand, and help him discover his identity and strengths. He is then in a better position to grow to be a competent, contributing member of society. Once our children achieve this, they will have reached what Abraham Maslow calls "self-actualization," when a person has fulfilled most of his needs, and likes himself and accepts others. Self-actualization means having satisfying and changing relationships, developing competence, self-direction, and a sense of values. A self-actualized person is one who comes close to reaching his potential and feels very satisfied with who he is and what he has accomplished and gives of himself to create a better world.

PERSONAL EXPERIENCE: BALANCING THE "SEESAW" OF SIBLING RIVALRY

You already know that personalities will influence how a child behaves. Steven's strong personality moved him to become *necio* and explode in anger over the things that bothered him. He was very quick-tempered and aggressive and those traits will help him in his role as fighter for justice and fairness. Sal's quiet personality and desire for eternal bliss kept his emotions restrained. He often clashed with Steven's boisterous personality. Through passive aggression, however, he tried to get even with his brother when Steven least expected it. Vanessa and Steven, at three years apart, have been inseparable. Vanessa was Steven's follower, but she would let him have it when she was fed up. These strong personalities showed me that sibling rivalry could be like a seesaw.

First, one child rises above her siblings to capture her parents' attention or to get what they desire until the other child forces his way to the top at the other sibling's expense. Vanessa learned quickly how to hold her own against her brothers. She would use her position as "the only girl" and the "baby" to reach the top of the seesaw and get mother or father to intervene until we realized that she was manipulating us. Still, Vanessa, through her negotiating ability, served as a mediator in the competition between her brothers. She turned out to be the one to bring about harmony in the house when her brothers fought. She had a clear sense of right and wrong at a younger age, unlike Steven, who was always looking to see what he could get away with. As the years passed, Steven settled down, Sal became more aggressive, and Vanessa became more unpredictable when she turned twelve. The sibling rivalry was transferred to Vanessa and Sal, probably because they became very much alike, and Steven would manage, when he could, to get on top of the seesaw as the "good kid." My family is typical of other families whose children's constant struggles to be on top bring about challenges for every parent who wants to take them from where they are to where they need to be.

A parent's role is to make sure that *each* child is at the top of the seesaw. Also, she is to get her children to find *un término medio*, a happy medium, in the seesaw of sibling rivalry that will bring some out of their shell and lasso others back in from out-of-bounds behavior. The balance will help our children gain autonomy, self-identity, and self-confidence. It will help them appreciate the value of interdependence. As frustrating as it might seem, it can be done. Children can alter their behavior. There are many strategies that can help you with sibling rivalry and that are intended to shape your children's behavior.

At times parents fall into the trap of being dragged into their children's arguments. It is so easy for parents to assume who is at fault in a conflict and to correct a situation that appears to be spiraling out of control. This authoritarian approach your *padre* may have used with you may, in certain situations, produce resentment and backfire later, especially if the innocent one is labeled guilty. You will have to save your energy for the bigger, more important issues. When I tried to intervene in disputes between my children, both sides would invariably decide that I had ruined their play. If I had just given them enough time, they later said, they would have solved their own problems. The child whose side I took defended the other one and complained that "everything was fine" until I came in. After several experiences watching my children end up laughing and hugging each other after a fight, I decided that I would begin to implement some new rules: Stay out of it and let them solve their own problems. As the *dicho* goes, *El mejor torero es el de la barrera,* The bullfighter that is in the bullring is the best one to fight the bull.

For example, there was to be no more *chismes,* or tattling, unless a dangerous or life-threatening situation presented itself. We were not to intervene, pick sides, or become referees or judges. We were going to let them work things out so that they would learn how to settle things on their own. The most that we would do as mediators would be to acknowledge how angry they appeared to be and help them identify the problem that needed solving. Then we would encourage them to find a resolution that satisfied both. It is important to remind your children that you have hope and faith that they can come up with a solution. In my experience, if they couldn't come up with a solution, I would present a few suggestions and ask them which sounded most fair. Together, we came up with rules and boundaries that became *la ley de la casa,* the law of the house. For example, there was a rule that said, "No hurting. Everyone must win, compromise, negotiate, listen, and try to understand." Another rule mandated, "You can disagree and get upset, but you must respect each other and love each other unconditionally."

When children are very young, you can help resolve conflicts by separating them and putting them in "time-out" in different rooms until they calm down. You may have to distract them with another activity. As they get older, they will have to learn to communicate and solve their own problems. When children are not able to settle their own problems, and if their disagreements really get out of hand, they may face consequences like a loss of privileges. They may be barred from watching television, using the computer, playing video games, or talking on the telephone. Be wary that too much punishment can weaken a relationship in a family.

With each episode of sibling rivalry, I tried to repeat the admonitions of my *abuelo* and my *mami.* They used to tell us not to fight and to try to solve our problems with understanding and forgiveness. They would say,

"You are sisters, you should love and care for each other. We are *familia* and that means people are to help one another. You cannot remain angry. You must forgive one another because we value family and we value each person within the family." Eventually, these words, together with many other lessons, guided our behavior.

Between siblings, a special bond develops over a period of time that comes from restraining one's needs and desires for someone else's pleasure and from a give-and-take that enables one to listen, understand, and empathize. Children should be encouraged to defend themselves and to express their opinions, but with the understanding that everyone has a legitimate point of view and that there are no winners or losers. Sometimes we got our way, other times we gave in, compromised, and negotiated. We had to develop the skills to communicate our needs. When *nuestros niños* realize that they will not always win and that they are not always right, they will then begin to understand what it takes to form bonds and successful, lasting relationships.

Those relationships require a give-and-take approach that incorporates patience and forgiveness. A home should not be a war zone, a football field, or an Olympic competition with clear winners and losers. It is a place where children can feel confident that everyone wins and where the good of the whole is more important than what one person can gain. The result of this kind of interaction is a family that is held together strongly because of unconditional love, trust, and mutual dependency.

El hogar prepares children to live in society. A home needs strong, loving parents who will give children the skills they need to live in harmony with other people who have different views and needs. Parents are responsible for setting the rules and values that will guide their children's behavior. Sometimes my children did not like the rules, but eventually they learned, as I did in my home, that the rules were established for their own good and the betterment of *la familia*. It is hard for a parent to be strong and stand firmly for what she instinctively knows is right. This is particularly painful when it means having to ignore the sad tears of a child, or the angry outburst of another who says, "*Ya no te quiero*," I don't love you anymore. Parents must be mature and firm in guiding their children in the right direction. Eventually *nuestros niños* will see the benefit in the long run when our guidance reaps what it was intended to sow. Every parent hopes that one day their children will confidently be able to make wise, prudent decisions.

You must consider the many factors that can produce sibling rivalry. Do you remember some of your own battles with your siblings when you were young? What brought them about? Did these episodes bring your siblings closer together? Was some rivalry healthy?

My relationship with my siblings is very strong today, because the good outweighed the bad, yet the bad was part of the growth. There can be some benefits to healthy competition and rivalry as we find in the *dichos No hay rosa sin espina* and *Más enseña la adversidad que diez años de universidad.* There were eight children in my family, but five of us were born one year apart from each other. I am the fourth of the first group of five siblings, all girls. Within that group, I was one of the youngest. I had three older sisters to take care of me, teach me, inspire and protect me. When my two older sisters married, I became the middle child, and a typical one at that. I was more aggressive, adventurous, and outgoing. I was always on center stage, striving to get my share of attention.

Because we were all siblings of the same gender, we argued about having to share toys, my mother's time, as well as clothes, jewelry, and hosiery when we got older. We also had a lot in common, such as an interest in clothes, make-up, and dating. We developed a very close relationship, a sense of healthy competition and a source of inspiration. Whatever the older siblings did, the younger ones had to do also, whether it was trying out for cheerleading, running for Sweetheart Queen, or going to college. My older sister Julia was a cheerleader, and three out of four younger sisters became cheerleaders after her. Julia ran for high school queen, and Susie and I followed and became queens in high school, and I, again in college. While my older sister went to college first, I was the first to graduate from college, and in this case, the older ones followed me. Writing this book, I have inspired one of my sisters to write her own book. Sibling rivalry is not always about releasing pent-up aggression. It can also offer healthy competition and motivation. Your *niños* can learn important values such as fairness, cooperation, kindness, sharing, patience, and justice.

My sisters and I spent holidays laughing over the sibling rivalry episodes. I admit, I started the *pleitos* most of the time. I knew that it would bother my sister if I took her things, but I did it anyway. Once I even sold one sister a box of pretty laced handkerchiefs that belonged to another sister. I was aggressive and usually out-of-bounds. I got into trouble many times and my mother knew that I probably instigated the fights. She tried very hard to keep me under control and make me more kind and considerate. She was hard on me and was not going to let me get away with too much. One day, my younger sister Yolanda boasted about how she could get my mother to get angry at me. "You want to see *mamá* get upset at you?" she asked. Before I could answer, she began screaming at the top of her lungs, "MOM! MOM!" as if someone were killing her. Just as she had predicted, my mother stormed in and let me have it. As my mother left, my sister had this great big grin that made me so mad.

What I learned from that episode was that children who are labeled as *peleoneros*, *buscapleitos*, *o buscapleitos* can earn a reputation that sticks with them and can be a source of torment even when they are not guilty. Another incident involved my sister Rosa Linda, who used to get upset if we did not meet her standards of cleaning. Susie was teased and taunted because she used to misplace everything, even though she would eventually find the things she lost. In spite of the harsh words and *batallas*, when the dust settled, we always remained *mejores amigas*. As much as we liked to tease each other, we would not tolerate anyone outside the family saying anything about our siblings. One day I overheard someone in school describe my cheerleader sister as having "*piernas de gallina*," chicken legs. I really got upset and defended her! The bond that exists between my siblings is so beautiful and one that I will treasure forever.

I, too, witnessed many episodes of sibling rivalry among my own children, but one episode that I remember vividly happened when Sal was five years old. He became *chipi*, or jealous, and felt threatened by the idea that he was going to be dethroned as the only child. I read books to Sal to prepare for our *chiquitín*, the new arrival, months before Steven was born. I bought him special gifts when I brought Steven home from the hospital and gave him special attention as the *tíos* and *abuelitos* arrived to greet the new baby. Regardless of all that I did, Sal took the arrival of his brother very hard. His body language told me that he had not accepted the change very easily. He wanted me all to himself. He would physically place himself between the baby and me whenever he heard me making *cariños* to Steven. When I asked him to be my little helper, things got better. But all the while, I knew he was thinking, "Why did he have to ruin it for me? I had it so great as the only child. Will my mother stop loving me?"

One day, in my presence, I saw him grab the baby's finger and bend it all the way back, producing an enormous *grito*. "You DO NOT hurt your brother!" I told him. Sal was frightened by what he had caused, and he never repeated it again. But as he got older, and Steven got into his things, the *pleitos* started. Sal had a great need for privacy, and I knew what was going to happen when I saw Steven's eyes light up as he saw his brother's things. The first five years of having a brother were very difficult for Sal, but he eventually accepted his brother and found a use for him. When his friends came over, Sal liked Steven to entertain the group. Unfortunately, it was then that Sal learned to get his brother into trouble by daring him to do things he wasn't supposed to do.

An important thing to remember when preparing for and dealing with sibling rivalry is to keep giving your children clear rules and guidelines, particularly when children are still too young to make proper judgments. I had taught my children that in case of danger or if someone was trying to hurt them to call 911. Sometimes the messages you send can be misinterpreted.

One day my husband called me and told me he had to leave for choir practice and he would leave the kids alone for 15 minutes. It was after school and my three children were watching television together in my bedroom when a spat turned into an argument, and Sal, then aged twelve, pushed Steven, who was seven, onto the floor. I had always told my children to take care of one another and to be respectful and considerate of each other's feelings, just as was done to me. Unfortunately, Steven remembered the question we would ask him over and over again: "What do you do when someone is hurting you? You call 911." This is exactly what our son did. I will never forget the experience of watching two police cars drive up to my house, sirens blaring and all, soon after I pulled into the driveway. The children had been together less than fifteen minutes. There on the porch were my three *angelitos*, looking very guilty with their eyes wide open. "Mom, you're never going to believe what Steven did now," Sal said. After they told me what happened, two police officers arrived, and *con mucha vergüenza*, I tried to explain that the whole episode was simply a case of sibling rivalry and that he had mistakenly dialed 911 because his brother hurt him. "Step aside, ma'am," he replied. "I have to speak to your son myself." Needless to say, when the officer learned what had occurred, Steven got the lecture of his life and would later think twice about how to deal with anger when things did not go his way.

I am sure you have your own adventures with sibling rivalry that have brought you embarrassment, joy, anguish, and anger. Yet, like with my siblings and yours, my children have become closer because of the ups and downs of sibling rivalry.

DISCIPLINE: *DE MALCRIADO A BIEN EDUCADO*

Cultures the world over hold different beliefs about what is acceptable and unacceptable behavior based on their own unique set of values. Since pre-Columbian times, Aztec parents played an important role in raising their children, teaching them to be obedient, well-mannered, self-disciplined, and most of all honorable. Jerry Tello, who runs a program in Los Angeles called Cara y Corazón, describes typical Aztec parental teachings to Hispanic fathers. Every morning after breakfast, Aztec children would receive instructions on how they should live. This included how to respect others, dedicate themselves to what was good and righteous, avoid evil, and refrain from perversion and greed. These principles were later reinforced by similar Christian values when the Spaniards arrived.

For Hispanic families through the ages, *disciplina* has been a major tool in socializing children. Richard Griswold del Castillo observed that for families in the nineteenth-century Southwest, *disciplina* was a defining aspect of life, whether in the public or private world. In that world, *respeto* was one of the most valued aspects of one's identity and was not to be diminished. To get their points across, parents at that time used to take their children to witness executions to show them what could happen when they committed misdeeds. My father-in-law took his children to *"las pizcas"* to pick *algodón*, cotton, in the fields to teach them how hard they would have to work if they did not get a college education.

In many families, *disciplina* is still considered the most effective way to move a child *de malcriado a bien educado*, from being spoiled to being well behaved. But while discipline remains an important part of raising children, it must go hand in hand with an understanding of children's stages of growth and of their basic needs.

During the early years, a young child believes that the rules that parents make are sacred and cannot be changed. Children will eventually test the limits and will struggle while acquiring autonomy and identity. If we want our children to become functioning members of society, we as parents need to provide the right kind of environment to help them to be able to make the right choices and to solve problems. Children need to learn values and build character.

You can learn more positive ways to get a child to be *bien educado* without the spankings, nagging, and put-downs. You can prevent the power plays, resentment, and outbursts. Following are some principles that will help you understand why children behave the way they do. Also listed are some strategies for producing more desirable behavior, such as cooperation and kindness. These strategies can help develop confidence and a positive self-esteem and help build positive relationships with others. As always, children will make some mistakes, but allow them to learn from those mistakes. You, too, will make mistakes and may revert to inappropriate strategies that do not work. Through sufficient practice, you will get better.

1. A Child Needs Unconditional Love, to Trust, and to Be Accepted

All children need unconditional love to feel a sense of security, self-confidence, and acceptance. That love will develop as parents learn to be responsive to their children's needs, as well as through many acts, such as giving a hug, kiss, or wink, or looking into their eyes and smiling. The bond between parent and child will become the basis for future social relationships. Love needs to be demonstrated to children unconditionally as they grow, regardless of what they say or do. *Odia el pecado y compadece al pecador,* You can hate the sin, but not the sinner.

2. A Child Will Behave the Way He Feels

A child's behavior is a reflection of how he feels. Irritability, similar to adults, can surface if he is hungry, sleepy, tired, sick, bored, scared, or sad. Also, he may be very sluggish or lethargic for lack of exercise. Stress, trauma, crises, or significant changes in his life, such as entering school, the arrival of a new sibling, dealing with divorce, moving to a new home, confronting racism and violence, or facing the death of a loved one, can affect a child's behavior. Tension can bring about physical symptoms like stomachaches, diarrhea, vomiting, excessive perspiration, or lack of energy. Some doctors believe that such symptoms can be psychosomatic, brought about by emotional stress. Others feel that pain associated with a feeling of lowered self-regard is manifested in signs of depression and hopelessness that can lead to overactivity, withdrawal from friendships and activities, school failure, drug use, and suicide. If you see your child experiencing these symptoms, seek psychological help for him at a child guidance center. Provide an environment where the child's needs are met. Make sure he is not allergic to anything, such as food coloring or caffeine. Support and help prepare him for changes in life that can be very emotional.

3. Having Realistic Expectations

Before you decide your child is *una niña malcriada* and is purposely making you upset, ask yourself if she is able developmentally to do what you expect. It is important to have realistic expectations of your children. For example, you should not expect a child to be potty trained at nine months when the average age for that milestone is about three years. Your child will not be able to share with others before the age of three. Before eight to twelve months of age, she cannot accept limits. During the "terrible twos" there will be a battle of wills between you and your toddler as she tries to become autonomous. Understand that children cannot be expected to sit still for a long period of time. Remember that they have an uncontrollable need to play, learn, explore, and experiment. It is not realistic if your child thinks that she can get everything she desires. It is important that you have realistic expectations and not push your child to become the person you would like her to become. Your child needs you to acknowledge and praise her interests, talents, and capabilities as you support her development.

4. Providing Appropriate Role-Modeling

Your child will learn what he sees and hears. He will learn what you value through your words and actions. If you teach him that it is not right to steal, and you eat grapes at the grocery store before paying for them or don't return things that are not yours, your child will be confused by what you say and do. If you want him to be considerate and patient and you push your way through a line, then you may be sending him one message through words and another through your actions. If you scream, pout, and throw things when you get angry, you are teaching him to follow that example. If you treat your child harshly, through physical or verbal abuse, your child will learn to do the same to others. The way you relate to your spouse will also teach him how to relate to others. You must model tolerance, kindness, patience, and love. Everything that a child sees, even outside the home, will make an impression on him and affect his behavior. Be aware of the violence, sex, and materialism that he may be exposed to on television, in the music he hears, in the video games he plays, and on the Internet. The media can be as dangerous as they are educational. Also, expose him to role models and friends with good character and integrity.

5. Being a Detective: Praising and Rewarding Good Behavior

When your child does positive things without being told, acknowledge her deeds, praise her actions, and reward her with treats or kind words. Always give your child positive attention, so that she will not have to misbehave to get noticed. This may mean having to look out for good behavior or breaking a particular behavior into parts and acknowledging each step with praise.

She will act in an unacceptable manner if she learns that it is the only way to receive attention. Negative remarks that embarrass, criticize, and ridicule will affect your child's self-esteem and your relationship as well. Give her space. Do not hover, nag, or provoke. There should be no manipulation, no power play, and no put-downs. A child has a great need for love and attention from at least one person who is crazy about her. So, be that person for your child by listening to her, acknowledging her feelings, and praising her good behavior.

6. Being a Coach to Encourage Desirable Behavior

Encourage your child to make good choices. If he comes home angry because of something that happened at school, ask him how he thinks he could have done it differently. Tell him that you have the confidence that he will solve his problems.

7. Knowing Your Children's Friends

As the child gets older, it is important that you know the friends with whom she associates. Invite her friends to your house. Get to know their families. When Spanish-speakers say, *"Dime con quién andas y te diré quién eres,"* they are warning about the influence bad company can impart.

8. Setting Clear and Consistent Rules

Children need rules and limits in life to provide the needed structure for their assertiveness and aggression. You must help your child understand the rules. A child by twelve months of age accepts your role in setting limits and establishing rules. Make sure that he knows what rules, principles, and values you want him to learn. Make sure that they are clear. Be consistent. Do not give in. Do not assume his responsibilities. He needs to learn how to accomplish a task. You may have to provide training and assistance. Teach him the desirable goals of your home and of a civilized society such as justice, fairness, and equity. Teach him that there are consequences to inappropriate behavior, especially between the critical years of one to eight.

9. Providing Spiritual Upbringing, Morals and Values

From the first year of life, your child needs to be exposed to standards of behavior, morals, and values that you consider important.

Your goal is to get her to be self-disciplined. Help her establish a sense of right and wrong and develop a mental image of a person who is *bien educada*.

10. Understand that each child is unique and responds to discipline differently based on his personality.

DISCIPLINE TECHNIQUES

1. Distraction

   When your very young child is headed for trouble, divert his attention. For example, if he screams because he wants something, take him outside to play on the swing, read him a book, or encourage him to blow some bubbles.

2. Withdrawal

   Take away the object that is causing the problems and explain why you are doing this.

3. Separation

   Physically separate a child who is misbehaving from the individual or the activity that has caused his frustration. Make one child go to one room and the other to another room.

4. Time-Out

   Direct the child to his room, until he is ready to settle down and behave or until he is ready to accept the conditions you've laid out.

5. The "Eyeball-to-Eyeball" Approach or *"Levanta la Ceja"*

   Look your child straight in the eye in a displeased manner, tell him "no!" in a firm manner, and shake your head. Lower your head, press your lips together, or raise one eyebrow, anything that will send the message that you are upset. Be firm and consistent, direct, honest, and serious. Don't joke around about things you don't like and want to change. Sometimes all you have to say is one or two words, "No!," "Stop it!," "Dishes," "Trash." You will get his attention and teach him that you are serious and mean business. Describe as succinctly as possible what needs to be done ("Put dirty clothes in the hamper," "Get your shoes on, now!") instead of giving him a long lecture.

6.   Effective Communication Skills

The first step in effective communication is for parents and children to calm down before they do and say things they may regret. If parents want to be able to teach, they must have patience while the child is trying to learn new habits, rules, values, and manners. Avoid criticizing with words like *tonto, llorona, bobo, dumb, stupid,* or *idiot.* Give "I-messages": "I did not like what you did. It made your brother very upset that you broke his toy." Avoid beginning sentences with words like "you" and "why" because many times these words will be followed by an attack on your child's character. These words will make your child defensive. Read body language and mirror feelings, so that you can demonstrate that you understand and value her feelings: "It seems like that makes you very angry." This will give her an opportunity to express herself and you to listen to what she has to say. Ask her if she has a solution. Make suggestions about alternative ways of doing things. Teach her the importance of knowing how to resolve the conflict so there are no losers and in a way that is fair to all.

Of course, there are times when you will have to draw the line and become authoritative. Some solutions may be as simple as setting *la ley de la casa,* the rules of the house. Tell her that it is time to pick up her toys instead of asking her whether she wants to do it. You may have to help her until she acquires the habit of picking up after herself. Other solutions involve bigger and more serious issues that can produce a confrontation. In these cases, the decisions and agreements are not always a win-win situation for the child at first, but will be better for her in the long run. Be sure when you do have a confrontation with your children that you have picked issues that are worth fighting about. On less important issues, you can be flexible and negotiate or give in. When it comes to the more serious matters, such as when a child does not want to get inoculations or when a preadolescent wants to stay out beyond the curfew, parents should stand firm on what they know their children need for healthy growth and development versus what they want. When you need to be unyielding, acknowledge your child's feelings and explain the reason behind the rules and actions. Tell her that what you are doing is for her own good and that you are taking action because you love her. She may not understand it now, but she will later. It would be helpful if the rules were established by the entire family at a family meeting. That way everyone understands and accepts the importance of the rules and agrees to abide by them.

When your child misbehaves, tell her that you love her, but that you do not like her behavior. Describe the action that you do not like, but do not attack the person or judge her character. Say things like, "I cannot let you behave in this manner. I have already told you that we do not hit." Give her the reason: "It hurts." "What you said hurt her feelings and it was very rude." Describe what you want her to do. Help her try to solve her problem or to behave in a certain manner. Children need to learn something every time they misbehave. Discipline is about teaching. It is better to encourage rather than force them and to help them learn from their mistakes, especially if the stakes are high.

7. Natural/Logical Consequences, and Contracts
A child needs to be helped to understand that there are consequences to his actions. If he doesn't put the dirty clothes in the hamper, there will be no clean socks or underwear. If he doesn't take care of his dog, he will not be able to keep his pet. If he doesn't come down to eat with the family, his food will be left in the refrigerator for him to warm up. If he does not behave, he will have to leave the party. If he does not do his homework or turn it in, he will make a bad grade. Sometimes children have to learn by failing. We as parents may not like to see this happen or to have to exercise our "tough love," but in order for *nuestros niños* to learn responsibility and self-reliance, sometimes we need to help them learn through their mistakes and always encourage them to persevere and to try again.

You need to help your child establish his own goals and objectives and help him figure out what it takes to achieve them. He could sign a "contract" with you, his teacher, or his siblings to achieve a certain behavior. We need to give him freedom and let him know we have faith in his judgment and in making the right decisions. This will lead to internal discipline, a consciousness of right and wrong, responsibility, and an intrinsic satisfaction from having accomplished his own goals or met his own standards.

8. An Opportunity to Make Choices and Find Alternatives
Children need to be given choices instead of hearing your ultimatums. You can say, "Do you want to take a bath right now or in ten minutes? Do you want to help me vacuum or dust the furniture? Which dress do you want to wear?" This is another way that you can help your child solve her own problems, become decisive, and learn to prevent confrontations. For example, you might say, "Your

teacher told me that you really misbehaved in the playground. It made me feel very upset that you hurt someone. You have a problem and I want you to tell me how you are going to solve it." If she does not have a solution, give her choices. "You must either realize that you are not to hit again or you will not be allowed to play." "I understand that you took something that did not belong to you. You know the rules about respecting people's property. What are we going to do about this situation?" "Tell me all the possible solutions that you can think of to solve the problem that you have of being tardy to school."

9. Rewards

Another technique for getting a child to do what you want is to reward him for good behavior. When he does something nice for his baby sister, like getting a bottle or diaper, you can tell him how thoughtful he was. You are reinforcing good behavior. Keep a chart and record every time he does something good by putting a happy-face sticker or a star by his name. When he earns a certain number of stars and stickers, he gets a treat, like an ice cream or gets to go to a movie. When a child makes the honor roll, he can select the restaurant where the family can celebrate together. They will feel good that the family's trip to the bowling lane or the camping trip came about because of their good behavior. Some parents reward good grades with money by giving a certain amount of money for an A and so much for a B. If you can afford it, a child can earn an allowance for doing chores around the house. This behavior-modification technique works up to a certain point. You have to select the rewards that can motivate children to behave in a certain manner. Unfortunately, the children may get satisfaction from earning the reward and not the internal satisfaction of learning, helping, or being kind.

10. Punishment—Deprivation of Privileges

Temporarily taking things away from children that you know they like, such as the privilege of watching TV, talking on the telephone, or playing video games, for misbehaving is another approach to correcting bad behavior. It is important that the children know what the rules are and that the consequences are directly related to the breaking of the rules.

There are times when you cannot follow through on logical consequences such as when a child has a tantrum at the grocery store and you will not be able to take her home with a cart full of groceries. You cannot let her stay home if she continues to miss the bus. You may have more luck if you deprive her of things you know that she would like later. For example, if she screams at the grocery store, she will not be allowed to pick her favorite cereal. She will not be allowed to go to the movies that she wanted to go to if she misses the bus again. Your child needs to realize that there are negative consequences for inappropriate behavior. You must follow through immediately after the infraction and be consistent every time. Another form of punishment is spanking, which can produce resentment, anger, a need to retaliate, a poor parent-child relationship, and family disharmony.

TO SPANK OR NOT TO SPANK: THE DISCIPLINE DILEMMA

Many Hispanics who grew up in families in which *una nalgada* or *un golpe* was the foolproof answer to bad behavior face a difficult dilemma today about the best way to discipline their *niños*. What they may not have been told is that many experts believe that when you spank your child, you are teaching him that physical violence is the only way to solve problems. You may admonish him not to hit his brother or sister when they are having a fight and to communicate his anger through words, but that lesson can be lost the minute *el cinturón* comes out.

Spanking is not a positive form of discipline. It teaches children to be violent and aggressive. It produces antisocial behaviors that will keep others from wanting to associate with your children. Physical punishment teaches our children that it is okay to lose control. Spanking does not produce guilt or motivation to do good. It does not build a sense of right and wrong. Spanking can produce rage and resentment. It stirs defiance, passive aggression, vengeance, and hurt feelings. If your child lashes out after a spanking, this can make you angrier and will escalate the conflict. As long as you are bigger, you may win, but at what cost? Spanking does not help the relationship nor help your child learn self-control. Spanking can also make you feel *sumamente culpable*, very guilty that you've crossed the line, when you did not intend to. Heaven forbid that your child wind up in the hospital or dead because you could not control your own emotions. Again, it is better to send him to his room or deprive him of privileges than to spank him.

If you resort to corporal punishment, you are teaching your child to use the most primitive part of the brain, the limbic centers at the base of the brain, which are used in moments of fear, passion, trauma, or crisis. Rather, help him use the prefrontal lobes in the neocortex region, located behind the forehead, which are used for thinking, planning, and analyzing. When a child is in an intense emotional state, his hormones force him to either "fight or flight." His heart beats faster, his blood pressure rises, and his large muscles get ready to react and attack. The limbic centers make us react without thinking while the prefrontal lobes analyze and assess the meaning of the situation and allow us to think, organize, and plan an appropriate response. Many animals use the primitive limbic centers to protect themselves from predators. But humans are blessed with a greater capacity to face conflicts.

More important, do everything in your power to establish and maintain a strong relationship of love and trust, so that if you sometimes lose your cool and do or say something you later wish you hadn't, your child will know that your good deeds outweigh your bad ones. When under stress, parents can easily revert to following the discipline techniques of their *padres*. If you administer a harsh *castigo* that may make you feel uncomfortable later, face your children afterward and say, "Perhaps I should have handled things differently. I am sorry. I just want you to know that what you did upset me because I love you and I desire the best for you." If you did or said something that you regret, it is okay to ask to be forgiven in order to keep the relationship strong.

What you do not want to do as parents is to hurt your children or kill their spirit and make them feel that they are not worthy of respect. Our language is so focused on words of respect like *mándeme, a sus órdenes, si Dios quiere,* and *para servirle*. This can be seen as respect and kindness coming from our strong religious upbringing. Those who use them may also be seen by outsiders as submissive and passive. Some people assert that this behavior is negative and attributed to the fact that we have been oppressed as a conquered people or because we are the country's last immigrants. Regardless of your viewpoint, most of us do not want our children to be overly aggressive and we demand they respect adults. But we need to respect our children's views and opinions as well. We must keep them confident and strong to help them be able to defend themselves against those who may mistake their manners and kindness for weakness. They need to feel good about themselves in order to be able to deal with discrimination and racism that, unfortunately, still exist in this country. As parents, we need to encourage our children to express their feelings and to experiment and explore with persistence and determination. Do not hurt your children emotionally or physically to the point that they do not value themselves. Children who are spanked or ridiculed will not be able to flourish and grow to become the confident children we want them to become. The challenge for parents is to maintain a balance between our strong cultural values while enabling them to know how to defend and assert themselves in a competitive world.

PERSONAL EXPERIENCE WITH SPANKING: KEEPING A BALANCE

Discipline can be effective if it is rooted in a strong relationship with the person administering the guidance. My grandfather Papayo assumed the role of disciplinarian after my father passed away. He had a great influence in my life as we developed a close relationship by doing things together. Just as he stood in for my father, I was his interpreter and translator when he had medical appointments or when he had to pay bills. For my knowledge of *inglés*, he used to reward me by buying me something that I needed, such as a pair of shoes, or by treating me to lunch at a nice restaurant. He was our spiritual leader, building a sense of right and wrong as he made sure we went to church every Sunday. He got personally involved in our spiritual growth by making us kneel down and pray, read the Bible to him, and sing *coros* (Spanish hymns). I remember how he used to get on his knees without fail every night and pray for each member of the family. I would wait anxiously by the door to hear my name called out. He would tell us stories of *La Revolución* and of his days in Mexico when he was a security guard at the presidential palace. A stoic, proud man with a nicely trimmed mustache, he always wore a brown wool coat and dark brown hat. He gave each of us much love and impressed upon us that in this country we had the opportunity to become anybody we desired. But, like my mother, he did not want us to lose the *valores* that would make us better people.

When it came to *la disciplina*, Papayo let us know exactly how we were to behave. He was very adamant about the value of *respeto*, especially to my mother, of knowing how to behave in public, and of planning for the future. One day, when I was just entering adolescence, I talked back to my mother, and he immediately came into the room with a belt in his hand. He had never hit me before. As he looked at me with his glassy, watery gray eyes, my grandfather said in Spanish, "Gloria, this is going to hurt me more than it is going to hurt you, but I have told you several times that you are to respect your mother." *Quien bien te quiere te hará llorar.* He who loves you makes you cry. I cried even before the belt touched my body, not because of the pain I would receive, but because I knew that I had disappointed the man whom I adored. Even my mother, who knew that I didn't mean what I said, was surprised at how this man, who had been as *fuerte* as a rock, could become so emotional. Because of my love for him and the dramatic point he made that day, I did indeed learn the meaning of *respeto*. It made such an impression on me that today when I hear teenagers talking rudely to their parents or grandparents, I am appalled because of how horribly those words go against the values that are ingrained in me. Hearing this disrespect was like scratching on a blackboard with a fingernail. I would not have learned those values and others had they not been taught to me from significant individuals in an atmosphere of love and respect. Today, my mother still receives my utmost *respeto*, and I, in turn, try to instill that principle in my children.

I know that as a child, with my curious, risk-taking personality, I could have been tempted to experiment with things that could have led me down the road of destruction had my mother and grandfather not been there to set limits and give me proper direction. I found out what an enormous challenge it is for parents of children living in the barrio to protect their children from harm. Yet as the saying goes, *Por la vereda no hay quien se pierda*, By the right path nobody will get lost. My mother, like my grandfather, made it very clear what was expected of me. Because she was consistent and maintained a warm and loving relationship with us, we trusted her *consejos* and followed them throughout the long and narrow road that she laid for us. Of course sometimes, like most children that age, I pretended not to hear the lectures and the admonitions. I complained whenever I was told to do things I did not want to do. However, like most young people, I wanted and needed someone to set the limits.

Many parents feel lost in the enduring debate over discipline. They may be concerned that spanking will have detrimental effects on their children's development. Many parents feel that they were spanked without any negative consequences and that perhaps a *golpe* or two may have even helped them when they were headed down the wrong path. But while some of us were fortunate that the corporal punishment we received did not negatively affect us, the same is not true for many children. In my case, spanking rarely occurred; and when it did, it did not cause serious pain. I was made to understand what I had done and to believe that it was done for my own good. It was also done in the context of unconditional love and acceptance. Although I was able to appreciate the discipline my grandfather gave me, not all children or spankings are the same. There may be times when parents, however unintentionally, cross the line.

For example, one of my sisters, whom we call the lawyer of the family because of her headstrong and daring personality, never forgot the anger she felt when a slap by my grandfather once caused her to bleed profusely from her nose. To this day, she says she still carries emotional scars because of the harsh discipline that my grandfather gave her that day. When the rest of my siblings and I speak lovingly about my grandfather, my sister says that she remembers only that he was abusive. What she does not always remember is that my grandfather was very concerned about the drug dealers and the many men who congregated in the housing project where we lived. In spite of the warnings not to leave the house without permission, she did it anyway. After several instances, my grandfather, driven by his own fear that something would happen to her, found no other way to impress upon her not to go. As far as my sister is concerned, my grandfather overstepped the bounds, injured her physically and emotionally, and irrevocably damaged his relationship with her.

Despite the volumes of advice against using corporal punishment, it is very easy to resort to spanking when all else fails, especially for those individuals who have grown up with physical punishment. Hispanics have *dichos* that reflect the Biblical passage "spare the rod and spoil the child." Spanish speakers also say, *Los padres que quieren a sus hijos, con más vera los corrigen*, Parents who love their children correct more earnestly with a *vera* (a tree of very hard wood). Also, *Si a tu hijo no le das castigo, serás su peor enemigo*, If you do not correct your child, you are his worst enemy. My mother believed in spanking us occasionally like my grandfather, and when I would get on her *nervios*, she would throw her *chancla* or try to use *el cinturón*. This approach did not always work as I got older, for I learned to run and dodge, and my mother did not aim very well. The *chancla* was her way of saying, "I've had it!"

Spanking may have a seriously negative effect on a child, and it generally does not work as a form of discipline. It certainly did not work on my sister or on my son Steven. I have to admit that my husband and I spanked him on the few occasions when we did not know what to do with his uncontrollable behavior. When we did, he was not fazed and would not even shed a tear. He would just glare at us with those flaming eyes of his. My husband and I realized that we would have more success getting through to Steven if we appealed to his heart and his mind instead. We stressed morals and values and exposed him to spirituality and to appropriate role models perhaps more so than with our other children.

I remember how my mother, grandfather, and older sister Julia used to apply the same strategies on me in attempts to teach me a sense of right and wrong. They would say, "Gloria, you know better than that. You have been taught right from wrong, and you know what you did was wrong." As long as people did not scream at me and as long as they explained to me in a calm, rational manner how my actions affected others, I listened. Adults could reach me more effectively when they appealed to my mind and heart just as my grandfather did when he was open and up-front about how my behavior affected him and others. Later when I was confronted with a tempting situation, I could still hear his voice, even when he was not around.

En tiempo de remolinos se ve subir la basura. This *dicho* warns parents to be aware of the times when your emotions seem to be rising out of control, and that you must take some time to calm down in order to handle a situation in a more rational manner. Realize that when you are tired or sick, or under stress, you tend to get more irritable. Sometimes I used language as a barometer to determine how upset I was in a given situation. When I switched from English to Spanish and my eyebrow went up, my children knew that I was very upset. "¡Salvador Julián!" I would scream. "¿*Qué estás haciendo? ¡Pórtate bien!*" Sometimes the English language just did not allow me to express my true emotions when I was upset. Since I spoke mostly Spanish the first six years of my life, my native language is my emotional language that I use to express my deepest feelings such as love, fear, and anger. A few of my bilingual friends have told me, "Boy, when my mother would speak to me in Spanish, I knew she meant business, and when she cursed at me in Spanish, "¡*mucho cuidado!*" Watch out!

Like most parents, *mi abuelo* loved my sister and believed that he had good intentions the day he slapped her. He was thinking of her welfare. Still, parents can easily cross the line, become abusive, and wind up doing something in a moment of rage that they later regret. In this country, where it is the law to report child maltreatment, 2.8 million cases are reported every year, and two thousand children die of child abuse and neglect. To help make sure parents at Avance do not find themselves in these situations, we advise parents never to spank their children and teach them more effective discipline techniques. Many parents who were spanked as children were steadfast in their belief that spanking was the best way to keep their children from becoming *malcriados*. We had to come up with alternative discipline techniques that would prove to be more effective. Although it is better to find more appropriate means to alter behavior than corporal punishment, if you find yourself in a situation that calls for *algo más*, I suggest you apply the following steps to lessen the negative effects of spanking on your child and on your relationship with him:

1. Count to ten or twenty.
2. Do whatever it takes to calm down: leave the room and go for a walk, try relaxation techniques, such as breathing and meditating to relieve stress and anger, or call someone you trust to vent your emotions.
3. After you have calmed down, explain to your child that you love *him*, but that you do not like the behavior.
4. Explain what behavior you want him to learn and why.
5. Never hit a child on the face or head. Never kick. Never throw objects at him. Do not use a belt.
6. If you have to spank, do it with a bare, open hand on his buttocks.
7. Try to make amends and reestablish the relationship by hugging him and telling him that you forgive and love him. For every negative action there have to be many more positives ones.

STYLES OF CHILD REARING AND CHARACTER DEVELOPMENT

According to R. R. Sears and E. E. Macoby in *Patterns of Child Rearing*, children are more likely to develop a conscience and suffer from guilt feelings if their parents use reasoning and guilt, or if they withdraw approval and affection. However, if they discipline their children with spankings, threats, or the withdrawal of privileges, the children tend to become more aggressive.

Diana Baumrind identified three child-rearing styles that include authoritarian, permissive, and authoritative. Children of *authoritarian* parents use punishment or guilt to follow absolute rules; they want to tightly control their children to adhere to a strict standard of conduct. The parents are detached, more controlling, and less warm than other parents. Their children tend to be more conforming, more unhappy, withdrawn, and distrustful.

Children of *permissive* parents are allowed to do anything they want. With few rules and hardly any punishment, they may grow up to become more anxious, uncertain, manipulative, and immature because they have not had a compass or road map to follow. Their behavior is motivated by external rewards and by avoiding punishment more than by internal gratification.

Many researchers agree that a child who grows up being rejected, without any training, exposure, or consistency to rules, values, and expectations, may grow to lack morals or become impulsive, egocentric, and vulnerable to delinquency. Delinquent children are described as guiltless, callous, and aggressive individuals who have failed to internalize any standard of moral conduct. Instead they may be stuck in the stage where they feel only a sense of fear that they will get caught or a feeling of inadequacy. Juvenile delinquency is associated with certain child-rearing techniques and patterns of family relationships. Regardless of socioeconomic status, juvenile delinquency can arise in any home where parents discipline harshly and sporadically, where they do not get involved in their child's life and do not adequately monitor and supervise the child's activities.

But *un carácter sano*, a healthy character, is born in a home that is consistently democratic and that has loving family relationships. Such a model is linked to the parenting style Baumrind identifies as *authoritative*. This model may differ from the model of *autoridad* that many people may have grown up with, but it does not reject the values behind it. Authoritative parents are loving, firm, demanding, consistent, and respectful in their discipline. They use lenient and rational discipline, explaining to the child the reasons behind their standards and positions. Authoritative parents allow the child to express himself and they respect his opinions, interests, and unique personality. Authoritative parents produce socially responsible children because (1) they explicitly confront children about things that could be harmful to them, (2) they are consistent in enforcing the commands and rules, (3) they are direct and honest and not manipulative and indirect, (4) they require obedience to authority, and (5) their consistent use of parental authority makes them attractive role models for their children.

RELIGION AND THE DEVELOPMENT OF CONSCIENCE AND DESIRABLE BEHAVIOR

Religious beliefs and practices, regardless of one's faith, can serve as strong tools for moral development. Each religion has value, and each espouses universal truths and standards for moral conduct. For my family, the Ten Commandments and the Bible serve as guides to proper behavior and teach us wisdom. Prayers are a source of inner strength. Children with a spiritual upbringing, including regular church attendance, acquire and reinforce some of the values and morals that are taught in the home. The Golden Rule exists in every religion.

Being filled spiritually will help children develop a strong sense of compassion and kindness as well as a conscience and a sense of guilt. Religion makes children aware of the good and evil forces tugging and battling for the child's will, intellect, and emotions to do good or bad things.

The good character in this battle is known by many names and is found in many Hispanic *dichos* guiding moral behavior and proper conduct. Parents use this powerful force to bring about a conscience in their children when they say, *Bien sabe Dios tus mañas aunque pienses que lo engañas*. This *dicho* signifies to children that they cannot get away with anything, because God is watching. *Déjaselo a Dios and Cosas a Dios dejadas, son bien vengadas are dichos* used to tell children to leave vengeance to God, helping children diffuse their anger.

The bad character that also tugs at the conscience because of fear is also known by many names: Satan, Lucifer, Beelzebub, *el Diablo*, or *Satanás*. There are *dichos* about him, like *El diablo no duerme*, The Devil never sleeps. The Hispanic culture is also rich with folktales about how easily people can be tempted by evil, a force that sometimes takes on the role of this character in a story to spur children to behave well.

"Not Only One But Two Devils," "The Devil Takes a Bride," and "*El Guapo Extranjero*" are part of a collection of folktales by Juan Sauvageau in *Stories That Must Not Die*. They are traditional Hispanic folktales about the devil that bring laughter and fear to children while imparting lessons in morality. The folktale "Not Only One But Two Devils" is about a man who was very cruel to his wife and children when he would get drunk. In desperation, his wife tells her two brothers that she will divorce her husband if he ever comes home drunk again. To teach the husband a lesson, the two brothers dress up like devils and frighten him, tying him up and pulling him into a small fire they had built by the road. They are warning him up before they take him to his eternal destination in hell because of the life he led as a drunk. He begs the devils to let him go and promises that he will never drink again. He was able to convince them to let him say good-bye to his wife and children and apologize for his terrible behavior. His wife accepts the husband's sincere apology and begs the devils to give him another chance. The devils agree but vow to take him straight to hell the next time he drinks again. The man never took another drink again.

"*El Guapo Extranjero*," The Handsome Stranger, is a story about a beautiful but vain girl who takes pleasure in hurting men. Her mother warns her not to play with men's feelings, but she laughs off the *consejo*. One evening, the mother, who senses that something terrible will happen to her daughter, begs her not to go to a ball. Finally, she decides to join her daughter, who is adamant about making an appearance. Close to midnight a very handsome man enters the ball and goes directly to the daughter, who blushes with pride, because she is chosen over all the girls. The handsome man dances with the daughter even after the music ends, spinning and spinning her around, faster and faster, until a cloud of smoke covers the couple. When the cloud disappears, the stranger is gone and the daughter is left on the floor, dead. Everyone still talks about how the "*guapo extranjero*" with whom the daughter danced was *Satanás*, the devil himself. This folktale is similar to the one children in my neighborhood used to tell except that the handsome man had rooster legs. This and others like "*La Llorona*" and the "*Lechusa*" were some of the scary tales that were told at every Halloween in the barrio.

BIEN EDUCADOS—WELL EDUCATED

As the first socializing agent, you are responsible for teaching your children as early as possible what you consider appropriate behavior, teaching them *la manera de vivir con relación al bien y al mal*. I think back to how my mother tried to socialize my siblings and me to become *bien educados*, to conduct ourselves *según las buenas costumbres* at home and in public. To my mother, being *bien educado(a)* meant having good character, integrity, and honesty. It went beyond getting a formal education and acquiring a college degree. She set a standard of conduct, *una manera de vivir*, that we were expected to meet and follow. "The number one rule of this family," she would say, "*es el respeto*." To have *falta de educación* meant to lack respect. We learned very early on that we were expected to respect our grandparents, our parents, and individuals in authority. She also stressed the importance of respecting those who were less fortunate, economically, socially, and physically. She would cite Benito Juárez's words that "*el respeto al derecho ajeno es la paz*," peace comes from respecting people's rights, to teach us not to take things that did not belong to us or not to damage what was not ours. She taught us the importance of self-respect and of feeling worthy of dignity and respect.

Apart from respect, a Hispanic child who is *bien educado* knows his manners. He says "please" and "thank you," does not interrupt, shares, and is empathetic and generous. He understands how to behave with different people in different circumstances. He knows when to talk and when not to, as illustrated in *dichos* like *Al hablar como al guisar, su gran-*

ito de sal. Speaking is like cooking, you have to have the right amount of salt, or the right amount and the right kind of words when you talk. Another *dicho* regarding talking is *Antes de hablar, es bueno pensar,* Think before you say anything. Some *dichos* advise that sometimes it is better to be quiet, *En boca cerrada, no entran moscas,* With a closed mouth, no flies come in, and *El poco hablar es oro, el mucho hablar es lodo,* It is like gold to be able to speak a few words, but it is like mud to speak a lot.

To be well socialized means to be well balanced. My mother wanted us to have pride and self-confidence, to achieve and to be competitive. But at the same time, she stressed the importance of humility, of never thinking we were better than anybody else. She always told us that we could become anything we wanted if we worked hard and got educated, but we were not to boast about our accomplishments, *ninguno diga quién es, que sus obras lo dirán,* because people would know about them if they were worth knowing by their works. *En árbol caído todos se suben a las ramas* and *Del árbol caído todos hacen leña* are *dichos* that teach Hispanic children that overthrown pride inspires only contempt, therefore be humble. Steven once questioned my mother's value of modesty when he told her, "But, Grandma, my football coach tells us to think we are better than everyone else so that we could get pumped up to win a game." She responded, as she often would, by saying, "Be brave like a lion, wise like an eagle, and kind as a dove. As a football player, people will know you are better if you work hard, develop, and use your fine talents and, most important, if you score more points than the other team." Like the *dicho* says, *En el modo de montar se conoce al que es jinete,* A man's horsemanship will be demonstrated in the manner in which he rides. Show that you are worthy through your actions, not your words.

In today's materialistic world, we may hurt our children when we give them everything they want. Our children can become like "snakes that will bite us" if we give them everything, like the *dicho, Todo el que a su hijo consiente, va engordando un serpiente.* I, too, am guilty of giving my children more than they need and have not been consistent at having them work for what they want. Children need to have a desire for something. They must learn to strive to earn what they want in order to appreciate it. Maybe because of our humble economic background, my siblings and I learned very early in life that we had to work for what we wanted and that we had to contribute to the family. From the wise words of our elders, we learned that we must appreciate what we had and what was given to us, for if we didn't, then we were not raised well, as is heard often in the *dicho, No es bien nacido, el que no es agradecido.* We also learned that *La felicidad es querer todo lo que tienes y no tener todo lo que quieres*, Happiness is wanting everything that one has, and not having everything one wants. Of course, if we wanted more, we knew that we had to work for it.

The value of work was really stressed in my family. I will never forget the summer of my sixteenth birthday. It was the first day of vacation and I was eagerly anticipating relaxing and lying on the sofa in front of the nice old-fashioned window watercooler in our home when my mother came in the room and said, *"¡Levántate y anda buscar trabajo! Get up and go look for a job."* I was bewildered since it was a month before I was of legal age to work, but she wanted to waste no time in getting me ready. As a girl, I had worked cleaning an elderly neighbor's home and selling the sequined earrings my mother made in addition to the many products that we would sell, like Stanley and Avon products and dresses from catalogs.

In my first job that summer as a waitress, I made more money from tips than I could ever imagine. My mother assured me that there would be even better jobs waiting for me later, that this was only the beginning. I later became a sales attendant. That job paid more, but required that I work Thursday evenings and take a city bus home. It was hard for my mother to let her children go out into the world of crime and violence, especially in the evenings. She would take a deep breath, leave us *en las manos de Dios*, and ask God to protect us against the dangers and temptations that we might confront. Like a sparrow in a nest, she let me fly, but I would sometimes see her waiting for me to get off the bus by the fence at our house where she would greet me with a *"Bendito sea Dios"* or *"Gracias a Dios."*

We were taught that each one of us had to contribute a percentage of whatever money we earned for the good of *la familia*. How often we heard my mother say, *"Cuando yo trabajaba, le entregaba todo a mi mamá."* When I was young," she would say, "I would give my mother my entire check, for she knew best *las necesidades de la casa*. She managed the family income and made sure each one of us got what we needed and wanted, including the dresses that she would let me put on lay-away and that we would pay *en abonos*." Because of her upbringing, my mother encouraged but did not demand that each one of us give her half of our earnings. All of her daughters obeyed without a question, except for me.

I questioned why I should give her money when some of my friends were getting an allowance from their parents. I thought that because she grew up during the Depression, my mother's family had to pool the family resources to survive, but I certainly did not see us as poor. It was not that I didn't want to contribute monetarily to *el bienestar de la familia*, I just wanted to have control over the money that I earned and wanted to determine where it went. I wanted to buy my mother the special things that I knew she would not buy for herself or for the house. She never complained and appreciated whatever I gave her. All year I would make payments for gifts I would put on lay-away to give her on her birthday or at Christmas. In retrospect, I now realize that my mother knew better what our needs were, but *cada cabeza es un mundo*, I have always wanted to be the boss and in control of things. My mother taught by example the importance of economizing, saving, and managing money, and many other mothers have taught through *dichos* like, *¡Ahorra! No hay poco que no llegue ni mucho que no se acabe; Guarda los centavos, que los pesos llegarán; Muchos pocos hacen un mucho. Save and economize, because no matter how little one saves, it adds up; No matter how much you have, it can be gone; and, Save the pennies and the dollars will follow, and Many little bits will add up to a lot.

My sister Rosa Linda was the only one in our family to carry on the practice of collecting a certain percentage of her children's earnings when they worked. Instead of fifty percent, like my mother, she collected a third. She did not really need the money to make ends meet, but she did it because she wanted to teach her children the lesson of giving of themselves and of helping their siblings who stayed at home to do the chores around the house. Her husband would take his sons to work with him when they were very young so that they could learn the trade of making cement sidewalks. He would give them each twenty dollars at the end of the day. As soon as her children gave her their share, she, in turn, gave the money to the younger ones. Like me, my sister had a headstrong child who also questioned the practice of giving part of his money. She responded to him by saying, "You have a responsibility to take care of your younger brothers and sisters."

Parents should teach their children important principles like having a strong work ethic, saving money, and being their brother's keeper. A child cannot learn the value of work overnight when she turns sixteen or when she graduates from college. The work ethic begins early in life. Children cannot suddenly take on the responsibility of caring for their brothers and sisters if asked to do so at the parent's deathbed. Instead, these values should be firmly established in children's minds when they are very young. Find ways to teach your children these important values, which take time, consistency, and ingenuity.

The value of education should also be stressed in the home. As siblings, my sisters and I were expected to help one another in our schooling. My mother's way of inculcating the importance of an education was to motivate us to pursue better jobs. Of course, she would say, *qualquier trabajo es bueno*, any job is good. *"Pero,"* she would always add, "But I want my children to work *en lugar respetable con aire acondicionado y alfombra*, in a place with air conditioning and carpet. Before we knew it, we were striving for something better and soon realized that the kind of jobs she was referring to required an education. She had such incredible influence over us to aspire for something better. She gently nudged us to dream and reach higher goals, but she never pushed us to do it. When I won a local beauty pageant as Miss Fiesta for San Antonio's Flambeau Parade, my mother nonchalantly suggested that I not stop there, but vie for the title of Miss America. How I laughed. By that time, I was determined to set my own goals and shape my own expectations. While I did not run for Miss America, I did graduate from college and became a schoolteacher in an air-conditioned room with carpet.

STAGES OF MORAL DEVELOPMENT: *EL DESARROLLO DE LA MORALIDAD*

You as a parent are principally responsible for teaching *las buenas costumbres* and *la enseñanza moral*. You are the one who will first teach your children *como vivir con relación al bien y al mal*. But where does one begin? Perhaps by knowing that children go through different stages of moral development. Parents should know and understand how children learn, grow, and develop and the many factors affecting behavior. They should be aware of the different stages of moral, intellectual, social, linguistic, and physical development. All of this information will set the framework for guiding parents' attitudes and practices in raising their children.

According to psychologist Jean Piaget, a child is first impulsive and has no concept of obligations or rules when he is very young. Remember when I mentioned how important it was at about eight months of age to start teaching children to have self-control? We have to help our child learn not to be so impulsive and do whatever he wants to do. Instead, we have to teach him to do what he needs to, *la conducta, los deberes de la vida*. When young, he accepts these rules as sacred and unchangeable. At the age of nine, rules can be more flexible and are founded on mutual respect. Lastly, a child develops an interest in rules.

Lawrence Kohlberg theorizes that a child does not initially realize he is separate from objects or parents. At the age of two, he starts affirming his separate identity. Remember the *"mío"* stage? This happens in children, as I illustrated with Vanessa. During this stage, your child may be impulsive and uncontrollable. This is followed by the "self-protective" stage, in which he anticipates short-term rewards and punishment. He will test the limits and do things that he knows he is not supposed to do. The *dicho*, *Carita de santo, los hechos no tanto*, applies to children at this age. Vulnerable, guarded, he tries to avoid getting caught. He will look around to see if his parents are present before committing *algo malo*. But *El mal y el bien en la cara se ven*. This stage is followed by the "conformist stage," during which he is able to connect his welfare with that of the family or group. He knows that to be a member of the family, he will need to do his part. Next, he will develop a sense of right and wrong and will need to evaluate situations in order to establish rules for himself. He develops his own standards and sees other people's points of view. The "autonomous stage" marks the period when a child develops a respect for autonomy and independence. Lastly, the "integrative stage" is the period of self-actualization, a time when a child feels secure and happy with himself and attempts to reach out to help others.

Girls and Hispanic children of both sexes reach this stage much earlier because of their uniqueness. As I mentioned earlier, Harvard professor Carol Gilligan explored the differences between girls and boys: Boys tend to be more competitive, more concerned with rules, striving for achievement and independence; girls, on the other hand, have a strong sensitivity toward others, are naturally more nurturing, and like to cooperate rather than compete or achieve at the expense of someone else.

As I was reading Gilligan's book, *In a Different Voice*, I concluded that those characteristics she describes for girls, to some extent, are related to the Hispanic mother's definition of a child who is *bien educado*. Hispanics traditionally have reinforced these same attributes (sensitive, nurturing, cooperative) as part of our culture. Gilligan says that boys, from the beginning of the Oedipal stage, want to separate from the mother; because of that urge, they are not as nurturing from that point on, striving for independence and autonomy. Not so for girls, she says. They, like Hispanics of both sexes, are very concerned with relationships and develop personalities in the context of attachment and affiliation with others. Would we categorize this as nature or nurture? I tend to believe it is how we socialize our children.

There is no question that I saw a difference between my daughter and my sons, yet I had the same dreams and expectations for my girl and my boys. At the same time, I wanted Vanessa to be healthily competitive and assertive, and my sons to be more nurturing and caring. The goal of a parent should be to help her sons and daughters to strike such a balance between the traditionally male and female qualities that researchers like Gilligan have defined.

When I was a child, my mother allowed me to be a tomboy. I used to shoot marbles, climb trees, and play competitive sports like baseball in the middle of the street with the boys in the barrio. I fought for my rights and questioned the rules of every game I played, from the line that we had to cross in the tug-of-war of *La Víbora de la Mar* to the parameters of *La Roña*. My daughter is as competitive as her brothers and can keep up with them in every sport. Yet I, like my mother, have emphasized the importance of being kind, considerate, and empathetic. In many respects, the world would be a better place if our children were less aggressive and competitive and more cooperative.

Teaching Values, Morals, and Customs: *La Enseñanza de la Moralidad y Costumbres*

Parents must determine what it means to them to be *bien educado*. Parents are the first teachers of morality, the first to impart values, morals, and customs. They are the first to transmit the behavioral and cultural values that influence the way their children should behave and the kind of life their children should lead. Therefore, it is crucial that parents have an image of how they want their children to behave. They should formulate and give voice to the expectations they have for their children. They should have an idea of what they want them to know. As the first socializing agents, parents shape children's behavior to conform to what they and society consider important. They set the foundation for the development of character, morals, and values. The parents must present a clear understanding of what is right and wrong and teach by example as well as by words.

A parent shapes a child's behavior whenever she teaches manners or appropriate behaviors such as: "Say please and thank you." "Don't pick your nose." "Cover your nose when you sneeze." "Do not interrupt." "Wait your turn." "Don't hit your brother." "Share." "Be nice." Teaching appropriate behavior is a form of socializing a child. Our children learn from the negative messages we give them as well. When you knowingly let a cashier undercharge you in the presence of your child or try to pass him off as a certain age to keep from paying adult prices at the movie theater, you are teaching him to say little white lies. As the *dicho* tells us, *Verdaderas a medias, mentiras enteras*, half truths equal whole lies. Little white lies and petty *robos* can easily grow into bigger ones. We cannot say "Thou shall not" with our mouth and "Thou shall" with our actions. Our actions have to correspond to our words, as we are told in the *dicho*, *Predicar con el ejemplo es el mejor argumento*.

Most parents will rear their children according to the way their *padres* brought them up. Those early lessons are not easily forgotten. Other parents will want to read and learn as much as possible about child rearing. The spiritual teachings learned in the home and places of worship such as the value of kindness, honesty, and compassion, actually serve as guides for behavior. The Golden Rule, "Do unto others as you would have them do unto you," is a tenet of many religions. It is regarded as a necessity for harmony and peace. Values such as fairness, kindness, generosity, responsibility, and respect should be taught as early as possible. For a civil and democratic society to flourish, it must be made up of people who embrace these virtues and principles. It is very important that parents comprehend what each of these virtues mean. Let your children know clearly what is expected of them. Assist them in understanding and acquiring these traits. It is the parents who must primarily teach their children these virtues and foster their children's spiritual and moral development.

Make a list of those qualities and virtues that you want your children to learn. Invite your spouse to do likewise. Make sure that you and your spouse rank these and agree on those you consider most important. Understand that you have to be flexible and realize that some values will clash with others due to lack of time and priorities. For example, cleanliness, orderliness, and organization sometimes may have to be set aside so that your family can experience joy, unity, and support for each other's growth and development. If you become so focused on achieving one virtue, there may be no time or energy left for other values you consider important.

As soon as you can, invite your children to get involved in establishing a list of the family values that each member of the family can agree to follow. Discuss the reason for each of these values and the natural consequences that may result if they are not followed: "If you do not have an orderly room, you will not be able to find things"; "You will sleep better if you change your sheets once a week." You might try role-playing situations so that your children can learn how it feels when they are not treated with kindness or when someone doesn't respect their property. Emphasize the opposite meaning of each of the values so that your children can recognize what not to do in certain situations, and why.

Children, depending on their age, may not have the same standards as you. Join them in cleaning their rooms when they are young. Make an effort to model for them what patience, kindness, and respect are. Always try to demonstrate the value of what you are trying to teach. For instance, you can make a family chart with the names of everyone in your family. Every time an action occurs that you want reinforced, put a gold star next to the name of the family member who demonstrates it.

Encourage, reward, and reinforce good behavior when it does occur. Use comments like, "It feels good to give, doesn't it?" or "Helping mow the neighbors' grass when they are out of town was a nice act of kindness; I am sure it will be greatly appreciated." Also, "Thank you for helping me set the table, I really appreciate it"; or "You did such a good job in putting the toys where they belonged."

Teaching Through *Dichos*

My mother and grandfather were very clear in the values they wanted to pass on to us. Like many Hispanics through the centuries, they taught us standards of behavior, virtues, and values by using *dichos*, proverbs that were used to build character. Authority and respect outside the family structure are earned through virtue and goodness, as stated in the *dicho*, *Con virtud y bondad se adquiere autoridad.* The kind of person you become is evident in your character, for *el árbol se conoce por su fruta.* As parents teach their children virtues, they are planting the seeds that their children will later harvest in a healthy, productive life. The following are values that my husband and I have tried to instill in our children accompanied by *dichos* that reflect those values.

Be Compassionate, Kind, and Sensitive

The greatest of all gifts you can give a child is your unconditional love, so that he can be compassionate to others. We want them to care for those in need, to be generous and appreciative. We want them to give of their time, talents, and resources for the benefit of others and to learn the meaning of forgiveness. As Mother Teresa said, we want them to love "until it hurts."

- *Ama a tu vecino y te amará.* Love your neighbor and he will love you back.
- *Ama a tu prójimo como a ti mismo.* Love thy neighbor as thyself.
- *Amor con amor se paga.* Love is repaid with love.
- *Amor de padre y madre, que lo demás es aire.* Only from the parents are we assured unconditional love.

- *Cortesía de boca, mucho consigue y nada cuesta.* Expressing courtesy will get you so much, and cost you nothing.
- *Costumbres y dinero hacen a los hijos caballeros.* Manners and money will make young men into gentlemen.
- *Cuando hay corazón hay lugar en la casa.* Where there is heart, there is room in the house.
- *El que da primero, da dos veces.* He who gives first, gives twice.
- *El que parte y comparte, se queda con la mejor parte.* He who divides something and shares will get the better part.
- *Haz bien sin mirar a quién.* Do good, without regard to whom.
- *La caridad para dar, empieza en el hogar.* Charity begins at home.

Be Hard-Working

We want our children to have motivation, determination, and perseverance, to use initiative and drive to improve themselves and to succeed. They must resist impulses and temptations and overcome obstacles and difficulties to reach their desired goals. We want them to be dependable, reliable, and responsible in completing a task (homework, chores, and hobbies) from beginning to end and do it in a proper and acceptable manner without being reminded or giving excuses. Children need to have a clear commitment to set realistic goals, plan, and take the necessary steps to achieve them. A person who is responsible is accountable for his actions and accepts the consequences. He realizes that he has a responsibility to know who he is and what his talents are, to uphold his name and his word, and to acknowledge his obligations to self, family, friends, employers, country, and those in need. He should use his time, energy, and talents wisely to achieve whatever goals he sets for himself. He should realize that his life is important and has purpose. There are many *dichos* in our language that enourage these virtues:

- *Al que madruga, Dios le ayuda.* The early bird gets the worm.
- *Cada cual es hijo de sus obras.* A man is known by his works.
- *Como siembras, segarás.* You will reap what you sow.
- *De lo dicho al hecho hay mucho trecho.* There is a big difference between saying and doing something.
- *El caballo corredor no necesita espuelas.* A person who shows initiative doesn't need to be led.
- *El trabajo es virtud.* Work is a virtue.
- *Hombre precavido, jamás vencido.* A prepared man is invincible.

- *No dejes para mañana lo que puedas hacer hoy.* Don't leave for tomorrow what you can do today.
- *Más vale pájaro en mano, que ciento volando.* A bird in the hand is worth more than a hundred in the sky.
- *Temprano se moja, tiene tiempo para secarse.* Stresses the importance of planning. You wet something early so that it will dry in time.
- *Trabajar para más valer, estudiar para más saber.* Work to have more value, study to have more knowledge.
- *Ninguno diga quien es, que sus obras lo dirán.* No one say who he is, for his works will say it.

Be Courageous and Responsible

Children need fortitude to hold steadfast to values and ideals and to be responsible for their actions. With this virtue, they will be able to say no to drugs, alcohol, sex, violence, and gangs. We want them to have the courage and confidence to take risks in order to learn, improve, and grow.

- *Cuando una puerta se cierra, dos mil se abren.* When a door closes (misfortune) there are two thousand opportunities that can open up.
- *Cuando todas las puertas se cierran, una ventana se abre.* When all the doors close, a window will open.
- *Cumple con tu deber, aunque tengas que perder.* Fulfill your duty (responsibility), even if you lose out.
- *Los cobardes mueren cien veces antes de morir.* Cowards will die a thousand deaths before they die.
- *Más vale morir parado que vivir de rodillas.* It is better to die courageously for one's ideals than to live a life of fear (on one's knees).
- *No des un paso adelante sin ver para atrás.* Don't take a step forward without looking back. Learn from your mistakes.
- *No hay mal que por bien no salga.* Something good comes from every bad situation.
- *No hay peor lucha que la que no se hace.* There is no worse struggle than the one that never occurs.

Be Educated

Knowledge is acquired from *consejos*, from experience, and from a formal education. With a good education, children will be able to think critically, analyze, solve problems, make good decisions, plan, and set future goals. They will be able to have confidence. Education es *la clave*, it is the key out of poverty and into a better quality of life. It is the vehicle for a civil society. Ultimately education is the key that can enable us to be free. It is said that in life people can try to take away all your possessions, strip you of your title, and deny you your next raise, *pero nadie te puede quitar tu educación*, no one can take away your education.

- *Dichos de los viejitos, son evangelios chiquitos.* The sayings of elders are like tiny gospels.

- *El alfabetismo es enemigo de la esclavitud.* Literacy is the enemy of slavery.

- *El error sólo es fracaso cuando no se convierte en experiencia.* It is a failure when one errs only if it is not converted into experience.

- *El hombre que sabe hacia donde va, el camino se abre para dejarlo pasar.* For the man who knows where he is going, the road will open to let him through.

- *El hombre que sabe dos idiomas vale por dos.* The man who knows two languages has the value of two people.

- *El niño aprende cada día cosas que no sabía.* A child learns every day things that he didn't know before.

- *El que adelante no mira, atrás se queda.* The person who doesn't see ahead will remain behind.

- *El que bien tiene, y mal escoge, por mal que le vaya, que no se enoje.* He who has a good thing and chooses a bad one, when things go wrong, should not be angry. If children choose not to take the right road, or they don't take advantage of the opportunities or advice that are before them, they should not get angry if things do not go well.

- *Lo que se aprende en la cuna, siempre dura.* That which is learned in the crib lasts forever.

- *Los libros nos dan la ciencia y la vida la experiencia.* Books gives us science, but life gives us experience.

- *Más sabe el diablo por viejo que por diablo.* The devil knows more because he is old than because he is the devil.

- *Mientras puedo, ¿quien dijo miedo?* As long as I can, who said fear? or Why should I be afraid if I can do it?

- *No hay que andarse por las ramas estando tan grueso el tronco.* Don't walk through the thin, flimsy branches when the trunk, or the right path, is so strong. Stay on the right path and remain focused.

- *No vengo a ver si puedo, sino, por que puedo vengo.* I did not come to see if I could do it; I came because I can do it.

- *Quien no oye consejos, no llega a viejo.* He who does not listen to advice does not reach old age.
- *Saber es poder.* To know is power. Knowledge helps one determine which course to take in life after considering all possibilities.

Be Frugal and Conscientious about Money

Children need to learn how to manage their assets, spend wisely, and save money for a rainy day.

- *¡Ahorra! No hay poco que no llegue, ni mucho que no se acabe.* Save money! There is neither "little" that does not come nor "much" that does not end. A penny saved is a penny earned.
- *Compra con tu dinero, no con el del banquero.* Buy with your own money, not with the bank's.
- *Cuentas arregladas, amistades largas.* Business arrangements are friendships at a distance. Stresses the importance of not borrowing from friends or lending to them.
- *El que nada debe, nada teme.* He who owes nothing has nothing to fear.
- *El que paga lo que debe, sabe lo que tiene.* He who pays what he owes, knows what he has; but those who do have debt become slaves to their debt.
- *Guarda los centavos, que los pesos (dólares) llegarán.* Save your pennies so that the dollars will come.
- *La ambición del dinero hace al hombre pecador.* The love of money makes a sinner. (The love of money is the root of evil.)
- *Poseer es ser poseído.* To possess (too much) is to be possessed.
- *Presta dinero a un enemigo y lo ganarás; préstaselo a un amigo y lo perderás.* Lend money to an enemy and you will gain a friend; lend money to a friend and you will lose him.

Have a Healthy Life

Leading a healthy life means eating well, exercising, and avoiding harmful habits like smoking, drinking, or consuming other substances that will hurt us. It means doing things in moderation. Being healthy means being happy and in good spirits. How one looks on the outside is how one feels on the inside. My husband and I want our children *que disfruten de la vida,* to enjoy life, because life is so short. We want our children to be able to laugh, have leisure time to meditate, and to stop to smell the roses and appreciate life's beauty and wonders. We want them to travel and meet people to learn about different cultures throughout the world. I want them to think, speak, learn, and grow in a peaceful, just, and democratic world.

- *Cada cosa se parece a su dueño.* Your outward appearance is a reflection of who you are.

- *Como te ven, así te tratan.* People will treat you the way they see you. Our children's outer appearance is important, but more important, they need to be healthy in body and soul, projecting confidence, self-acceptance, inner strength, and character.

- *Desayuna bien, come más, cena poco y vivirás.* Eat a good breakfast, a heavy lunch, and a light dinner, and you will live longer.

- *El que mucho abarca, poco aprieta.* The person who tries to do too many things will accomplish few and hurt himself physically. Everything should be done in moderation, because if you don't, it will affect your health.

- *La que come manzana, se cría sana.* She who eats apples will grow healthy.

- *Salud y alegría crían belleza.* Health and happiness bring out beauty.

- *No te apures, para que dures.* Don't worry so that you can have a long life.

- *Si quieres vivir sano, acuéstate y levántate temprano.* If you want to live healthily, go to bed early and wake up early.

- *Se come para vivir, no se vive para comer.* One eats to live, not the other way around.

- *Tanto baja el cántaro al agua hasta que se quiebra.* One took the water container to the well too often, until it broke. Everything in moderation.

- *Una onza de alegría vale más que una libra de oro.* An ounce of happiness is worth more than a pound of gold.

Be Successful through Friendships and Relationships

We want our children to be successful, social, and to have many good friends. We want them to feel they belong and are able to contribute to society as individuals, parents, workers, neighbors, and citizens. We want them to have many successful relationships and be loyal to family, friends, neighbors, the Latino community at large, and to the country.

Relationships can serve as a mutually beneficial source of support and companionship, because we are interdependent on one another and no man is an island, sayings that have many Spanish equivalents:

- *Acompáñate con los buenos y serás uno de ellos.* If you hang around with good people, you will be like them.
- *Amigo en la adversidad, amigo de verdad.* A friend in need is a friend indeed.
- *Aquellos son ricos, que tienen amigos.* Those who have friends are rich.
- *Entre más amistad, más claridad.* The closer the friendship, the better the understanding.
- *El caballo y el amigo no hay que cansarlos.* We should tire neither horse nor friend.
- *El que a buen árbol se arrima, buena sombra le cobija.* He who gets close to a good tree will get good shade.
- *La amistad sincera es un alma repartida en dos cuerpos.* Sincere friendship is two bodies sharing one soul.
- *¿Quién es tu hermano? Tu vecino más cercano.* Who is your brother? Your neighbor who is closest to you.
- *Vida sin amigos, muerte sin testigos.* One who lives without friends will die alone, without people present at his funeral to provide testimony.
- *El pueblo unido jamás será vencido.* A united people will never be defeated.

Be Orderly and Organized

- *Cada cosa tiene su lugar, y todo en su lugar.* Everything has its place and everything in its place. Children need to learn to organize their possessions, time, and thoughts in a structured manner. They need to set priorities, make schedules and plans, and develop systems, procedures, and routines in life. They need to be considerate and respectful of others by being quiet and orderly.

Be Respectful, Honest, and Just

As parents, we want our children to treat people with dignity and respect by being fair and just. Similarly, we want them to know that they, too, are worthy of dignity and respect and that they have, under the U.S. Constitution, rights to life, liberty, and the pursuit of happiness.

We want them to be familiar with the Constitution and the Bill of Rights so that they can protect themselves and others against injustice and inequality. We want them to be cautious, alert, and aggressive when it comes to someone trying to take advantage of them or cause them harm. Children must learn to respect themselves, their unique talents, their parents, neighbors, people in authority, and the laws.

- *Tu conciencia es testigo, juez, y jurado.* Your conscience is witness, judge, and jury.
- *El respeto al derecho ajeno es la paz.* Peace will come if we respect what is not ours. Being honest is a very important virtue.
- *Bienes mal adquiridos, a nadie han enriquecido.* No one gets rich from being dishonest.
- *Detrás de la desconfianza está la seguridad.* Behind mistrust is security. Be cautious, alert, and aggressive when it comes to dealing with those who are trying to take advantage of you.
- *De juez de poca conciencia, no esperes justa sentencia.* From a judge with little conscience, don't expect a just sentence.
- *Para ser justo, hasta con el diablo.* Be just with everyone, even with the devil.
- *Más vale mancha en la frente que mancilla en el corazón.* It is better to be ugly and good than handsome and with a blemish in your heart (bad).

Be Religious, Have Faith, and Be Strong Spiritually

My husband and I want to instill in our children a strong sense of faith, hope, and confidence that comes from their religion and spiritual growth. We want them to know that God loves them and will always be with them, and that they can turn to Him for help. Also, that God created each one uniquely and for a purpose. When things go wrong, we want them to know that they can turn to God, for He can turn any negative situation into a positive one. When one is confronted with a terrible loss or misfortune, he can get strength from his faith. One day as I was writing this section of the book, I learned that my best friend of 30 years and my right-hand person at Avance for twenty years, my *comadre*, my neighbor, Carmen Prieto Cortez, had died in a terrible car accident. I had just finished reading this section to my children, including that we had to ask God to help us accept what we cannot change, when the unfortunate call came. Through that tragedy, I was able to show my children how faith can help a person endure, cope, and accept the suffering and pain that is an inevitable part of life.

- *Ayúdate que Dios te ayudará.* Help yourself for God will help you. He will provide for all our needs. He will help us endure any setback, rejection, humiliation, or anger.

- *Cosas a Dios dejadas son bien vengadas.* Things left to God are well avenged. Leave vengeance to God. We want our children to pray for guidance, wisdom, inner strength, and peace to God, *La Virgen de Guadalupe*, and the *Santitos*.

- *Dejarse en las manos de Dios.* Leave things that we cannot control in God's hands.

- *Dios habla por el que calla.* God speaks for him who refrains from speaking, who holds his tongue for the sake of peace.

- *El que no habla, Dios no lo oye.* God will not hear him who does not speak.

- *El hombre propone y Dios dispone.* God's will may be different from man's desires.

- *No hay mal que por bien no venga.* Out of something bad will come something good.

- *No se mueve la hoja sin la voluntad de Dios.* Things, like the movement of the leaf, do not occur without the will of God.

- *Tiene más Dios que darnos, que nosotros que pedirle.* He will provide for all our needs. God has more to give than we have to ask.

- *Cada quien es como Dios lo hizo.* Everyone is like God made him.

- *Cuando Dios no quiere, Santo no puede.* When God doesn't will it, not even a saint can help.

- *Como el arco iris, siempre sales después de la tempestad.* (Hope) is like a rainbow after a storm. (Can also refer to a faithful friend who always comes to help after a misfortune.)

Teaching Through Folktales

Folktales are not only regarded as some of the best keepers of our language and cultural memories, they are also great helpers in the process of socialization, they teach our children the sometimes difficult lessons about how to interact with other people and what happens when virtues are tested or pitted against one another. Many Hispanics have grown up hearing the stories of *Juan Bobo* and learning from his mishaps. These stories are just a few of the countless folktales of Latin America (as well as those that have been modified over generations and adapted in the U.S.) that contain important societal messages you can share with your child.

Some folktales try to answer in whimsical ways the *porqués* or the whys of life, such as why the sky is blue or how the toad got his spots. In this latter tale, captured in a collection by Genevieve Barlow, *Legends from Latin America/Leyendas de Latinoamerica*, an adventurous toad sneaks into the guitar case of a musical crow to attend a gathering of his feathered friends in the sky. When he is discovered at the party, the toad is promptly tossed out of the heavens and falls to the earth on a pile of pointy rocks that scar his once smooth skin forever. But to this day, the inquisitive and courageous little toad is admired by all the animals for his daring flight, and his spots are regarded as a mark of bravery.

Sometimes old stories provide basic lessons in survival and appreciation for one's blessings. In the story "Count Your Blessings," retold by Teresa Pijoan in *La Cuentista*, a very poor father goes out on a cold day with an ax to look for firewood for his family and accidentally falls into a well. He hits his head and when he awakes, he confronts a rattlesnake face-to-face. Staring intensely into each other's eyes, both the man and the snake think that they will be killed by the other. The man tells the snake that there is no need for both of them to freeze to death, and throws the snake out of the hole. The snake returns with his children and, tied together, they pull the father out. Both families return to the man's house, and in spite of the few pieces of wood that warm the house, the snake and the father have lots of blessings to be thankful for: life, family, and friends.

"How the Brazilian Beetles Got Their Coats," retold by Elsie Eells in William Bennet's *The Moral Compass*, teaches about using one's God-given talents and having the confidence to venture out into the world despite the odds. The beetle got his beautiful colors as a reward for outracing the big rat. Instead of running the race, the beetle uses his wings to fly to the victory line. "No one said we had to run," he tells the cocky rat, as he reveals his concealed assets. Because this insect chose to use his gifts, beetles have beautiful colorful coats while rats continue to have a dull gray coat.

Mothers and grandmothers for centuries have used the Mayan folktale "The Story of Mariano the Buzzard," in James D. Sexton's book, *The Mayan Folktales: Folklore from Lake Atzlán*, to teach children to work and not be lazy. The folktale is about a married couple who are very lazy and hardly have anything to eat. Mariano, the husband, would lie in the grass looking up at the sky and long to be like a buzzard so that he wouldn't have to work for his food and could hover about looking for dead animals. One day the buzzard overhears the man and they agree to trade places by exchanging jackets. The real buzzard realizes he doesn't want to be a human, takes off his human jacket in front of the man's wife, and flies away. The wife believes that her real husband had turned into a buzzard because of his laziness. When her husband returns home as a buzzard, he tries to talk to his wife, but can't. The wife is so upset and annoyed at the sounds the buzzard makes, that she grabs a piece of firewood and kills it.

"The Late Bloomer," found in The Moral Compass by William J. Bennett, is a Mexican folktale about a cactus that is distraught over its ugly appearance and its lack of usefulness and purpose in the hot desert. The moon joins a chorus of animals who mock the cactus, and boast about their usefulness. Then suddenly, at the tip of the cactus, a beautiful glorious flower blossoms like a brilliant crown and releases a wonderful fragrance. Everyone stops to admire the beautiful cactus for they have never seen such beauty. Then the voice of the Lord acknowledges the cactus's patience, and tells it, "The heart that seeks to do good reflects my glory, and will always bring something worthwhile to the world, something in which all can rejoice—even if for only a moment."

These are just a few of the tales that have been passed on from generation to generation and have helped to shape the way Hispanic children learn the values, morals, and beliefs of their ancestors, while exercising their imaginations. A trip to almost any neighborhood public library can uncover a wealth of Hispanic folk stories, either in books or in audiotapes. Many storytellers often perform at libraries, museums, and community centers. Get one of Joe Hayes's many great books on folktales.

Teaching through Letters and Poems

Another way to teach or reinforce morals and values is by writing letters or poems to your children that will reach their souls and help renew your relationship with them at major milestones. Similarly, children can use letters to express their feelings. Following are two letters, one that I gave my son Steven when he took part in a religious camp and one to my husband from our son Sal when he was older.

Dear Steven,
     This weekend is a time for you to be away from family and friends to reflect and renew your Christian vows. It is also a time for you to communicate with God about the direction and purpose of your life and to ask him for His blessings.
     This retreat gives me an opportunity to tell you how much I love you, Steven, and to tell you how much you mean to me and how happy I am that you are my son. I have always told you that you are very special and

that God has a very special purpose and plan for your life. He made you so compassionate, brilliant, witty, adventurous, and handsome. You have a personality that makes you stand out wherever you are. You have always been surrounded by many friends that seem to follow you and respect you as a leader. You have never been concerned over material things and have been satisfied with whatever we have been able to provide for you. What I admire most about you is your drive and determination. When you want something, you go after it by working hard, sometimes even staying up all night or being out in the hot sun. Whether it is in the classroom or on the football field, your performance reflects your quest for excellence. You have been strong enough to resist temptation that is out there in this world: cigarettes, drugs, alcohol, sex, and gangs. Your father and I are so proud that you have not brought harm to yourself, nor pain and suffering to the family. We are proud of how well you are learning to speak Spanish and how well you dance to the Latin beat. We love your high regard for life, people, animals, and the environment. You are naturally funny and have brought laughter and joy to others. When I am tense and tired, you make me laugh.

Steven, all of these wonderful attributes God has given you for a reason. You have all the right ingredients to become someone very special in the future. You were a wild stallion when you were young. I prayed that you would be able to restrain those uncontrollable impulses and grow into the fine, mature, respectable, and responsible young man that you are becoming. You will need to always possess integrity and character, if you are to succeed and to fulfill your purpose in life.

Ask God to fill you with His Grace and Spirit to begin the rest of your life walking the Christian walk with good morals and values. Jesus Christ came down to earth to show each one of us how to live. He was patient, kind, and full of peace, joy, and love. He used the gifts God gave Him to heal and to help the poor, the weak, those who couldn't see, and the little children. Steven, you should strive to be as much like Jesus Christ as you can. I love you and will be thinking of you as you grow spiritually in Christ.

Love,
Mom

Dear Dad,

So, how's the retreat so far? Hopefully, it's going good for you. I am kind of glad that I was told to write you a letter, since I rarely am up-front and open like this. I guess I am not really one to show much emotion, but I know that you know how much I love you.

As a matter of fact, tonight I was just talking to a friend and I was telling her how I don't know how I would be able to go on with life, without you, Mom, Steven, or Vanessa. I have realized that I have the perfect family. I mean, I know at times we argue and fight, but when it really comes down to it, I know that we honestly love and care for each other much more than most families could even dream of. I also know that I may not be perfect at times, but I am so glad that you and mom have instilled in me the values and morals needed to be a successful and prosperous person both in the world and in God's eyes. When my friends see how much we love each

This is a poem my husband wrote and set to music for my daughter on her first birthday and will sing on her *Quinceañera*.

Vanessa, Mi Princesa

Tengo una niña muy linda
Que nos mandó el Señor,
Para completar la familia,
Y darle mucho amor.

Se llama Gloria Vanessa,
La que me inspira a cantar.
Le gusta oír mi guitarra,
Para ponerce a bailar.

Nació ya con dos hermanos,
Que siempre la van a cuidar.
Con Salvador y Esteban,
El amor nunca le faltará.

(Coro)
Y cuando está dormidita,
No hay otra princesa igual.
Le cantan los angelitos,
Con música celestial.

Mi muñequita tan linda,
Eres un gran placer.
Vanessa, mi Princesa,
Que siempre tengas tu querer.

Ya que se está desarrollando,
Sus gustos se proclamarán.
Expresa con una voz fuerte,
"Démen leche con un pan."

Se divierte con sus libros.
También trata de escribir.
Pero cuando llega su padre,
Sus brazos le va a pedir.

Vanessa es muy cariñosa,
Abrazos y besos ya da.
No le quites su juguete,
Porque su modo cambiará.

Le gusta ver pajaritos,
Cuando cantan su canción.
Camina con sus pacitos,
Con gracia y precaución.

Sus labios son muy pequeños,
Los ojos relumbran de amor.
Y con sus dientitos de perla,
Come con mucho sabor.

Su pelo es muy fino y chino,
Se ve bien con aprendedor.
Y cuando usa sus gorritas,
Ya se ve como una flor.
(Coro)

Es linda como su madre,
Le gusta la atención.
Y el pobre con quien se enamore—
Cuidado con su corazón.

Y cuando se encuentre un hombre
Que quiera hacerla feliz,
Le damos consejos de padres,
Que ese amor no deje cicatriz.

Las aspiraciones de un padre
Para su linda mujer,
Serán que goce de la vida,
Su mejor trate de hacer.
(Coro)

Anuncian ya las trompetas,
Las puertas se van abrir;
Para que entre mi Princesa,
La Reina del porvenir.

other and how close we are as a family, they say, "Man Sal, you've got it made." I want you to know that I don't take that for granted at all. I thank God every day that I am fortunate enough to have been born into such a loving and caring household and that I am just beginning to realize just how much you all really do care for us.

One of these days I hope to be as good a parent to my kids and as good a husband to my wife as you are. It must have been tough to put up with us as teenagers. It really hurts me to know that I caused you all such grief, and for that I would like to apologize. In closing, I just want you to know that I really, really love you and I am extremely appreciative for all that you have and will ever do for me.

Your loving son,
Salvador Rodriguez

DISCRIMINATION AND PREJUDICE

Helping your child function in the world means preparing him to confront the people in it who may refuse to accept him, perhaps even hate him, simply because of the color of his skin, the sound of his surname, the language he uses, his accent, or his beliefs and cultural practices. Racism can manifest itself in a number of ways and its seeds can be planted very early in life. Though some acts of racism may fade from your children's memories, there are less visible scars that can last a lifetime. A child exposed to prejudice, whether directed at him or at another person, can suffer a crippling blow to his self-esteem, his sense of belonging, and his sense of trust in the world. His ability to achieve in many areas of life may suffer under those circumstances. Socially, discrimination can affect the child's willingness to associate with other people later in life out of fear of being rejected and alienated. It can cause him to stereotype others by thinking that all members of a group hold the same beliefs. Your child needs to know that both *lo bueno y lo malo* exist in every group and that racism and prejudice are not a reflection of his own shortcomings but are born out of the ignorance of others.

From the way lands were taken away from *nuestros antepasados* through illegal and racist means, to segregated and unequally funded schools, separate public facilities, and chronic exploitation in the world of work, Hispanics have experienced their share of historical discrimination and racism. Today, racism and discrimination may be more subtle and less easy to define. They may arise in such forms as immigrant bashing, continued inequality in educational opportunities, and the so-called "English Only" movement, which is attempting to deny us the right to speak our language. Usually in hard economic times that bring about uncertainty and insecurity, there tends to be a scapegoat for the conditions. Hispanics, particularly since we are the most recent immigrants, are the first to be blamed for society's ills, a point that is important to make as you talk to your children about issues related to prejudice and discrimination.

Personal Experience with Discrimination

When I was growing up, I was confronted with a situation where one individual, whom I call "a gatekeeper," could have changed the course of my life because of his actions. In spite of the fact that I made A's and B's and was a leader of my school, my high school principal told the representatives of a war on poverty college program, entitled Project Teacher Excellence, that he did not recommend me for the program because "I was not college material." In spite of his recommendation, I was still accepted and successfully graduated in three and a half years and included in *Who's Who in Colleges and Universities*. I later took a graduate course with this man, when we were both getting our principal's certificate.

Being a parent, I again had to deal with many "gatekeepers," in my children's education, teachers or counselors who thought my children did not belong in certain classes, programs, or schools. When Sal was in the third grade at a very prestigious private school, it became very evident to several of us that a particular teacher felt that Hispanics and Blacks should not be in that school. One year, his grades dropped from almost all A's three years in a row to two D's. I found out that the teacher had been picking on my son and an African-American girl, neither of whom, she may have thought, belonged in that school. One day I dropped in to the school without notice and found out that Sal had been put out in the hallway. Eventually he told me that he had been placed out in the hallway the first two weeks of school. After complaining to the headmaster and asking a counselor to help make the teacher aware of her actions and its effects on her students, the teacher's behavior changed and my son's academic performance improved. I experienced something similar with my two other children, when they were not allowed to take advanced classes or to be included in gifted and talented programs. On those occasions, I let it be known to the "gatekeepers" that I wanted the key to let my children in. I succeeded, but only after I had convinced them that my children deserved an opportunity to participate in enrichment classes.

As Hispanics, we have to confront the fact that our children will probably experience discrimination. We have to help them learn to deal with it, for it can happen when and where they least expect it, like at camp, for example. My son Steven was taking part in a camp with Anglo and Hispanic young people and heard one of the Anglos say in a loud voice, "We'd better take care of our things because the Mexicans like to steal." Other comments that my son has heard are: "Frito Bandito," "Beanie," and "Wetback," and "Is your back wet from crossing the Rio Grande?" In an attempt to get Steven in trouble so that he would not play in an important football game, a white student cracked a raw egg on Steven's head. It was his Anglo and Black football friends who came to his defense. When my son Sal was in college at Texas A&M, two Anglo students were fighting outside campus and their Hispanic friend tried to separate them. The police came and arrested the Hispanic. One year a poster was tagged to the wall of my Sal's college that read, HISPANICS AND BLACKS GO BACK TO MEXICO AND AFRICA WHERE YOU CAME FROM. All of these occurrences have been topics of many conversations on the subject of discrimination in my home.

When there are so many stereotypes in the media depicting Hispanics as hoodlums, members of the Mexican mafia, prostitutes, Don Juans, drug dealers, and low-riders, it is not surprising that such negative attitudes exist among young people. On television and in the movies, too often Hispanic roles are restricted to maids, nannies, gardeners, or sexy voluptuous mistresses, which can make our children feel they are not worthy of professional jobs. Hispanics are depicted as lazy, shiftless people who wear sombreros and ride donkeys. Many Hispanics have been disturbed by characters like Speedy Gonzalez, Chiquita Banana, and Juan Valdez. In the 1960s Hispanics organized to complain about the Frito Bandito, and recently some Hispanics became offended by the Taco Bell commercials displaying the Spanish-speaking pointed-ear Chihuahua Pinky, saying "Yo Quiero Taco Bell." He may be cute and many people love Chihuahuas, but it is what he says, how he says it, and what he is wearing (the costume of a revolutionary) that convey subtle feelings of how some Anglos perceive Latinos. A Jack-in-the-Box commercial about beans and what happens to people who eat them was certainly not funny to me.

What Hispanics like me want is for our culture to be more accurately and respectfully portrayed. We do not want a creation of new stereotypes associated with funny animals with squeaky voices or talking green jalapeños. That is making a subtle mockery of our culture. We need more positive role models and images on television and in the media that will inspire and motivate our children and make them feel proud of who they are. We as a people must do our part to educate the general public about what it truly means to be Hispanic.

Fortunately, today there are more movies being written, directed, and cast by Hispanics that feature our people in more positive roles and contain stories that more accurately reflect our culture's beauty and strength. In their attempts to capture the $350 billion Hispanic market, corporations are now engaging Hispanic-marketing firms to create commercials that effectively capture the positive aspects of our culture, such as our devotion to family and the virtue of respect.

Even as middle-class professional adults, many of us have felt the effects of immigration bashing. Once I was trying to get my luggage down from a storage compartment in an airplane that had just arrived in San Antonio from New York, when a very rude man pushed me aside and said, "Proposition 187, here we come to Texas. *You all* should go back to Mexico where you came from." It did not matter that I was in first class or wearing a professional-looking suit; I was still part of a category of people that this man detested because we are Hispanic. I gave him a look of disapproval and chose to ignore him.

A professional acquaintance of mine from Colombia shared with me her experience living in an upper-middle-class neighborhood in Michigan where she was the only Hispanic. She came from a large family whose members of the extended family would visit her often. The neighbors could not believe that anything but drug dealing was going on in her home, and they reported her to drug authorities, who sent a drug agent to her home. I have heard of instances in which prominent and middle-class Hispanics have been told to go to the kitchen when they entered parties or asked to show their green cards when they are in fact legal citizens. Many have been redlined or denied loan applications for housing in predominantly white areas. Despite the Supreme Court order in 1954, and Title VI and VII of the Civil Rights Act enacted by Congress in 1964, which prohibited unfair and discriminatory practices in public accommodations, such as schools, employment, credit, housing, or any institution that receives federal funds based on race, national origin, creed, and color, we still see propositions in the ballot box trying to deny our *gente* their rights.

Whether we live in the barrio or the suburbs, whether we are rich or poor, many of us will be affected by the negative attitudes that persist regarding Hispanics. We are undergoing a great amount of change from internal and external forces that can threaten our people in the future and we must prepare our children to be ready to confront these changes. One is the demographic shift in the United States that is creating many opportunities as well as challenges for the growing number of Hispanics. The other is that Latin America is gaining more economic importance globally because of treaties like the North American Free Trade Agreement (NAFTA). Either we can stand by the wayside and allow these changes to overtake us, or we can be involved in making sure that policies that are being adopted are sensitive to Hispanics.

As parents, we must listen to our children's verbal and nonverbal messages, discuss these issues openly with them, and teach them how to confront them in a nonviolent manner. We, as parents, are responsible for teaching our children to be kind and to be respectful. We can help them get fortitude through our spirituality and through the unity of our people. However, we have to make them aware that harassment and discrimination do exist in our country and around the world for any number of reasons. Sometimes the best way to confront racism and discrimination is to look into the past at how it has affected different people. Talk to your children about how other groups have also been victims of discrimination like the people in Chiapas, Bosnia, Rwanda, Somalia, and Germany.

We did not only talk to our kids about the atrocities that man has committed to man, we wanted them to see it with their own eyes. One year my family took a vacation to Germany with the intention of taking our children to the Dachau Concentration Camp so that they could see firsthand the atrocities that occurred to the Jewish people during the Holocaust. My children toured the actual gas showers and ovens where countless Jewish people perished. I explained to my children that the concentration camp had been preserved so that people from around the world could see what happened and would make sure that history not repeat itself. I wanted them to be sensitive about how all people are treated, including how others treat Hispanics. This trip, taken when he was very young, had an impact on Steven when he was older. Many years later, he came home from a history class upset because of their discussion on Proposition 187. There had been discussions about how ID cards were going to be issued to identify Hispanics who were not American citizens. "First, they will make us identify ourselves with these ID cards, just as the Jewish people were made to identify themselves with the Star of David. Then they will put us in concentration camps. We must speak out against it now, before it is too late," he said.

As you move into multiethnic communities and your children attend schools with more young people of different backgrounds, you will have to help your children learn that there will always be people who might say or do things to them that could cause them pain. Your child may one day come home crying because someone called him "greaser," "spic," "beaner," or "wetback," or because someone told him that he needs to go back to Mexico, Cuba, Africa, or Puerto Rico, or "wherever you people came from." Hateful words can cause our children great pain and affect their self-worth. Be ready to help your child understand that there are different kinds of people in the world, just as my mother taught me.

People who say those things often come from parents who have not taught their children to be kind and considerate or to respect their fellow man. They may not have received love and kindness. Sometimes a child who uses racial epithets does not even know what he is saying, but is merely repeating what he has heard from his parents. *No dice la criatura sino lo que oye tras el fuego,* The child only repeats what he hears by the fire, *en el hogar.* Individuals who have a great deal of hate and who target people they consider weak or vulnerable are individuals who are not secure or confident, and have not learned to care and empathize. Because of their insecurity, they try to get their sense of superiority and power from taking advantage of and manipulating others. They may insist they are superior to others, but in reality, it is they who feel unloved and inferior. Following are ways to help your child cope with discrimination and racism. In addition, refer to the Resource List at the back of the book for information on organizations that deal with complaints of discrimination and civil rights violations.

1. Nonviolence and Tolerance Begin in the Home

El buen juez por su casa empieza. Justice begins at home. The elimination of discrimination begins at home, as we teach our children morals and values, including brotherhood, mutual respect, and social responsibility. We must help our children channel their aggression in a constructive manner. When children experience their first conflict with siblings, they are beginning to learn to solve their disputes and to live harmoniously under one roof. That concept must be extended outside the family, so that they can learn to live together with different people from diverse groups, whether it be on the baseball field, at school, in the community, or in one's world.

We must teach our children to be proud of who they are, where they came from, and where they are going. The best tool we can give our children against hateful, destructive attitudes and behavior is to give them a solid inner strength that comes from our love, acceptance, and support and from a strong spiritual upbringing. As the saying goes, *Cuando el viento sopla, el árbol se limpia,* and after the dust settles, what remains are these attributes that keep one standing strong and firmly grounded. We need to help our children become resilient, tenacious, and bold and help them learn to possess an inner fortitude to ignore people who try to hurt them. Regardless of what others say to your children or about them, assure them that you are there to support them. Help them express their feelings by talking, by writing, or by just punching a bag or kicking a ball specifically used for releasing emotions. Children need to know that they may be rejected, ridiculed, and hurt in life because of their ethnicity and the best defense sometimes is to file a complaint, from the lowest level of authority all the way to the Supreme Court.

We have to teach our children that at some point in their lives they may have to take a stand against hatred that is expressed by some people. Discuss how different people have historically been discriminated against. Expose them to Hispanic leaders, like Dr. Hector Pérez García, founder of the GI Forum, and César Chávez, activist for farm workers, who fought against social injustice and discrimination. In addition, discuss how great leaders like Martin Luther King, Jr., and Mohandas Gandhi were able to create social change through peaceful means.

2. Know Your Rights

Saber es poder. To know is power. Know that you can defend and support your own children's rights to dignity and respect and equal protection under the law. When my children were young I complained to authorities when they were treated unfairly. I encouraged them to solve their problems and to speak for themselves when they were older. Know that you have rights and resources to help you if your child is discriminated against. Your children cannot learn in school if they are scared. Go to your school board representative or even to the Office of Civil Rights (OCR) in Washington, D.C. (See the Resource List at the back of the book for address.) According to OCR, you have 180 days after an incident to file a complaint by giving the following information: (1) your name and address, (2) general description of the person injured by the act(s) or class of person injured by the alleged discriminatory act(s), (3) the name and location of the institution that committed the alleged discriminatory act(s), (4) a description of the alleged discriminatory act(s) in sufficient detail to answer what it was, when it took place, and what you believe to be the basis of the act(s) (race, color, national origin, sex, handicap, or age). If you face a problem that is very serious and is happening to more than one individual, remember you are stronger in numbers. You can organize a group to complain or file a civil action suit together.

You and your family have rights in this country against harassment and discrimination. If you or a member of your family encounters discrimination or harassment from immigration officials, go to the Immigration and Naturalization Service (INS) Processing, Holding, and Public Access area to get a complaint form or call the toll free number from the Resource List in this book. It is against the law to retaliate against a person who files a charge of discrimination, who participates in an investigation of discrimination acts, or who opposes an unlawful employment practice. Know your civil rights.

3. Parents Are the First Models and Teachers of Nonviolence

El buen padre en la casa comienza. Good parenting begins at home. Parents teach through word and action. Parents must be good role models of tolerance, patience, kindness, and compassion. By restraining oneself from administering corporal punishment, discussing the reasons behind a certain position, and working toward a solution, parents are teaching children to do likewise when they want to make a point. Some *dichos* that parents can use to teach their children empathy and compassion include *Sea grande o chica, la espina pica,* A thorn, whether it is big or little, still hurts. This teaches that it may not be obvious on the surface what a person is feeling. Another *dicho, Sólo el que carga el costal sabe lo que carga o lleva adentro,* reminds us that only the holder of the sack knows what's inside. Do not tell or laugh at racial, handicap, or ethnic jokes and do not permit your children to do so. Speak up against anyone who does. Do not condone racist remarks with your silence.

3. Discuss the Subject of Discrimination Openly

Hombre prevenido nunca fue vencido. A man who is prepared will always be spared. You should sensitize your children very early in life to the fact that discrimination and racism are still alive and that they may be victims of it. Encourage your children to discuss issues related to discrimination, whether they be incidents they have experienced or problems of the world that need to be addressed with more mutual respect, compassion, and cooperation. Teach your children to speak up against hate and discrimination. Even if the discrimination and hatred is not targeted at them, they must be taught not to be afraid and to take a stand against it. Share with them the words of Pastor Martin Niemöller, president of the World Council of Churches, who spent several years in a concentration camp for opposing Hitler:

In Germany they came first for the Communists, and I didn't speak up because I wasn't a Communist. Then they came for the Jews, and I didn't speak up because I wasn't a Jew. Then they came for the trade unionists, and I didn't speak up because I wasn't a trade unionist. Then they came for the Catholics, and I didn't speak up because I was a Protestant. Then they came for me, and by that time, there was no one left to speak up.

4. Encourage Your Children to Serve and Do Community Service

Quien no sirve para servir, no sirve para vivir. One's life should be devoted to service, for a person who does not serve is not living right. Children should be encouraged to serve. They should be sensitized to the plight of people in their communities and in the world, beginning with the poor, homeless, elderly and handicapped individuals in their hometown to people suffering from natural disasters and hunger in faraway lands. Children learn to coexist and care for their fellow man when they have given of their time, talents, and energy to help someone less fortunate. Encourage them to help tutor children, organize recreational games for handicapped children or children of the barrio, or teach classes like piano to those in need. Invite them to join you in serving the homeless in soup kitchens or delivering presents to the poor. Adopt a family in need so that children will know how benevolent actions can make a difference in the lives of people and how much appreciation can result from such acts of kindness. Have them feel the satisfaction that comes from doing something good without expecting anything in return. Tell them *Haz bien y no mires a quién*, Do good without noticing to whom.

5. Teach Conflict-Resolution Skills

Vale más perro vivo que leon muerta. A live dog is better than a dead lion. Help your children learn to resolve their problems in a constructive manner. Encourage them to role-play situations in which they must think through what they would do if confronted with a particular situation. It is not easy to avoid some situations when one is being ridiculed or taunted. *Más vale un cobarde en casa que un valiente en la cárcel o en el cementerio* is another *dicho* used to teach children to get away from a situation before they become a dead or regretful *valiente*. It is best to stay away from danger, *porque jugar con fuego es peligroso juego*, playing with fire is dangerous.

6. Analyze and be Critical of What Your Children Watch on Television

El diablo no duerme. El que evita la tentación, evita el pecado. These are but a few of the dichos that Hispanic mothers use to help their children become aware of vices that exist in the world. Children need supervision and guidance. Do not allow your children to watch television without any type of monitoring system. Sit down and watch television with them and discuss the different stereotypical images, hatred, and violence that are presented on television. Control which programs they can watch. Children who watch violence on television have been known to become violent themselves and to lash out after watching such a program. Protest and write to the producers of programs, commercials, and music that are offensive and violent. Do these activities with your children. I, along with many mothers, was greatly concerned when the tapes and articles on the Monica Lewinsky/Clinton scandal hit the airwaves, the Internet, and newspapers. This exposed our children to subject matter they were not prepared to handle. I felt powerless at first when the bombardment of unwelcome information enetered the privacy of my home. But we managed to turn the events into a mode for constructive dialogue and the resulting discussions with our children centered on the acts of the President as well as Congress and how we felt they had used poor judgment.

7. Encourage and Foster Respect for Diversity

Has bien sin mirar a quien. Be kind to everyone regardless of who they are. Encourage your children to associate with children from other ethnic, racial, and religious groups so that they can break down stereotypes for themselves and have a greater understanding of and respect for differences. Encourage them to go to camps, schools, or programs where there are children from different backgrounds and sensitive leaders, so that your children can learn to live together in harmony. Travel when you can so that your children can be exposed to different people and diverse cultures. The best way to attack stereotypes that result in prejudice and discrimination is through knowledge and information.

THE BEST OF BOTH WORLDS

Not all Hispanics rear their children in the same manner, nor do we all agree on the primary values we want to inculcate, but probably every Latino parent will agree that our shared culture is rich in traditions and values, which include loyalty to family, children, and community, as well as respect, compassion, obedience, interdependence, cooperation, spirituality, and (for many) preservation of the Spanish language. Hispanic parents in the United States are also socializing their children in the dominant Western culture, which stresses competitiveness, aggressiveness, assertiveness, individuality, independence, and, of course, the English language. Although these values may sometimes clash, there is merit in possessing both to bring about a cultural balance.

My mother was talking about the need for balance when she would share messages like these: *No te creas mucho y ten orgullo*, Be humble and proud. *Ten respeto y espera respeto*, Respect others and expect to be respected. While determination, aggressiveness, and assertiveness are characteristics that should be upheld, as they are encouraged in the Anglo world, we must ask our children and ourselves to what end they will be used. Will they be used solely for the good of the individual or can they also be used for the common good of the family and of the community? Will they be used to maintain our freedom, democracy, equality, and justice? As parents, we need to help children develop a sense of competence, autonomy, and independence and help them feel they can participate and contribute to society. But remember, too, that if every child were brought up being self-centered, believing he should be completely autonomous and independent, always thinking of number one, he would not consider himself a part of anything. What kind of society would we live in? Our *niños* need to learn that they exist in a social world where people must rely on each other if they are to live and prosper in a harmonious civil society.

While both worlds advocate the work ethic, I believe that Hispanics traditionally work to live rather than live to work, a principle that is important to remember. Achievement and accomplishment have been ingrained in the Hispanic psyche for generations, but not at the expense of destroying personal relationships, which we strongly value. This nation needs more people possessing the values and morals that are so ingrained in the Latino culture. We need the skills of negotiation, compromise, and sensitivity to avoid total annihilation. We need caring and moral leaders who look out for the common good, who know the importance of cooperation and interdependence.

At the same time, we should strive to uphold our rights, dignity, and place in society. One of our rights is the right to speak Spanish in addition to English. If we are to succeed in the decades to come, we will need to communicate in both languages. Business and political leaders will be expected to be bilingual if they want to communicate with the fastest-growing segment of this country's population and with citizens of Latin American nations that are more connected to our country than ever before.

We need to teach our children to be socially competent, to be able to move back and forth between the Hispanic and Anglo worlds, dealing with different people in different situations. My husband is a good example of this. When he spoke to his parents or the elderly *viejitas* in the barrio, he spoke to them in Spanish in a respectful manner. When he spoke to me, he spoke in a colloquial manner, in both English and Spanish, mixing the languages because he knew we could communicate in both languages with ease. When he spoke to his engineer friends, he spoke in a very professional, technical manner that only they could understand. When he went to the barrio, he would greet his friends with *¡Órale, bato! ¿Qué tal?* Because of his social and language skills, he was able to communicate with many people in different circumstances. He didn't have to reject his roots, his culture, or his family and friends. He was a better person because he had the ability to switch if he needed to, depending on the setting.

One does not have to completely assimilate, or give up one's culture and language to succeed in a world where there are "majorities" and "minorities." To reject one's culture or language is to reject oneself. As parents, we want our children to become bilingual and bicultural, to get the best of both worlds. We want them to be kind and compassionate, but we also want them to be assertive and demand their rights and place in society. While we want them to value humility, they must not be so humble that they do not assert their constitutional rights to life, liberty, and the pursuit of happiness. They can be bilingual and bicultural and have the capability of moving in and out of both worlds.

Part Three

The Three Pillars of

Effective Parenting:

Marriage, Family,

and Community

Chapter VII

El Matrimonio: Marriage

Contrato,
Compromiso, y
Comunicación

THE HISPANIC WEDDING

De un buen matrimonio, florecen las semillas, From a strong and healthy marriage the child will blossom. This simple, yet profound *dicho* reflects the notion that is central to the Hispanic view of family. Like a plant that thrives and becomes strong from nourishment in a rich soil, a child's strength comes from the bond between husband and wife. The love and respect that is expressed to one another will enable the child to go forth into the world to grow and flourish. That is why it is so critical to maintain a strong and healthy marriage. The bond between husband and wife in *el matrimonio* is a fundamental building block to effective parenting. The stability in marriage is one of the pillars for successful parenting.

In a Biblical parable about the sower and the seed, we are told that the seed that falls on rocky ground will not develop well for lack of moisture. The seed that falls among thorns will grow but eventually be choked by thorns and die. However, the seed that falls on good soil will develop strong roots and produce a hundredfold. If gardeners are committed to producing a good crop, they must plant the seed in rich, healthy soil and nurture it so that the plant will thrive. A marriage rooted in love, trust, and respect becomes the rich soil that will help children grow and develop well.

Today Latino families in the United States are undergoing enormous transformations and pressures that can place great stress on a marriage and on parenting and ultimately on the child's environment. The roles, expectations, and responsibilities of Hispanic mothers and fathers, while grounded on the experiences of our parents and caregivers, demand a new set of skills and perspectives. In many ways, these parenting approaches differ greatly from those our *padres* used on us. For too many couples, education, career, and community involvement must be balanced against the parent's responsibility to create a nurturing home environment to ensure their children's success. Buried within each of these issues is the mitigating factor of culture. While we all want our children to excel in a primarily English-speaking world, many of us want them to maintain a sense of their native language and culture, which connects them to the past and to the future. We expect our children to succeed in a society where competition, autonomy, and individual success are prized. At the same time, we want to instill in them the traditional virtues of cooperation, *respeto*, and *familismo* (loyalty to the family). Without guidance, the journey to raise children in a bicultural world can produce anxieties and uncertainty and can upset the delicate soil needed for healthy growth and development.

This book is about helping Latino parents understand that it is possible to raise their children successfully in the U.S. without abandoning traditional cultural values. With regard to marriage, this means entering a lifelong commitment that espouses the traditional notions of permanence, obligation, and *familismo* in such a way that does not negate personal needs and goals. Within this new framework for Latino families, equal partnerships can be based on three essential elements: contract, commitment, and communication.

While I encourage readers to do everything in their power to preserve their marriage, "for the sake of the children," as our parents did, I recognize at the same time that the problems we face today are not the same as the ones our parents confronted. The traditional support networks are not there for many mobile Hispanic families as they were thirty years ago. In addition, some Latino single parents have been able to do an appropriate job of rearing their children, despite the odds. Nevertheless, what is important for the purpose of this book is to explore the idea that strong marriages produce better outcomes for children than broken, unhealthy ones. Throughout my twenty-five years of working with families, I have observed that if marriages are strong, one will generally see positive outcomes in the children.

As I mentioned before, Urie Bronfenbrenner of Cornell University once said that every child needs at least one person in his life who is crazy about him. But as countless studies have shown, two united parents are better than one, economically, educationally, emotionally, and physically for both parents and children. For example, the Coleman Report, a groundbreaking nationwide study of 570,000 schoolchildren in 1965, found that the nuclear family had a stronger influence on student achievement than any other factor, including quality of curriculum, books, buildings, and teacher-training programs. This means that no matter how superior the teachers and curriculum may be in school, your child's success will be influenced more by the experiences she receives in *la familia*.

But the effects of a healthy marriage and family go much further than the academic arena. It also gives our children the interpersonal skills to communicate and form social relationships with others. Parents who respect and support each other are teaching children such basic values as loyalty, honesty, and responsibility, which are essential for a civilized society. Conflicts occur in all marriages, but when these are resolved in a thoughtful and rational manner, parents are modeling the virtues of tolerance, compromise, cooperation, and kindness. They also espouse the virtues of compassion and generosity when they listen to each other and work together to find ways to fulfill each other's needs and goals. These "prosocial" behaviors determine how successful children will be in relating to others in society, particularly members of the opposite sex, later in life. One might say that the state of the marriage is a reflection of the state of society at large, since the family is the basic unit of society. One of the best qualities a person can have in dealing with others is *confianza*, a healthy sense of confidence, which occurs by growing up in a family that sticks together in good times and in bad.

Every marriage will have its ups and downs. If parents don't acknowledge this from the start, they can easily give up and their marriage will fail, as it does in 65 percent of new marriages in the United States. Put strategies in place to cope with the many challenges that come with raising children in a bicultural world, where the pressures from both sides can be overwhelming. As was stated earlier, according to demographic data from the U.S. Department of Health and Human Services, 64 percent of Hispanic households with children are headed by two parents. However, the fact that it has become easy in this country to walk away from a marriage poses a challenge to our values of a strong family. The so-called "no-fault" divorce policy allows a spouse to break the marriage contract easier than breaking a rental agreement or a contract to purchase a refrigerator or a car.

Parents should ask themselves in times of insecurity and doubt, Is this marriage worth saving? Given that this person is the father or mother of my children, is that important enough that I should put forth the effort to work things out? Could I find another partner who will be worse than my spouse? As the saying goes, *No te vayas de Guatemala a Guatepeor*, Don't go from a bad to a worse situation. If you are tempted to leave your spouse and children for another woman or man who appears more tempting, *No dejes el camino por la vereda*, Don't leave the familiar (main) road for an unfamiliar side road, or Don't leave a marriage of many years for another that could fail. *Vale más malo por conocido que bueno por conocer*, It is better to stick to the familiar rather than to something that is unknown. How will I feel about my actions ten or twenty years from now if I do get a divorce? What are the effects of divorce on my children, my health, economic status, and emotional stability? What about the relationships that we have built together through the years? Will I lose contact with our mutual friends or the extended family? Is it worth it?

While many of these questions are difficult to answer, some studies have tried to examine the effects of divorce on parents and children. In Judith Wallerstein and Sandra Blakeslee's book *Second Chances: Men, Women and Children a Decade after Divorce*, the authors found that divorced men are twice as likely to die from heart disease, stroke, and cancer. They are four times as likely to die from an automobile accident or suicide, seven times more likely to die from cirrhosis of the liver or pneumonia, eight times more likely to die by murder, and ten times more likely to have psychiatric illness. Although divorced women are less prone to physical illness than single unmarried women, they suffer from more chronic conditions and spend more days in bed. They are two to three times more likely to die in a given year from cancer of the mouth or digestive organs, lung, or breast.

EFFECTS OF DIVORCE ON CHILDREN

Children of divorce see their family income drop 37 percent. Ten years after their parents' divorce, one out of three males and one out of ten females exhibit delinquent behavior. Children of divorced parents are almost twice as likely to demonstrate poor school performance than children from two-parent homes. Women raised in single-parent families are 64 percent more likely to have children out of wedlock themselves. Those women who do marry are 92 percent more likely to end up divorced than women from two-parent families. Inmates in state prisons are twice as likely to have grown up in single-parent homes. Daughters between the ages of twelve and sixteen who live with unmarried mothers are at least twice as likely to become single parents themselves. Studies have linked mental illness, suicide, physical illness, drug abuse, cigarette smoking, homelessness, juvenile crime, and school failure to broken marriages.

Sometimes parents think that by divorcing, they will have an opportunity to find a better mate and that conditions will get better. Sometimes this does occur, but more than half of the children of divorce witness physical violence between their parents, whereas before the divorce most had never experienced violence in the home.

I want to make it clear that I am not saying that every marriage should remain together regardless of the circumstances, for there are indeed important exceptions to consider. My point is simply that knowing the negative consequences of divorce should warrant some deeper consideration before couples decide to make the big leap. What you might think of as an exit clause, or a "safe way out," can often result in more problems and suffering. Many younger generations of Latinos today, not fully committed to the cultural view of marriage that reinforces its permanence, opt to test out other alternatives. They might try living together with their partners before they marry or simply not marrying at all. More and more young people go into these situations thinking that they will learn something about their future spouse that will help prepare them for the commitment later. But this belief finds no support in recent studies.

According to the National Survey of Families and Households by the University of Wisconsin, among the 14,000 people interviewed who were living with their mates, there was a 50 percent higher divorce or separation rate compared with marriages without premarital cohabitation. Nearly 40 percent of couples living together broke up before they even reached the altar. The average duration of their relationship was 1.3 years. So, where do the answers to a solid marriage lie? *Simplemente en el contrato, compromiso, y comunicación*, in the contract, commitment, and communication between two people. It all begins with an individual's examination and disclosure of his or her own values, expectations, and hopes before one marries.

PERSONAL AND PREMARITAL INVENTORY: *ANTES QUE TE CASES, MIRA LO QUE HACES*

While this book is primarily intended for parents who have children under the age of twelve, it is also designed for those individuals who are seriously thinking about marriage with the intentions of one day having children. To that group of individuals I tell you what my mother told me and my siblings: "*Antes que te cases, mira lo que haces*," Before you marry, think of what you are doing. As a young, single woman, I wanted to be very careful about choosing the person with whom I would share the rest of my life. I wanted my marriage to last. I had a list of characteristics that I was looking for in a mate, and I tested them on every man I dated.

I could not believe how close my husband came to my ideal man. We were *como agua para chocolate*, like water for chocolate; it seemed like we were meant for each other. One day I announced to my family that I was madly in love and that I had found the perfect man. Then my voiced dropped and I abruptly said, "W-e-l-l, except for *one minor trait*." He was shorter than I expected my prince charming to be. I remember going to Father Albert Kippes, the Catholic priest who eventually married us, for some guidance. I told him, "Father, I think I found the perfect man, except for one minor thing." He replied, "I don't want to hear about it now. On one side of a sheet of paper, write down all the things that you like about him; on the other side list the things that you don't. Then we'll talk."

I followed his instructions, filling the left side of my list with so many things I liked about Sal. On the right side, I listed the one thing: *que era chaparro*. Father Kippes laughed when he saw my list. "The things that are important, like his character, will not change," he said. "Physical attributes do. We all get short, fat, and bald as we get older. We may lose a leg or an arm in an accident. But the heart will always remain constant." He looked at me and emphatically told me to marry him. *Dicho y hecho*, just as Father Kippes recommended, I did, and on June 17, 1997, we celebrated 25 years of marriage. *¡Qué aguante!* Of course, I am joking, for it has seemed like only yesterday that we took our marriage vows.

One of the best pieces of advice that can be given to anyone who is thinking of marriage and having it last is to take a premarital inventory offered by the pastors and counselors of many churches to determine how compatible you are. *Si no escoges el mejor, por lo menos no el peor*, If you do not choose the best, at least do not choose the worse. You want someone who will help you provide the best kind of environment for your children. There will be stresses in any relationship, but the more you know about each other, the better relationship you will have later. Even on your own, you can take stock of personal expectations, hopes, and attitudes. Make a mental list (or on paper) of those things that you value most in life and want to pursue: an education, career, and/or family. Discuss what things are important to you and what things you will not tolerate, such as adultery. All of the items that you lay out will be used later to create a plan for your marriage, to set goals, and to negotiate a common ground. Couples who are thinking about marriage should discuss their views on the roles and responsibilities that each person will assume before entering the marriage contract. The earlier you realize where each one stands on such issues as finances, education, and career paths and the number of children you want the better able you will be to resolve conflicts later on. If not carefully thought through, the questions and doubts may very likely turn into resentments and hostility and can easily erupt into a host of problems.

Some of the questions you should ask yourself are:

- Will I take my husband's last name or keep mine?
- Will both parties have an equal opportunity to pursue educational and career goals?
- Is each person willing to move to a new city or country if the other is offered a job or an educational opportunity?
- How will the finances be divided? Will they be shared equally, or will each person be expected to contribute a "fair share"? Is one person willing to support the other for years if necessary? How much will we save or invest? Will we have credit cards? How many? Up to what amount?
- Of the many household tasks that have to be done to maintain an orderly home, who will do what? Should we get outside help?
- Will there be children? If so, when? How many? How will they be disciplined? Will they be bilingual? What traditional beliefs and practices do we want to pass on to them?
- What role will members of the extended family play?
- Where are we going to live? Are we going to live near our support system, including our parents' homes, or farther away?
- Are we going to maintain certain traditional beliefs and practices?
- Which religion will we practice? If we choose to maintain different religions, which one will our children practice when young?
- What will I do if my spouse becomes an adulterer, an alcoholic, or an abuser?
- Where and how do we celebrate important holidays (Christmas, Mother's Day, Easter)?

- And what about *la suegra* y *el suegro*, the in-laws or the stepchildren? How will we make sure to keep the relationship strong?

Other essential issues include sexual relations, friendships, and use of leisure time. The roles and responsibilities will range from such complex matters as discipline to something as seemingly trivial as doing the dishes. As difficult as many of these subjects may be to discuss, talking them through can be extremely helpful in exploring common ground. Even things that appear minuscule can become significant issues that could break a relationship later.

For those who are already married, as the popular *dicho* goes, *Te casaste, te fregaste*. Now it is important to make it work out. Following are some tips, some observations that can help you maintain a strong marriage.

LATINAS: *LA SACRIFICADA* AND THE "SUPER-MOM"

Hispanic women today are redefining and asserting their position in society. Throughout history, Latina mothers were revered as the heart of the family, the nurturers, the stabilizers, and the ones who took on the enormous task of keeping the family together. But their authority never rivaled that of their husband's, who had *la última palabra* in the home. The model of being *sacrificada*, self-sacrificing and submissive, continues to affect Hispanic women's positions in the United States. It was a model I grew up with in my barrio, one that everyone from my grandmother to my mother—up until the time my mother became a Jehovah's Witness—took on without question. Her new religion gave her the strength to become assertive in the name of doing "Jehovah's work."

Later, as a mother and a working professional, I knew that equality, cooperation, and communication were going to be essential in my family and that negotiating an equal partnership was not going to be easy. Latina women today demand and expect to be treated as equals, *con dignidad y respeto*. They are driven, as any American, to make the most of the freedoms and opportunities that life in this country affords them. Nevertheless, a host of barriers, both outside and inside of the family, have made this a difficult journey. As a result, many Hispanic women face enormous difficulties in assuming new roles to accommodate a world of two cultures with two sets of expectations. It is very easy to feel overwhelmed.

My brother-in-law who is married to my sister Yolanda told me early in their marriage that he would only allow her to work if the house was clean and if a plate of warm food was waiting for him when he came home from work. My sister-in-law, Hope, a very traditional woman, is at her husband's beck and call. She is considered *pura mujer* (all woman) in the eyes of some. Her husband snaps his fingers and not only does she jump, but so do her daughters. She has accepted the traditional role with hardly a complaint or adjustment, except for one important difference: she works full-time, not because she wants to, but because the financial demands of the family make it necessary. For some, this arrangement may still be satisfying. But to a growing number of Hispanics, it presents a troubling scenario.

In the rapidly changing social landscape of the United States, Hispanic women are taking advantage of new roles and experiences. More and more, they are discovering their potential outside the home. According to the U.S. Department of Labor, Hispanic women make up one of the most rapidly growing groups of women in the workforce in the United States. Their participation in employment increased by 65 percent between 1986 and 1996. Certainly these dramatic shifts have enormous implications for the structure of the family. Unfortunately, these changes are not readily discussed, and with more women waiting longer to have children, the issues of work and family are not always clarified early on in the marriage.

I did not mind playing a traditional maternal role when I had only one child and a staff of four, for as a nurturing person, I wanted to give of myself to everyone I could. When both my immediate family and my Avance family grew, I knew I could no longer be everything to everyone and still maintain my sanity. I came to terms with the fact that I was not a super-mom and I didn't want to be. Only when I protested did my husband begin to assume more responsibilities in taking care of the children and helping me around the house. He did not mind playing with the children, bathing them, and cooking for them. What he hated was housework. Through the process of communication, instead of keeping quiet, I let him know all the things that needed to be done and how I didn't have the time or energy to do everything. Just as I have spoken up for children and families through the years and have fought for the survival and growth of Avance, I found myself applying this assertiveness in my own home with the people that I cared for most. My husband carried more of the load in our attempt to keep an orderly home, but he refused to do the dishes until we got a dishwasher, and even then, he had something against those dishes. As my children grew older, the workload was divided among all the members of the family, as well as getting domestic help who came in at least once a week to do the major work that we hated to do—like the bathrooms!

I have joined the ranks of many other women and men who are convinced that real changes must occur in several corners of society in order for Hispanic women to gain the economic and social footing they deserve. Breaking discriminatory barriers in education and in the workplace and making employment policies more helpful to working mothers are two examples of changes that need to take place. Within the family, some reevaluation on the part of our men regarding their roles will also be necessary to help women find some middle ground between being *la mujer sacrificada* and the super-mom. The most important part of the process of redefining and asserting *"nuestro lugar,"* our place, as mothers, wives, and productive workers in the next century is strengthening our voices and being heard in the family and beyond.

THE HISPANIC MAN: RETHINKING THE MACHO MODEL

For generations, *machismo* has been associated with a man who is very firm and domineering in the home. He is someone who lives by his own laws and is never questioned by anyone, particularly not by *su esposa*. While this profile is a familiar one, there is much more to the model of *machismo*.

The root word for *macho* comes from the pre-Columbian Náhuatl word *mati*, "to know" and *macho*, "to be known." Among the Aztecs, valor and bravery were virtues men strived for to achieve prominence and recognition. Hispanic men today are still being recognized for their bravery as they hold many Congressional Medals of Honor for valor. Also, according to author Earl Shorris, the values, or *virtu*, that the Aztec men wanted to be known for included "courage, vigor, fortitude in adversity, public achievement, order, discipline, happiness, strength, justice and above all assertion of one's proper claims and the knowledge and power needed to secure their satisfaction."

The negative aspects of *machismo*, it is said, came about after the conquest, during which men, as leaders of the society, lost their names, religion, culture, and families. In many ways, they lost their identities and self-respect. The man who has a need to display his positive virtues but can't, hides under a mask of alcoholism. He inflicts violence and terror on family and friends whom he perceives weaker than him. He cannot express his anger to his "*patrón*," even an unjust one, and he won't stand up against blatant discrimination. This may lead to alcoholism to numb the pain or to family violence to release the anger.

There is an Aztec legend that illustrates the phenomenon of hiding in a mask of shame and guilt. There was a good monk of Tula, whom the evil god, Tezcatlipoca, tricks into getting drunk. Not in his right mind, Tula sexually abuses his sister. The next morning, ashamed, he hides his face with a jade mask, goes to the sea, and sets his boat on fire. He then turns into a feathered bird named Quetzalcoatl. This legend is analogous to what has happened to many Hispanic men who have been stripped of their identity, dignity, and self-respect because of oppression, discrimination, or an inability to provide for the family. All of us want our lives to have meaning and purpose. But when a man cannot even provide basic needs for the family or know who he is, he hides under the mask of shame and diverts his anger onto the people he loves. That is why it is so critical that society afford all of its citizens, including men, the educational opportunities and jobs to properly fulfill their fatherhood role as providers. It is also important that Hispanics from an early age know who they are and be proud of their culture.

In this country, there is more of a balance between the mother, who has generally been seen as the one who nurtures and educates the children, and the father, who has traditionally been seen as the provider and disciplinarian. If this balance occurs, both should be honored and revered by the children for their role in rearing the children and in keeping the house together. *De un buen matrimonio, florecen las semillas*. Children will blossom when there is a strong marriage. They will feel a sense of security when parents demonstrate love and respect for each other.

However, when the Hispanic woman is made to feel weak by an insecure man who expresses his feelings of inadequacy by physically and emotionally abusing her, the family shifts out of balance and becomes dysfunctional. Sometimes the man, who cannot find an adequate paying job to support the family, finds that he cannot handle the load himself and he masks his insecurities of not being able to take care of his family with the negative aspect of *machismo*. Each family needs two strong individuals, supporting each other and doing whatever it takes to keep the family functioning well.

The way to make parents strong is to apply the ancient Náhuatl practice referred to as Etzli-Yollotl, or *cara y corazón*. Each individual must have *cara* (dignity and respect) and *corazón* (confidence and love) in order to function well. The Aztec Náhuatl people believed that if a person was hurting, perhaps because of misfortune or war, he had to regain his strength through *cara y corazón*. He was to get healed in order to become a *macho* again.

Just as our ancestors were able to consider the positive aspect of *machismo* as an outward manifestation of virtue, today, people like family therapist Jerry Tello from Los Angeles, California, are reevaluating what it means to be a Latino man. Tello developed a Hispanic men's network and a fatherhood program called *Cara y Corazón* to help Hispanic men heal from the pain that comes about because of discrimination and lack of education or marketable job skills and employment. He is trying to get them to regain their *cara y corazón* so that they can be better fathers, husbands, workers, and citizens. According to the *Codice Florentino*, the Aztecs believed that the man who is mature "has a heart solid as a rock, and has a wise face.... He should be able and understanding." When a person is described with phrases like *"No tiene cara para hablar"* and *"No tiene corazón,"* he is said to not have face or heart, or that he lacks character. But to have *cara y corazón* is to be wise, able, self-disciplined, and compassionate, to be the ideal man, *"un hombre noble."*

In his book *La Morenita: Evangelizer of the Americas*, Father Virgilio P. Elizondo points out that Aztec children were accepted into the clan from birth and given a *cara*, a face, or knowledge of the traditions and ways of the group that gives them dignity and respect, and a *corazón*, a heart that would incline them in the direction of self-discipline and goodness. From a very early age, Aztec children were taught the concept of *virtus*, to dedicate themselves to what was good and righteous, to avoid evil and refrain from perversion and greed. Also, the principles of moderation and self-control were also taught. In a passage taken from the Náhuatl text of the *Codice Florentino*, an Aztec father taught his son to abstain from having sex by comparing the child to a maguey plant. "If it is opened before it has grown and its liquid is taken out, it has no substance. It does not produce liquid, it is useless. Before it is opened to withdraw its water, it should be allowed to grow and attain full size. Then its sweet water is removed all in good time." The Aztec lesson is concluded with, "before you know woman you must grow and be a complete man. And then, you will be ready for marriage; you will beget children of good stature, healthy, agile, and comely." Our ancestors taught us that the real *macho* is well socialized and taught to have self-control before and after marriage, the antithesis of the negative aspect of being macho.

While some negative aspects of the image of manhood do exist in Latino culture, as they do in many cultures, we must remember that for Hispanics, *un hombre noble*, as it was first taught to our forefathers, is someone who is a leader and a protector. Today, Hispanic fathers can still be people who govern their children, but they can also be people who nurture and are not afraid to show affection to *la familia*. These are qualities that, in and of themselves, should be upheld, not dismissed or belittled as being *"de las viejas,"* for women. Husbands and fathers must explore the part of the macho that stresses respect, pride, and responsibility. Although the Hispanic woman is revered for being the one who traditionally holds the family together, it is important that the man share a place of honor by becoming more involved in the nurturing and education of his children.

In his book *Fatherlessness in America*, David Blankenhorn, social scholar and president of the Council on Families in America, which I am a member of, wrote that not so long ago when a father died, society underscored the father's role by going to the family with assistance and emotional support. I grew up in just such a community. When my father died, it was not one single person but many men and women in the barrio who felt the obligation to take his place. They, along with my mother, assumed my father's role as disciplinarians, providers, spiritual advisors, role models, and mentors. This is clearly described in the *dicho, El muchacho maleriado donequiera encuentra padre*. Unfortunately today, Blankenhorn says, when a father leaves, in many families his exit is accepted with indifference. Fatherlessness, he observes, has become just another social problem beyond our reach. It is too often seen as another fact of life.

Today, in many ways, the expectations of the Hispanic male are greater than ever. As we prepare to become the largest minority group in the United States, Hispanic men, like their women partners, face the immense challenge of keeping their *familia* strong at a time when adverse economic and social forces seem to be tearing families apart. Too many of our Hispanic youth are becoming fathers too young or falling prey to the lure of gangs and guns in attempts to get some meaning and purpose in their lives. The Hispanic macho must revert to his valor and strengths, to *luchar, aguantar, y sacrificar por el bienestar de la familia y de los niños*. There will be no greater battle won nor a greater recognition gained than when both mothers and fathers do everything possible within a strong marriage to help their children succeed in life. *Un hombre noble* is one who is strong enough to keep his family together, in harmony, and functioning well.

My mother believed that a husband brought *respeto al hogar*. She believed that many people take advantage of single women, especially in the barrio. She remarried five years after my father died because of the importance she placed on having a man in the home for protection, security, and companionship. For her, a married couple was a symbol of respect and well-being. Her philosophy is corroborated by research that links strong marriages and families with good physical and mental health. It acts as a protection against poverty, youth homelessness, juvenile crime, and sexual abuse. Research also demonstrates that having a supportive husband can serve as a buffer for the effects of stress and depression.

Speaking for myself, I know that I would not be able to keep the schedule I do, nor accomplish nearly as much as I have, without the love and support of my husband. He has encouraged me, has believed in me, has been my reality check and my sounding board. He has always stood by me, been my strength, and helped me realize my highest goals and dreams. Sal and the children have been my stabilizing force and my refuge from the outside forces and stresses of life. I feel so fortunate and blessed that my husband has been very supportive of my personal development and that he doesn't feel threatened by my accomplishments. He is just a very secure and self-confident man.

As for his parenting role, my husband has also taken it very seriously. When I was working late, traveling, or working on my doctorate degree and my book, he assumed the major parenting role. My husband has made bottles, changed diapers, and taken our children to and from the doctor when they were sick. He has cooked for them, attended teacher conferences with me and without me, and been the children's coach. My children have established a strong relationship with their father because of the precious time he has spent with them.

Many husbands have allowed work commitments to keep them from becoming involved with their children, and they have missed out on a great opportunity of feeling the same satisfaction, gratification, and love that mothers get in giving of themselves to their children. The *dicho, Sin dolor, madre sin amor*, without pain, a mother without love, can be applied to a father as well. Fulfilling your child's needs and helping him or her flourish, in good times and in bad, will develop a relationship that is priceless. Children do not just want their physical needs met or to be showered with material things. They need and want both parents' time, support, emotional assistance, and guidance. There must be unconditional love from both parents and both should be responsible for meeting their children's needs for healthy growth and development. Fathers need to savor the joy and fulfillment that comes from being involved in their children's lives. At the same time, though they often assume the role of the Hispanic matriarch, mothers need to let go of some of their responsibilities and help their men find ways to assume their equal share of child rearing. When I did this, my husband learned to be closer to his children, understanding them as individuals and forging important bonds of love and trust with them. These things, he tells me, have enriched his life tremendously, both as a father and as a human being.

DOING AWAY WITH THE "UNSPOKEN" TRADITIONS

As young men, Hispanic boys in some families are often encouraged to be sexually active and are generally spared the consequences of their actions. My mother-in-law would tell her neighbors, "*Cuiden a sus pollitas, porque ahí vienen mis gallos,*" take care of your daughters because my boys are coming. Men, as well as women, should be sexually responsible, a lesson that needs to be taught in the home when they are young. Many times when my children and I watched *telenovelas*, I found myself having to point out how opposed I was to infidelity. We watched the *telenovelas* together as a way for them to learn Spanish. What they saw, in addition, were portraits of unfaithful husbands who made a sport out of having extramarital affairs. My daughter and I became furious at the men for mistreating the women and at the women for not being more assertive.

Earlier I talked about some of the positive aspects of *machismo* that are often overlooked as well as those things that need to be added to our culture's definition of Hispanic male identity. Nevertheless, another very real factor linked to *machismo* that must be discussed is the unspoken tradition of adultery and abuse. Its roots come from the belief that basically the man was like a rooster, free to do as he pleased, and it was the woman who had the responsibility to protect herself. Infidelity is tolerated in Latin America and still persists in the United States. I learned that in Mexico it was common for a man to take on "*una sancha,*" a mistress on the side, and to father one or several illegitimate children. As a young man in Mexico, my grandfather was once a frequent womanizer. His wife tolerated his *actos de sinvergüenzas* for many years. Back then, her choices were few. It was not until my grandfather changed from a lukewarm Catholic to a devout Pentecostal that my mother and my grandmother saw a profound transformation in him. But this was not always the outcome for other families. As long as their formal duties to their families were not neglected, men were generally forgiven for extramarital affairs. At times, women who dared to take a stand would be met with punishing blows from their husbands.

Throughout my life and especially in my work, I have listened to Hispanic women talk to each other in hushed tones about the problems they faced with their husbands. Though the situations varied, many times the words were the same. *"Pues uno tiene que aguantar,"* one has to take it, they would say, or *"Ya me tocaba sufrir,"* I was meant to suffer. Today such a notion is no longer acceptable. There is not a single justification for a woman to remain with a man who is abusing her, whether it be emotionally or physically. I have urged some mothers at Avance who were victims of physical abuse not to tolerate such acts of brutality. *"¡Tú no eres una pelota para que te pateen!"* "You are not a ball to be kicked around," I would say. "You are a human being with feelings and rights. What your husband has done to you is wrong, and he needs help. He will not change his behavior until he gets help. Think about yourself, and most important, think about your children." As soon as I mentioned the children, the women would take a more critical look at their situation and take appropriate action.

María was a mother of six who would come to Avance black and blue, wearing sunglasses and long-sleeve shirts to hide her black eyes and bruises. When I confronted her about her injuries, she never admitted that her husband caused the marks. But as she came to the classes and learned about the options that were open to her, she began to understand and appreciate her worth and potential. Eventually she left her husband, completed high school, and went on to earn a college degree. Later she admitted that spousal abuse had existed for generations in her family and that she never knew that things could be different until she came to Avance. She said that by coming to Avance she learned that she did not have to live in the "rut" she was in.

It is important that women who are in these situations take steps to get out immediately. In the United States, abuse is grounds for divorce. Period. *Punto final.* The same goes for adultery. This behavior should never be accepted as a way of life. You deserve to be treated with *dignidad y respeto.* Through education, advocacy, and a legacy of legal victories, our society has succeeded, to some measure, in ending the silence around domestic abuse and has worked to give more women the tools to take action against it. But these outlets are only successful insofar as women have the strength to take the first step. The emergence of sexually transmitted diseases and AIDS has also reinforced for women the importance of fidelity in the marriage now more than ever. Women cannot afford to be submissive with regard to their lives. They must stand firm against all forms of abuse, including adultery, because it is their well-being and the well-being of their children that are at stake. One of the most important things to consider in making decisions about your relationship is that it is teaching your children how a man and a woman should treat one another. If you remain in an abusive relationship, your actions, or lack of action, serve as a model for your children.

TIMES ARE CHANGING—*LOS TIEMPOS CAMBIAN*

Through the years, I have seen Hispanic women becoming more assertive and Hispanic men more involved *en las cosas del hogar*, something that was not seen two and three decades ago. If men helped their wives they would do it only if no one saw them. My sister Rosa Linda's husband used to pull down the window shades whenever he helped her make tamales for Christmas because he did not want the neighbors or family to see him "*con las manos en la masa.*" Though he loved homemade tamales, he was forced to accept the fact that, with her share of the duties raising five children and holding a full-time job, my sister couldn't make them without his help. Over time, he was able to do these things without giving a second thought to what others might be thinking.

COMMUNICATE, COOPERATE, AND NEGOTIATE

More and more you find couples communicating openly, negotiating, compromising, and realizing that some things have to be different. As couples take this path of negotiation, along the way there will be disagreements. Placing marriage on a solid foundation requires tremendous communication and conflict-resolution skills. In our twenty-five years of married life, my husband and I have had our share of arguments. In moments of anger, disappointment, frustration, or tension, many people tend to say things they do not mean. I learned this right after our honeymoon when I found myself declaring, "I want a divorce," after our first argument. In fact, to this day I cannot recall why I was so upset. Fortunately, like our parents, my husband and I both shared the same fundamental belief that our marriage was going to be forever, *hasta la muerte*, till death do us part. We determined on the day of our disagreement that the word "divorce" did not exist in our family and that we would never bring that up again as an option. We were determined to make our marriage work.

Sometimes we had disagreements over unfinished projects, financial management, disciplining our children, and, yes, even once, a fleeting moment of petty jealousy. At other times, the conflicts were over use of leisure time and housecleaning. It's natural for couples to have arguments. However, it is not healthy for one party to keep everything inside. All couples must develop a strategy and their own "language" to use with one another in times of conflict. Some steps that we followed were:

- When tension is high, take a moment to calm down. Go to another room, take a walk, listen to music, anything that you know will soothe your nerves. You'll find it easier to communicate your feelings after taking a moment to calm down.
- Use some of that time to reflect on the other person's point of view, without condemning your own.
- Though it is often difficult, try to find the words and the time for each person to state his or her position and come up with some possible solutions. Evaluate the solution to see if it can work for both of you.
- Communicate needs and concerns clearly, *sin vergüenza y con confianza*, without embarrassment and with confidence. Don't be afraid to say that you were wrong or that you are sorry.
- Never put down, blame, or make the other person feel guilty.
- Always try to reestablish the relationship and communication before you go to bed.

Only when we followed these strategies did we realize that what had appeared at the time to be *insoportable*, intolerable, turned out to be relatively insignificant or a simple misunderstanding. We learned to accommodate, change bad habits, or give in to the other's desires. To reach common ground, one has to learn to communicate, cooperate, and negotiate. If there is an overarching message throughout this lesson, it is that a good marriage is based on a give-and-take.

HANDLING CONFLICT THROUGH COOPERATION: THE HISPANIC MATRIARCH—*LA DOÑA*

It is not good for man to be alone. I will make a helper suitable for him. Then the Lord made woman.... A man will leave his father and mother and be united to his wife, and they will become one flesh. (Genesis)

De decir y hacer, hay mucho que ver, It is easier said than done for a Hispanic husband to leave his family after he marries. When a Hispanic woman marries her husband, she marries her husband's family, and all the relatives for two generations. (See the chapter on *La Familia*). This is also true for the Hispanic man.

Regardless of how much couples work together to break down barriers between themselves and resolve conflicts, they may still face clashes outside the nuclear family, particularly with older members of *la familia*. For me, these clashes were most vivid with my mother-in-law, who was very much like me in personality. The matriarch in a Hispanic family has a strong relationship with her children, especially her sons. While Hispanic fathers are made to think that they are *los reyes de los castillos*, the kings of their castles, it is very clear that in most Hispanic families the women, in many ways, are the head of the clan. They are the clever ones who tend to rule and make major decisions.

This belief is captured in whimsical ways in Hispanic folktales in which women take the dominant role. For example, in "In the Days of King Adobe," a story told by Joe Hayes in his book *Watch Out for Clever Women, Cuidado con las Mujeres Astutas*, an elderly woman outsmarts two men who tried to steal her ham, for which she had saved her money for a long time in order to buy it. The woman, who had overheard that the men had stolen her ham, switched the ham that they had already put in their bag with bricks. The next day, the men tell her laughingly that they had dreamt of a king named Hambone the First. She told them she, too, had a dream of a king named Hambone the First, but that in her dream, the people threw him out of the kingdom and replaced him with Adobe the Great. The two men did not know what she was referring to until they discovered the bricks in their bag. They realized what the woman meant and vowed never to be mean to old women again—especially clever Hispanic women!

"The Day It Snowed Tortillas" is another folktale told by Joe Hayes that illustrates the cleverness of a woman who always gets her husband out of trouble. After she tells her husband not to tell anyone about the gold they found by the road, he does, and inevitably, the robbers who lost the money come looking for it. Anticipating their visit, she hides the gold and makes a great number of tortillas and tells her not-too-clever husband that it had snowed tortillas. When the robbers come to the house to ask for the gold, she tells them she does not know what they are talking about. When they turn to her husband, he asks his wife, "Where is the gold that we found the day before it snowed tortillas?" The robbers dismiss the couple as crazy and leave without the gold.

While being strong and clever is certainly an asset, it can sometimes be the cause of conflict when a mother and daughter-in-law are both trying to get their points across. I still recall how my mother-in-law came to our house one day with a bundle of homemade tortillas and said to my husband in a tone that seemed directed more to me, "*Pobrecito, mi hijito. Aquí te traje unas tortillitas calientes.*" My poor son, I brought you some warm tortillas. I thought to myself, when one has limited time and can buy tortillas almost as delicious as homemade ones at the grocery store, why make them? But I ignored the comment and enjoyed the tortillas with my husband.

After I was in a car accident that totaled my car, my mother-in-law threw me yet another *piedrita*, another innuendo, when she told me that God was trying to tell me that my place was "*en la casa*" caring for her son and grandchildren. It was not easy to refrain from saying anything to *mi suegra* out of respect. Nor was it very easy to "undo" some of the habits my husband had adopted in her home. When my husband first uttered those dreaded words "Men *do not* wash dishes," I knew both of us were going to be making a lot of adjustments and compromises. But over time, we managed to strike a balance that suited both our needs and expectations. One of the most difficult steps to that balance comes with knowing how to stand firm with disapproving family members, particularly those who traditionally command the utmost *respeto*.

My mother-in-law was *La Doña*. Every Sunday she expected us to go to her house after church for a brunch with her seven other children and their families. She would have a feast waiting. If we failed to show up, I knew that she would look to the *nuera*, her daughter-in-law, as the guilty party. Occasionally she called family meetings to which everyone was required to show up and to agree with her position on any number of subjects. After the announcement of our engagement, *mi suegra* called the family together for such a meeting with the express purpose of planning our wedding. I was shocked and angry, but I refrained from speaking throughout the gathering until it came to the selection of the color of my bridesmaids' dresses. Though I had always wanted pink, I found myself settling on yellow just to contradict my mother-in-law's choice of pink. The meeting went on for a couple of hours, and I could not believe what was happening or that my husband allowed it to happen. Salvador, who was used to his mother's domineering way, did not see anything wrong with the way things were being handled.

When we returned to my house, I told Salvador that although I loved him very much and wanted to marry him, I was not going to go through with the marriage if his *mamacita* was going to be running our lives.

Granted, our wedding day was just one day out of many we would share as husband and wife, but to me it was a moment that would define the rest of our lives together. When we arrived at my house, I appealed to his sense of reason and fairness as I left him alone to think the situation over. I knew that I had to find a way to resolve a potential clash that could have hurt our new family without abandoning the *respeto* I felt I owed my mother-in-law and the extended family. When I returned, Sal agreed to thank his mother and respectfully ask her to let us plan our wedding. Though she was hurt initially, his mother understood that she had overstepped her bounds with this "*caprichosa,*" who was very much like her. (Unfortunately, because I was so stubborn, my bridesmaids wore yellow dresses instead of the pink ones that I truly wanted!)

My own mother proved to be just as suggestive as Sal's. I remember how adamant she was about my not wearing the ivory gown I had picked out to match my ivory Spanish floor-length lace veil. To my mother, not wearing a white gown or not having orange blossoms on your veil implies that you are not a virgin, and it would be scandalous to openly declare it to those in attendance. "*¡Ay, qué vergüenza!*" were the words I saw written all over her face, although I had nothing to be embarrassed about. Since I was steadfast about wearing the dress, she spent the whole night sewing "*azahares*" (pearl orange blossoms) on my veil. "*Azahares significan que la novia es honrada y decente,*" she said. For some people, *las costumbres* are very important. Together Sal and I managed to embrace other traditions typical of a Hispanic wedding. We had a set of *padrinos* and *madrinas*, thirteen dimes to symbolize prosperity, and a *lazo* to symbolize unity. The music included an *Ave María* and the song "We've Only Just Begun." There was *gallina en mole, mariachis,* and a dollar dance. There were so many relatives and friends and, of course, the children in the middle of the dance floor dancing by themselves or with their parents. But in the end, one of the most special moments for us was when we knelt down in front of both sets of parents and received *la bendición*, the sign of the cross, from them. Then we knew that our marriage was bound to succeed.

Years later, as I reflected on these two women's strong characters and steadfastness, I was able to look closely at my own words and actions. Now I have been professionally trained to understand the importance of giving young people the space they need to grow. Yet, I hear myself laying down *la ley* on how things should be done around the house, at times not allowing my children to question my authority and wisdom. When a person continues to do something in spite of the fact that she knows better, the cultural influences become apparent. As a future mother-in-law, I have to remember the *dicho, Guarda tu ayuda para quien te la pida.*

I cannot give my future daughters-in-law advice unless it is requested. I will have to be sensitive, while still maintaining my role as *Doña* in holding the extended family together. Knowing my strong personality, I am sure it will not be easy.

We can hold on to the traditional values cherished by our parents without giving up our own expectations. Think for a moment about the qualities of your parents that you most admired. Perhaps it was their resilience when faced with difficult circumstances, their resourcefulness, or their pride in their identity. Maybe you value their sense of loyalty to *la familia*, their *amor* for each other, their sense of respect, their hope.

Now think about the situations in your life where these qualities can serve you most. It might be in dealing with people outside your family, with your spouse, or with children you have, or hope to have. You'll find that with negotiation and a willingness to make decisions together as husband and wife, traditional values do not necessarily need to conflict with your new roles, but can actually enhance and strengthen them. Looking to your parents as the ultimate and absolute ideal, however, may not allow you to confront new realities in a bicultural world. After all, upon closer inspection, the control of the home is not always what it seems.

My mother, for example, always let my stepfather believe that he was *el jefe*, the head of the house. In front of family and friends, and particularly in front of strangers, she assumed a passive role. But in private, my stepfather always deferred to my mother on major issues such as moving to a new house or dealing with problems associated with the children. My sister Yolanda, who is married to the traditional *mejicano*, fascinates me with her ability to make her husband believe that every decision that is made within the family is his idea, when in fact it is hers. She never wanted him to lose his seemingly prominent role and respect for being the "head" of the family. She felt it was important, at least for maintaining the peace in the family, to keep some semblance of tradition, though on her own terms. Her experience, though different from my own, has made me aware of how one's culture shapes the balance of power in a marriage. I learned that couples can make adjustments that work to everybody's advantage.

I always believed that my husband and I each had an equal role in our home, until I heard my children remind me that "Dad is the man of the house. He makes the rules." I am convinced that there are certain cultural nuances that will remain with us.

In every family, whether one's parents are allowed to play an active role or not, there remains in each of us ways of thinking and acting that reflect our parents' attitudes and approaches to life's problems. What is important is that we become aware of these influences, and learn how to adjust them to new situations. With a better understanding of the ways that you have been conditioned to approach parental authority, you can begin to develop new tools to shape and strengthen the relationship between you and your spouse in a way that is beneficial, both to you and to your children.

The process is never an easy one, and many times, it calls for negotiation and cooperation from both sides, or at other times, just going with the flow. During the first of my husband's family gatherings that I attended before our marriage, I remember feeling bothered by the fact that all the men were sitting together in one room, playing their *guitarras y trompetas* and singing or watching football. All of the women were in the kitchen preparing the meal, talking about their children or planning the next family gathering and just *comadriendo y chismeando*, talking and gossiping. I questioned this arrangement because I wanted to be with my future husband. Breaking the cultural norm, I sat with Salvador and received deep subtle sanctions from everyone except him. After a while, I felt so uncomfortable that I eventually found myself wandering back to *"mi lugar,"* my place, with the women in the kitchen. The lesson I learned that day: A *la tierra que fueres, haz lo que vieres,"* In the land that you go, do as you see, or, *Cuando en Roma, haz como los romanos,* When in Rome do as the Romans. I had to get used to the fact that while I was at my in-laws' home, *los hombres* were the performers and entertainers and the women were the audience and cheerleaders. We were, at least in appearance, supposed to serve our men and children, before we thought of ourselves. I went along with it and served my husband before I served myself. That was one world, but *my* home, I knew, would be different. And it has been, for on occasions not only has it been my husband who cooks, but he has been the one who serves me. But most of the time, we serve the meals together, along with the children.

In the continuous string of potential conflicts that arose throughout our marriage, I won some battles in the name of principles that I felt were important, and I lost others that were more negotiable. If you feel secure in a relationship in which each partner has an equal voice, and each one is willing to make certain sacrifices for the other, it will be easier to make concessions from time to time. Again, the lesson to be learned is that marriage is a give-and-take. For both sides, there is some truth to the saying, *Más vale doblarse que quebrarse*, It is better to compromise than to lose completely. And I am here to tell you that even if you bend a little, if the bond is strong enough, it won't break. Compromising does not mean giving up!

Over the years, as my husband and I adapted cultural values to new situations, we learned to negotiate roles, responsibilities, and expectations and resolved to communicate our feelings and concerns. It has become much easier for our children to follow the example. Though my boys sometimes tease me by saying that they would rather marry a woman like their Aunt Hope, the aunt who jumps when her husband snaps his fingers, they feel more comfortable cooking and vacuuming or working around the house if they see their father doing it. My daughter, who has always demanded that she be treated the same as the boys, is encouraged by us to pursue her goals, assert her needs, and express her individuality. Above all, our children have learned that it is okay to make mistakes, for they have witnessed their mother and father go through their share of obstacles as we navigated through new experiences, creating and testing new rules along the way, and still end up *triunfando*. They understand that they are between two worlds, and because of our experiences, they will be better equipped to carry on new roles within a marriage, *cuando les toque*, when it is their time.

Chapter VIII

La Familia: Family

Con Familia Hay Amor y Sabiduría

Almost two decades before Dan Quayle attacked the character Murphy Brown for having had a child out of wedlock, producing the debate about the importance of an intact family, I traveled around the country speaking about the importance of the family and how all families needed support to remain strong. I realized back then that many Hispanic parents were being negatively affected by societal forces, and this in turn was having a harmful impact on marriages, families, and children. I began the Avance Family Support and Education Program to strengthen Hispanic families in some of the poorest communities of this country, and to direct national attention to the problems tearing many families apart. When I received a "distinguished working mother" award from *Working Mother* magazine, I was asked by my local newspaper how I felt about this honor. I said that next to God, I loved my family and I found my job as a parent very gratifying for I have always considered the role of motherhood one of the most important. Also, the hopes and dreams I have for my children I have for all children. The outcomes that I advocate for Avance children are the ones I want for my own children: to see them become responsible, compassionate, and competent individuals.

The family is the basic unit of society. It is within the family that a fragile, dependent infant survives, develops, and discovers his identity, talents, and interests. His potential can only be reached, and his place under the sun can only be determined, if the family meets his basic needs and lays a solid foundation developmentally. A family should be a place where a child learns to trust, where he feels protected and has a sense of worth, a sense of belonging. It should be a place where important values are learned and character is formed, where culture and heritage are handed down. Family should be a safe haven where members of the family feel a sense of warmth and belonging. It is a place where people can find refuge from the stresses of life and enjoy each other's company as they create wonderful memories together. People can relax here, express their emotions, and test their limits as well as a multitude of emotions. The family becomes the incubator from which all future relationships with other people will result. It will be the testing ground for learning to control one's impulses and emotions and learning how to deal with frustrations and failures. The family, if it is strong, will adequately prepare the child to become a productive, contributing member of society.

In the Latino culture, *familia* is sacred. One just has to enter a Latino home and look at the walls to determine what they value most. There you will find dozens of pictures of children, grandchildren, parents, *abuelitos, tios, primos*—the entire extended family. My mother-in-law's living room was filled with family pictures that were divided by categories. On one wall were those of all the grandchildren, on another were graduation pictures, and yet another displayed women in their bridal gowns. There was a section set aside for the brave sons and uncles in uniform who had gone off to war. A framed full-page color photograph that appeared in the newspaper of me as Miss Fiesta of San Antonio hung in the section of her house that my mother-in-law called "the wall of fame," along with awards received by other members of the family. On a wooden door frame, one could read the names and respective heights of every child spanning several years. Family members' handprints were molded into cement sidewalks, just like the movie stars' handprints are in Hollywood. All of these things sent a message that *el orgullo del hispano está en la familia*, a Hispanic's pride is in his family.

This sense of family pride was no different in my mother's home. As children, we also felt important when we saw our place in the family's gallery of pictures. In a neighborhood, where there were negative influences on the streets, none of us felt that we needed to belong to a gang to achieve a sense of belonging, because we knew we already had a place in *la familia*. My sister Yolanda, who became a licensed interior designer, learned that it is not "proper" to display family pictures in a living room. Nevertheless, because of the value we have for the family, our pictures are usually the centerpieces of the decor, regardless of who says that it is not proper. As a professional, middle-class Hispanic person, I keep my family pictures in my living room among the other paintings and floral vases.

Familia consists of as many as three generations of relatives under the watch of a strong and loving grandmother and a most revered grandfather. It is referred to in Larissa Lominitz and Marisól Pérez-Lizaur's book *A Mexican Elite Family, 1820–1980* as the "grandfamily." When one marries a Hispanic, one marries into two generations of *familia* from both the father and mother's side of the family. Part of Latino culture means that *la familia* supports parents in preparing *nuestros niños* to go into the world to become competent, responsible, and productive members of society. Children are never totally independent from *la familia* for their emotional, economic, and social needs and for their sense of identity. This includes shared rituals, close social interactions, economic assistance, emotional support, and shared celebrations. The Hispanic family revolves around at least one of the grandparents. When both grandparents die the eldest son or daughter becomes the head of the new grandfamily.

PROXIMITY TO THE PARENTS

After we got married, my husband and I moved near my in-laws' home. Being Hispanic meant that being close to *familia* was very important. While it is common to see non-Hispanics moving out of the home and often far away as soon as they reach legal age, one would generally find the opposite experience among Hispanics. This was true for our parents; my mother lived next door to her father. After my father and grandmother died, my mother moved next to my uncle's house and my uncle built a room in his house for my grandfather so that both he and my mother would take turns caring for him when he got older. My husband's grandparents and parents and their married daughters lived within a span of three blocks. In spite of the fact that both my husband and I were professionals, we chose to live one block from my in-laws in the barrio for one year. We rented a house until we were able to save enough money for a down payment on our first house, which was less than two miles from my mother's. So many of my non-Hispanic friends are amazed to know that most of our siblings live in the same city, and the one or two siblings from each side of the family who do not, reside in the same state.

Today, it is more common when people become acculturated and more economically secure to move away from their parents. More Hispanics move out of town to take advantage of educational and economic opportunities. Others want to move away to find their own identity and independence, apart from the family. What is still typical, though, is that many choose not to move too far away from *la familia*.

I have also seen many young, professional Hispanics move away from home, only to return close to home after getting an education or work experience. They tell me that they value their relationship with family more than money, fame, and glory. For them to return home is not to give up something but to have a fuller life, with career and family.

Hispanic parents trying to raise their children according to the traditional norm of keeping them close to home until they marry, meet with conflict as they merge with a majority culture that advocates early independence, self-reliance, and separation. I lived with my family until I got married. My husband moved away from home to attend college, but when he became a professional engineer, he went back home to live with his parents so that he could save money to start his own family. Though I expect the same to happen to my son, I see that this generation of children on both sides of the family adhering to the overwhelming pressure of acculturation. They are talking not only about wanting their own apartments but about living together with boyfriends or girlfriends. "*Cómo cambian las cosas*," how things change, and "*¡Qué vergüenza!*" for shame, are often heard among the older *viejitas* in the barrio. It gets harder for us as parents to raise our children with certain standards and values when their peers and their peers' parents do not see anything wrong with cohabitation.

During one spring break, my son Salvador brought home a group of college friends for the weekend. This wasn't out of the ordinary, except that this time it included an unmarried couple who expected to sleep together in my house. Steven and Vanessa, then thirteen and ten, wanted to know how I was going to handle the situation. Both my husband and I stood steadfast in our values and told my son that his friends had to sleep in different rooms. I realized as a parent that values slowly die unless one is consistent and firm in one's beliefs. Your young children will learn what you value by your actions or lack thereof.

THE "CENTRALIZING WOMAN"

In *A Mexican Elite Family, 1820–1980,* the Gomez family, like most Hispanic families, regarded their entire life, including business and social prestige, as blessings that were bestowed solely for the sake of their children. Like the Gomez family, generations of Hispanics have been structured around one person, the "centralizing woman," who organizes the activities and brings the family together. Often that person is the grandmother. Today those responsibilities can be divided among many. For example, every year my sister-in-law Lupe would buy twenty parade tickets so that the family could sit together during San Antonio's annual fiesta parades. She helped my mother-in-law organize family gatherings, and told everyone what to bring. When my mother-in-law passed away, Dolores, the eldest daughter, assumed her role of keeping the *familia* together. Every New Year's Eve, the family gathers at her house to eat the traditional *buñuelos* and *menudo* along with a table spread with all kinds of food.

In my family, since my Jehovah's Witness mother does not believe in celebrating religious activities and birthdays, I became the organizer, and Lisa, my niece, helped me by taking over when I was tied up with work. Every year at the family's Thanksgiving celebration, Lisa prepares the list of family members for exchanging gifts for Christmas. She sends out a family newsletter with information on special events and birthday reminders.

The "centralizing woman" is considered the most respected figure in the genealogy because of her traditional role of gathering and transmitting family information and because she is consulted as an authority on family lore and traditions. The centralizing woman circulates information and organizes and promotes social events. That tradition still continues as women today gather around the kitchen table or at family meetings to plan the next social event. I learned from the Rodriguez clan very early on that in their family, birthdays are celebrated with a meal and a cake, and the clan will undoubtedly show up with presents in tow. My sister-in-law Dolores, like Lisa, has mailed out family newsletters briefing relatives on all the happenings. Now, with the advent of the Internet, the family can communicate more often. With chat rooms and digital cameras that can transmit pictures through computers, *la familia* is much closer than before.

When an out-of-town member of the family comes for a visit, the centralizing person will notify all members and organize a family celebration. If a member of the family is getting serious about a boyfriend or girlfriend, the centralizing person organizes a gathering that will bring the family together to meet the "special person." This happened with my niece Mónica when she suddenly became serious over a man she met through the Internet. Boy, did *la familia* want to know who this stranger from Canada was! I felt sorry for him. Here was this very nice six foot four-inch *pelirrojo*, redheaded, *güero* who got a chance to see what came with the package of marrying a Hispanic. After he passed the interrogation with flying colors and survived the shock, a wedding shower was planned, and the entire *familia* was there at the ceremony to celebrate.

ECONOMIC SUPPORT

Another aspect of the Hispanic family that still exists in Latin American countries today is the strong economic network among family members. Many Hispanic-owned enterprises are run by family members. One reason for this, I believe, is that such businesses allow the freedom to be involved in family and community affairs as well as to use the business as a vehicle to help others, especially family members.

In *A Mexican Elite Family, 1820–1980*, having family on the payroll was a way of continuing to take care of members of the family, especially the women. If family members were part of the business, then the boss would understand when they would be late or had to be absent to attend to family matters. This is true of my brother Tony, who works in the family-owned barbershop. He has the freedom to leave the workplace to get involved in his children's lives. An Avance board member, Jose Medellin, has his wife, several of his brothers, and his daughter, the future president of the company, running his multimillion-dollar printing enterprise while he gets actively involved in the community and enjoys life. Since he was a young man, his mother told him that as the eldest he had the responsibility of taking care of his brothers and sisters. In his twenties, he moved the entire family from Laredo to San Antonio to live with him and he has fulfilled his mother's request ever since.

Sometimes Hispanic family members want to work together for support. For twenty-five years, I have worked alongside my older sister Julia at Avance. She came on board as a volunteer when an employee abruptly quit the day before Avance's opening. Julia's talents, creativity, and loyalty and commitment to the people we serve were valued, and she was asked to remain by my supervisor. Before I worked at Avance, my sister Susie and I taught first grade in the same school for two years.

EMOTIONAL SUPPORT: *EL APOYO DE LA FAMILIA*

There is no better safety net for parents and children than *la familia*. I often called members of the extended family to support my husband when he was fulfilling the "Mr. Mom" role, and sometimes just to see how he and the children were doing. He did fine, but I wanted a back-up in case of emergencies. At other times, the extended family played the role of child-care provider. My mother and sister used to care for Vanessa at my house during her first year of life. Sometimes a relative would ask to take one of the children on an outing. We welcomed these invitations when my husband and I needed some time for ourselves. Just as the extended family came to my aid, I, too, would reciprocate when I was needed. After the divorce I used to pick up my sibling's young children and take them out to parades or outings with our family, just as my *tíos* did for me when my mother was a single parent.

There are times when your siblings can serve as mediators and help you when you or your children need to cool down after testing the limits and testing your patience. How I appreciated when my siblings and in-laws spoke to, counseled, and prayed with my children when their behavior needed to be brought under control. This kind of support can be a means of reinforcing the messages you are trying to get across to your *niños*. Family members can be the impartial parties that enable the family to resolve conflicts and allow the lines of communication to remain open. My husband and I resolve our own conflicts with our children, but those few times when relatives intervened were the times we *really* needed them. My husband and I were just too close to the situation. Usually the eldest in the extended family would assume the role of mediator, in the absence of the grandparents. On a more frequent basis, the grandparents called to check on the grandchildren, reinforcing desirable behavior or admonishing against undesirable ones. When I tell my children their grandmother wants to talk to them on the telephone, they say, "here comes the sermon," because my mother always quotes the Bible. "Yes, grandma," said Vanessa. "OK, uh-hum. Yes, I love you, too. Here, Steven, it is your turn." One of my nieces went to live with my mother for a time when she was going through her rebellious teenage years, just as my son went to stay at my sister's house for one day in order to calm down. Children may ignore or reject a parent's *consejos*, but they generally do not reject the counsel of the extended family. They will listen to an *abuelita* or to a *tía* who shows impartiality and some understanding.

Julia Álvarez, author of the book *How the Garcia Girls Lost Their Accents*, wrote about the advantages of having a large Latina family. Her family had enough people in it, she revealed, that whenever one relative was angry at her, there was always someone else to turn to. One just has to look at a few *telenovelas* to see how the extended family is full of outlets for children.

All parents face trials and tribulations. The family is important in helping one cope, endure, and overcome life's challenges when they occur. I experienced this extraordinary assistance when I lost Sonya Yvonne, my first child, who died of a congenital heart defect three months after birth. Relatives from both sides of the family gathered at the hospital with us for hours during the delicate operation that we had hoped would save her life. They left only when we were told that the operation was a success and that the worst was over. Unfortunately, seven hours later, my daughter of three months died, but the family never left us alone after that until they were certain that we could cope with our tragedy. How I wanted to go to sleep and be depressed, but they would never let it happen. My mother was right by my side for days and told my sisters to do the same throughout that very difficult first week. She knew what I was experiencing, because she, too, had lost a child soon after birth. The extended family from both sides, as well as friends, were taking turns bringing food, trying to make us talk or to cheer us up. With time and support, the pain subsided and we moved on with our lives.

My sister Susie experienced a terrible ordeal when gang members tried to entice her twelve-year-old daughter to join them. After Susie left her daughter with a friend at a skating rink, the friend unknowingly led her to a gathering of gang members. For seventy-two hours the gang tried to brainwash my niece by telling her that they were her new family and they would take care of all her needs. Everyone from both sides of the family came to her rescue. My sister Yolanda and her family flew in from Dallas to San Antonio to offer their support. My seventy-two-year-old mother joined another sister, Rosa Linda, to look for my niece at sites where her friends from the barrio said gang members congregated. Relatives joined law enforcement officials, including the FBI and my brother-in-law's brothers, who were policemen, to assist us in trying to track her down. Some relatives brought food, others made flyers, and still others contacted church members who held an around-the-clock vigil for my niece. Ultimately, it was Susie's husband and my brave sister, Rosa Linda, who met the abductors face-to-face and persuaded them to release my niece. Fortunately, because of the profound unity of *la familia*, the gang members couldn't devour my niece as they have been able to do with so many children who may not have had the benefit of a strong family.

CELEBRATIONS AND RITUALS

Our extended family has also been the source of wonderful memories and joyous times. I recall the weekend gatherings at my mother-in-law's home where cousins frolicked about the yard while the adults talked, ate, or participated in such group games as basketball, baseball, and volleyball. The *familia* also sat together at the annual parades to cheer siblings and cousins marching in bands. The entire clan attended graduations and award ceremonies together. When other families had a few people in attendance, we had the *abuelitas, tíos, tías, primos*—at least twenty people—all taking pictures of the honoree. We went to see each other's children play sports or dance folkloric dances at fiestas.

The family would travel in a caravan of cars on vacations, on picnics, or to visit out-of-town family members. The campouts were especially enjoyable and delightful. Every inch of the picnic tables was covered with food. While some of the older men barbecued and some of the older women prepared the rest of the meal, the children went along with the rest of the adults to play sports, go swimming, hike, or look for creatures like frogs and snakes. The best part of the outing was just sitting in front of the campfire listening to the crackling of the fire, looking up at the stars in the evening, and waking up in the morning to the fresh pine-scented air and to the smell of bacon cooking. The next day, sunburned and exhausted, the family campers would sit around playing cards or board games.

It seemed that we would come up with any reason to celebrate or to come together as a family. Once we attended a luau held in honor of *mis suegros* before they went to Hawaii to visit a son who was on furlough from Vietnam. My sister-in-law and their newly born son joined my inlaws. I also remember a welcome-home gathering with *mole* and *enchiladas* served on fine china for a niece who returned from Germany. In these and other ways, we tried to reinforce the idea that everyone is special in the *familia*, and no one is ignored. Hispanics are taught very early, by accompanying their parents, that one is to visit the elderly members of the family, the widows, and those who are sick.

I often hear at professional meetings that many of today's problems are related to the breakdown of the family, and the urgent need to strengthen the extended family is often proclaimed. I have stood up at these meetings and proudly described to others the way in which my family and other Hispanics have maintained a strong connection to *la familia*. Unless we recognize the extended family as a strength, we, too, will lose it, with all its benefits.

The benefits that you and your children can derive from a strong extended family are worth the time and effort it takes to maintain certain traditions, customs, and values that bind the extended family and keep its members strong. Celebrating with our loved ones gives us opportunities to build supportive relationships. It helps us connect with our roots, family, friends, and neighbors, and with our spiritual side. By coming together as a family, we share joyous memories that enrich our lives. It helps us escape, as my son says, "even for a moment," from the troubles and woes of everyday life. It can be as uneventful as a telephone call to a relative on his birthday, which says you care, or a holiday celebration that takes a great deal of planning and preparation.

When I realize all the time and effort that it takes to keep our families and traditions strong, I think of how easy it could be to give up and watch them slowly fade away with all that makes us unique and strong. You, too, may have realized early on as a parent, as my husband and I did, that you do not want to raise children without the support of the extended family and a strong social support network of caregivers and friends outside the family. Parenting can be an awesome responsibility and an overwhelming task, if you try to do it alone. Most families have trials, tribulations, and a very demanding schedule. You will be better able to handle some of these challenges or have a richer parenting experience with the help of relatives who can influence and show so much love to your children.

NUCLEAR FAMILY VERSUS THE CLAN

As far back as the earliest hunting and gathering experiences of agrarian societies, it was the responsibility of the clan to maintain families and care for the children. Bruce Perry of the Baylor College of Medicine in Houston has remarked about the evolutionary significance of the clan. He says that throughout history, human beings have been programmed to work and play in groups.

Many Hispanics face obstacles when they sometimes have to choose between maintaining proximity to the extended family in one city, and accepting a job in another state or attending college far away. If you have left your extended family behind in another city, it is important that you stay in contact with them through letters, visits, the Internet, and telephone calls. Today advancements in technology, such as E-mail and faxes, make it easier and fairly inexpensive to keep in contact with family members around the world. Some families organize newsletters to keep one another informed on family activities. Visit your loved ones at least on special occasions so that your children can experience some of the traditions of *la familia*. Invite your family to visit you and together involve your children in trying to keep certain traditions alive, such as making *tamales, buñuelos, pasteles*, and other treats.

Since industrialization, more women have been working and more families have become separated because of mobility and immigration. Many parents are now faced with the difficulty of having to rear their children within the nuclear family alone. Like most families where both spouses work, Hispanics who have lost touch with the extended family are finding the task of rearing children an awesome and overwhelming experience. Today it is even more crucial that the nuclear family function well.

One approach you can take to help make this happen is to draw up a creed or mission statement with your family. Stephen R. Covey, noted management consultant and author of *The 7 Habits of Highly Effective Families*, recommends the mission statement as a way to help families outline shared objectives and values. For Hispanic families, a mission statement is ideal for raising children in a bicultural world where traditional values and expectations can sometimes clash with other norms. The document could serve as a *contrato* that is designed to help family members navigate both sides of the cultural divide. They can decide together what they believe are the goals of *la familia* and what each person should strive for in his or her own life. Family members can even set the guidelines for what they believe is acceptable and unacceptable behavior. In helping to set these parameters, your children will be clearing a path for themselves to explore interests and talents, develop character, and become secure, wise, compassionate, hard-working, and respectful individuals. The mission statement encourages family members to create a loving, supportive, comfortable, and orderly environment, a place where members can develop in every way. If everyone in the family has a stake in the mission statement, they will work hard to bring about the ideal family you envisioned together. Family members should have a common understanding of the importance and purpose of the family unit and make a commitment to do everything possible to preserve it and to make it function well. According to Stephen Covey, the mission statement becomes a guide for thinking and for governing the family. "When the problems and crises come," he writes, "the constitution is there to remind family members of the things that matter most and to provide direction for problem solving and decision making based on sound principles." Twice every year, Covey's family members evaluate their family mission statement to see what they need to work on to accomplish their goals and put their values into practice.

It is not easy to have many members of the family live harmoniously under one roof. In our two-career family, we were finding life very chaotic at times until we dealt with the important issues like changing traditional roles. We found ways to organize our limited time, dividing our responsibilities in a more equitable manner. Each family member has different personalities, needs, and interests that can easily conflict with each other. Communication is vital to planning events that meet everyone's needs and interests. It is important to have tools to coordinate and organize family activities.

One such tool that we have found very useful is a family calendar, which keeps a record of daily events. It is difficult to remember what days I am going out of town, when Sal has choir practice, when Vanessa and Steven had basketball and football games, or when Sal was coming home from college as well as birthdays and our anniversary. A calendar can also be useful for taking care of logistical details that need to be considered in planning an event. Many activities require a division of duties among different members of the family and a good mailing list of family members who must be invited to special events.

Another useful tool in keeping a family strong is family meetings. During these gatherings, we are able to use our calendar as a guide for many discussions on topics ranging from grades to visiting grandma. This is when major decisions affecting all members of the family are discussed: family trips, big purchases, moving, parties, or something someone did that will have an impact on other members of the family.

Because many families have harried schedules, it is important that they come together to share a meal as often as they can. A meal—without the TV in the background—is a time for giving thanks for the day's blessings and a time for communication to take place. This is the time when everyone can help in the preparation of the meal and in the cleanup afterward.

Families can do much to build their own traditions and confront problems together. They can take journeys together to learn about new cultures and explore different parts of the world. We have had unforgettable family vacations to Mexico, Europe, and Africa, and throughout the United States, and my husband and I have been to South America and Israel together. Even when our children were not with us, we shared our experiences with them after trips.

But a family trip does not have to be a vacation to the four corners of the world. Even your backyard can be an adventure if you plan fun, stimulating activities for your children. While our family trips to other countries have broadened our childrens' worldviews, my children say that the best times they have had were when we went hiking or camping in parks and on beaches. It was in these natural settings, the snow-capped mountains, the grassy hills, the invigorating springs, waterfalls, and brooks as well as the gorgeous extraordinary flowers, that we felt most moved by our surroundings. Fishing, boating, and swimming were a must in the summer. The children liked to camp out and gaze at the stars, listen to the stillness of the night, and smell the fresh air. As they grew older, they took up golf and tennis. Many times, they brought along their friends to have a good game of basketball.

Through these experiences, we learned that relationships can blossom only if people work at them and devote time together to nurture them. These *lindos recuerdos* with my family and extended family are ones that I will treasure forever. As Barbara Bush once said, "It is not the number of cases that you have won, or the meetings that you have attended that you will remember and cherish, but the time that you had with those that mean so much to you: family and friends." For Latinos, it is loyalty to *la familia* that has enabled many of us to survive, succeed, and lead a fuller, richer, and happier life. We must do what we can to maintain a strong extended family. The value of the family is one of our strongest assets and another foundation for effective parenting.

Chapter IX

La Comunidad: The Community

El Muchacho
Malcriado
Dondequiera
Encuentra Padre

A well-known Mexican *dicho*, *El muchacho malcriado dondequiera encuentra padre*, stresses the important role that people in the *pueblo* have in rearing children. Within our culture, if a child misbehaves it is everybody's responsibility to correct him and teach him the appropriate ways of behaving. All children belong to the community and everyone in it has a responsibility to care for them and look after their well-being. There is much concern and attention placed on children. Neighbors take time to notice what they are up to and to correct them if they are up to no good. For this to work well, *vecino* must know *vecino* like a brother. *¿Quién es tu hermano? Tu vecino más cercano*, Who is your brother? Your closest neighbor. *Amigo en adversidad es amigo de verdad*, A friend in need is a friend indeed. These *dichos* emphasize the important role that neighbors have in taking care of each other, especially our children. Neighbors must develop trust, unity, and communication. They must come to some mutual agreement that they are collectively responsible for their children's welfare.

The barrio where I grew up was structured with these ideas in mind. Everyone knew everybody by his or her first name. There was a great sense of community in which *vecino* helped vecino. Neighbors borrowed milk, *huevos*, and tools from one another. They protected each other's homes, supported each other's efforts, attended each other's celebrations, and took care of one another's children. Growing up, we could never get away with anything, because the neighbors would eventually relate our *maldades y travesuras* to our mothers before we got home. One day when I lingered after school to talk to a boy, my mother knew exactly what I was up to by the time I got home. A neighbor told her, "*¡Ay, Luz! Ten cuidado, porque a Gloria le gustan mucho los muchachos, y si no te cuidas, se te va a casar muy jóven!*" ("Oh, Luz! Be careful, because Gloria loves the boys and if you do not watch it, she will marry very young!") Because of their concern, I was the last one in the family to marry! If I wore too much makeup or if my skirts were too short, my mother would hear about it from the neighbors. The day I began to hang around with bad company, my mother knew about it. There is truth to the *dicho, El muchacho malcriado dondequiera encuentra padre.* Each one of us can remember the *viejitas del barrio* and the concerned *vecinas* who worried about us.

From the times of our ancestors, the community has taken care of its children. The Aztecs accepted the children from the village into the clan and gave them *cara y corazón.* They socialized them, teaching them the traditions, to be self-disciplined and obedient. They helped them develop their unique personalities and identities. It was the group that gave the child life and sustained him. The child, in turn, had to do his part in making sure that the community survived and functioned well. In *La Morenita,* Virgilio Elizondo writes that the survival and well-being of the group was the responsibility of each and every member of the group. Each knew his duties and responsibilities to make the group function well.

Through the years, something happened to the spirit of the strong Hispanic *pueblo.* In too many communities, Hispanic children are no longer at the center of the village. Many are not known by their neighbors, and apathy and indifference are pervasive. Children are undervalued and ignored by the larger community. As a result, many of our children have fallen prey to crime and violence because of inattentiveness and neglect on the part of parents, neighbors, and community leaders. Somehow, the sense of community is being lost in all neighborhoods, rich and poor. Distrustful parents keep their children locked up in the house and they do not know or communicate with their neighbors. In many communities today, parents are socially isolated and become depressed as a result.

One of my goals in establishing Avance in 1973 was to re-create in poor neighborhoods the sense of community that I experienced as a child and that I am still experiencing in my neighborhood, where doctors, professors, businessmen, and businesswomen live side by side and support each other. I realized that family and community were important factors that enabled my mother to stay strong, which in turn helped her to be able to parent more effectively.

In the Mirasol Housing Project, where the first Avance Program was established in San Antonio, the people in the community were so isolated from one another that delinquent teenagers and drug dealers were given free reign over the streets. Mirasol had become a neighborhood where parents neither knew nor talked to one another. Drug dealers set up shop on street corners, in vacant buildings, and around schoolyards. They vandalized homes and cars and terrorized the people who lived around them. After many years of feeling as though their homes were under siege, most people were too afraid to do anything to change things for fear of retaliation. When one brave mother of three, who was one of the first mothers to join the Avance program, had the courage to stand up and complain to housing officials about the appalling activities she saw all around her, the consequences were severe. A few days after I met her, I learned that some gang members dragged her out of her house and killed her in front of her children and neighbors, using her death as an example of what could happen to others who complained about their terrible *maldades*. The parents had slowly surrendered their rights and lost their liberty. Not even locked doors or wrought-iron protectors could keep the villains out of their homes. Day by day, the community worsened.

I have seen this same scenario develop in communities throughout the United States. When neighbors stop talking and supporting one another, the neighborhood starts to deteriorate and disintegrate. The bad element takes over. Parents lose control of their streets. Over time, parents feel helpless, depressed, and disempowered. They are too weak to show their love, to discipline, or to pass on traditions to their children and help them develop and grow into strong adults. As in the parable in the Bible that compares children to seedlings, these seeds fall on rocky ground, and when they grow, they wither or are stunted for lack of a safe, stimulating, and nourishing environment.

It became increasingly clear to me as I was implementing Avance that I had to look much further than simply educating parents on a one-on-one basis about child growth and development. Improving their knowledge and skills in parenting was not enough. Their neighborhoods were in a state of deterioration and falling prey to drugs and violence. Their schools were crumbling as institutions of learning, with inadequate teachers and resources. Businesses were moving away because of the violence where even the police were afraid to enter the community, leaving the parents, especially single parents, to fend for themselves. The children would never have much of a chance to succeed living under these conditions.

However, I also knew from having grown up in the same neighborhood that in designing a program to help children and families, I would not be starting from scratch. Unlike those who had written off the neighborhood, seeing only the scars of poverty and apathy, I knew that in the barrio there was much strength to build on. Beneath the fear and frustration, I knew there remained a great love for the children and a great devotion to family and community that had been ingrained in their souls through generations.

With her 1995 best-selling book, First Lady Hillary Rodham Clinton helped to repopularize the notion that "it takes a village to raise a child." But for Hispanics, the idea that the *pueblo* is closely tied to the well-being of families and children has always been an integral part of our culture. In fact, neighbor helping neighbor is a tradition that has played perhaps the biggest role throughout our history, both in our homelands and in the United States. For example, in the late-nineteenth-century Southwest, Richard Griswold del Castillo observed that Mexican communities formed *mutualistas,* or mutual aide societies. These were groups of families that pooled their resources to assist each other in times of crisis, whether it was an illness, death, or financial ruin. In New York City, according to Virginia Sanchez Korrol, a variety of associations, including *hermandades,* or brotherhoods, were organized to help new immigrants from Puerto Rico. Although designed as social safety nets, these groups were also a way for people to come together for family and community celebrations. They were the natural webs of assistance, before they were called "social support networks" that held families and neighborhoods together. These informal systems were similar to the Settlement Homes that were sponsored by the government to support people who landed in Ellis Island. These arrangements helped them learn the language and find a home and a job and taught them how the American system worked. In some communities, Hispanics have had to do these things mostly on their own, based on the value they have for helping *nuestra gente* or for having a strong community. However, in other communities where there is apathy of people and government, you see communities in a state of decline.

Several generations later, this sense of community has, unfortunately, diminished. Churches, too, are changing. They used to extend more direct support to the downtrodden, the widow, and the orphan. In many churches, the second collection, traditionally for the poor, is not even taken up. With both parents working, it has become more difficult for people to give of themselves to their community. Hispanics' tradition of *compadrazgo*, or god-parenthood, is not the same tradition it was for our *antepasados*. Today *compadres* who are chosen as *padrinos* do not always have the time to fulfill their role as "co-parents" after the *bautismo*.

Through Avance, we have been able to rekindle the spirit of *compadrazgo* and the *pueblo* in the Mirasol community and many others throughout Texas and the United States. We introduce parents to their neighbors and provide a place and a reason for them to meet and to learn about how to keep their children healthy, happy, and successful in school and in life. Because of the love, hopes, and dreams that parents have for their children, mothers and fathers come to a nine-month-long parenting program. Beginning with the simple act of coming together, the parents are able to fortify themselves and their families against the influences of gangs, drugs, and guns and against the dark cloud of isolation, hopelessness, and despair.

Through attending Avance classes, the parents of the first program began talking openly about some common problems they were experiencing at home and in the community. Then they organized support groups to look for common solutions. In the process, they realized they could not solve everything by themselves. Avance families banded together and formed a Community Watch program to protect each other's homes and report break-ins when they occurred. Tired of watching their neighbors' homes being broken into day after day, a group of parents organized to record the response time of the police. When the police waited until seven A.M. to respond to a burglary call that had been reported at eleven o'clock the night before, the Avance parents passed out flyers, held meetings, and came up with strategies to hold neighborhood and city officials more accountable for what was happening. They held a press conference to raise public awareness about the problem. The next morning, there were so many police officers in the neighborhood, I was nearly run over by them. Eventually, most of the drug dealers got the message that they couldn't continue to flourish in this neighborhood and left. Perhaps they went to a more vulnerable community where neighbors didn't know one another, didn't communicate, and didn't have a commitment to support each other.

Little by little, more changes began to happen. In a neighborhood where more than one thousand children did not have a single swing to play on, the parents organized and forced the housing officials to set funds aside to build a playground so that their children could have a safe place to go. There was still the ongoing threat of retaliation, but over time, parents realized that they outnumbered the gangs and that together they were more powerful than any drug dealer. Through their efforts, they had learned the meaning of the *dicho, Un lápiz se puede quebrar muy fácil, pero muchos juntos no se pueden,* A single pencil is easily broken, but many held together can't be. Through unity, the parents got stronger. Today, parents proudly wear special T-shirts and rings that signify membership in the "Avance family." They celebrate holidays together, hold neighborhood parades, come to each other's aid in times of crisis, care for each other's children, mourn each other's losses, and share in each other's victories.

In the Avance Rio Grande Valley Chapter, we witnessed the deplorable living conditions that some of the *colonia* families had to endure. With no paved streets, running water, or sanitation services, most families lived in "third world" conditions. Many children are being born with brain damage and physical defects because of the toxic wastes that the *maquiladoras* have been allowed to dump into the rivers along the border. The lack of enforcement of some environmental policies makes life a nightmare for most. Children cannot even play safely in the streets without being exposed to contamination. As a result, Hepatitis B cases have been recorded to be three times more prevalent in this area than throughout the state of Texas. Hepatitis A is also greater among Hispanics than Blacks and Anglos in Texas. Just as they did in San Antonio, the Avance parents organized and went to county government officials to demand that pipes be installed in their neighborhoods for running water. Their request was granted. The lack of buildings to provide services to parents in this rural area did not keep us from making a difference. Once the parents heard about the successes in the nearby community, they too organized, and a group of mostly mothers (and a few skillful fathers) remodeled an old, run-down building to house an Avance project.

With every mutual act of assistance, the Avance families rekindle their spirit of hope and community. They acquire knowledge and skills. They strengthen their social support networks. They learn that members of the community need to do their part bringing about adequate policies, programs, and services that would help them in their jobs as parents. The *pueblo* has grown beyond a small geographic area. Communities today include many people, organizations, and institutions. But as was true of our *antepasados*, children must be at the center of our world where everyone values them and cares for their well-being.

Today, I live in the suburbs with other Hispanic, Anglo, and African-American professionals and I see that many parents have taken this same sense of community with them. I see our children feeling free to visit the neighbors' yards and homes and playing games while adults are watching. Parents occasionally borrow tools, ladders, eggs, and milk. We take care of each other's children, share carpooling duties, take each other to the airport, and keep a watchful eye on each other's homes while on vacation. I see my neighbors making themselves available to check on the health of the elderly neighbor, care for pets, and mow the neighbor's grass when they are out of town. Sometimes, they just chat outside, just as our parents did in the barrios. We also organized a Neighborhood Watch, and once a year neighbors come together at the end of the block and have a picnic. Our close neighbors have an extra key to our houses in case of emergencies.

CHURCHES

For Hispanics, the link between church and family has always been very strong. Some of my earliest memories of the church are of the men and women who did their part to keep the congregation strong. I remember *El Hermano* Garcia, who, at the request of my grandfather, used to come to our house to take my siblings and me to the weekly services at his small Protestant church. He took a special interest in watching out for us and other members of the community. One day when I was eleven, he asked me if I would help a bedridden single mother who had just had a baby, perhaps my first act as a family advocate.

It was one of my grandfather's primary goals to make sure that each of us was filled with the spirit that he believed changed his life when he came to the United States. Even though we were baptized Catholic, he took us to tent revivals in the Pentecostal community. I remember feeling awestruck by the intense energy from the crowd of faithful believers who swayed to the rhythmic sounds of drums and cymbals filling the air. Some would fall to the ground, "slain in the Spirit," others would lift up their hands in prayer, buoyed by their faith. At the end of the service, I remember how relieved and happy everyone seemed, as though a tremendous burden had just been lifted off their shoulders. There at the church, and in their homes, *los hermanos* would lay hands over those who were hurting and would pray for them. Somehow, the people seemed to get well, and they in turn later joined the group of intercessory healers. This loving congregation was a community of simple people reaching out and helping one another, including parents with young children.

Churches can do more to reach out, support, and strengthen families, whether through Marriage Encounters, counseling, or spiritual services that all families need in order to more effectively deal with life's *obstáculos*. In addition to a house of worship, the church must serve as a fellowship center where relationships are formed, where values and morals are taught and reinforced. Some of the activities offered by the church include family groups for divorced or separated parents, youth activities, and different types of ministries like visiting the sick in the hospitals or, like my brother-in-law Jim, visiting the prisoners in jail. *Hay que lograr*. Take advantage of the many support organizations found in churches that are meant to foster good values. Today, many Catholic church members are active in social justice issues, as we see in Ernesto Cortez's Citizens Organized for Progress (COPS) and South Texas' Valley Interfaith organization. In Newark, New Jersey, Monsignor William J. Linder of New Communities Corporation is involved in economic development. He has been instrumental in bringing day care, job training, and job placement, as well as a grocery store and a credit union, to a poor community. He takes his Christian vows of helping his fellow man very seriously.

Many parents are sending their children to religious schools for the very purpose of coming together with families of similar religious beliefs and values. Members of the church, fraternal, and civic organizations could work together to help families.

SCHOOLS

The structure and quality of schools also affect a child's future tremendously. For decades, the structure of families has been changing with increased mobility and with women entering the workforce. However, too many schools have not responded to those changes. Schools are still designed for the agrarian family, whose children needed to be off for three months to harvest crops. Many school buildings are vacant in the evenings, and children are left to fend for themselves while parents are working. Some grandparents and the extended family are no longer as readily available to assist in this important child-care role. Policies that allow schools to remain open year-round and for longer periods in the day to support the working family should be adopted on a broader scale. Some school districts today do offer alternate school calendars that extend schooling year-round with numerous smaller breaks.

The decisions that our leaders make regarding teachers' salaries, teacher qualifications, and student-teacher ratios will also have a bearing on children's ability to learn. Teachers play an important role in molding a child's character and self-esteem. I was most fortunate to have had three outstanding schoolteachers who positively affected me during a very vulnerable period in my life. When I received the Woman of the Year Award from our local newspaper, I thanked my sixth and seventh grade schoolteachers, Mr. Ben Mata and Mr. and Mrs. Daniel Villarreal, and my high scool teacher, Mr. Don Connell, whose words of encouragement and support made the difference to me and many kids in the barrio.

While the Coleman Study stressed the importance of the family in the education of the children, many Hispanics in poor communities have been negatively affected by the quality of the school buildings, lower teacher salaries, limited science and mathematics courses due to the inability to attract and afford qualified teachers for these courses, and limited educational resources, such as computers and library books. As a member of the Presidential Commission on Educational Excellence for Hispanic Americans, I listened to the numerous testimonies of people who described the deplorable learning conditions that many Hispanics have been forced to endure because they live in poor areas. There is so much disparity that affects learning between schools in affluent and poor areas. For example, the Edgewood Independent School District that I attended took the school finance inequity case to the Supreme Court under *Edgewood v. Kirby* (*United States v. Texas, 1971; Edgewood ISD, et al. v. Kirby, et al., 1987*). In 1970–71, per pupil per year expenditures for a student in Edgewood was $418.00 and in Alamo Heights it was $913.00. Hispanics for years have been attempting to address a more equitable financing of schools. Instead of dealing with adequately funding and supporting poor schools, we see a push for vouchers for nonpublic schools, jeopardizing the survival of school districts such as Edgewood. Albert Cortez from Intercultural Development Association and Al Kaufman from Mexican American Legal Defense and Educational Fund (MALDEF) have for decades been advocating for better educational equality and opportunities for Hispanics.

One educational option that Hispanic parents may want to explore is charter schools. These institutions, which now exist in communities across the country, are special public schools set up by local groups, teachers, and parents that try to provide alternatives to traditional educational systems. Many focus on the needs of children from diverse background with curricula that incorporate a child's language and culture. The National Clearinghouse for Bilingual Education monitors the creation of charter schools and keeps a list of them on their website.

THE BUSINESS OF HELPING YOUNG PEOPLE

When I was growing up in the barrio, the businessmen in the community supported the children. Don Benito Romo would give us free *pollitos pintados*, free colored chicks that became our pets until my grandfather killed them for a Sunday meal by wringing their necks. Local businesses helped the children in the barrio earn extra money by supporting their entrepreneurial spirit and giving them jobs.

I found out early on that I had a talent for selling. I sold beautiful sequined earrings that my mother made as well as products from dress catalogs, Avon, Stanley, to name a few. Not only would neighbors buy whenever I knocked on their doors, but the owners of the corner drive-in restaurants allowed me to sell the earrings to their customers. I remember the Anglo man who delivered the ice and the Anglo school maintenance supervisor, whom I befriended. Both would say, "Here comes the girl with the million-dollar smile." They would always buy earrings from me every time they saw me. Heaven knows to whom they gave all those earrings.

I lived near a cemetery where there were several floral shops owned by the same extended family. Several of my siblings worked for "Chelo" Alejandro, who was so nice and patient. I was hired as young as nine years of age by her mother, *la Señora Elizondo,* to do odd jobs at one of the floral shops. I will never forget *la Señora Elizondo.* On my first day of work, she complained in front of the customers about the quality of my sweeping. The broom was probably twice as big as I was. However, because I did not appreciate being talked to in that manner, I immediately quit after having worked a few hours. I demanded my prorated pay of $1.00 a day. I was adamant then, as I am today, that people should be treated with dignity and respect. I felt then that only my mother could reprimand me. But now, I realize that she, like other community business owners, felt she had a responsibility to teach *los jóvenes* to get ready for the world of work. When a similar incident happened to me years later as a sales attendant, when I didn't measure up to my supervisor's standards of folding sweaters, I was hurt by her reprimand, but I remained and learned the correct way to fold sweaters.

Today, small family-owned businesses are being replaced by large corporations. Still, businesses can and should do more to support young people. They can sponsor community groups and local events. They can encourage employees to participate in mentoring programs for young people or set up scholarship funds. One of the best examples of corporate participation in the well-being of Hispanic youth is the National Hispanic Scholarship Fund. Begun by Ernest Robles, the fund now receives donations from several corporations. This financial aid has given thousands of young people a helpful start in their education and has given hope for young parents who want the best for their children. Professional associations should encourage and help mentor children to explore and strive for careers. Through the Texas Alliance of Mexican-American Engineers, my husband, as well as other professional engineers, mentor youth in areas like math and science. Manuel Berriozabal from San Antonio initiated the award-winning program called Texas-Prep and Prep-Proyecto, a prefreshman and middle school engineering program supported by the government, military, colleges, and business sector that prepares many Hispanic students to enter careers in math and engineering.

Avance receives direct and in-kind support from the public and private sectors. Businesses have contributed to us financially as well as by donating vans and playground equipment. They have provided funds for purchasing toys for the children, sponsored Christmas and Thanksgiving events, and repaired our buildings. Their employees have worked as volunteers and mentors, and they have adopted children, families, and entire centers. We have had speakers and mentors come to Avance to inspire and motivate the youth.

Beyond contributing to worthwhile efforts and encouraging their employees to do community service, employers should make it easier for Hispanic parents to find ways to create a place of work that is friendly to la familia, including flexible scheduling (flex time), family friendly leave, split shifts, on-site child care, maternity or parental leave, and adequate pay with benefits. Many large corporations allow employees time off to visit their children's school.

By supporting employees with family-friendly policies, employers reap their own benefits with a more productive workforce, less absenteeism, and higher retention. By investing in children, the business sector as a whole contributes to a healthier and stronger community.

GOVERNMENT

While I don't believe that the government should play a dominant role in the lives of children, I do believe that our public agencies and elected officials can and should do much more than they do now to support families. In 1989, I joined Hillary Clinton as part of a twelve-member delegation to France to learn about the country's day-care system, which is considered one of the most successful because of the support of government and business sectors. In France, we learned that 95 percent of children between three and five years of age attend free, universal child care. We watched youngsters using amazing outdoor and indoor playground equipment that promoted creativity, gross motor development, social play, and learning. I was particularly impressed with the well-designed buildings and the quality of programs and staff, whether in low- or middle-income communities. The French day-care teachers are considered professionals, and they are paid as such. The field is competitive, requiring extensive schooling. Employees have an opportunity to move up the career ladder with more training. Unlike in the United States, they have a low staff turnover rate.

Most impressive to me was the way the French devised a comprehensive system that linked child care with the nation's health care and social service systems. All families with two or more children, regardless of their income, received a family allowance if they obtained prenatal care and showed that their children were receiving scheduled immunizations and physical examinations. Child-care centers had public doctors assigned to each facility. France also supports their families with benefits such as sixteen weeks of maternity leave.

When the American delegation met with business and political leaders of France and asked them about their spectacular child care system, they seemed surprised at the curiosity and explained that they simply couldn't afford not to invest in the country's greatest resource, their young children. "We are preparing the future workers, leaders, and citizens," they told us. We can learn from this and many other countries that support families more than we do. With the new Family Leave Policy, Americorp Programs, increases in funds for child care and college financial aid, and a higher minimum wage, our country is beginning to make positive strides.

The government has a responsibility to address the social and economic problems of society. The work at Avance is about empowering people to help their children, themselves, and their communities and is partially supported by the government. Political leaders must realize that supporting parents with knowledge and assistance in child growth and development, literacy, and job training is a good use of taxpayer dollars and an investment in the nation's most important and valuable resource: its people.

We are affected by policies, laws, and regulations that government enacts. Some of these laws affect the quality of the food we eat, the air we breathe, the water we drink, the music we hear, and the movies we see. While we are making some strides in some very good family policies, such as the Family Leave Act, which benefits all Americans, other policies have not been very good for Hispanics. We have become the latest targets of immigrant bashing because of the recent immigration laws that have been enacted. Historically, in times of economic unrest, immigrant groups have been the scapegoats for the country's economic woes. Proposition 187, together with the English Only movement and a repeal of Affirmative Action, negatively affects Hispanics. The Unz initiative, or Proposition 227, in California stressed the elimination of bilingual education. Fortunately, these actions have united many Hispanics to speak out for their rights. Organizations like MALDEF and Lulac use the courtroom as a means of seeking justice and equal rights for Hispanics.

As parents, we must be actively involved in the political process and teach our children by example the importance of exercising our rights as citizens to vote. We must cast our vote and get our relatives and friends to do likewise. There is so much power in the vote and each vote does make a difference in the policies, laws, and programs that are supported and that affect you and your family. Willie Velasquez taught us *que su voto es su voz.* Southwest Voter and Education Fund is available to help you get registered to vote and teaches you how to use the voting machines. Also, attend forums where different candidates will state their positions on important issues. Question how they stand on issues affecting children and families. We must elect ethical, responsible, and sensitive individuals who will make prudent decisions that will support all its citizens, preserve our democracy, and support the human rights of people across the world. It is also critical that we start preparing a group of Hispanic youth now to assume the future political leadership roles to ensure that Hispanics' special needs and interests are adequately addressed in the local, state, and national governments.

MEDIA: THE END OF NINJA TURTLE MANIA AND SPEEDY GONZALEZ

It is incumbent upon the government to come up with policies that support the family, such as keeping airwaves more decent *para la familia*. Media organizations also have a social responsibility to regulate offensive material including CDs, movies, and television programs that undermine parents' efforts to instill positive values, morals, and self-esteem in our children. Regardless of how prepared you are as a parent or how hard you try, your efforts may be regulated by other forces from the community at large.

The violence that is passed off in movies as "young people's entertainment" is sometimes difficult to avoid, no matter how hard you try. Even when I forbade my son Steven from going to see the Ninja Turtle movies, because he had a tendency to practice his karate kicks on his sister, I still could not shield him from the impact of these creatures, whose images were emblazoned on backpacks, watches, toys, piñatas, and costumes.

Violence is so entrenched in popular culture that few people could see the negative influence that the Ninja Turtles or Power Rangers were having. There was so much pressure on me as a parent not to deprive my children of what they considered harmless action figures. I couldn't believe what I was hearing as I tried to protect my child from those influences. Others saw the Ninja Turtles as heroes, while I saw them as too aggressive and violent. I stood steadfast, but it wasn't easy. One day six-year-old Steven fell prey to a marketing blitz and tried to steal a Ninja Turtle watch from a store and enticed his three-year-old sister to join him. We made him return both watches to the storeowner and personally apologize for what he had done.

Years later, I was at a meeting in which U.S. Senator Paul Simon said that Japan would not allow the Ninja Turtle movies to enter their country with all that violence and mentioned how the producers responded by making a version of the Ninja Turtle movie without the violent parts. In our country, it seems that we generally accept violence without question and have already become desensitized to it. Children are being affected by all the violence, as was seen in a recent shooting rampage of two young students at a middle school in Arkansas that ended in four deaths and many injured. Some people believed that a similar violent scene that the two children had seen in a movie had influenced their behavior.

In addition to these dangers, the media is filled with many negative images of Hispanics. Earlier I mentioned some of these images.

Hispanics have been portrayed as lazy people wearing sombreros or riding donkeys or low-rider cars, as villains, maids, or gangsters. Speedy Gonzalez, the Frito Bandito, Chiquita Banana, and Juan Valdez produce stereotypical images of Hispanics just as Amos and Andy depicted blacks when I was growing up.

Today's children are exposed to too much sex, materialism, and vulgarity. Children today, as in my time, will imitate what they see. The image of the father as irresponsible, incompetent, and weak is illustrated in programs like *The Simpsons* and *Married with Children*. Is it any wonder that fathers, both Hispanic and otherwise, may have difficulty getting through to their children with the image of fatherhood modeled on these programs? What a difference from *Father Knows Best*, a program in which the father was seen as a strong, responsible, decisive, and compassionate leader of the house. The *Beavis and Butthead* program is the antithesis of *The Waltons* with defiance and disrespect used as a basis for comedy.

There are some very good educational programs on television, such as *Sesame Street* and programs on the Discovery Channel. However, parents also need to control the amount of television that their children are allowed to view. Parents must determine what they believe in, and inculcate these values in their children through the programs they watch. They cannot allow them to be subjected to the immorality and violence on television, radio, advertisements, compact discs, tapes, and the World Wide Web.

I attended an Aspen conference with leading media executives who tried to tell Hispanic leaders in attendance that the media simply mirrors American culture and that it was demand that drove the production of movies, records, and products that many parents consider offensive. They added that our country's First Amendment does not permit censorship of their products. I disagree. Just as one cannot cry out "fire" in a movie theater when there is no fire, the entertainment industry, too, has a corporate responsibility not to project the kind of behavior that leads to violence. Media executives must work to make certain that their products reflect the kind of culture and character that we all want for our children and for our country .

Certainly, the media is a powerful force that can work against the values we try to instill, but you are not powerless to protect your children. You can join other parents to protest violence, sex, and profanity in the media. If we don't complain and if we continue to purchase products that do not reflect our values, the entertainment media will see our inaction as a sign of approval. Together, we can be the voice for our children and for our society.

COMMUNITY ORGANIZATIONS: KEEPING THE HISPANIC *PUEBLO* ALIVE

This country is a place where local organizations and individuals play a big role in supporting children and families. Society needs to have community resources to support parents who have special interests and concerns. These include organizations that support parents with handicapped children, parents whose children were abused or killed, alcoholic parents, and single parents, to name a few. We must come together as a community to help those who are hurting and need support. If one child in the community suffers, we will all suffer. If one child is vulnerable, we all become vulnerable. Sometimes the problem has to stare us in the face for us to take action, as one of the most prominent men in San Antonio found out coming out of a Spurs basketball game one night. A group of gang members put a gun to his head in front of his four grandchildren. Later he spoke out against the violence and began to organize the community to address this problem.

Alexis de Tocqueville, a great French political thinker, wrote in his book *Democracy in America* in 1835 that our democracy and the virtues of freedom are associated not only teaching our children lessons that will prepare them for freedom but also with civic participation. He wrote of the thousands of associations that existed in America at that time that provided entertainment, taught morals, distributed books, and founded hospitals, churches, prisons, and schools—all of which brought about a better civil society to help in the preservation of our democracy. He warned us, though, that our democracy would be imperiled by an individualistic cultural view and if these civic associations ceased to exist or if children were not taught important virtues.

For parents, this means that they must find time to be involved in their community, from belonging to the PTA to unions, clubs, and local neighborhood organizations. It means attending town or city hall meetings and letting elected officials know what you feel is needed for your community to stay strong, whether it is a streetlight, a park, a library, better streets, a better drainage system, or improved police protection. You have the power to organize a group of people to make sure your voices are heard by your elected officials. If elected officials do not respond to community needs, you have the power to replace them. Together you have a stronger voice and a great deal of strength to have the political officials represent you effectively. This is true democracy. Government is for the people and by the people. Unfortunately, for too long there has been too much apathy among the people. Fewer and fewer people vote or get involved in community activities. If this continues, we will be allowing self-interest and an individualistic culture to thrive at the expense of our democracy. Parents must come together to make sure that children and families are at the forefront of every decision government makes in the United States, from the environment, to the food we eat, to the advertisements, movies, and music our children are exposed to. It is time that parents are seen and heard. It is time for them to have an active voice in the quality of life of their communities, the quality of their schools, and the kind of government they want. This can only come about if we hold our elected representatives accountable and become involved in community affairs.

As parents, we should do all we can to keep nonprofit institutions alive and support them. These organizations are run by caring volunteers who are concerned about their community. From national organizations such as the Red Cross, the March of Dimes, and Mothers Against Drunk Drivers to organizations that predominantly help Hispanics, like Avance, SER, and Cara y Corazón, many groups are involved in supporting families and individuals. The National Latino Children's Institute, Intercultural Development Research Association, the Tomás Rivera Center, HACU, and the National Council of La Raza are also advocating for our families and children every day. Attitudes, knowledge, behavior, and entire lives are being changed because of the support that comes from nonprofit community-based organizations.

Some community-based organizations that serve Hispanic families are cited in the back of the book. These include organizations that help immigrants learn how the American system works, similar to the Settlement Homes of yesterday. There are organizations that help Hispanics who have been the victims of discrimination and other groups that will help them with their civil and legal rights. Fraternal and civic organizations like ASPIRA, League of United Latin American Citizens, GI Forum, the Mexican American Legal Defense and Educational Fund (MALDEF), and the Puerto Rican Forum have organized to address the special needs of Hispanics. There are youth programs and cultural groups that teach your children art, *mariachi* music, and folkloric dancing. There are nonprofit organizations that help parents learn English, obtain citizenship, earn high school equivalency degrees, attend college and job training programs, and help them find jobs. Others provide parenting workshops, early childhood programs, and mental health and counseling services.

Sometimes the best help we can get comes not from organized groups or community programs but from the simple acts of generosity, words of wisdom, and guidance of ordinary men and women who serve as mentors and who serve on boards of these nonprofit organizations. Remember that the Spanish word for village, "*el pueblo,*" can also be translated to mean "the people." It is each individual doing his or her part to make a community not just a place where people sleep and eat, but a place where they can live and enjoy their freedom.

The changes that have come about in Avance have been ripples in a pond, each one bringing about one positive reaction after another. It all started with the love that I received from my mother and grandfather, who had, in turn, received it from their parents. That love generated compassion and concern for others. It brought about a vision and a passion to do what I could to improve the conditions of Hispanics through Avance. From the cooks to the bookkeepers to the managers to volunteer community leaders and funders who shared my vision, together we pooled our tremendous energy and compassion to give light and hope to the people of Avance. Despite enormous obstacles related to poverty or discrimination, Hispanics can build many defenses within the community if they are supported by a caring community.

From that caring community will come more pebbles that will generate more ripples in the community. For example, we must strengthen the bond between husbands and wives, who are children's first teachers. We have been able to enhance the love between parents and their children. Through warm and nurturing parent-child interactions, their children will become more compassionate and will be able to produce their own series of ripples by giving of themselves to bring about a better world. We have also been able to have an impact on how neighbor relates to neighbor. When *vecinos* know each other's names and feel comfortable calling on one another *en tiempos de adversidad,* in times of need, they become stronger and can accomplish great things together. When adults take notice, show concern, and care for all children, in many communities, this country will become an even greater nation, one that we can all be proud of.

As I look back at all the positive changes that have taken place in the barrios over the last two-and-a-half decades since Avance has been in existence, I am convinced that if these things could happen in some of the poorest communities in the United States, they can certainly happen in all communities, wherever they may be. We must keep in mind that the "village," the Hispanic "pueblo," does not end with a strong marriage, the nuclear extended family, or the corner *tiendita*. It consists of schools, churches, businesses, government, the media, individual volunteers, and community organizations all working together to find ways to make a better future for *nuestros niños*.

Resource List
for Parents

ADVOCACY AND SUPPORT GROUPS

ASPIRA
1444 I Street N.W., Suite 800
Washington, DC 20005-2210
(202) 835-3600
An advocacy group for Hispanic youth that provides educational support and promotes leadership, with offices in Bridgeport, Chicago, Miami, Newark, New York, Philadelphia, and Río Piedras, PR.

AVANCE
301 S. Frío, Suite 380
San Antonio, TX 78207
(210) 270-4630
Provides comprehensive, community-based family support and education services to predominantly Hispanic families. This includes early childhood, parenting education, father/married couples program, literacy, home visiting, and job training services. Has chapters throughout the state of Texas and in Kansas City. Also provides training and technical assistance and disseminates information and bilingual parenting curriculum to individuals and organizations throughout the United States and Latin America.

Cara y Corazón
3270 Richview Drive
Hacienda Heights, CA 91745
(626) 333-5033
Provides training to organizations and individuals on the Cara y Corazón Fathers' program and the Hispanic Men's Network using the Náhuatl practice known as "Etzli-Yollotl."

Catholic Big Brothers
45 E. 20th Street, 9th Fl.
New York, NY 10003
(212) 477-2250
Links young people ages seven to eighteen who come from single-parent families with adult volunteers who can serve as role models.

Council of Latino Agencies
2309 18th Street N.W., Suite 2
Washington, DC 20009
(202) 328-9451
This group brings together twenty-nine Latino-oriented community organizations, from multicultural high schools to bilingual health services, in the Washington area through joint educational and advocacy programs.

Educational Equity Concepts
114 East 32nd Street, Suite 306
New York, NY 10016
(212) 725-1803
Multicultural educational materials, with an emphasis on disability.

Girls Incorporated
National Headquarters
30 East 33rd Street
New York, NY 10016-5397
(212) 689-3700
www.girlsinc.org
A national organization that provides educational and other programs to help girls realize their potential. Has more than one thousand affiliates across the country.

Hispanic Association of Colleges and Universities (HACU)
4204 Gardendale Street, Suite 216
San Antonio, TX 78229
(210) 692-3805
fax: (210) 692-0823

HACU@Hispanic.com
www.HACU2000.org
Provides educational opportunities to Hispanics.

Intercultural Development Research Association (IDRA)
5835 Callaghan Road, #350
San Antonio, TX 78228
(210) 684-8180
Provides education research and educational services for Hispanic
Americans. Involved with policy issues related to bilingual education and
school finance.

La Leche League International
P.O. Box 4079
Schaumburg, Il 60168
(847) 519-7730
or call (800) LALECHE to find a representative near you.
www.lalecheleague.org
Provides information and support to women who want to breastfeed.

National Catholic Educational Association
1077 30th Street N.W., Suite 100
Washington, DC 20007-3852
(202) 337-6232
A source of information and support to groups and individuals concerned about
Catholic education from kindergarten to the graduate level.

National Clearinghouse for Bilingual Education
U.S. Department of Education Office of Bilingual Education and Minority
Language Affairs
Information is available through the World Wide Web and through a weekly
news bulletin *Newsline*.
www.ncbe.gwu.edu

**National Coalition of Hispanic Health and Human Services Organizations
(COSSMHO)**
1501 Sixteenth Street N.W.
Washington, DC 20036
Phone (202) 387-5000
www.cossmho.org
Has a membership of numerous health and social service organizations serving
Hispanic communities. Offers services that include education and research in
maternal and child health and immunizations. Also has a prenatal and Radon
hotline.

National Council of La Raza
810 First Street N.E., Suite 300
Washington, DC 20002-4205
(202) 289-1380
fax: (202) 289-8173
Seeks to improve opportunities for Hispanic Americans and conducts research
on issues affecting Hispanics, including immigration.

National Hispanic Scholarship Fund
One Sansome Street, Suite 100
San Francisco, CA 94104
(415) 445-9930
Awards scholarships to Hispanic undergraduates and graduate students.

National Information Center on Deafness
Gallaudet University
800 Florida Avenue N.E.
Washington, DC 20002-3695
(202) 651-5052
www.gallaudet.edu

National Latino Children's Initiative
1611 W. 6th Street
Austin, TX 78703-5059
(512) 472-9971

Parents Helping Parents
3041 Olcott Street
Santa Clara, CA 95054-3222
(408) 727-5775
Helps families of children with special needs, including those with disabilities
and serious illnesses.

Parents Without Partners
401 N. Michigan Avenue
Chicago, IL 60611-4267
(312) 644-6610
A support group for single parents. Has chapters throughout the country. (Dues
range from $17 to $45.)

Puerto Rican Family Institute
145 W. 15th Street
New York, NY 10011
(212) 924-6320
Assists families with a variety of services including psychological counseling.

Puerto Rican/Hispanic Genealological Society
25 Ralph Avenue
Brentwood, NY 11717-2424
(516) 834-2511
Helps those who want to research their family's history. (Annual dues are $20.)

Service Employment and Redevelopment, SER Jobs for Progress
100 Decker Drive
Irving, TX 75062
(972) 541-0616
A support to families with an emphasis on employment of youth and adults.

Southwest Voter Registration and Education Project
403 E. Commerce, #220
San Antonio, TX 78205
(210) 222-0224
Concerned with educating Hispanics about the importance of registering to vote and exercising their right to vote.

The Hispanic Mother-Daughter Program
Arizona State University
P.O. Box 870512
Tempe, AZ 85287-0512
(602) 965-6547
Geared to eighth-grade girls in local communities and their mothers. It strives to build strong mother-daughter relationships as it encourages both to pursue higher education.

MARRIAGE

Marriage Enrichment and Family Life Conferences
For information call (800) 795-LOVE
Marriage Enrichment: (800) 634-8325 or
Family Life Conference at (501) 223-8663.

National Marriage Encounter
4704 Jamerson Place
Orlando, FL 32807
(407) 282-8120
(800) 828-3351
Offers weekend retreats for married couples and clergy to promote communication and religious growth.

PREPARE/ENRICH
Offers workshops for engaged couples.
P.O. Box 190
Minneapolis, MN 55440
Offers workshops for engaged couples.

Worldwide Marriage Encounter
2210 E. Highland, No. 106
San Bernadino, CA 92404
(909) 863-9963
Has sixteen regional groups. Holds weekend retreats for Catholic couples to explore their relationships and their faith.

DISCRIMINATION AND CIVIL RIGHTS

American Civil Liberties Union
132 W. 43rd Street
New York, NY 10036
(212) 944-9800
fax: (202) 244-3196
Defends the right of all citizens as guaranteed in the Constitution and the Declaration of Independence.

American GI Forum
2711 W. Anderson Lane, #205
Austin, TX 78405
(512) 302-3025

Center for Democratic Renewal
P.O. Box 50469
Atlanta, GA 30302
(404) 221-0025
Monitors activities of hate groups and helps communities fight hate violence.

Center for the Study of Biracial Children
2300 S. Krameria Street
Denver, CO 80222
(303) 692-9008
Conducts studies and disseminates information on biracial children and how they are doing in a racially conscious society.

Lulac (League of United Latin American Citizens)
701 Pennsylvania Avenue N.W., #1217
Washington, DC, 20004
(301) 589-2222
www.lulac.org
Works to promote the well-being of Hispanic Americans across a range of areas
including economic empowerment, education, health, and civil rights. Offers a
network of educational counseling centers for youth across the United States.

Mexican American Legal Defense and Educational Fund (MALDEF)
634 South Spring Street, 11th Fl.
Los Angeles, CA 90014
(213) 629-2512
Defends the civil rights of Hispanics in such areas as education, employment, immigration, and voting rights. Also conducts leadership training. Offices in Chicago,
Los Angeles, Sacramento, San Antonio, San Francisco, and Washington, D.C.

National Alliance Against Racist and Political Repression (NAAPR)
11 John Street, Suite 702
New York, NY 10038
(212) 406-3330
(212) 406-3542
Opposes human rights oppression and seeks to end the harassment and depor-
tation of illegal immigrant workers.

Northern California for Immigration Rights
995 Market Street, Suite 1108
San Francisco, CA 94103
(415) 543-6767 or (415) 243-8215
fax: (415) 243-8628
Advocacy and support group for immigrants.

National Institute Against Prejudice and Violence
31 S. Greene Street
Baltimore, MD 21201
(410) 328-5170
fax: (410) 328-7551
Opposes violence and intimidation motivated by prejudice through research, education and training, and dissemination of information on programs and legislation.

National Network for Immigrant and Refugee Rights (NNIRR)
310 8th Street, Suite 307
Oakland, CA 94607
(510) 465-1984

Composed of coalitions of organizations interested in supporting and advocating for immigrants and refugees. Works to promote just immigration and refugee policies.

New York Association for New Americans (NYANA)
(212) 425-5051
(888) 2-HALT-DV
webmaster @ nyana.org
Provides education and job training services to immigrants and refugees, monitors policies, and disseminates information about policies affecting immigrants and refugees.

President of the United States
The White House
1600 Pennsylvania Avenue N.W.
Washington, DC 20500
(202) 456-1414
or call (202) 456-1111 to give your stand on an issue

Puerto Rican Legal Defense and Education Fund
99 Hudson Street, 14th Fl.
NewYork, NY 10013
(212) 219-3360
Works to safeguard the civil rights of Puerto Ricans and other Latinos. Areas of work include education, employment, and housing. It also refers legal questions to other agencies.

U.S. Commission on Civil Rights
1121 Vermont Avenue N.W.
Washington, DC 20425
(202) 376-8177
Gathers facts regarding discrimination or denials of equal protection of the laws because of race, color, national origin, or other factors. Reports to Congress and the president the effectiveness of federal laws and equal opportunity programs.

U.S. Department of Education Office of Civil Rights
Customer Service Team
Mary E. Switzer Building
330 C Street S.W.
Washington, DC 20202
(202) 205-5413
fax: (202) 205-9862
Enforces statutes that prohibit discrimination in programs and activities that receive federal financial assistance, which include discrimination on the basis of race, color, national origin, handicap, or age.

United States Immigration and Naturalization Services
1-800-755-0777
Responsible for enforcing the laws regulating the admission of foreign-born persons to the U.S. and administers naturalization benefits and refugees. Accepts complaints of discrimination or harassment by immigration officials.

CULTURAL ORGANIZATIONS

Association of Hispanic Arts
173 E. 116th Street, 2nd Fl.
New York, NY 10029
(212) 860-5445
Promotes Hispanic arts through assistance to organizations and individual artists and promotes community performances and exhibitions that reflect Hispanic history, culture, and social issues.

Bilingual Foundation of the Arts
421 North Avenue, #19
Los Angeles, CA 90031
(213) 225-4044
Sponsors Spanish and English theater productions based on the work of Hispanic artists, including a touring group for young people in schools.

Campanas de América
1422 Buena Vista
San Antonio, TX 78207
(210) 224-0258
Promotes and teaches the instrumentation of *mariachi* music to over three thousand schools throughout the country.

Caribbean Cultural Center
408 W. 58th Street
New York, NY 10019
(213) 307-7420

Fine Arts Latin Assn., Inc.
1123 Jocalyn
Houston, TX 77023

Florida Museum of Hispanic and Latin American Art
40006 Aurora Street
Coral Gables, FL 33146

(305) 444-7060
www.latinweb.com/museo
Places an emphasis on learning through the arts with such activities as courses, lectures, music, and book presentations.

Grupo de Artistas Latino-Americanos
P.O. Box 43209
1625 Park Road N.W.
Washington, DC 20010
(202) 234-7174

Guadalupe Cultural Arts Center
1300 Guadalupe Street
San Antonio, TX 78207
(210) 271-3151
www.guadalupeculturalarts.org
A community arts institution that includes a variety of programs geared to young people and families.

Hispanic Fashion Designers
1000 Thomas Jefferson Street, N.W. #310
Washington, DC 20007
(202) 337-9963

Houston Society of Flamenco Arts
7016 Culmore
Houston, TX 77087
(718) 640-1089

Instituto Cultural Mexicano
600 Hemisfair Plaza
San Antonio, TX 78204
(210) 227-0123

Latino Resources at the Smithsonian
For a brochure on items in the Smithsonian collections by and about Latinos, write to:
Smithsonian Institution
SI Building, Room 153, MRC 010
Washington, DC 20560
www.si.edu/resource/tours/latino/start.htm

Mexican Fine Arts Center Museum
1852 W. 19th Street
Chicago, IL 60614
(312) 738-1503
Contains a collection of Mexican folk art. Holds performances and lectures.

BOOKS AND CASSETTES FOR YOUNG CHILDREN

Alacon, Francisco X. *From the Bellybutton of the Moon/Del Ombligo de la Luna.* San Francisco: Children's Book Press, 1998. $15.95.

Alacon, Francisco X. *Laughing Tomatoes and Other Spring Poems/Jitomates Risueños y Otros Poemas de Primavera.* Illustrated by Maya Christina Gonzalez. San Francisco: Children's Book Press, 1997. $15.95.

Castañeda, Omar S. *Abuela's Weave.* Illustrated by Enrique O. Sanchez. New York: Lee & Low Books, Inc., 1993. $15.95.

Cepellín, Ricardo Gonzalez. *Rondas Infantiles.* Cepellín DML-C9355. 1996 Orfeón Videovox, S.A.

Cisneros, Sandra. *Hairs/Pelitos.* Illustrated by Terry Ybañez. New York: Alfred A. Knopf, 1994. $15.00. Softcover $6.99.

Compañía Fonográfica. *Coro del Valle de México. Juegos y Rondas Infantiles.* Internacional, S.A.

Delacre, Lulu. *Arroz con Leche: Popular Songs and Rhymes from Latin America.* English Lyrics by Elena Paz. Musical arrangements by Ana-Maria Rosado. New York: Scholastic, 1989. $15.95. Softcover $4.95.

Delacre, Lulu. *Vejigante Masquerader.* New York: Scholastic, 1993. $15.95.

Delgado, Emilio. *Fiesta Musical.* Niños Catalog, NS 415, 1994. $72.95.

Delgado, María Isabel. *Chave's Memories/Los Recuerdos de Chave.* Illustrated by Yvonne Symank. Piñata Books, Arte Público Press, University of Houston, 1996. $14.95.

Dorros, Arthur. *Abuela.* New York: Dutton's Children's Books, 1991. $15.99. Softcover $4.99.

Dorros, Arthur. *Tonight Is Carnaval.* Illustrated by members of the Club de Madres Virgen del Carmen of Lima, Peru. New York: Dutton Children's Books, 1991. $4.99.

Elizondo, Evangelina, Yolanda Del Campo, y Conjunto de Carlos Oropeza. *Juegos Infantiles. 15 Éxitos. Coro Label.* Compañía Fonográfica. Internacional, S.A. de C.V. Sanctorum No. 86-B. Argentina, Mexico D.F.C.P.

Garcia, Maria. *The Adventures of Connie and Diego/Las aventuras de Connie y Diego.* San Francisco: Children's Book Press, 1987. $14.95.

Garza, Carmen Lomas. *Family Pictures/Cuadros de familia.* San Francisco: Children's Book Press, 1990. $14.95. Soft cover $6.95.

Garza, Carmen Lomas. *In My Family/En Mi Familia.* San Francisco: Children's Book Press, 1996. $15.95.

Gonzalez, Lucia. *The Bossy Gallito/El Gallo de Bodas.* Retold by Lucia M. Gonzalez. Illustrated by Lulu Delacre. New York: Scholastic Inc., 1994. $14.95.

Gonzalez, Ralfka, and Ana Ruiz. *Mi Primer Libro de Dichos/My First Book of Proverbs.* San Francisco: Children's Book Press, 1995. $15.95.

Harper, Jo. *The Legend of Mexicatl.* New York: Turtle Books, 1998. $15.95.

Hayes, Joe. *La Llorona.* El Paso: Cinco Puntos Press, 1986. $5.95.

Hinojosa, Tish. *Cada Niño. Niños* catalog, NS 8032.

Jaramillo, Nelly Palacio. *Grandmother's Nursery Rhymes/Las Nanas de Abuela.* Niños Catalog, NS 1115. $15.95.

Lachtman, Ofelia Dumas. *Pepita Talks Twice.* Houston: Arte Público Press, 1995. $14.95.

Lachtman, Ofelia Dumas. *Pepita Thinks Pink/Pepita y el Color Rosado.* Houston: Arte Público Press, 1998. $14.95.

Martinez, Alejandro Cruz. *The Woman Who Outshone the Sun/La Mujer que Brillaba Aun Más Que el Sol.* San Francisco: Children's Book Press, 1991. $14.95. Softcover $6.95.

Mora, Pat. *A Birthday Basket for Tía.* Illustrated by Cecily Lang. New York: Macmillan Publishing Co., 1992. $13.95.

Mora, Pat. *Pablo's Tree.* Illustrated by Cecily Lang. New York: Macmillan Publishing Co., 1994. $14.95.

Mora, Pat. *Delicious Hullabaloo/Pachanga deliciosa.* Illustrations by Francisco X. Mora. Houston: Piñata Books/Arte Público Press, 1998. $14.95.

Mora, Pat, and Charles Ramírez Berg. *The Gift of the Poinsettia/El Regalo de la Flor de Nochebuena*. Houston: Piñata Books, 1995. $14.95.

Orozco, José-Luis. *De Colores and Other Latin-American Folk Songs for Children*. Illustrated by Elisa Kleven. New York: Dutton Children's Books, 1994. $17.00. *De Colores* (cassette). *Niños* catalog, NS 2131. $10.95.

Pfister, Marcus. *El Pez Arco Iris*. Switzerland: North-South Books Inc., 1994. $16.95.

Ramirez, Michael Rose. *The Little Ant/La Hormiga Chiquita*. Illustrated by Linda Dalai Sawaya. New York: Rizzoli, 1995. $12.95.

Sáenz, Benjamín Alire. *A Gift from Papá Diego/Un Regalo de Papá Diego*. El Paso: Cinco Puntos Press, 1998. $10.95.

Soto, Gary. *Chato's Kitchen*. Illustrated by Susan Guevara. New York: G.P. Putnam's Sons, 1995. $15.95.

Soto, Gary. *Too Many Tamales*. Illustrated by Ed Martinez. New York: G.P. Putnam's Sons, 1993. $14.95.

Tripp, Valerie. *Josefina Series of the American Girls Collection*. Middleton: Pleasant Co, 1997. $5.95.

Winter, Jeanette. *Diego*. New York: Dragonfly Books, 1991. $5.95.

Intermediate Books

Barlow, Genevieve. "The Toad's Spots." In *Legends from Latin America/Leyendas de Latinoamérica*. Illustrated by Robert Borja and Julia Scarf. Lincolnwood (Chicago), Illinois: National Textbook Company, 1995.

Lankerford, Mary D. *Quinceañera: A Latina's Journey to Womanhood*. Photographs by Jesse Herrera. Brookfield, CT: Millbrook Press, 1994. $20.90.

Nye, Naomic Shihab, ed. *The Tree Is Older Than You Are: A Bilingual Gathering of Poems & Stories from Mexico*. With Paintings by Mexican Artists. New York: Simon and Schuster, 1995. $19.95.
Phillis, Tashlik, ed. *Hispanic, Female, and Young: An Anthology*. Houston: Piñata Books, 1994. $14.00.

Sources for Bilingual Books

These are just a handful of sources for bilingual books. Since this is a growing field, there are more publishers and bookstores where bilingual books are available:

American Girls Collection. *Josefina* Collection. Pleasant Company. 8400 Fairway. Middleton, Wisconsin 53562, 1-800-845-0005. www.americangirl.com Bilingual Books for Kids. P.O. Box 653, Ardsley, NY 10520, (800) 385-1020. www.bilingualbooks.com

Cinco Puntos Press, 2709 Louisville, El Paso, TX 79930, (800) 566-9072.

Children's Book Press, 246 First Street, Suite 101, San Francisco, CA 94105, (415) 995-2200, (800) 788-3123.

Lind, Beth Beutler. *Multicultural Children's Literature: An Annotated Bibliography*. Grades K-8. Jefferson, NC: McFarland & Company, Inc., 1996. $34.50

Piñata Books/Arte Público Press, University of Houston, Houston, TX, 77204-2090, (800) 633-2783.

Scholastic, 55 Broadway, New York, NY, 10012, (212) 343-6100.

Turtle Books, 866 United Nations Plaza, Suite 525, New York, NY 10017, (212) 644-2020, (800) 788-3123.

DICHOS BOOKS

Aranda, Charles. *Dichos: Proverbs and Saying from the Spansh*. Santa Fe: Sunstone Press, 1977. $4.95.

Aroroa, Shirley L. *Proverbial Comparisons and Related Expressions in Spanish*. In Folklore Studies 29. Los Angeles: University of California Press, 1977.

Burciaga, José Antonio. *In Few Words/En Pocas Palabras: A Compendium of Latino Folk Wit and Wisdom*. San Francisco: Mercury House, 1997. $14.95.

Cobos, Rubén. *Southwestern Spanish Proverbs*. Sante Fe: Museum of New Mexico Press, 1985. $11.95.

Coca, Benjamí. *Book of Proverbs*. Montezuma: Montezuma Press, 1983.

Gómez Maganda, Alejandro. *¡Como Dice el Dicho! Refranes y Dichos Mexicanos*. Mexico City: Talleres Litográficos E.C.O., 1963.

Martinez Perez, José. *Dichos: Dicharros y refranes mexicanos*. Mexico City: Editores Mexicanos Unidos, 1981. 30 pesos.

Rivera, Maria Elisa Diaz. *Refranes Mas Usados en Puerto Rico*. Puerto Rico: Editorial de la Universidad de Puerto Rico, 1984. $11.95.

Sellers, Jeff M. *Proverbios y Dichos Mexicanos/Folk Wisdom of Mexico*. San Francisco: Chronicle Books, 1994. $9.95

Index